Perspectives on
Learning Disabilities

Perspectives on Learning Disabilities

Biological, Cognitive, Contextual

EDITED BY

Robert J. Sternberg
Louise Spear-Swerling

with a foreword by
Keith E. Stanovich

Westview Press
A Member of the Perseus Books Group

Copyright © 1999 by Westview Press, A Member of the Perseus Books Group

Published in 1999 in the United States of America by Westview Press, 5500 Central Avenue, Boulder, Colorado 80301-2877, and in the United Kingdom by Westview Press, 12 Hid's Copse Road, Cumnor Hill, Oxford OX2 9JJ

Library of Congress Cataloging-in-Publication Data
Perspectives on learning disabilities : biological, cognitive, contextual / edited by Robert J. Sternberg and Louise Spear-Swerling
   p. cm.
Includes bibliographical references and index.
ISBN 0-8133-3175-7 (hardcover)
ISBN 0-8133-3176-5 (paperback)
  1. Learning disabilities. 2. Learning disabled children—
Education. 3. Learning disabilities—Physiological aspects.
4. Constructivism (Education) 5. Context effects (Psychology) in children. I. Sternberg, Robert J. II. Spear-Swerling, Louise.
LC4704.P476 1999
371.92'6—dc21   98-11327
                                                                   CIP

PERSEUS
POD
ON DEMAND   10 9 8 7 6 5 4 3

Contents

Foreword

Keith E. Stanovich

This volume makes a timely appearance in the checkered history of learning-disabilities research. As is well known to researchers, the field of learning disabilities is littered with dead ends, false starts, pseudo-science, and fads. For decades the field rambled on from one incoherence to another. Educational practices without intellectual foundation became entrenched (see Snider, 1992; and Stahl & Kuhn, 1995 for some cogent examples). Thus the field has been characterized by what has been termed a "cart before the horse" development (Stanovich, 1991). Educational practice simply took off before a thorough investigation of certain foundational assumptions had been carried out.

In the 1990s, however, there is some reason for optimism: Hard-won progress has become discernible on the research front. This progress is still much more apparent in the research domain than in the domain of educational practice—all the more reason for the appearance of this volume. It amply reflects how we have made our progress—by attacking this complex phenomenon at a variety of levels (biological, psychological, social) and by seeking converging trends. It is rare to see work from all three perspectives brought together in the same volume. To see, for example, Grigorenko's summary of biological foundations, Torgesen's conceptualization of phonological reading disability, Pressley's and Samuels's prescriptions for education practice, and the trenchant social and organizational critiques of Christensen and Skrtic. The reader thus has an unusual opportunity to see our collective progress and disagreements.

It is of course by now a cliché to say that learning disabilities can be studied from many different levels of analysis. For example, reading disability may be approached from the perspective of the neurophysiologist interested in brain processes; from the perspective of the cognitive psychologist interested in isolating information-processing functions that explain reading ability; and from the perspective of the social-constructivist theorist interested in how social structures define, support, and suppress certain literacy acts based on the social value assigned to various activities. The issue of contention is whether the views deriving from the different perspectives can be *integrated*. Several chapters in this volume demonstrate that in the past ten years there has been a remarkable amount of convergence of findings at the biological and cognitive levels. Integrating these findings with the perspective of the social constructivist has proven more difficult. Nevertheless, Spear-Swerling and Pressley take some important steps in that direction, as does Sternberg in his epilogue. I would like to encourage these efforts, and I see this volume as a contributor.

Anyone familiar with the learning- and reading-disabilities field is aware that we have made the fundamental error of turning the debate about levels of analysis into a zero-sum game where the assumption is that a gain for one framework somehow diminishes the respect given to another. For many years, biologically oriented theorists, information-processing theorists, and social-constructivist theorists did not talk with each other; the various explanatory frameworks often treat each other as hostile competitors. In contrast, the chapters by Olson, Hynd and colleagues, and Torgesen amply illustrate the progress that can be made when cross-talk between the cognitive and biological researchers is encouraged.

Nevertheless, it is still not uncommon to see inappropriate hostility toward neurological findings in some parts of the reading-research community. The motivation to counter neurological findings often reflects the fear that inappropriate conclusions about causation will be reached. Critics argue that neurological explanations are often mistakenly seen as specifying causation, when in many cases they are ambiguous on this issue. But note that the right course for critics of neurological findings is not to try to *deny* the neurological differences but instead to question their interpretation in a causal model.

Likewise, when an information-processing theorist causally links a process such as phonological coding ability to reading skill, what is really being said is that phonological coding has been identified as a *proximal* cause of reading-ability differences (see Gough & Tunmer, 1986); in most cases, we do not know how the phonological differences arose. Interestingly, an identified difference in brain structure, although a little more distal, is still in some sense a proximal cause because the origin of the brain-structure difference is often itself unknown—being some complex combination of genetic structure (see Olson's chapter) and a multitude of environmental experiences (again, see Olson's chapter) that are in part a function of how the social milieu reacts to the brain differences as they manifest at the behavioral level. And here, of course, is where socioconstructivist views come in.

Brain differences may exist that cause functional processing variations of the type related to school and academic behavior, but the socioconstructivist perspective emphasizes that the context in which the differential behavioral outcomes occur and how these differences are interpreted by society can have enormous consequences for children (see Christensen's chapter). In a discussion of Matthew effects in education (Stanovich, 1986), that is, poor-get-poorer effects in reading achievement, I outlined how certain social structures can set up particularly bad interactions between the processing abilities with which a child approaches the task of reading and the educational milieu in which those abilities will be evaluated. Two examples that I employed were (1) ability grouping within classrooms and schools and (2) political and social structures that dictate poorer educational environments for the economically disadvantaged. Both social policies ensure that it is just those children who are at risk for school difficulty who are provided with suboptimal educational resources.

As a further example, consider the work of Stevenson and his colleagues (Stevenson, Stigler, Lee, Lucker, Kitamura, & Hsu, 1985; Uttal, Lummis, & Stevenson, 1988) on cross-cultural differences in educational achievement. His samples of Japanese and Taiwanese children outperformed his American sample, particularly in the area of mathematics; yet basic information-processing differences, at least of the type revealed by common psychometric instruments, were virtually nonexistent. One looks to differences in cultural and school contexts for the explanation of the differential performance.

Thus, socioconstructivist or interactionist perspectives (see Spear-Swerling & Sternberg, 1996) have helped us view learning disabilities from a broader perspective than would have been possible if we relied solely on neurological perspectives. Similarly, it is well known that via cognitive and neuropsychological processing analyses, (1) extensive progress has been made in linking word-recognition problems to processing difficulties in the phonological domain (see the Siegel, Torgesen, and Wagner and Garon chapters); (2) some of the more distal causes of these proximal difficulties have begun to be identified (see all of the chapters in Part 1); and (3) intervention methods based on this functional processing difference have met with some success, but we still have much to learn about remediating the most severe cases of reading disability (see chapters by Olson, Pressley, Siegel, and Torgesen).

Perspectives are not monolithic. Sometimes they do not automatically embody the assumptions that we so readily assume. Take as an example Ehri's (1987, 1995) work on how knowledge of spelling patterns allows children to gain awareness of phonological distinctions. Her work may well be identified with the information-processing framework, particularly because it shares the analytic bias of that framework. But in a paper on the genesis of reading disability published in the *Journal of Learning Disabilities*, Ehri (1989) argued that the distal cause of the orthographic and phonological processing differences that she identifies is almost entirely instructional, and she explicitly rejects approaches that emphasize inherent neurological differences as a distal cause. Her theoretical stance thus shows that there is not necessarily a connection between the analytic functional approach and the endorsement of purely biological distal causes of reading disability.

Or consider the Colorado Reading Project and the Olson group's work on the best way to present the reader-generated feedback in their computer-aided reading system (Olson & Wise, 1992; Wise & Olson, 1995). Much of the theoretical foundation for this work again reflects the information-processing perspective. But consider some of the other properties of the Olson group's computer-aided reading techniques. They emphasize the reading of whole texts, and the presence of reader-generated help in the form of spoken words in the text allows older readers to read age-appropriate materials. Thus, this educational innovation had a concern for presenting coherent language to readers and a concern for the sources of some of the motivational and self-esteem problems that are present in many older less-skilled readers. These concerns are not commonly associated with the information-processing framework, but the work of the Olson group clearly demonstrates that it is not antithetical to this framework.

As a final example, consider one interesting finding discussed by Shaywitz, Shaywitz, Fletcher, and Escobar (1990). It appears that when epidemiologically based sampling methods and regression-based statistical definitions are used, the ratio of boys to girls in a sample of dyslexic children is much lower than the ratio that characterizes school- and clinic-based samples. This evidence of differential sex ratios depending upon the source of the classification should, I submit, be of intense interest to researchers using a socioconstructivist perspective to understand how disabilities are partially cultural constructs. The lesson taught by this example is that evidence deriving from one framework can be of utility to a different research perspective even when workers within the two frameworks are not consciously attempting to interact.

In the complex community of scholars and teachers concerned with learning disabilities, there no doubt exist numerous obstacles to paradigm integration and collaboration. It may be difficult for practitioners, school administrators, and curriculum representatives not to take sides in paradigm disputes relevant to educational, social, and political positions that have already been staked out. But one service that the research community can provide, surely, is a context for a more dispassionate and open-minded consideration of existing approaches to understanding learning disabilities. This volume contributes immensely to this goal.

Several chapters rightly warn the reader that the term *learning disabilities* is a confusing mix of scientific theory, political advocacy, and service-delivery convenience (see particularly the chapters by Torgesen and by Wagner and Garon), and thus the domain in which the term is used must always be kept in mind. For example, Torgesen warns that "the concept of learning disabilities, from a scientific point of view, is not threatened by our current inability to show that a majority of school-identified LD children have intrinsic cognitive limitations resulting from neurological impairment. Historically, it is almost certainly true that the field of learning disabilities as a social/political movement has *overgeneralized* the concept of learning disabilities in order to create improved education opportunities for the largest possible number of children." Wagner and Garon reiterate this warning by conjecturing that less than 3 percent of learning-disabled children will meet medical-model criteria—vastly less than the 20–30 percent estimates that educational personnel concerned with service delivery advocate. I worried about just these implications over a decade ago when I warned that "reading ability forms a continuum, and the farther up on it the poor reader resides, the less likely it is that he/she will be characterized by a qualitatively different syndrome. Logically, the wider the net that is cast by the term reading disability, the vaguer the term will become, and the difficulties in distinguishing poor-reading children with the label from those who do not carry it will increase" (Stanovich, 1986, pp. 114–115). At the time, my thoughts on the matter contained a large dose of speculation, but now, as the chapters in this volume illustrate, our use of the term *learning disability* can be guided by much more rigorous scientific evidence. The uncertainty that remains is whether the field will choose to use that evidence.

Finally, it must be admitted that much of the progress in our field has been a funny type of "negative" progress. What I mean is that we have spent much research effort simply falsifying earlier assumptions about learning disabilities that had become unquestioned background assumptions of the field. Much of this "negative progress" work is well represented in this volume. Most notable (see the Siegel chapter) is work in the past decade indicating that the basic assumption that discrepancies between intelligence and achievement demarcated a neurological and cognitively distinct group of poor learners is questionable (see Fletcher, Shaywitz, Shankweiler, Katz, Liberman, Stuebing, Francis, Fowler, & Shaywitz, 1994; Francis, Shaywitz, Stuebing, Shaywitz, & Fletcher, 1996; Stanovich & Siegel, 1994). This work has begun to cause a conceptual revolution in the learning-disabilities field (see Spear-Swerling chapter and Stanovich, 1996). Similarly unsettling have been the empirical indications mentioned previously that long-standing assumptions about gender ratios of learning disabilities (see Shaywitz et al., 1990) and about the assumed discreteness of learning disabilities (see Wagner and Garon chapters) are incorrect. This work on the fundamental characteristics of learning disabilities has laid the foundation for a more scientific model unencumbered by unverified assumptions carried over from the field's service-delivery function—a function, as many contributors note, that is often at odds with the scientific understanding of learning disabilities.

References

Ehri, L. C. (1987). Learning to read and spell words. *Journal of Reading Behavior, 19,* 5–31.

Ehri, L. C. (1989). The development of spelling knowledge and its role in reading acquisition and reading disability. *Journal of Learning Disabilities, 22,* 356–365.

Ehri, L. C. (1995). Phases of development in learning to read words by sight. *Journal of Research in Reading, 18,* 116–125.

Fletcher, J. M., Shaywitz, S. E., Shankweiler, D., Katz, L., Liberman, I., Stuebing, K., Francis, D. J., Fowler, A., & Shaywitz, B. A. (1994). Cognitive profiles of reading disability: Comparisons of discrepancy and low achievement definitions. *Journal of Educational Psychology, 86,* 6–23.

Francis, D. J., Shaywitz, S. E., Stuebing, K., Shaywitz, B. A., & Fletcher, J. M. (1996). Development lag versus deficit models of reading disability: A longitudinal, individual growth curves analysis. *Journal of Educational Psychology, 88,* 3–17.

Gough, P. B., & Tunmer, W. E. (1986). Decoding, reading, and reading disability. *Remedial and Special Education, 7(1),* 6–10.

Olson, R. K., & Wise, B. W. (1992). Reading on the computer with orthographic and speech feedback. *Reading and Writing: An Interdisciplinary Journal, 4,* 107–144.

Shaywitz, S. E., Shaywitz, B. A., Fletcher, J. M., & Escobar, M. D., (1990). Prevalence of reading disability in boys and girls. *Journal of the American Medical Association, 264,* 998–1002.

Snider, V. E. (1992, Jan/Feb). Learning styles and learning to read: A critique. *Remedial and Special Education, 13(1),* 6–18, 30–33.

Spear-Swerling, L., & Sternberg, R. J. (1996). *Off track: When poor readers become "learning disabled."* Boulder, CO: Westview Press.

Stahl, S. A., & Kuhn, M. (1995). Does whole language or instruction matched to learning styles help children learn to read? *School Psychology Review, 24,* 393–404.

Stanovich, K. E. (1986). Matthew effects in reading: Some consequences of individual differences in the acquisition of literacy. *Reading Research Quarterly, 21,* 360–407.

Stanovich, K. E. (1991). Discrepancy definitions of reading disability: Has intelligence led us astray? *Reading Research Quarterly, 26,* 7–29.

Stanovich, K. E. (1996). Toward a more inclusive definition of dyslexia. *Dyslexia, 2,* 154–166.

Stanovich, K. E., & Siegel, L. S. (1994). The phenotypic performance profile of reading-disabled children: A regression-based test of the phonological-core variable-difference model. *Journal of Educational Psychology, 86,* 24–53.

Stevenson, H. W., Stigler, J. W., Lee, S. Y., Lucker, G. W., Kitamura, S., & Hsu, C. C. (1985). Cognitive performance and academic achievement of Japanese, Chinese, and American children. *Child Development, 56,* 718–734.

Uttal, D. H., Lummis, M., & Stevenson, H. W. (1988). Low and high mathematics achievement in Japanese, Chinese, and American elementary-school children. *Developmental Psychology, 24,* 335–342.

Wise, B. W., & Olson, R. K. (1995). Computer-based phonological awareness and reading instruction. *Annals of Dyslexia, 45,* 99–122.

Preface

The goal of this book is to present alternative perspectives on learning disabilities, concentrating on what we believe to be the three most promising and widely adopted: biological, cognitive, and contextual. Obviously, these perspectives are not the only ones theorists and practitioners have on learning disabilities; nor are they mutually exclusive. On the contrary, most experts view learning disabilities as phenomena that can be understood at multiple levels, including the three emphasized in this volume.

The book was written with several different audiences in mind: students, scholars, practitioners, and parents of students with learning disabilities. Authors were asked to write at a level that would be accessible to the lay reader. At the same time, some of the concepts are technical, and there is no way around the clear expression that sometimes requires the use of appropriate technical terms. We believe the book will serve a useful function for individual readers and for courses with the goal of conveying to students the diversity of perspectives that constitute the field of learning disabilities today.

There are many books today that deal in one way or another with learning disabilities, and we hope that our book occupies a unique niche in its merger of several characteristics: (1) the presentation in a single volume of three sometimes diverging perspectives; (2) the selection of individuals who are world-renowned for their expertise in representing these perspectives; (3) a level of presentation that is accessible and useful to readers with a diversity of backgrounds; (4) a balance in presentation of theory, research, and suggestions for practice that will make the book appealing to people with different needs; and (5) an attempt to provide in the book only seriously thought-out scholarly positions rather than the sometimes mindless "hype" that one sometimes finds in the field and that represents personal opinions that seem to be backed by neither theory nor data nor even any remotely rational argument.

Although the book is divided into parts that represent the alternatives in perspective previously mentioned—biological, cognitive, and contextual—they may be read in any order. Similarly, the chapters within a part may be read in any order. In any case, many chapter authors connect two or even all three of these perspectives. Further, the number of chapters in each part of the book reflects the number of authors contacted who actually provided chapters rather than the number of individuals from each perspective who were invited to contribute.

We are grateful to Dean Birkenkamp, who originally contracted the book for Westview, and to Cathy Murphy, our current editor at Westview, for their support of the project, and to Marcus Boggs for his continuing support throughout this and other projects. We also thank our students and colleagues who have enabled us to develop and explore our interest in learning disabilities. Robert Sternberg's contribution to editing the volume was supported in part by grants (R206R50001 and R206A70001) from the Javits Program of the U.S. Office of Educational Research and Improvement.

Robert J. Sternberg
Louise Spear-Swerling

PART ONE

Biological Approaches

1

Genes, Environment, and Reading Disabilities

Richard K. Olson

First, what is the nature (cause or causes) of learning disabilities? The answer to this initial organizing question for the book is addressed in this chapter from a behavioral-genetic perspective on reading disability. It will be shown that reading disability often tends to run in families. More compelling evidence from identical and fraternal twins shows that the familial pattern of transmission is due to both genetic factors and shared-family environment. Second, how are reading disabilities most effectively diagnosed? This question is addressed from both a behavioral-genetic and medical-genetic perspective. It will be shown that some component skills in reading have stronger genetic influences than others and that the degree of genetic influence may vary depending on characteristics such as disabled readers' IQs, phonological decoding, and age. Current evidence from analyses of disabled readers' DNA suggests the future use of genetic markers and ultimately specific genes for the early diagnosis of risk for reading disability. Third, how are reading disabilities most effectively remediated, and to what extent is remediation possible? It will be strongly argued that evidence for genetic influence, even very strong genetic influence in some cases, should not discourage our best efforts in remediation. However, the genetic evidence and results from training studies suggest that some extraordinary environmental intervention may be needed for many disabled readers.

The research reported from the Colorado twin and computer-remediation projects was supported by NICHD grant Nos. HD 11683 and HD 22223.

Definition of "Reading Disability"

Large differences in literacy among countries and many of the differences within countries are due to cultural variation in instruction and reading practice. For example, one elementary school in an impoverished area of Denver recently showed average reading scores at the 13th percentile on a nationally normed test. Another school in a more affluent Denver neighborhood had average reading scores above the 80th percentile. It is likely that most if not all of this difference in reading performance is due to environmental factors. A major factor in this example may be the high number of children in the low-performing school whose first language was not English.

The behavioral-genetic studies with families and twins discussed in this chapter have often limited the range of environmental influence on literacy by excluding children from environments or language backgrounds that would obviously constrain reading development. These studies tend to select disabled readers with adequate schooling (for normal readers), average or above-average levels of socioeconomic status, and English as the first language. Individuals with some obvious environmental cause for a reading disability such as signs of brain damage (i.e., seizures) or poor school attendance are excluded. Cases with extremely low IQ are also excluded. Thus reading disability is unexpected from the individual's known environment and general intelligence. However, many relevant aspects of the family environment are not directly assessed in most studies. There may be considerable variation in factors such as parental expectations regarding literacy, television viewing habits, books in the home, children's preliteracy activities, lead exposure, or some other environmental influence that is shared by the family but not always identified in behavioral-genetic studies. Analyses of data from identical and fraternal twins show that differences in shared-family environment do have a substantial influence on many cases of reading disability.

Because reading ability in the population is normally distributed (Rodgers, 1983; Shaywitz, Escobar, Shaywitz, Fletcher, & Makuch, 1992), the severity criterion for reading disability is arbitrary and varies somewhat across studies. The studies reviewed in this chapter typically selected subjects who were more than about 1.5 standard deviations below the population mean (i.e., below the 10th percentile) in their sampling areas.

Rate of Familial Incidence and Prediction of Children's Reading Disabilities

Evidence from a number of family studies has shown that if a child is diagnosed with reading disability, there is a higher than normal probability that other family members will also be reading disabled (cf. Finucci, Guthrie, Childs, Abbey, & Childs, 1976; Hallgren, 1950; Gilger, Pennington, & DeFries, 1991; Vogler, DeFries, & Decker, 1985). The exact probability seems to depend on a variety of factors, including the severity of the child's reading disability and the type of assessment for other family members' reading skills. For example, when the parents' diagnosis for reading disability is based on self-report, the familial incidence tends to be lower than when the diagnosis is based on the direct measurement of parents' reading skills (Gilger et al., 1991).

Most studies of familial incidence first diagnose a child with reading disability using a severity criterion that would identify 5–10 percent of children with normal intelligence and educational opportunity. Then the investigators attempt to use a similar severity criterion to diagnose reading disability in the parents. Evidence for the familial nature of reading disability is based on parental rates that are substantially above the 5–10 percent rate estimated for the population. Hollis Scarborough (personal communication, 1997) computed the average rate of reading disability among parents across eight family studies that included a total of 516 families. The rate across studies varied from 25 percent to 60 percent with a median value of 37 percent. Thus all studies found rates for reading disability among parents of reading-disabled children that were significantly higher than expected in the normal population. The median proportion of reading disability among fathers (46 percent) was slightly higher than the median proportion among mothers (33 percent).

Results from these family studies suggest that evidence for parents' reading disabilities could be used to predict a greater than normal risk for their children. A few studies have attempted to directly estimate this prospective risk. Finucci, Gottfredson, and Childs (1985) found that of 115 parents who had attended a special school for disabled readers when they were children, 36 percent reported that at least one of their children was reading disabled. Scarborough's (1990) study of children with one or two reading-disabled parents found that 31 percent of their second-grade children were eventually identified as reading disabled by their schools. When the diagnosis of reading disability was based on Scarborough's extensive test results, which showed that reading was at least 1.5 standard deviations below the population mean, the rate was twice as high (62 percent). (A higher than school identification rate when children are actually tested is a common result in large epidemiological studies [Olson, Forsberg, & Wise, 1994; Shaywitz, Shaywitz, Fletcher, & Escobar, 1990].) In contrast, Scarborough found that only 5 percent of children were reading disabled if both parents were normal readers.

In summary, studies clearly show that parents' reading disabilities predict a higher than normal rate of reading disabilities in their children

(31–62 percent vs. 5–10 percent). Although parents' reading disabilities are not completely predictive of their children's reading disabilities, the substantially greater risk at least warrants very close monitoring of their children's progress in early language and literacy development.

Evidence for the partial familial nature of reading disability is necessary but *not* sufficient evidence for inferring genetic influence, because families also share their environments. As discussed earlier, most family studies attempt to eliminate obvious environmental risk factors such as different native languages, low socioeconomic status, and unusually poor schools. Nevertheless, there could be a variety of less obvious environmental risk factors associated with the reading disabilities of both parents and children. For example, parents with reading disability sometimes express the concern that they might environmentally transmit their negative attitudes about reading to their children. The next section reviews results from behavioral-genetic studies with twins that attempt to separate the proportional influences due to genes and shared-family environment.

Twin Studies of Genetic and Environmental Influences on Reading Disabilities

The Twin Method

Twins who are raised together share their family environment. This is true for both monozygotic (MZ) "identical" twins and dizygotic (DZ) "fraternal" twins. However, MZ and same-sex DZ twin pairs differ markedly in their genetic similarity. MZ twins develop from the same sperm and egg and are therefore genetically identical. DZ twins develop from two different egg-sperm combinations and share half their normally segregating genes, on average (Plomin, DeFries, & McClearn, 1990). Ordinary siblings also share half their segregating genes, but their different birthdays may lead to less shared-environment influence compared to MZ and DZ twins. If MZ twins share their reading disabilities significantly more often than same-sex DZ twins, it is assumed that the greater genetic similarity of MZ twins is responsible.

Of course, genes can be expressed only through their interaction with the environment. This interaction begins with the complex process of embryological brain development and ultimately extends to genetic effects on the children's selection of their reading environment. For example, genetic effects on early brain development resulting in unusual difficulties in learning to read could ultimately cause a child's frustration with and avoidance of reading practice.

In contrast, relative ease in learning to read due to favorable brain development could lead to much more reading practice and enjoyment of literature. Such child-selected environmental differences could have a strong impact on reading development. Because the cause of this environmental selection is genetic, behavioral-genetic analyses include any effects of this or any other genotype-environment correlation in their estimation of total genetic influence. Implications for the remediation of genetically influenced reading disabilities are considered in the final section of the chapter.

Twin Concordance Rates for Reading Disability

Several early twin studies of reading disability found that MZ twin pairs shared their reading disabilities significantly more often than DZ twin pairs (Bakwin, 1973; Hallgren, 1950; Zerbin-Rudin, 1967). When an MZ or DZ twin pair shares a disorder, such as reading disability, diabetes, or schizophrenia, the twin pair is referred to as "concordant" for the disorder. If only one twin of a pair has the disorder, the pair is referred to as "discordant." In Hallgren's classic study, the concordance rate for MZ and DZ twins was 100 percent and 52 percent, respectively. This extreme result suggested that nearly all cases of reading disability are due to genetic factors. Other studies have reported smaller differences in MZ-DZ concordance rates, but with the exception of Stevenson, Graham, Friedman, and McLoughlin (1987), all find a significantly higher concordance rate for MZ pairs (DeFries & Alarcon, 1996).

The ascertainment of disabled readers in the early concordance studies may have been biased by a higher tendency to report concordant than discordant pairs (Harris, 1986). The ongoing Colorado twin study of reading disability reduces this potential referral bias by ascertaining reading-disabled twins in grades 3–12 from school performance records and then giving the twins an extensive battery of tests in the laboratory (DeFries, Filipek, Fulker, Olson, Pennington, Smith, & Wise, 1997). DeFries and Alarcon (1996) reported that the unbiased concordance rate for reading disability in this sample is currently 68 percent for 186 MZ pairs and 38 percent for 138 DZ pairs. This is a highly significant difference, but it is somewhat smaller than the extreme differences found in some earlier and potentially biased studies.

Differences between MZ and DZ concordance rates can provide evidence for significant genetic etiology, but they do not provide precise estimations of the relative magnitude of genetic and environmental influences. Also, concordance rates are insensitive to the degree of twins' reading deficits below and above the severity criterion for a categorical diagnosis of reading disability. When reading disability is defined as the lower 10 percent of the population in reading skills, there is still a very large range of reading deficit within this group. Also, there is a large range of reading ability between the criterion level and the normal mean. A regression analysis developed by DeFries and Fulker (1985) is sensitive to this variability above the criterion level. Their basic regression model yields direct estimates of the proportion of genetic influence on the disabled group's reading deficit.

Assessment of Genetic Influence from Cotwin Regression to the Population Mean

The DeFries and Fulker (1985) analysis defines reading-disabled twins as those who fall below a selected severity criterion, usually the lower 10th percentile relative to a normal sample of twins. In this type of behavioral genetic analysis, twins that meet the selection criterion for reading disability are called "probands." In cases where a twin pair is discordant for reading disability (one member of the pair is disabled and the other is not), the twin that does not meet the criterion for reading disability is called the "cotwin."

The DeFries and Fulker (1985) analysis compares the degree to which reading performance of the MZ and DZ cotwins regresses toward the population mean. The population mean is defined by the average performance level in a comparison sample of normal twins. Cotwins' regression to the population mean is indicated by the amount their scores fall above the criterion level for reading disability, toward the population mean. To aid in understanding how the analysis works, three extreme examples of MZ and DZ cotwin regression are given that would indicate exclusive influence from (1) genetic factors, (2) shared environment, or (3) nonshared environment.

If reading disability is completely due to genetic influence, both members of the genetically identical MZ pairs would be affected probands: There would be no cotwin regression to the population mean. However, that result alone would not prove a genetic influence because MZ twins also share their family environment. A comparison must be made with DZ twins who also share their family environment but who share only half their segregating genes on average. If reading disability were completely due to genetic influence, many of the genetically dissimilar DZ pairs would have a cotwin that did not meet the selection criterion. The expectation for complete genetic influence is that MZ twins show no regression and DZ cotwins regress halfway to the population mean, on average.

If reading disability were entirely due to shared-family environment, both MZ and DZ pairs would have two probands and no cotwin regression to the mean. This is because both types of twin pairs share their family environment.

The third extreme example is that if reading disability were due entirely to some nonshared environmental factor, both MZ and DZ cotwins would be expected to average nearly complete regression to the population mean, constrained only by the defined rate of reading disability in the population. Nonshared environmental factors among twins could include such things as selective gestational or birth problems, nonshared illnesses, or head injury. Test error is also included in behavioral-genetic estimates of nonshared environment.

The actual patterns of cotwin regression to the mean for reading and related skills fall between the previous extreme examples and yield proportional estimates of the balance of genetic (h^2_g), shared environment (c^2_g), and nonshared environment (e^2_g) influences. The subscript "g" for each of the three estimates indicates their reference to the average *group* deficit. The estimates from these behavioral-genetic analyses do not specify proportional influences for any individual within the deviant group.

When the DeFries and Fulker (1985) regression analysis was recently applied to a composite measure of reading that combined the Peabody Individual Achievement Tests (PIAT, Dunn & Markwardt, 1970) for reading comprehension, word recognition, and spelling, the estimated proportion of genetic influence (i.e., heritability) on the group deficit was 56 percent, or $h^2_g = .56$ with a standard error of .09 (DeFries & Alarcon, 1996). Thus there is a 95 percent probability that the true group h^2_g for the composite PIAT measure of reading disability is between .38 and .74.

It should be noted that this estimate for genetic influence on the group deficit in reading is specific to the Colorado sampling constraints. If a broader range of reading environment (i.e., poor inner-city schools) had been included in the sample, it is likely that the influence of shared environment would have been higher than genetic factors in the average group deficit. If the range of the twins' reading environment had been more constrained, it is likely that genetic influence would have been higher. An average population estimate of genetic influence on individual differences in a behavior is jointly influenced by the range of relevant genetic variation and by the range of relevant environmental variation.

Genetic and Environmental Influences on Specific Skills in Reading and Language

Olson, Forsberg, and Wise (1994) extended the DeFries and Fulker (1985) genetic analysis to derive estimates of the proportion of influences from genetic factors (h^2_g), shared-family environment (c^2_g), and nonshared environment (e^2_g) for several separate reading and language skills.

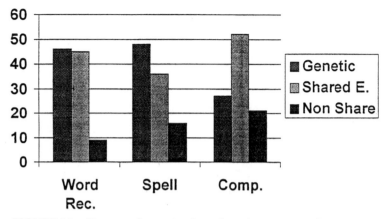

FIGURE 1.1   Percent of genetic, shared-environment, and non-shared-environment influences on disabled readers' group deficits in PIAT word recognition, spelling, and reading comprehension.

Probands (twins below the 10th percentile) were separately selected for each of the PIAT tests of word recognition, spelling, and reading comprehension that DeFries and Alarcon (1996) used in their composite measure. Proband membership in the three deviant groups largely overlapped because of the positive correlations between the PIAT tests. However, the correlations were far enough from 1 to allow for some differences in proband group membership and in average genetic influence across the tests. The results from the separate PIAT analyses are presented in Figure 1.1. Both word recognition and spelling had substantial and similarly high levels of genetic and shared-environment influence. However, for reading comprehension, shared-environment influence was high (52 percent) and genetic influence was low (27 percent). The specific vocabulary and world knowledge needed to correctly answer the PIAT comprehension questions may have been strongly influenced by the twins' shared school and home environment. In contrast, the rate of growth in word recognition and spelling appears to have been more constrained by genetic factors. Which of these measures is most appropriate for the diagnosis of reading disability? If the interest is in reading disabilities with significant genetic influence, the word-recognition and spelling measures would be most useful.

Olson, Wise, Conners, Rack, and Fulker (1989) examined genetic influences on group deficits in word recognition, phonological decoding (oral reading of nonwords), orthographic coding (selection of words from word-pseudohomophone pairs such as rain-rane), and a measure of phoneme awareness that was similar to Pig Latin. In this small twin sam-

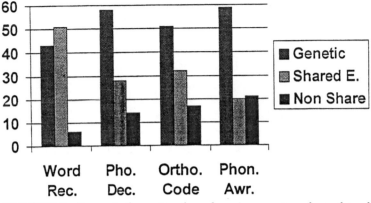

FIGURE 1.2   Percent of genetic, shared-environment, and nonshared-environment influences on disabled readers' group deficits in PIAT word recognition, phonological decoding, orthographic coding, and phoneme awareness.

ple, there were significant genetic contributions to the group deficits in word recognition, phonological decoding, and phoneme awareness but not in orthographic coding. It was argued that deficits in the orthographic task may have been more influenced by shared-environment differences in print exposure (Stanovich and West, 1989). However, in larger twin samples analyzed by Olson et al. (1994) and in more recent unpublished analyses, it is clear that there is also substantial genetic influence on the group deficit in orthographic coding.

The current estimated levels of genetic influence depend somewhat on the criteria for proband selection. The estimates in Figure 1.2 are based on the selection of probands on the individual variables regardless of their school history for reading disability. When proband selection is further constrained by school history, as in DeFries and Alarcon (1996), genetic influence is about 10–15 percentage points higher and shared-environment influence is about 10–15 percentage points lower. It is not clear which approach is most appropriate, so the most conservative approach for genetic influence is used here.

Current estimates of genetic influence are substantial and statistically significant for group deficits (–1.5 SD [standard deviation]) in PIAT word recognition (204 MZ, 151 DZ pairs), phonological decoding (187 MZ, 124 DZ pairs), orthographic coding (162 MZ, 114 DZ pairs), and phoneme awareness (137 MZ, 101 DZ pairs). It appears that genetic influence might be somewhat higher for phonological decoding and phoneme awareness compared to word recognition and orthographic coding, but the contrasts are not statistically significant. The influence of shared environment is statistically significant for all variables except phoneme awareness. Shared-environment influence is higher for the group deficit in word recognition compared to the other variables. This may reflect a greater role for shared-environment differences in print exposure in the development of word recognition. Phonological skills and the high precision of orthographic representations required for correct responses in the orthographic choice task appear to be less influenced by shared environment.

Gayan, Datta, Castles, and Olson (1997) noted that the heritability estimates for word recognition and phonological decoding seem to depend on whether fluency is included as a part of the assessment. An experimental measure of time-limited word recognition (correct responses had to be initiated within two seconds) yielded a higher heritability estimate for the group deficit ($h^2_g = .55$; $c^2_g = .40$) compared to the untimed PIAT test of word recognition ($h^2_g = .44$; $c^2_g = .47$). Similarly, the high heritability and low shared-environment estimates for phonological decoding in Figure 1.2 ($h^2_g = .58$; $c^2_g = .28$) are based on deficits in the combined z scores for percent correct and latency on correct trials. In comparison, heritability for the percent of nonwords read correctly was much lower and shared environment was higher ($h^2_g = .41$; $c^2_g = .45$). It seems that shared environment plays a stronger role in limiting disabled readers' accuracy in word recognition and phonological decoding, whereas deficits in accuracy and fluency combined are relatively more influenced by genetic factors. If the diagnosis of genetically based disabilities in word recognition and phonological decoding is a goal, measures of speed should be included in the test battery. The implication of these results for the remediation of reading disabilities is considered in the final section of the chapter.

Genetic Covariation and Independence Across Measures

Are the same genes involved in disabled readers' correlated deficits in word recognition, phonological decoding, orthographic coding, and phoneme awareness? The answer is partly yes and partly no. Olson and colleagues (1994) reported significant genetic covariance among the measures in bivariate extensions of the DeFries and Fulker (1985) twin regression model. Gayan and Olson (1997) performed a different type of genetic analysis to estimate specific and shared genetic influences for individual differences on the measures. The results showed a common genetic influence across all measures, consistent with the earlier results from bivariate analyses of group deficits. However, there were also specific, nonshared genetic influences for individual differences in each of the measures. This significant independent genetic variance for each of the measures indicates that differences in disabled readers' profiles of component reading and language skills may have a partly genetic basis.

Converging on Genetic Influence for Individual Disabled Readers

It is important to reiterate that the previously presented behavioral-genetic twin analyses do not provide information about the balance of genetic and environmental influences on any individual with reading disability. These studies only estimate the average relative influences for the reading-disabled group. Within the group, some disabled readers' deficits may be primarily due to their genes, some may be primarily due to shared environment, and some may be due to a closer to equal influence from both factors. However, we can look for interactions among other subject variables and the average degree of heritability for reading deficits. If significant interactions are found, this information could be used to make more accurate probability statements about the degree of genetic etiology for an individual's reading disability.

Gayan, Datta, Castles, and Olson (1997) found that when they assessed the heritability for the disabled group's deficit in PIAT word recognition, depending on the probands' level of phonological decoding, probands with relatively low phonological decoding had a significantly higher average genetic influence on their deficit in PIAT word recognition compared to probands with relatively high phonological decoding. They suggested that relatively severe deficits in phonological decoding are strongly influenced by genetic factors that place a genetically based constraint on the growth of word recognition. Extremely poor phonological decoding would lead to frequent decoding errors when children independently attempt to read unfamiliar printed words. In contrast, disabled readers with relatively good phonological decoding compared to their word recognition may have deficits in word recognition that are more due to shared-environment deficits in print exposure.

Olson, Forsberg, Gayan, and DeFries (in press) proposed a similar explanation for an apparent difference in genetic influence on deficits in word recognition, depending on subjects' full-scale IQ scores. In this analysis, subjects with relatively high IQs compared to their word recognition had a stronger average genetic influence. Shared environment was a relatively stronger influence for subjects whose IQ scores were lower (see Figure 1.3). Olson and colleagues suggested that a poor home and educational environment could be jointly responsible for the concurrent expression of low IQ and low word recognition. In contrast, disabled readers with higher IQ scores were more likely to have a relatively good educational environment, and their failure in reading would be more likely due to genetic constraints.

The final example of individual variation in genetic influence is a fascinatingly complex interaction between genetic influence, age, and mea-

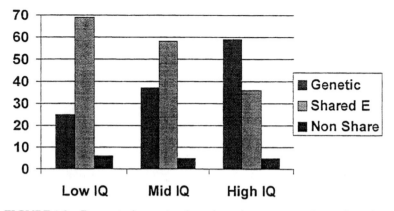

FIGURE 1.3   Percent of genetic, shared-environment, and nonshared-environment influences on disabled readers' group deficits in word recognition across three levels of WISC-R IQ.

sures of reading and spelling reported by DeFries, Alarcon, and Olson (1997). They found that genetic influence on PIAT word-recognition deficits tends to decline across the eight-twenty-year age range of the cross-sectional Colorado twin study, whereas genetic influence on PIAT spelling deficits tends to increase with age. It was suggested that correct reading of the high-level items in the PIAT word-recognition test was more dependent on amount of print exposure compared to the shorter, more phonologically regular, and orally familiar items at lower levels of the test. In contrast, the higher-level spelling items in the PIAT test may demand a level of precision in subjects' orthographic representations that is more constrained by genetic factors.

The previous three examples indicate that estimates of the likely proportional genetic influence on individual disabled readers' reading and spelling deficits can be improved through knowledge about other subject characteristics. However, a direct analysis of disabled readers' DNA may ultimately provide much more precise knowledge about likely genetic influences on an individual's reading disabilities. Some progress toward this goal has already been made. Cardon, Smith, Fulker, Kimberling, Pennington, & DeFries (1994) analyzed the DNA from same-sex DZ twins in the Colorado study and from an independent sample of extended families that included several disabled readers. They found that in both samples, there was significant evidence for the linkage of many cases of reading disability to the HLA (immune system) region of chromosome 6. This apparent linkage needs to be replicated in additional samples before we can have strong confidence in its validity and have a good estimate of the proportion of reading disabilities that may be influenced by the gene or genes in this area.

Current linkage analyses of a new set of DZ twins from the Colorado study suggest that the results of the earlier study will be replicated and that the strongest linkage to this area is for probands with the most severe deficits in orthographic coding, phonological decoding, and phoneme awareness.

At least one independent study has reported linkage to a similar region of chromosome 6 (Grigorenko, Wood, Meyer, Hart, Speed, Shuster, & Pauls, 1997). The strongest linkage in this region was for deficits in a reading-related measure of phoneme awareness. Deficits in word recognition were more strongly linked to a region on the short arm of chromosome 15. The authors argued that deficits in component skills in reading and related language processes are linked to different regions of the genome. This is certainly possible in view of the partially independent genetic effects found through behavioral-genetic analyses for different component reading skills (Gayan & Olson, 1997). However, it appears from the report by Grigorenko and colleagues that *differences* in the strength of linkage for phoneme awareness and word recognition would not be significant at either locus. Cardon and others (1994) did not find significant linkage for reading disability on chromosome 15, but an earlier study by Smith, Kimberling, Pennington, and Lubs (1983) did find significant linkage here. It is not entirely surprising that different linkages emerge in different samples. It seems likely that there will be more than one important genetic contribution to reading disability across the population (Smith, Kimberling, & Pennington, 1991). Whole-genome scans made possible by the human genome project may help locate several additional regions of the genome that account for some significant proportion of genetically influenced reading disabilities.

Following the confirmation of linkage for reading disability to the HLA region of chromosome 6 and the short arm of chromosome 15, a search through the millions of base pairs in these regions must be undertaken to find the gene(s) responsible, identify the protein(s) that are coded by the gene(s), and ultimately understand the developmental pathway from gene(s) to brain structure and function that lead to genetically based reading disabilities. Prior to our complete understanding of the specific gene(s) and their developmental pathway, it may soon be possible to use reliable DNA markers that are close enough to the responsible genes to identify children who are at a high genetically based risk for reading disability. This information could then be used to begin preventative measures before the child experiences reading failure and frustration in school.

Implications of Behavioral-Genetic and Linkage Results for Education

Educators are often wary of behavioral-genetic studies. They may be concerned that evidence for genetic influence will be mistakenly used to account for the poor average reading performance of disadvantaged racial or ethnic groups. They may also be concerned that evidence for genetic influence will be used as an excuse for educational policymakers to give up on disabled readers, assuming that their problems with reading are absolutely determined by their genes and without hope for remediation. It must be emphasized that these are clear mistakes in the interpretation of the evidence for genetic influences on reading disabilities.

First, the behavioral-genetic evidence has nothing to say about differences in reading performance between different racial or ethnic groups because it is impossible to disentangle the effects of the substantial environmental differences between these groups (e.g., different dialect, different first language, socioeconomic level, etc.). Second, even if the genetic influence on some individual reading disabilities proves to be very strong, this only implies that some extraordinary environmental intervention may be required. Someday this intervention may be partly biological, perhaps through the manipulation of neural transmitters, as in the successful treatment of some attention-deficit disorders with Ritalin. At present, the behavioral genetic evidence has some important implications for educational policy.

One implication is that some children may be poor readers in spite of their parents' and schools' provision of an environment that is quite adequate for reading development in normal children. Many parents and their children with reading disability feel a high level of guilt about the problem. The parents may feel that they have failed to provide their children with a "good" environment for reading development. Whereas this may be true in some cases of reading disability, it is clear that there are strong genetic influences in many cases. Many parents are often quite relieved when they learn that the problem may have originated in their genetic makeup rather than in their failure to provide a good environment for their children.

A "good" or "normal" environment for reading development may not be nearly enough for some children to reach a functional and enjoyable level of literacy. The direct manipulation of brain processes through medical intervention is a future possibility, but we must rely on our best educational efforts now. These efforts may include special types of prereading and early reading instruction and they may also need to include a significantly greater amount and intensity of accurate reading practice to compensate for some disabled readers' biological liabilities. Some of this additional support might be efficiently provided through computer-based exercises and reading practice (Wise & Olson, 1995). The behavioral-genetic evidence can help parents and educators understand why this extra effort is needed for many children with reading disability.

I will close the chapter with some reflections on how results from recent training studies with disabled readers may be related to some of the genetic influences that have been described. Recall that one likely pathway for genetic influence in many children is early failure and frustration with reading and a subsequent low level of reading practice. Thus some children may be initially slowed in their reading development because of prior biological and environmental constraints, and their rate of growth is slowed further by the avoidance of reading in favor of more enjoyable and less frustrating activities. Interventions that provide well-motivated, structured, and accurate reading practice may therefore show significant improvement for many disabled readers, including those who get off to a bad start because of negative genetic influence.

The benefits of structured and accurate reading practice for disabled readers in the schools were clearly shown in a study by Wise and Olson (1995). Children in the second to fifth grades who were in the lower 10 percent of their class in word recognition were trained for a half hour each day over a semester, for a total of twenty-five hours. This training occurred during times that the children would otherwise be in their regular reading class. A common core of two different training programs described further on included the reading of interesting stories on the computer. The stories were selected so that most of their words were not too far beyond the child's reading level. Accurate reading of difficult words was supported by synthetic speech when children targeted the words with a mouse. This structured reading experience resulted in an average gain over the semester of about ten standard-score points on several measures of word recognition. This was an impressive improvement for these children during a relatively brief training period, although most were still well below the mean for their class. Our observations suggested that the amount of accurate reading during the training periods was substantially greater than most of these disabled readers would have experienced in their regular reading class.

Unfortunately, follow-up testing one and two years after the end of training indicated that subjects' growth rate in word recognition returned to the slow rate experienced before training (Olson, Wise, Ring, & Johnson, 1997). Their structured practice in accurate reading was clearly beneficial during training, but apparently it did not improve most children's poor reading habits after training. More needs to be done to ensure that disabled readers maintain a high level of reading practice over the long term and achieve a level of reading fluency that is high enough to support their continued enjoyment of reading. Olson and colleagues noted the need to provide much longer training in the schools to bring disabled readers closer to the level of their peers. It will also be important to work with the families of disabled readers to boost their accurate reading practice at home, possibly with the assistance of computer-based reading programs in the home.

Other results of the Wise and Olson (1995) study may be understood with reference to the strong genetic effects reported earlier for deficits in phonological decoding and phoneme awareness. One of the two training conditions explicitly targeted the subjects' deficits in these skills. The other group practiced comprehension strategies while reading both on and off the computer. Subjects in the phonologically trained group showed substantially greater improvement in their accuracy for reading nonwords and in several measures of phoneme awareness. Thus it seemed that we had remediated much of their deficit in phonological skills. Unfortunately, this apparent improvement in phonological skills was not accompanied by a similar expected advantage in growth for disabled readers' word recognition during training. At the end of training, there was a trend favoring the phonological group on the untimed PIAT measure of word recognition, but the other group was significantly better on our measure of time-limited word recognition. Olson, Wise, Johnson, and Ring (1997) reviewed several other recent studies that found a similar dissociation between growth in disabled readers' phonological skills and word recognition when similar treatment comparisons were made at the end of training.

Follow-up tests for the Wise and Olson (1995) subjects, one and two years after training, found no significant differences in any of the word-recognition measures, although the phonological group retained a significant superiority in nonword reading accuracy and phoneme awareness at least through the first year following training (Olson, Wise, Ring, & Johnson, 1997). These results seem inconsistent with the view that better phonological decoding skills should provide a "self-teaching" mechanism that would support more rapid growth in word recognition (Share, 1995).

What are we to make of these results from a genetic point of view? We have seen that individual differences in phonological decoding and phoneme awareness are phenotypically and genetically correlated with reading and spelling in the population (Olson et al., 1994; Gayan & Olson, 1997). In most normal readers, phonological skills emerge as a consequence of learning how to read even if they are not given much explicit instruction. In disabled readers, phonological skills tend to lag significantly behind their development in word recognition unless explicit instruction is given (Rack, Snowling, & Olson, 1992). However, raising disabled readers' performance in nonword reading and phoneme awareness to a level consistent with or better than expected from their word recognition does *not* mean that we have created the same reading process seen in younger normal children at the same level of reading development. The normal children's integration of their phonological skills in the reading process may be much more natural and automatic, requiring less explicit attention for their use during fluent reading. In contrast, the phonological awareness and decoding skills learned by disabled readers in many training programs may be less well integrated and automatized (Sternberg & Wagner, 1982).

The high shared genetic influence on deficits in fluent phonological decoding and reading may help explain why it is difficult for many training methods to penetrate to the level of phonological processing that may be responsible for this genetic covariance. New and more intense training methods may be needed to improve disabled readers' automatic phonological processes, facilitate their transfer to fluent reading, and implement the automatic "self-teaching" function that seems to support the rapid growth of word recognition and spelling in normal development. The amount of print exposure required for the development of fluent reading may still be greater than in normal readers but less than would be required without the strengthening of disabled readers' automatic phonological processing.

References

Bakwin, H. (1973). Reading disability in twins. *Developmental Medicine and Child Neurology, 15*, 184–187.

Cardon, L. R., Smith, S., Fulker, D., Kimberling, W., Pennington, B. & DeFries, J. (1994). Quantitative trait locus for reading disability on chromosome 6. *Science, 266*, 276–279.

DeFries, J. C., & Alarcon, M. (1996). Genetics of specific reading disability. *Mental Retardation and Developmental Disabilities Research Reviews, 2*, 39–47.

DeFries, J. C., Alarcon, M., & Olson, R. K. (1997). Genetics and dyslexia: Developmental differences in the etiologies of reading and spelling deficits. In C. Hulme & M. Snowling (Eds.), *Dyslexia: Biological bases, identification, and intervention* (pp. 20–37). London: Whurr.

Defries, J. C., Filipek, P. A., Fulker, D. W., Olson, R. K., Pennington, B. F., Smith, S. D., & Wise, B. W. (1997). Colorado Learning Disabilities Research Center. *Learning Disability Quarterly, 8*, 7–19.

DeFries, J. C., & Fulker, D. W. (1985). Multiple regression analysis of twin data. *Behavior Genetics, 15*, 467–473.

Dunn, L. M., & Markwardt, F. C. (1970). *Examiner's manual: Peabody Individual Achievement Test.* Circle Pines, MN: American Guidance Service.

Finucci, J. M., Gottfredson, L., & Childs, B. (1985). *Annals of Dyslexia, 35*, 117–136.

Finucci, J. M., Guthrie, J. T., Childs, A. L., Abbey, H., & Childs, B. (1976). *Annals of Human Genetics, 40*, 1–23.

Gayan, J., Datta, H. E., Castles, A., & Olson, R. K. (1997). *The etiology of group deficits in word decoding across levels of phonological decoding and orthographic coding.* Paper presented at the meeting of the Society for the Scientific Study of Reading, Chicago, 3/23/97.

Gayan, J., & Olson, R. K. (1997). Common and specific genetic effects on reading measures. *Behavioral Genetics, 27,* 589.

Gilger, J. W., Pennington, B. F., & DeFries, J. C. (1991). Risk for reading disability as a function of family history in three family studies. *Reading and Writing: An Interdisciplinary Journal, 3,* 205–217.

Grigorenko, E. L., Wood, F. B., Meyer, M. S., Hart, L. A., Speed, W. C., Shuster, B. S., & Pauls, D. L. (1997). Susceptibility loci for distinct components of developmental dyslexia on chromosomes 6 and 15. *American Journal of Human Genetics, 60,* 27–39.

Hallgren, B. (1950). Specific dyslexia: A clinical and genetic study. *Acta Psychiatr Neurolog Scand, 65* (Suppl): 1–287.

Harris, E. L. (1986). The contribution of twin research to the study of the etiology of reading disability. In S. D. Smith (Ed.), *Genetics and learning disabilities* (pp. 3–19). San Diego, CA: College Hill Press.

Olson, R. K., Forsberg, H., Gayan, J., & DeFries, J. C. (in press). A behavioral-genetic analysis of reading disabilities and component processes. In R. M. Klein & P. A. McMullen (Eds.), *Converging methods for understanding reading and dyslexia.* Boston: MIT Press.

Olson, R. K., Forsberg, H., & Wise, B. (1994). Genes, environment, and the development of orthographic skills. In V. W. Berninger (Ed.), *The varieties of orthographic knowledge I: Theoretical and developmental issues* (pp. 27–71). Dordrecht, Netherlands: Kluwer Academic.

Olson, R. K., Wise, B., Conners, F., Rack, J. P., and Fulker, D. (1989). Specific deficits in component reading and language skills: Genetic and environmental influences. *Journal of Learning Disabilities, 22,* 6, 339–348.

Olson, R. K., Wise, B., Ring, J., & Johnson, M. (1997). Computer-based remedial training in phoneme awareness and phonological decoding: Effects on the post-training development of word recognition. *Scientific Studies of Reading, 1,* 235–253.

Olson, R. K., Wise, B., Johnson, M., & Ring, J. (1997). The etiology and remediation of phonologically based word recognition and spelling disabilities: Are phonological deficits the "hole" story? In B. Blachman (Ed.), *Foundations of reading acquisition* (pp. 305–326). Mahwah, NJ: Erlbaum.

Plomin, R., DeFries, J. C., & McClearn, G. E. (1990). *Behavior genetics: A primer.* San Francisco: W. H. Freeman.

Rack, J. P., Snowling, M. J., & Olson, R. K. (1992). The nonword reading deficit in developmental dyslexia: A review. *Reading Research Quarterly, 27,* 28–53.

Rodgers, B. (1983). The identification and prevalence of specific reading retardation. *British Journal of Educational Psychology, 53,* 369–373.

Scarborough, H. S. (1990). Very early language deficits in dyslexic children. *Child Development, 61,* 1728–1743.

Share, D. L. (1995). Phonological recoding and self-teaching: Sine qua non of reading acquisition. *Cognition, 55*(2), 151–218.

Shaywitz, S. E., Escobar, M. D., Shaywitz, B. A., Fletcher, J. M., & Makuch, R. (1992). Evidence that reading disability may represent the lower tail of a normal distribution of reading ability. *New England Journal of Medicine, 326,* 145–150.

Shaywitz, S. E., Shaywitz, B. A., Fletcher, J. M. (1990). Prevalence of reading disability in boys and girls. *Journal of the American Medical Association, 264,* 998–1002.

Smith, S. D., Kimberling, W. J., Pennington, B. F., & Lubs, H. A. (1983). Specific reading disability: Identification of an inherited form through linkage analysis. *Science, 219,* 1345–1347.

Smith, S. D., Pennington, B. F., & Kimberling, W. J. (1991). Screening for multiple genes influencing dyslexia. *Reading and Writing: An Interdisciplinary Journal, 3,* 285–298.

Stanovich, K. E., & West, R. F. (1989). Exposure to print and orthographic processing. *Reading Research Quarterly, 24,* 402–433.

Sternberg, R. J., & Wagner, R. K. (1982). Automatization failure in learning disabilities. *Topics in Learning and Learning Disabilities, 2,* 1–11.

Stevenson, J., Graham, P., Friedman, G., & McLoughlin, V. (1987). A twin study of genetic influences on reading and spelling ability and disability. *Journal of Child Psychology and Psychiatry, 28,* 229–247.

Vogler, G. P., DeFries, J. C., & Decker, S. N. (1985). Family history as an indicator of risk for reading disability. *Journal of Learning Disabilities, 18,* 419–421.

Wise, B. W., & Olson, R. K. (1995). Computer-based phonological awareness and reading instruction. *Annals of Dyslexia, 45,* 99–122.

Zerbin-Rudin, E. (1967). Kongenitale Worblindheit oder spezifische dyslexie (congenital word-blindness). *Bulletin of the Orton Society, 17,* 47–56.

2

The Biological Foundations of Developmental Dyslexia

Elena L. Grigorenko

As you read these words, you are not experiencing any conscious effort on your part. On the contrary, you let the words transport you from reading per se into the world of ideas and imagination. You allow the words to link to each other and create a story, and what you experience and comprehend is the story, not single words. This description is suitable only for a person who has mastered reading, for whom the process of reading words has become automatic. The experience of reading is completely different for children who have just learned how to read, for adults who are trying to master reading in a foreign language, and for those who have general difficulties in mastering reading in their native language.

At first glance the Browns are a typical American family. Adam is a carpenter and Kate is a school speech specialist. They have five children: two boys, 12 and 6, and three girls, 11, 9, and 6. The youngest kids are twins. What makes the Browns different is that several of them have trouble reading.

When Adam was a child, that is, more than twenty years ago, he had serious problems at school related to his inability to master reading. Fortunately, his parents were well-off enough to send him to a reading specialist, who worked with him for over four years, helping him to learn how to read. Adam made it through high school but did not even consider the idea of going to college—it was difficult for him to picture himself wading through all those books and papers one needs to read in order to get a college degree. Now his oldest boy and nine-year-old daughter have similar problems. Adam's older daughter seems to be doing well in school: She earns straight A's at school and just loves reading. The other two kids, his twins, are simply too young to judge. Adam says that he is worried about them, though. His older children are getting help, but it is quite expensive, and it would be difficult for the family to manage if four kids needed help with reading. Adam, however, will do anything in his power to help them; that was what his family did for him.

Adam says that his dad was always very supportive of him. Adam's father himself had a brother and sister who had difficulties with reading and writing. Adam's aunt, Gloria, is still alive, and her Christmas cards are notorious in the family for the number of spelling mistakes in them. For better or worse, Gloria married a man who also had trouble mastering reading. Gloria told Adam that her husband's family also had a history of reading problems.

Adam's Uncle Jack passed away a long time ago. Adam remembers that Jack's wife read him newspaper highlights every morning. They had five children, four of whom got a college education, and one, just like Adam, always had difficulties with reading.

Adam's brothers did very well at school. The oldest, Stan, is a lawyer, and his daughter is very smart. She is only five but already knows how to spell the word archaeologist. As a child, Mike, the youngest brother, went to see the same reading specialist Adam did. These lessons helped Mike a lot. Mike is an engineer, but both of his daughters did not do well in school. Kate never made it through high school, and her son is also having difficulties with reading. Mary graduated from high school but did not even want to hear about going to college. At school she worked really hard in order to get through reading and writing assignments: She put a lot of time into her homework and always complained that everything that involved reading and writing took too long.

The Browns are not a real family. They are a prototype of many families in which reading problems are transmitted from generation to generation; the Browns do not resemble any particular family, yet they have something in common with each of them. Families similar to the Brown family led scientists to formulate a hypothesis that certain types of reading problems run in families and therefore appear to be hereditary. This hypothesis, formulated initially by Hallgren in 1950, has attracted much attention among researchers and has introduced a new aspect into the search for the biological bases of dyslexia. Research on the hereditary mechanism of dyslexia has been closely linked both to the development of behavioral models of dyslexia and to attempts to understand its underlying biological grounds. And the more researchers know about developmental dyslexia, the more apparent it becomes that the data accumulated within three paradigms of studying it (behavioral, behavioral-genetic, and neuropsychological) converge, that findings from one paradigm contribute to progress in another paradigm, and that multidisciplinary researchers' efforts help to understand the mechanism and the course of developmental dyslexia.

The goal of this chapter is to offer an interpretation of recent findings gleaned from the field of research on the biological basis of reading and developmental dyslexia. This interpretation arose from evidence drawn from three distinct sources: research on developmental dyslexia in different populations around the world, brain research on reading and dyslexia, and genetic research on reading and dyslexia. This evidence is structured to address three questions: (1) Are there families like the Browns in populations that speak different languages? (2) Is there a biological trait, a biological "foundation," that runs in families like the Brown family and manifests itself in various behaviors ranging from the inability to comprehend a newspaper headline to making spelling errors? and (3) What do we know about the familiality of developmental dyslexia, and do we know enough to hypothesize why and how this condition gets passed from generation to generation in the Brown family and comparable families?

Miscellaneous Details

A Range of Definitions

As it appears from the description of the hypothetical Brown family, the spectrum of their reading problems is quite broad, extending from spelling errors to serious difficulties with the reading of single words. This variability is very real and is reflected in a major problem in the field of dyslexia studies—namely, the definition of dyslexia. If the complexity of a studied phenomenon were measured by the number of terms and concepts used to define and investigate it and these data were analyzed, dyslexia would no doubt score somewhere in the top 5 percent. The number of terms used in the investigation of dyslexia is especially remarkable when one takes into account the brief period during which there has been awareness of specific reading failures. According to Richardson (1992), the first mention of dyslexia-like problems was found as late as in eighteenth-century medical literature, where dyslexia was viewed as a type of aphasia. During the next 200 years, the condition of specific reading failure was variously referred to as *word blindness* (Kussmaul, 1877), *dyslexia* (Berlin, as cited in Richardson, 1992), *congenital word blindness* (Morgan, 1896; Hinshelwood, 1917), *strephosymbolia* (a disorder of twisted symbols; Orton, 1928), *specific reading disability* (Eustis, 1947), *reading disability* (Kirk & Bateman, 1962), *specific developmental dyslexia* (Critchley, 1970), *unexpected reading failure* (Symmes & Rapoport, 1972), *specific reading retardation* (Berger, Yule, & Rutter, 1975; van der Wissel & Zeger, 1985), *poor reading* (Olson, Kliegl, Davidson, & Foltz, 1985), and possibly by many other terms that have not yet been noted by historians of science.

Along with not agreeing on how to refer to this condition in general, researchers have run into another difficulty. Could it be said that various problems observed in the Brown family are different manifestations of one condition or that they are different conditions that just happen to co-incide in one family? Does poor spelling have the same root as difficulties with reading single words? Translating these questions into one, formulated in the language of genetic studies, could it be assumed that the phenotype (the behavioral manifestation of the underlying genetic structure, genotype) transmitted in the Brown family is singular, or are these multiple phenotypes, not necessarily related to each other? The current inability of the field to provide a definite answer to this question constitutes a major shortcoming of the extant studies of developmental dyslexia: Most of the studies conducted so far are characterized by imprecision and variability in the definition of the reading phenotype.

The Working Definition

The quilt of definitions covering the body of developmental dyslexia is a research subject in itself. Without engaging in a complicated debate on what dyslexia is and what it is not, I shall in this chapter use the following working definition of developmental dyslexia: Developmental dyslexia is a complex, biologically rooted behavioral condition resulting from impairment of metalinguistic phonological ability and manifested in difficulties related to mastering reading at the level of population norms under conditions of adequate educational and normal developmental environment.

The belief underlying this definition is that every human being who is in adequate health and is developing in an adequate social environment will learn how to speak; and similarly, every individual will learn how to read. Whereas language acquisition is driven by powerful internal developmental forces that are evolutionarily fixed as exclusively human ones (by language instinct in Pinker's [1995] terms), the mastery of reading is less predetermined yet is biologically controlled. The possibility of learning how to read is biologically orchestrated and evolutionarily fixed. The ability that drives the development of the "reading organ" is the metalinguistic ability of processing phonemes. In other words, the assumption here is that acquisition of normal reading skills is biologically grounded. This "grounding," however, is a two-way dynamic path between the biological foundation and the peculiarities of societal practices regarding the process of learning how to read.

To illustrate, when a tulip bulb is planted, there is a high probability that a beautiful flower will develop from the bulb. However, in the course of a sprout coming out and the tulip growing, many things can go wrong. The bulb itself could look just fine but be a carrier of deleterious genes, challenging the development of a sprout. The soil might be poisoned. There might not be enough sun. Similarly, the development of the "reading organ" might be jeopardized both by a malfunction in the biological programs setting up the possibility for such an organ to develop and by inadequate environments in which the formation of the "reading organ" takes place. The biological mechanisms leading to distortions of the "reading organ's" development might not be the same mechanisms that are responsible for normal reading development.

The Working Hypothesis

If reading is a product of the "reading organ," whose development is evolutionarily predetermined, this organ should have an identifiable seat (or a number of seats) in the brain. The "reading organ" is a functional organ that develops as a result of interaction between its biological substrate and the linguistic and educational environments in which the development takes place. The development of the reading organ is orchestrated by a number of cognitive abilities, one of which is metalinguistic phonological ability. A working hypothesis defended in this chapter states that reading, by the means of various cognitive processes involved, is rooted somewhere in the brain; and those brain circuits could have been established to carry their function by the genes. Moreover, reading ability might relate to a set of genes that help wire it in place. If these genes and the functions they carry are disrupted, reading suffers, whereas other cognitive functions (e.g., thinking) might remain primarily intact. Another possible explanation is that reading involves a number of cognitive processes that are rooted in different areas of the brain and that the malfunction of different genes in the process of brain development results in the cascade of events impairing reading-relevant cognitive processes.

Present gaps in our understanding of the biological mechanisms of both reading and dyslexia, unfortunately, do not permit the verification of the working hypothesis. Reading is a uniquely human skill, and this uniqueness hampers the identification of suitable animal models. Moreover, most people feel somewhat resistant to their brains being injected with chemicals, speared with electrodes, surgically operated upon, or split, sliced, or stained. Neither do they appreciate the idea of tampering with their genes. What is left for researchers is to puzzle over pieces of data accumulated through different studies and to impose their working hypotheses on the existing relevant evidence, estimating the fit between theory and data.

In this chapter the suggested working hypothesis is supported by evidence accumulated from three different types of research: studies of reading and developmental dyslexia in different languages; studies of the brain bases of reading and developmental dyslexia; and genetic studies of reading and developmental dyslexia.

Developmental Dyslexia: Language-Specific or Language-Free?

According to a survey of data collected in 26 countries, the percentage of school-age children with dyslexia ranges from a low in Japan and China (1 percent) to a high in Venezuela (33 percent), with an overall median rate of 7 percent (Tarnopol & Tarnopol, 1981). In English-speaking countries, children with reading problems constitute about 20 percent of the school population; in Scandinavian countries, about 10 percent, and in Germany, about 5 percent (Glezerman, 1983).

Three different hypotheses can be formulated to explain the varying incidence of reading problems in different countries. According to the first hypothesis, the observed differences in incidence are attributable to definitional differences or educational practices. For example, there are no characters in Chinese or Japanese whose meaning is equivalent to the term *reading disability*. In Asian countries, as another example, it is more likely that reading problems would be credited to lack of proper experience, not trying hard enough, not being adequately taught, or not being motivated enough, rather than to disability (Stevenson, Stigler, Lucker, Lee, Hsu, & Kitamura, 1982). Similarly, French psychologists have suggested that the major causes of dyslexia are motivational and cultural rather than linguistic (LeFebvre, 1978).

The second hypothesis suggests that language and orthography play an important role in reading disability (e.g., Mann, 1985; Read, Zhang, Nie, & Ding, 1986). The highest frequency of reading disability is observed in English-speaking countries. English is notoriously irregular. It is possible that very different language-processing deficits will be associated with dyslexia in languages that embed regular and easy-to-master rules of grapheme-phoneme correspondence and minimize a probability of phonological coding errors (Frost & Bentin, 1992; Taylor, 1981). Languages differ in their phonological characteristics, such as the complexity and variety of syllable types (Mattingly, 1985) and the transparency and consistency with which the orthographic representations map onto the phonology. In so-called *phonologically shallow* orthographies, the only sources of constraints on letter sequences are constraints on sound sequences (i.e., orthography represents phonology almost directly). In so-called *phonologically deep* orthographies, restrictions on letter sequences are related not only to phonological constraints but also to the etymology and morphology of the written language. For example, it has been sug-gested that "the syllabary of Japanese provides consistencies between symbols and their pronunciation, and that the ideographs of Chinese and Japanese offer possibilities for response to whole units that do not exist in alphabetic writing systems such as English" (Stevenson et al., 1982, p. 1165). The orthographic hypothesis was initially supported by an early study of Rozin, Poritsky, and Sotsky (1971), in which they showed that children who had serious difficulties in learning how to read in English were much more successful in reading Chinese characters to which En-glish words had been associated. This finding, however, was not con-firmed in population-based studies of reading disability in Japan and Tai-wan (Stevenson et al., 1982, 1987). The results challenged orthography as the major determinant of the incidence of reading disabilities across cul-tures. The researchers emphasized that there appeared to be more simi-larities than differences among children with reading problems in the United States, Japan, and Taiwan (Stevenson et al., 1982, 1987).

Finally, the third hypothesis is related to both of the previous ideas but presents a different explanation. This hypothesis is based on four lines of converging evidence. First, the majority of modern models of reading, most of which were developed in the English language, put phonological awareness at their center. Recently, even those models that include phonological processes but also stress the importance and independence of orthographic processes (e.g., dual-coding models of reading, Col-theard, 1978; Coltheard, Curtis, Atkins, & Haller, 1993; Paap, McDonald, Schvaneveldt, & Noel, 1987; Paap & Noel, 1991) have been challenged. Several studies (e.g., Lukatela & Turvey, 1991, 1993, 1994; Perfetti & Bell, 1991; Van Orden, 1987) have obtained evidence for an early and strong influence from assembled phonology in conducting any lexical opera-tions. Second, there is now compelling data that an individual's under-standing of the phonological structure of words is an important predictor of success in learning to read in many alphabetic orthographies besides English (e.g., Cardoso-Martins, 1995; Cossu, Shankweiler, Liberman, Katz, & Tola, 1988; Durgunoglu & Oney, submitted; Lundberg, Olofsson, & Wall, 1980; Wimmer, Landerl, Linortner, & Hummer, 1991). Third, by now a certain consensus has been formed around the converging evi-dence that phonological impairments play a causal role in the genesis of difficulties in mastering reading in English (e.g., Bradley & Bryant, 1993; Bryant & Bradley, 1985; Frith, 1985; Stanovich, 1988; Torgesen, this vol-ume). And finally, a number of studies have investigated the role of phonological impairment in the genesis of reading failures in "easier" than English writing systems (Wimmer, 1993, 1996).

Two observations made in these studies are especially important: (1) developmental dyslexics in more shallow languages show significantly lower error rates than dyslexics in phonologically deeper languages but still differ significantly from their matched normally reading peers in reading speed, and (2) the best predictor of reading performance in poor readers is the quality of their nonword reading, which is considered to be an indicator of phonological ability. In general, European definitions of dyslexia are very close to English-American ones. Dyslexia is viewed as a developmental disorder, the central deficit of which is phonetic-processing problems, in the Netherlands (Bouma & Legein, 1980; Walraven, Reitsma, & Kapper, 1994), France (Bailly, 1990; Tomatis, 1967), Poland (Krasowicz, 1993), Switzerland (Wright & Groner, 1992), and Italy (Cassini, Ciampalini, & Adriana 1984). According to Hoien (1989), dyslexia in Norway is also viewed as a behavioral problem to which language is central, and successful reading requires the recognition of symbols, sounds, and spelling patterns. Lundberg (1985) conducted a large-scale epidemiological study of reading disability in Sweden. The results were largely in agreement with current Anglo-American reading research, although the researcher applied a broader assessment battery and attempted to approach reading disabilities within a developmental context that is comparatively rare in other countries. Ramaa, Miles, and Lalithamma (1993) studied dyslexics who speak Kannada, a Dravidian language of South India, and found that these children showed the same pattern of specific dyslexia found in children who speak European languages. In addition, it has been observed that dyslexics in any language have difficulties mastering any second language, suggesting, again, that the dyslexic impairment is language-free. In the United States, for example, this finding is embedded in educational policies regarding disabled readers: Many diagnosed dyslexics are allowed get their college degrees without meeting foreign-language requirements.

Thus these four lines of evidence converge around the interpretation of phonological abilities as a metalinguistic ability, the manifestation of which is moderated by a given linguistic system. Just as spoken languages differ in the complexity of their phonological structure, so written languages differ in their representations of spoken languages. Just as characteristics of spoken languages affect the patterns of development of phonological processes, so those patterns, in turn, affect the development of reading skills. These observations permit formulating the third hypothesis regarding the varying incidence of developmental dyslexia in different languages. It appears that the mechanism leading to difficulties

associated with mastering reading is universal and is related to the metalinguistic ability to decompose words into sounds and link phonemes to
graphemes. The manifestation of reading problems, however, will be different in different languages depending on the phonological demands
imposed by a given linguistic system. Think of an analogy: A person who
is musically tone-deaf might not be aware of his or her deficit until asked
to sing; and when asked to sing, dealing with a simple melody will be
much easier than dealing with a complex opera aria.

If we are willing to accept the third hypothesis as the working hypothesis, that is, if we believe that there is a metalinguistic phonological
deficit that is biologically based and whose behavioral manifestation
varies depending on the challenge imposed by a phonological structure
of a given language, then it is logical to suggest that there should be a
distinct signature of this deficit at a biological rather than a behavioral
level. In this regard the distinction between the deep and the superficial
phenotypes of dyslexia (Pauls, Naylor, & Flowers, 1992) appears to be
very useful: The superficial, behavioral phenotype of dyslexia might
cover a wide spectrum of behavioral manifestations varying in different
languages and depending on the amount of remediation, whereas the
deep biological phenotype (e.g., certain structural or functional patterns
of the brain) would remain distinct and identifiable even after years of remediation.

So it appears that the existence of dyslexia is recognized across many
cultures and continents. Even though the amount of cross-cultural and
comparative research on developmental dyslexia is rather limited, the
majority of results supports a consistent pattern in specific dyslexia that
does not depend on any one writing system or geographic location. Thus
the differences in the rates of incidences of dyslexia throughout the
world can most likely be explained not by low prevalence of this disorder
in different cultures that results from different underlying language-spe-
cific dyslexic deficits but rather by the interplay of two factors: the
phonological structure of a given language and the societal attitudes toward the disorder. The results presented earlier suggest the possibility of
constructing a culture-free definition of dyslexia (Wood, Felton, Flowers,
& Naylor, 1991), central to which is, probably, the biological basis of this
condition. It appears that the Brown family might exist in any society,
speaking any language. The basic dyslexic impairment is language-free.
However, its manifestation is language- and culture-dependent. Only in
a situation where (1) the phonological structure of the language is challenging enough to impose a serious obstacle for dyslexics, (2) the frequency of normal reading in a given society is high enough so that failures are noticeable, and (3) there is a societal demand to master this skill
that is backed up by an adequate number of professionals, is dyslexia

noted by educators, psychologists, and biologists, its prevalence studied and its etiology investigated.

Studies of Brain Structure

The Neuropathology of Dyslexia

Postmortem studies have been performed on the brains of four dyslexic men. Three men had histories of language delay, and one had a history of seizures. All four men showed unusual symmetry in the planum temporale (posterior aspect of the superior temporal lobe), a structure relevant to normal language function (Galaburda, Sherman, Rosen, Aboitiz, & Geschwind, 1985). A postmortem study of three dyslexic women (Humphreys, Kaufman, & Galaburda, 1990) with comorbid attentional disorders, psychiatric disturbances, and head injury also reported a highly symmetrical plane in all subjects. In normal individuals, a distinct asymmetry is usually seen in this brain structure, which is larger on the left side of the brain in 65 percent of the population, and larger on the right in 11 percent. At the microscopic level, the dyslexic brains were found to have significantly more misplaced and unusually organized nerve cells, which, presumably, reflects the failure of neurons to reach their normal cortical targets during fetal development. The presence of an unusually symmetrical plane is the most consistent neuropathological finding in dyslexia to date. This symmetry is not due to a decrease in the size of the left planum but results from an increase in the size of the right planum. Galaburda and colleagues (1985) hypothesized that this results from reduced cell death during fetal development, which leaves an excessive number of surviving neurons in the right planum, forming anomalous connections and resulting in a "miswiring" of the brain. Thus it is proposed that dyslexia is an outcome of anomalous neural development, the trigger of which might occur at the prenatal stage of development. Furthermore, these authors suggest that dyslexia could have its beginnings in the interaction between the prenatal chemical environment and the maturation rate of the relevant areas of the brain. This interaction could result in anomalous cell migration and organization. For example, it has been shown that neurons in various structures of the dyslexic thalamus are smaller than expected (Galaburda, Schrott, Sherman, Rosen, & Denenberg, 1996). This structural abnormality may be related to the temporal processing abnormalities described in the auditory system of language-impaired children (e.g., Tallal & Piercy, 1973).

More recently, in addition to unusual symmetry, small vascular events and other injuries have also been suspected as being related to dyslexia (Galaburda, 1990). It has been proposed (Galaburda et al., 1996) that these ischemic injuries are produced by autoimmune damage of vessel walls, leading to cortical injury, scars, and disrupted blood flow.

Another line of evidence is drawn from studies of brain-damaged patients and studies of brain asymmetry. For example, it has been shown that isolated-right-hemisphere patients show little capacity for phonological processing (Zaidel & Peters, 1981). Moreover, patients with acquired dyslexia resulting from extensive left-hemisphere lesions tend to demonstrate extremely poor decoding skills but adequate orthographic and semantic judgments, suggesting that these patients rely mostly on right-hemispheric processes in reading (Coltheard, 1980; Schweiger, Zaidel, & Dobkin, 1989). The results of visual hemifield experiments with neurologically normal individuals also suggest that phonological processing is associated predominantly with left-hemispheric functions (Cohen & Freeman, 1978; Parkin & West, 1985) and that the advantage of the left hemisphere is smaller for women than for men (Luh & Levy, 1995; Lukatela, Carello, Savic, & Turvey, 1986; Pugh et al., 1996)

Neuroanatomic Imaging

Roentgenographic computerized tomography and, more recently, magnetic resonance imaging have been used to examine cerebral asymmetries in dyslexia, particularly posterior hemispheric asymmetries. Based on neurobiological theory that implicated the importance of the central language areas, computerized tomographic magnetic resonance imaging studies have provided evidence that links deviations in normal patterns of posterior asymmetry (left greater than right) to dyslexia (Flowers, 1993; Hynd, Semrud-Clikeman, Lorys, Novey, & Etiopulos, 1990; Rumsey, 1992). Whereas normal brains favor the left planum temporale and posterior region, dyslexics appear to have a higher incidence of symmetrical or reversed posterior asymmetry that is due to increases on the right side (Duara et al., 1991), although other researchers report decreases in the size of the left planum (Hynd et al., 1990; Larsen, Hoien, Lundberg, & Odegaard, 1990). However, Leonard and colleagues (1993), in their recent study of nine dyslexics, found no anomalous interhemispheric symmetry, although some subjects with dyslexia had an anomalous intrahemispheric asymmetry owing to a significant shift of right planar tissue from the temporal to the parietal bank. Similar exaggerated asymmetries were mentioned in another study (Tzeng, 1994). In addition, Leonard and colleagues (1993) found that dyslexics were more likely to have cerebral anomalies such as missing or duplicated gyri bilaterally in the planum and parietal operculum, presumably reflecting disturbance in cell migration resulting from genetic or developmental causes. Researchers have also examined different regions of the brain in attempting to find the biological basis for dyslexia. For example, in a recent study of 16 dyslexic and 16 control subjects, Hynd and colleagues (1995) found that the corpus callosum was significantly smaller in dyslexics. Thus these studies, though providing overall support to a neurobiological model of dyslexia, are marked by some inconsistency in terms of their specific findings. Certain methodological flaws, such as small populations and varying diagnostic criteria used to identify dyslexic subjects, may collectively contribute to the somewhat discrepant results (Hynd & Semrud-Clikeman, 1989). However, even though the presented findings should be considered only as suggestive of potential structural differences in dyslexics as compared to control populations (Filipek & Kennedy, 1991), the researchers consistently find the presence of developmental anomalies in dyslexic brains, which, on its own, is a rather strong indication of the underlying biological bases of dyslexia.

Functional Brain Studies

Electrophysiological Studies of Dyslexia

A number of studies were designed (e.g., Hughes, 1985) to gain some insight into dyslexia-specific EEG correlates of phonological coding. Results of childhood electrophysiological studies showed a clear physiological deficit in children with reading disability. These deficits manifested themselves as longer latencies in the evoked potentials and a reduced amplitude at a number of latencies (e.g., Harter, Diering, & Wood, 1988; Harter, Anllo-Vento, Wood, & Schroeder, 1988). Researchers found greater theta activity and less beta power at parietal, central, and frontal sites to be characteristic of dyslexia (Ackerman, Dykman, Oglesby, & Newton, 1994; Duffy, Dencka, Bartels, & Sandini, 1980; Flynn, Deering, Goldstein, & Rahbar, 1992; Lubar, 1991; Pricep, John, Ahn, & Kaye, 1983), indicating that adequate readers process verbal stimuli more actively. Adult electrophysiological studies of dyslexia also pointed to reduced amplitudes and smaller differences in the waveforms of evoked potentials to words versus flashes (Preston, Guthrie, Kirsch, Gertman, & Childs, 1977).

Functional Neuroimaging

Incredible recent advances in neuroimaging technology have made it possible to detect and investigate cortical regions and their activation patterns associated with performance of complex cognitive tasks (e.g., Demonet, Price, Wise, & Frackowiak, 1994; Petersen, Fox, Posner, Mintun, & Raichle, 1989; Shaywitz et al., 1995). New functional brain-imaging methods are being applied to test hypotheses of cortical dysfunction in both normal reading and dyslexia. This technology enables study of patterns of cortical activation (e.g., glucose utilization, blood flow, and oxygen consumption) elicited by various cognitive challenges. The goal of such studies is to determine what areas of the brain get activated while performing the operation of reading and whether dyslexic individuals activate the brain regions involved in reading, language, and phonological coding in a way similar to normal readers.

A number of investigators using functional magnetic resonance imaging utilized subtraction methodology, which employs a list of increasingly difficult tasks with each consecutive task including a preceding task as a subcomponent. By measuring the brain activity during the performance of such a set of increasingly difficult tasks and subtracting the index of activation associated with a lower-level task from the level of activation associated with a higher-level task, researchers quantify the brain activity by creating brain activation maps. These maps outline correlations between task performance and regional activation. For example, Pugh and colleagues (1996) decomposed the holistic process of reading into a number of distinct visual and linguistic processes (i.e., line, letter case, nonword rhyme, and semantic category judgments) and investigated whether these processes employ different cortical regions. These researchers (Pugh et al., 1996) examined six cortical regions located in the frontal, temporal, and occipital lobes. The frontal-lobe areas included the inferior frontal gyrus (centered in Broca's area), the prefrontal dorsolateral, and the orbital gyrus. The temporal-lobe areas included the superior temporal gyrus and the middle temporal gyrus. Finally, in the occipital lobe, the extrastriate region was investigated. The study, by pointing to increased activation of the brain under various subtraction conditions, rooted different visual and linguistic processes to different brain areas. Thus orthographic processing made maximum demands on the extrastriate region, phonological processing activated both the inferior frontal gyrus and the temporal lobe, and semantic processing engaged the superior temporal gyrus more than did either phonological or orthographic processing.

Findings from recent studies (Howard et al., 1992; Law, Kanno, & Fujita, 1992; Petersen et al., 1990; Shaywitz et al., 1995) seem to be converging around the involvement of Brodmann's Area 37 in object recognition, where the object category can include letters and words. These findings were extended further in the study of Garret, Wood, Flowers, and Absher (1997). The researchers applied the positron-emission tomography methodology in order to register brain activity during performance of the letter-recognition task. The remarkable result of this study was that Left Brodmann's Area 37 and the left angular gyrus generated metabolic activity that was inversely correlated with task performance. This link between better performance and less activation suggests that increased activation may indicate inefficient processing and thus may be related to failure to inhibit completing activity, recruitment of resources exceeding those necessary for a given task, or the brain's immaturity reflected in its inability to activate locally rather than globally.

Thus recent studies of associations between brain regions and various procedural components of reading in accomplished readers indicate that reading is a holistic process rooted in the brain and link various reading subcomponent processes to different brain regions.

Finally, the most crucial piece of evidence critical for the argument in this chapter comes from comparative brain metabolism studies of normal and dyslexic readers. Only a few studies of dyslexics have been conducted utilizing functional neuroimaging methodology. Two early studies (Hynd, Hynd, Sullivan, & Kingbury, 1987; Rumsey et al., 1987) reported differences in the brain responses of dyslexic and control subjects to cognitive tasks, but neither had enough evidence to conclude that left-hemisphere activity is abnormal in dyslexia. Flowers, Wood, and Naylor (1991) found that left-hemisphere superior temporal blood flow is positively related to orthographic accuracy. This correlation was found only at the left superior temporal region. Notable is the fact that this finding was replicated in two independent samples. In addition, reading performance, as diagnosed in childhood, was significantly positively related to blood flow in Wernicke's Area and, negatively, to the flow in the angular gyrus. Flowers (1993) also noted that generalized low EEG waveform and high-angular gyrus blood flow were correlated with each other and were distinct characteristics of dyslexic brains. In addition, this "brain profile" was independent of reading improvement from childhood to adulthood, suggesting that it might be related to early reading problems. Similarly, Rumsey and colleagues (1992) found that the left temporoparietal cortex near the angular gyrus was less likely to be activated in dyslexic men when going from rest to rhyme detection. Furthermore, dyslexics showed a decline in accuracy of detection compared to control subjects.

Other researchers (Wood, Flowers, Buchsbaum, & Tallal, 1991) found that dyslexics, when reading, demonstrate unevenly spread metabolic activity throughout the brain, whereas metabolism in normal individuals tends to be more equally distributed. In addition, patterns of metabolism in dyslexics are also different from those in controls. Subsequent to their earlier work, Garret, Wood, Flowers, and Absher (1997), comparing patterns of brain metabolism in accomplished readers and dyslexic ones, found metabolic differences (relative to matched controls) in the thalamus and the posterior inferior-temporal cortex. Specifically, dyslexics showed decreased metabolism in two right-hemispheric regions, Brod-mann's Area 37, and the thalamus.

One of the most exciting lines of the brain research on reading is re-lated to links found between patterns of brain activation as quantified through regional changes in cortical metabolism registered while per-forming cognitive operations and independent behavioral measures on tasks viewed as reflecting those cognitive operations. For example, Pugh and others (1997) found strong associations between patterns of brain ac-tivation and peculiarities of performance in the lexical decision task. In detail, those individuals who showed greater extrastriate and inferior frontal right-hemispheric activation tended to be slower in rejecting non-words and more sensitive to the phonetic regularity of real words. Garret and Wood (1997) detected strong relationships between variation in thal-amic metabolism, especially in the left hemisphere, and variation in in-dexes of reading ability such as single-word reading.

To summarize, studies of both structural and functional brain differ-ences in normal readers and dyslexics have accumulated evidence sug-gesting that dyslexic subjects are different from controls. The consistent finding of abnormal, excessive left temporoparietal or angular gyrus acti-vation in the brains of dyslexics indicates that abnormal reading perfor-mance has a specific mechanism that is different from the mechanisms of normal reading. It appears that an abnormal reader does not simply show characteristics of an extreme on the normal distribution but instead demonstrates features that are either suppressed or not at all present in the normal population (Wood, Felton, Flowers, & Naylor, 1991). In addi-tion, functional studies of brain regions engaged during the performance of cognitive tasks that are considered models of subcomponent processes involved in reading in normal subjects link different processes to differ-ent areas of the brain. Moreover, these links appear to be valid when the patterns of brain activation are correlated with performance on behav-ioral tasks. And most important for the present discussion, there is con-verging evidence suggesting that the phonological process is rooted to a particular brain area (temporal gyrus) and that the patterns of activity in this area vary for dyslexic versus normal readers.

Linking these general findings back to the Browns, one could hypothe-size that what has been transmitted in this family is a deep brain-based phenotype of dyslexia. The observed phenotypic variation in manifesta-tions of dyslexia might be explained by the degree of impairment and time and amount of remediation offered. The sensible investigation would be one on whether dyslexic family members have a distinct brain phenotype and whether a similar "brain signature" exists in those indi-viduals who do not have behavioral signs of dyslexia but whose children do (e.g., Mike Brown and his two daughters). Recent advances in neuroimaging techniques allow us to conduct noninvasive studies and thus make it possible to study not only healthy adults but also children and elderly persons. There is no doubt that within the next few years researchers will conduct family neuroimaging studies that search for brain correlates of poor reading transmitted in dyslexic families.

Is Dyslexia Hereditary?

A number of converging lines of evidence suggest that developmental dyslexia (or at least some of its forms) is hereditary; one type of evidence comes from twin studies (also see Olson, this volume); another comes from family studies of dyslexia.

Studies of Twins Reared Together

In describing twin studies relevant to understanding the role of genes in the etiology of dyslexia, it is necessary to distinguish between (1) twin studies of concordance rates, which utilize a design where twin pairs are recruited based on one of the individuals in the pair having dyslexia and the rates of concordance (both twins having dyslexia) and discordance (only one twin having dyslexia) are determined and (2) twin studies of reading achievement where both twins are recruited simultaneously. These two types of studies provide qualitatively different information: The research of type 1 allows an evaluation of the hypothesis of the hereditary basis of dyslexia as a clinical condition, whereas the research of type 2 can estimate heritability coefficients for the transmission of various indicators of reading performance.

Concordance Rate Studies

In the first twin study of dyslexia, Hermann (1959) found that all 10 (100 percent) identical (monozygous—MZ) twin pairs were concordant for reading disability in contrast to only 11 out of 33 (33 percent) fraternal (dizygous—DZ) pairs. Zerbin-Rudin (1967) summarized several case studies of MZ and DZ twins in which at least one member of every pair had reading problems. She reported that in a sample of 17 MZ and 34 DZ pairs, the concordance rates were 100 percent and 35 percent, respectively. Bakwin (1973), through a population-based twin registry at a local mother-of-twins club, selected 62 pairs of twins in which at least one twin was dyslexic. The concordance rates were 84 percent for MZ pairs and 20 percent for DZ pairs. Decker and Vandenberg (1985) reported similar concordance rates (85 percent and 55 percent, respectively, for MZ and DZ pairs) for a sample selected in the frame of the Colorado twin study of reading disability. DeFries, Fulker, and LaBuda (1987) also presented evidence for a significant genetic etiology of dyslexia by applying multiple-regression analysis to data collected from a sample of 64 pairs of MZ twins and 55 pairs of DZ twins, in which at least one member of the pair was reading disabled. Thus unless there is something about being an MZ twin, besides having an identical genetic makeup, that could lead to co-occurrence of reading failures in both twins, all of these studies suggest that genetic factors are important in developmental dyslexia. Indeed, rather high MZ concordance rates, in comparison to the DZ concordance rates of just under 50 percent found in these studies, indicate the presence of genetic influences in developmental dyslexia.

Twin Studies of Reading Achievement

It has been suggested that the etiology of dyslexia may not be distinct from the etiology of the normal distribution of reading skills (cf. Perfetti, 1984; Spear-Swerling & Sternberg, 1996). Stanovich (1990) noted that dyslexia exists on a continuum rather than as a discrete entity, and the borderline between disordered and normal functioning may therefore be somewhat arbitrary. If so, causal influences resulting in dyslexia should be essentially the same as the ones important for the development of normal reading performance. Based on this consideration, researchers applied the classic twins-reared-together design to estimate the relative impact of genetic and environmental effects on the etiology of normal reading achievements (Olson, this volume).

A vast number of studies have reported MZ and DZ twin correlations for various measures of reading performance (for review, see Grigorenko, 1996). MZ correlations are uniformly greater than DZ correlations, suggesting the presence of genetic influence. However, heritability estimates have varied. Some of this variability can be attributed to the fact that in the majority of studies the sample size was relatively small, so the standard errors of the h^2 (broad-sense heritability coefficient, which points to the estimated proportion of the genetic component in the phenotype variation but does not provide any more information beyond this assertion) estimates are relatively large. In addition some twin studies suggest that only certain reading-related skills are inherited. Thus it has been shown that reading recognition, spelling, digit span, and phonological coding show significant heritability, whereas reading comprehension, perceptual speed, and orthographic coding do not (Olson, Wise, Conners, Rack, & Fulker, 1989). For example, for reading recognition, heritability has been estimated as 45 percent (Brooks, Fulker, & DeFries, 1990). Heritability estimates for spelling have ranged from approximately 21 percent to 62 percent (Brooks et al., 1990; Petrill & Thompson, 1994). Altogether, for various reading factors and scales, heritability estimates range down from 79 percent (Martin & Martin, 1975) to 10 percent (Canter, 1973).

When multivariate analyses were applied, researchers showed that heritability coefficients estimated jointly for word recognition and phonological coding were substantially higher than for word recognition and orthographic coding (DeFries et al., 1991). The low heritability and genetic covariance estimates for orthographic coding suggest that this skill is most likely influenced by environmental forces. Thus researchers concluded that what is inherited appears to involve the phonological aspects of reading disability. However, this conclusion was challenged in the recent study of Hohnen and Stevenson (1995), who found strong genetic influence on both phonological and orthographic components of reading processing.

Wadsworth, Gillis, and DeFries (1990) employed multiple-regression techniques to test a hypothesis, suggested by Stevenson and others (1987), that the genetic etiology of reading disability may differ as a function of age. The obtained heritability estimates varied for younger and older twins. This finding was consistent with the hypothesis that genetic factors may be less important as a cause of reading disability in older children (DeFries, Olson, Pennington, & Smith, 1991). However, the sample was not large enough to obtain statistically significant differences between the estimates. This research group also studied the genetic and environmental causes of the phenotypic association between reading performance and verbal short-term memory (Wadsworth, DeFries, Fulker, Olson, & Pennington, 1995). Results of bivariate behavioral genetic analyses indicate that both reading ability and verbal short-term memory are highly heritable and that a substantial proportion of their phenotypic correlation is due to common genetic influences.

In summary, all twin studies suggest that some components of reading performance, most likely phonological coding, show high broad-sense heritability estimates, suggesting the involvement of genetic factors. However, these findings should be interpreted cautiously because estimates of heritability (and conversely, estimates of the contribution of environmental factors) have varied across studies and measures. In addition, the base rates of reading disability could be different in a population of twins and the population of singletons. For example, in the 1975 Australian nationwide study of school performance, Hay and colleagues (Hay, O'Brien, Johnston, & Prior, 1984) showed that by the age of fourteen only 42 percent of twin boys had achieved adequate standards of literacy compared with 71 percent of single-born boys.

Familiality of Dyslexia

Researchers characterize developmental dyslexia as an etiologically and functionally heterogeneous clinical condition (Ellis, 1985; Jorm, 1979) that nonrandomly aggregates in families with some subtypes having a genetic etiology (Finucci, Guthrie, Childs, Abbey, & Childs, 1976; Hallgren, 1950). The risk for reading disability is greater among relatives of dyslexic probands than in the general population (Childs & Finucci, 1983; DeFries & Decker, 1982; Olson, this volume; Pennington, 1991; Wolff & Melngailis, 1994). Studies of familial risk report that 40 percent of boys and 18 percent of girls with an affected parent show dyslexia (Pennington & Smith, 1988). This incidence rate approximates a sevenfold increase in boys and a twelvefold increase in girls over the estimated population risk (Rumsey, 1992).

What Is the Pattern of Transmission of Dyslexia?

In order to understand the pattern of transmission of developmental dyslexia in families with reading problems, researchers conducted a number of segregation analyses, fitting different statistical models corresponding to various patterns through which the genes can be transmitted in families. Some investigators have concluded that familial dyslexia is transmitted in an autosomal (not sex-linked) dominant mode (Childs & Finucci, 1983; Hallgren, 1950), whereas others have found only partial (Pennington et al., 1991) or no support for an autosomal or codominant pattern of transmission. These findings were interpreted as suggesting that specific reading disability is genetically heterogeneous (Finucci et al., 1976; Lewitter, DeFries, & Elston, 1980). Researchers (Pennington et al., 1991) also conducted complex segregation analyses of a qualitative dyslexic phenotype. These phenotypic scores were obtained by applying discriminant weights estimated from an analysis of the Peabody Individual Achievement Test (PIAT) Reading Recognition, Reading Comprehension, and Spelling subtest. The results suggested that dyslexia was transmitted in a mode consistent with a major gene (additive or dominant).

Gilger and colleagues (Gilger, Borecki, DeFries, & Pennington, 1994) reported on genetic segregation analyses performed on a quantitative phenotype (derived as in Pennington et al., 1991) of members of families ascertained through normal, nondisabled readers. The findings indicated the presence of familial transmission of the phenotype in which a significant amount of variance could be attributed to a major gene.

Thus there is no consensus in regard to the mode of transmission of dyslexia. Some researchers suggest that specific reading disability is likely to be polygenic and influenced by the environment (Decker & Bender, 1988). A general model-free approach to polygenic phenomena, quantitative trait loci (QTL) mapping, has been applied (Cardon et al., 1994; Fulker et al., 1991) to allow the localization of individual genes that contribute to the development of dyslexia, which is presumed to be defined by multiple genes.

In addition to working with "pure" dyslexic phenotypes, researchers studied patterns of familiarity of psychological and neuropsychological traits relevant to reading disability. For example, Ashton and colleagues (Ashton, Polovina, & Vandenberg, 1979; Borecki & Ashton, 1984) reported on the presence of major gene effects for spatial and vocabulary tests. Wolff and Melngailis (1994) have started a family study of dyslexics wherein, along with using traditional means of diagnosing dyslexia, they have studied deficits of temporal organization on tasks of bimanual motor coordination and motor speech, assuming that these impairments may identify one developmentally stable, physiologically plausible, and linguistically neutral behavioral phenotype in familial dyslexia. Decker and DeFries (1980) studied the response of dyslexics to tests of right and left hemispheric functions. They found that parents and siblings of the reading-disabled probands demonstrated patterns of deficits in reading and cognitive processing speed but not in spatial reasoning.

Moreover, researchers point to some additional facts that appear to be related to the familial nature of dyslexia. For example, Wolff and Melngailis (1994) found that sibs in families with two affected parents are at greater risk and tend to be more severely impaired than sibs in families with one affected parent. These findings point to a possibility of the importance of additive genetic effects that might play an important modifying role in familially transmitted developmental dyslexia.

Several studies have suggested that assortative mating may be an important factor in studying dyslexic pedigrees (Gilger, 1991; Wolff & Melngailis, 1994). Thus examination of dyslexic families with two affected parents may "disclose dimensions in the etiology and pathophysiology of developmental dyslexia that would not be apparent if such families were excluded" (Wolff & Melngailis, 1994, p. 130). Moreover, Hanebuth, Gilger, Smith, and Pennington (1994) showed that a child's risk for dyslexia is conditioned upon the current parental reading skills. Even though the mechanism of this effect is yet to be understood (and it is clear that the effects of genes and family environment are confounded in these families), this finding is clinically useful (Smith, 1992). Thus a health-care practitioner or educator should always consider the family history of a child because the prognosis for a child of a once-affected, adequately compensated adult is much better than that for a child of a once-affected, still-affected adult.

In sum, a convincing amount of evidence has been accumulated suggesting that at least some proportion of developmental dyslexia has a genetic basis. However, it should be noted that the precise mechanisms of the transmission of dyslexia are not clear. In addition, in interpreting family data, researchers are always aware of the fact that estimates of genetic variance may not be reliable because of shared environmental family experiences and attitudes that can inflate the indices of genetic similarity.

Which Genes Are Involved in the Transmission of Dyslexia?

The ultimate goal of a genetic study of a monogenic condition is locating and isolating the responsible gene. The absence of expression of this gene in individuals with a trait, or direct demonstration of a correlation of mutations in the gene and in the phenotype, constitutes powerful evidence that the gene plays an important role in causing the studied characteristic. Once located, the protein product encoded by the gene may permit a physiological explanation for its role in normal processes or diseases. Research may eventually lead to the development of new interventions (both biological and nonbiological) that may lessen the effects of dysfunctional gene products. Finally, the isolation of a gene might allow for gene therapy, replacing a "defective" mutant gene with a normally functioning copy (Billings, Beckwith, & Alper, 1992; Kidd, 1991).

Using current molecular techniques of linkage analysis, investigators have carefully studied selected family trees (pedigrees) of dyslexic individuals in which developmental dyslexia reoccurs in different generations. The results of one early study suggested that a major gene for dyslexia was located on the short arm of chromosome 15 (Pennington et al., 1991; Smith, Kimberling, Pennington, & Lubs, 1983; Smith, Pennington, Kimberling, & Ing, 1990). Fulker and colleagues (1991) followed up these findings by selecting from the original extended-family study a sample of siblings who represented lower levels of reading ability. They applied multiple-regression techniques, and their results also pointed to chromosome 15. However, subsequent molecular linkage studies, which included the same dyslexia pedigrees, refuted the original findings (Lubs et al., 1991; Rabin et al., 1993; Cardon et al., 1994). Furthermore, independent investigators who examined Danish families with an autosomal dominant pattern of transmission for dyslexia were also unable to replicate the chromosome 15 finding (Bisgaard, Eiberg, Moller, Neihbar, & Mohr, 1987).

A screen of other regions of the genome revealed chromosome lp as a locus that provided moderate evidence for linkage to dyslexia (Rabin et al., 1993; Smith et al., 1983). Coincidentally, Froster and colleagues (1993) have identified a German family in which dyslexia and delayed speech development cosegregate with a balanced translocation (rearrangement of chromosomal material) between chromosomes 1 and 2. This observation suggests linkage to a gene on the distal region of the short arm of chromosome 1 or the long arm of chromosome 2. However, in at least one subsequent study (Cardon et al., 1994), interval mapping analyses of the Rh region markers yielded no evidence for linkage at any location.

Lubs and colleagues (1991) identified a family with a translocation with a fusion of chromosomes 13 and 14. Six of the seven family members with the translocation also have dyslexia; however, there is one dyslexic member of the family who does not have the translocation. Thus, this family provides a possible clue that there might be another gene associated with dyslexia on chromosome 13 or 14. These researchers also conducted random genome testing that included selected markers on chromosomes 1–4, 6, 8, 9, 11, 13, 14–16, and 18–21 (Lubs et al., 1991). No significant results were obtained.

A number of investigators (Hansen, Nerup, & Holbek, 1986; Hugdahl, Synnevag, & Saltz, 1990; Lahita, 1988) hypothesized a possible association between dyslexia and autoimmune disorders. Results of their studies have suggested that rates of autoimmune diseases are elevated in relatives of dyslexic probands and that the incidence of dyslexia is increased in relatives of probands having autoimmune illness. Although the causal basis of the association is unknown, the evidence for association from these independent studies points to the human leukocyte antigen (HLA) complex, located on the short arm of chromosome 6, as a candidate region (Pennington, Smith, Kimberling, Green, & Haith, 1987). Interval mapping of data from two independent samples of 114 sib pairs, with at least one disabled, revealed evidence for linkage between reading disability and the HLA region on chromosome 6 (Cardon et al., 1994). Analyses of corresponding data from an independent sample of 50 dizygotic twin pairs also provided evidence for linkage to the HLA complex. However, these findings do not hold for reanalyses when dyslexia is defined as a categorical condition according to clinical (DSM-III-R-based) diagnosis (Cardon, et al., 1994). In addition, the continuous diagnosis, used in this study, was based exclusively on the perceptive vocabulary and verbal IQ measures. Thus whereas the applied methodology seems very promising for the analyses of continuous traits, the analyzed trait, even though it is associated with specific reading disability, may reflect an overwhelming influence of verbal IQ.

Both of the earlier genetic findings (chromosome 6 and chromosome 15) have been replicated in an independent sample of dyslexic families (Grigorenko et al., 1997). What is especially interesting is that both genetic regions—the chromosome 6 region, located in the neighborhood of the human leukocyte antigen (HLA) complex, and the chromosome 15 region, associated with the production of 2-microglobulin—are loci implicated in human autoimmune disorders. This link might suggest that some autoimmune disturbance of the developmental organism might be a primary insult to the brain that in turn results in disturbances of the blood flow to various regions of the brain, including those engaged in reading.

In summary, linkage studies have pointed to some regions of interest that are spread on a number of chromosomes throughout the human genome. None of these findings can be referred to as "the true result," and more research in the same regions is needed. When these findings are translated to the level of individual disabled readers, like those members of the Brown family described previously, three observations are important. First, differential linkage of different phenotypes to different chromosomal regions might be indicative of the genetic heterogeneity of developmental dyslexia. It might be that the genetic cause of reading problems in Adam's family is different from the genetic cause of dyslexia in the family of Gloria's husband. Moreover, there could be different genetic causes of dyslexia within Adam's family itself—such genetic heterogeneity might be the reason for all the different behavioral manifestations of reading problems seen among the Browns. Second, similar remediational efforts within a given family might have differential success. Whereas Mike completely compensated for his childhood reading problems, Adam carried them, even though to a lesser degree, throughout his life. These individual differences in receiving and responding to remediational help are matters for special investigation. The third observation has to do with the degree of severity of developmental dyslexia, even within one family. As is obvious in the case of the Browns, severity varies. One more unanswered question is why this is so.

Three converging lines of evidence have been reviewed to support the working hypothesis of the nature of developmental dyslexia suggested in this chapter. To reiterate in broad terms, the working hypothesis assumes that a metalinguistic deficit, characteristic of dyslexics in any language, is linked to a brain pattern that results from specific genetic mechanisms. This hypothesis is an empty frame that yet needs to be filled with concrete scientific results and robust, replicable findings. Much work remains! The last issue to be addressed here concerns the kind of scientific speculations about the nature of developmental dyslexia that are permitted by the working hypothesis formulated at the beginning of the chapter.

Reaching Beyond the Evidence

Developmental dyslexia is one of many common familial disorders that does not conform to simple Mendelian expectations. Genetic explana-

tions of dyslexia have had to rely mostly on evidence from twin and segregation studies, but these results intersect consistently in the hypothesis
of the presence of the genetic endowment for dyslexia. In addition, the
structural and functional studies of dyslexic brains point to traces of genetic influences during brain development. Moreover, the rapidly accumulating evidence suggesting that developmental dyslexia is language-
free, at least in one of its forms relevant to phonological impairment, also
suggests a possibility of universal genetic mechanisms governing the
manifestation of dyslexia across different linguistic systems.

Thus because the results of different avenues of research converge and
lead to the same conclusion, the role of genes in the etiology of dyslexia
appears to be significant. Yet the path from the belief that genes are important to identifying specific genes influencing specific behaviors is not
a straight or simple one. However, there are many ways in which genetic
studies of specific disabilities might turn out to be very productive.

First, it might occur that some genetic causes of dyslexia become understood prior to the discovery of neuropsychological and behavioral
profiles specific to dyslexia. This would lead to more precise phenotype
definition and subtyping. The identification of etiological correlates
might contribute to differential diagnosis; then, if subgroups of dyslexic
individuals who show physiological or genetic abnormalities are found,
a specific set of cognitive or neuropsychological characteristics representing an important behavioral diagnosis and practical recommendations
would follow (Decker & Bender, 1988; Smith et al., 1990). For example, if
a familial subtype of dyslexia turns out to be linked to the immune system, that finding would be important in regard to treating dyslexia as
well as for delivering the message to the public that an abnormal immune system may manifest itself through reading problems.

Second, dyslexia is a type of neuropsychiatric disorder that, following
traditions of classic human genetics, might be useful in attempts to understand the normal functioning of the human brain (Kidd, 1991). As
mentioned, there is constant debate in the field about whether dyslexia is
a qualitatively different condition or simply a unique combination of individual differences, many of which happen to be distributed below two
standard deviations on the normal curve. Distinct subtypes suggest distinct causes for different reading disabilities, such as localized brain impairments or single-gene inheritance patterns. Continuous distributions
suggest multiple causes and polygenic models of inheritance (DeFries &
Decker, 1982; Pennington et al., 1990). This is also true for the distribution
of reading ability. If disabled readers are distinctly separated from the
normal distribution of reading ability, single-gene factors or some unique
environmental insults will be likely. An alternate view is that due to polygenic inheritance patterns and/or continuously varying environmental

influences, disabled readers are very low in the specific cognitive skills needed for normal reading, just as superior readers may be very high in these critical skills (Olson et al., 1985, p. 50). Again, through utilizing genetic studies, a reverse movement is possible—if genetic causes of dyslexia are understood first, then the individual-differences-versus-qualitatively-different-condition debate might be resolved.

Third, the hypothesis formulated by Galaburda and supported by others (Chase & Tallal, 1991; Hynd, 1992), which states that dyslexia is a disorder of brain development rather than a disorder of metabolism/function in a structurally normal brain, appears to be more and more plausible in the context of current findings in the field of developmental genetics.

In recent years, a great deal has been learned about the differentiation of individual nerve cells, their organelles, and their synaptic contacts (Rakic, 1988, p. 33). However, the meaning of these events is still not understood in terms of building a complex cellular assembly such as the neocortex. Sutcliff (1988) maintains that tens of thousands of genes are expressed in the adult brain alone. In addition, there are many genes that control the development of the brain and the differentiation of various neurons. For example, researchers have just started investigating the ways in which genes guide the movement of neurons to the cortex, having discovered a number of mutations derailing neurons on their journey to the highly ordered cortex (Barinaga, 1996). To date, molecular neurobiologists have identified only a diminutive portion of the genes that could, by malfunctioning, cause structural and/or functional abnormalities in the central nervous system. The field is at the stage where, once more, we recognize our ignorance: Virtually nothing is known about genes that control the differentiation of neurons or those that control the establishment of connections. Evidence is accumulating that certain multigene families (homeogenes) participate in pattern formation and segmentation in animal development (Dressler & Gruss, 1988; Melton, 1991). Mouse and drosophila models will help to decipher the role of highly evolutionary conserved genes called homeoboxes in the control of gene expression, in diverse regulatory context, and in embryonic pattern formation (Shashikant et al., 1991). The DNA-binding properties of the protein products of homeobox genes, the patterns of their expression, and the high precision of their functions suggest that these genes may form systems that are highly specific and effective in terms of envisioned information. "Such a system not only would be cybernetically regulating the expression of its component genes, but also might be responsive to input (environmental) information, and, in turn, function to coordinate the patterns of expression of effector genes. Presumably, effector genes would be those directly involved in growth and morphogenesis, as, for instance, genes encoding growth factors, receptors, structural proteins, etc." (Kappen, Schughart, & Ruddle, 1989, p. 251).

Fourth, the aforementioned plasticity of genetic systems and their ability to utilize environmental information are indicative of the existence of the complex sequence of bidirectional, interacting causes that make it almost impossible to separate definite roles of genotype and environment unless a major gene is identified. According to the findings discussed in this chapter, dyslexia is, most plausibly, a complex condition that emerges at the intersection of biological and environmental influences, reflecting and responding to both detrimental and remediational effects of nature and nurture.

Modern neuroscience is revising its view of the brain. It suggests that richness of environment is essential for maintaining healthy neurons and viable connections among them (Baringa, 1992) and that learning actually modifies the physical structure of cells, not just their chemical contents (Purves, 1988). The plasticity of the human brain and its dependence on environment can provide an explanation for why remediation efforts work in dyslexia cases. The hardware-software metaphor previously often used in regard to the living brain does not really hold anymore, since evidence in animal research has accumulated to support the fact that experience continues to alter the connections throughout life. More and more fascinating details are learned every day about the links between genes and the brain. For example, Goodman and colleagues (Davis, Schuster, & Goodman, 1996; Schuster, Davis, Fetter, & Goodman, 1996a, 1996b) might have found a solution to the central mystery of plasticity. Their research is concerned with the question of how changes in gene expression in a neuron that has many axons and many synaptic connections can alter the strength of only some of its synapses. Goodman and colleagues' studies suggest that the neuron nucleus manages the assembly of synaptic structure, whereas local biochemical factors in individual axons determine where in the nerve cell the synaptic structure gets placed. And other researchers have suggested that the cells on the other side of the synaptic connection become engaged in the completion of the synaptic renovation (Roush, 1996).

On the basis of what we have learned from modern molecular biology, nothing is driven exclusively by genetic or environmental forces (cf. Wahlsten & Gottlieb, 1997). Under appropriate conditions, the gene is transcribed into messenger RNA and then translated into a polypeptide molecule that may function as an enzyme, hormone, or structural element of a cell. The gene codes for the sequence of amino acids in the polypeptide and a gene metabolic activity can be documented by molecular techniques that allow us to determine the presence of antibodies specific for the protein in question or even to look at the complementary

DNA probes that bind to a specific sequence of the mRNA molecule. The modern results are indicative of the fact that most genes are active for restricted periods of time and in limited areas. The gene itself is subject to control by its surroundings and cannot govern itself. The stimuli switching a gene on or off are transmitted by the cytoplasm of the cell (Blau et al., 1985) and can originate in the external environment of the animal (e.g., Zawilska & Wawrocka, 1993). A variety of environmental stresses provoke a cascade of events that turn on a class of "immediate-early" genes, which in turn unleash a diverse multitude of further molecular events (Sager & Sharp, 1993). Learning and memory involve the controlled actions of numerous genes (Kaczmarek, 1993). Thus environment regulates the actions of genes, and genes, via changes in the nervous system, influence the sensitivity of an organism to changes in the environment.

From what can be predicted now, the immediate future of research on complex human traits will be devoted to studying the complexity of the interaction between genes and environment. Regarding dyslexia, this shift of paradigms might help to understand the phenomenon of compensation. Remediation matters even when the condition is genetically determined! Nevertheless, the theoretical realization of this complexity of gene-environment interactions does not lead researchers to a direct understanding of the biological basis of the functioning of genetic webs. Moreover, only knowledge of specific genes, their functions and surroundings, can help us to understand learning, memory, intelligence, language, and reading. There can be no meaningful and valid representation of the biology of the human brain and behavior without positive knowledge of the genes involved. The only way is to try to find these genes.

Finally, studies of the biology of dyslexia and its genetic grounds might help us to understand the puzzle of the evolution of the human brain in general and of human higher mental functions in particular. It is possible that reading, as a skill, underwent remarkable changes in the course of human history. The universality of complex languages and their written representations is a discovery that impels linguists and psychologists to wonder whether linguistic systems are not just a cultural invention but also the product of a specific trajectory of human development. And like any developing structure, reading might have reshaped, and this reshaping might have been caused by (or be a cause of) some corresponding change in the brain. For example, Saint Augustine, the Christian theologian (AD 400), when writing about the bishop of Milan, Saint Ambrose, remarked with astonishment upon the fact that Ambrose could read silently, not pronouncing any words aloud (Augustine, 1978, 6.3). Speculating on this remark, historians (Gavrilov, 1985) have suggested that in those times, the majority of readers knew only how to read aloud; they did not practice reading silently to themselves. It is plausible that comparative genetic studies of populations whose linguistic systems differ will reveal some clues about the evolutionary path of normal and dyslexic reading in modern civilization.

The field of genetic research on neuropsychiatric conditions is on the verge of a breakthrough. Detection of genetic factors associated with psychiatric disorders has not progressed at the pace originally hoped for and anticipated in the frame of "old" views of complex disorders (Berg, Mullican, Maestri, & Shore, 1994). In the late 1980s, investigators hoped that the theory of Mendelian inheritance would serve as a strong theoretical background for discoveries of major genes operative in complex human conditions and that the only problem on the path to these discoveries was the relative weakness of laboratory methodologies. Since the late 1980s, the study of complex human disorders has been marked by the astonishingly rapid and extensive development of new laboratory techniques and methods of data analysis, but no comprehensive conceptualization of the biology underlying complex human disorders has been proposed. Moreover, since about 1993, the field has experienced a number of dramatic discoveries of genetic mechanisms of various neuropsychiatric conditions, many of which deviate from Mendelian laws. As dialectics predict, now is the time for conceptual developments. It is hoped that this expected reconceptualization in the field of neuropsychiatric genetics will also lead to finding the missing interlinkages within the triad of "behavioral manifestations of dyslexia–underlying brain patterns–respective genetic mechanisms" and bring us closer to an understanding of the laws of the normal and abnormal development of the "reading organ."

References

Ackerman, P. T., Dyckman, R. A., Oglesby, D. M., & Newton, J.E.O. (1994). EEG power spectra of children with dyslexia, slow learners, and normally reading children with ADD during verbal processing. *Journal of Learning Disabilities, 27,* 619–630.

Ashton, G. C., Polovina, J. J., & Vandenberg, S. G. (1979). Segregation analysis of family data for 15 tests of cognitive ability. *Behavior Genetics, 9,* 329–348.

Augustine. *Confessions.* New York: Penguin Books, 1978.

Bailly, L. (1990). La dyslexic en 1990 [Dyslexia in 1990]. *Perspectives Psychiatriques, 24,* 269–272.

Bakwin, H. (1973). Reading disability in twins. *Developmental Medicine and Child Neurology, 15,* 184–187.

Barinaga, M. (1992). The brain remaps its own contours. *Science, 258,* 216–218.

Barinaga, M. (1996). Guiding neurons to the cortex. *Science, 274,* 1000–1001.

Berg, K., Mullican, C., Maestri, N., & Shore, D. (1994). Psychiatric genetic research at the National Institute of Mental Health. *American Journal of Medical Genetics (Neuropsychiatric Genetics), 54,* 295–299.

Berger, M., Yule, W., & Rutter, M. (1975). Attainment and adjustment in two geographical areas. II: The prevalence of specific reading retardation. *British Journal of Psychiatry, 125,* 510–519.

Billing, P. R., Bechvith, J., & Alper, J. S. (1992). The genetic analysis of human behavior: A new era? *Social Science and Medicine, 3,* 227–238.

Bisgaard, M. L., Eiberg, H., Moller, N., Neihbar, E., & Mohr, J. (1987). Dyslexia and chromosome 15 heteromorphism: Negative lod scores in a Danish sample. *Clinical Genetics, 32,* 118–119.

Blau, H. M., Pavlath, G. K., Hardeman, E. C., Choy-Pik C., Silberstein, L., Webster, S. G., Miller, S. C., & Webster, C. (1985). Plasticity of the differentiated state. *Science, 230,* 758–766.

Borecki, I. B., & Ashton, G. C. (1984). Evidence for a major gene influencing performance on a vocabulary test. *Behavior Genetics, 14,* 63–79.

Bourna, H., & Legein, C. P. (1980). Dyslexia: A specific recoding deficit? An analysis of response latencies for letters and words in dyslexics and in average readers. *Neuropsychology, 18,* 285–298.

Bradley, L., & Bryant, P. E. (1983). Categorizing sound and learning to read: A casual connection. *Nature, 301,* 419–421.

Brooks, A., Fulker, D. W., & DeFries, J. C. (1990). Reading performance and general cognitive ability: A multivariate genetic analysis of twin data. *Personality and Individual Differences, 11,* 141–146.

Bryant, P. E., & Bradley, L. (1985). *Children's reading problems.* Oxford: Blackwell.

Canter, S. (1973). Some aspects of cognitive function in twins. In G. Claridge, S. Canter, & W. I. Hume (Eds.), *Personality differences and biological variations: A study of twins.* Oxford, England: Pergamon Press.

Cardon, L. R, Smith, S. D., Fulker, D. W., Kimberling, W. J., Pennington, B. F., & DeFries, J. C. (1994). Quantitative trait locus for reading disability on chromosome 6. *Science, 266,* 276–279.

Cardoso-Martins, C. (1995). Sensitivity to rhymes, syllables, and phonemes in literacy acquisition in Portuguese. *Reading Research Quarterly, 27,* 153–162.

Cassini, A., Ciampalini, L., Adriana, L. (1984). La dislessia in Italia. Strumenti di rilevazione e incidenza in alcune regioni (Dyslexia in Italy: Detection instruments and the incidence in some regions). *Eta Evolutiva, 18,* 66–73.

Chase, C. H., & Tallal, P. (1991). Cognitive models of developmental reading disorders. In J. E., Obrzut & G. W. Hynd (Eds.), *Neuropsychological foundation of learning disabilities* (pp. 199–240). New York: Academic Press.

Childs, B., & Finucci, J. M. (1983). Genetics, epidemiology and specific reading disability. In Rutter M. (Ed.), *Developmental psychiatry* (pp. 507–519). New York: Guilford.

Cohen, G. & Freeman, R. (1978). Individual differences in reading strategies in relation to handedness and cerebral asymmetry. In J. Requin (Ed.), *Attention and performance VII* (pp. 411–28). Hillsdale, NJ: Erlbaum.

Coltheard, M. (1978). Lexical access in simple reading tasks. In G. Underwood (Ed.), *Strategies in information processing* (pp. 151–216). London: Academic Press.

Coltheard, M. (1980). Deep dyslexia: A right hemisphere hypothesis. In M. Coltheard, K. Patterson, & J. C. Marshall (Eds.), *Deep dyslexia* (pp. 326–380). London: Routledge & Kegan Paul.

Coltheard, M., Curtis, B. Atkins, P., & Haller, M. (1993). Models of reading aloud: Dual-route and parallel distributed-processing approaches. *Psychological Review, 100*, 580–608.

Cossu, G., Shankweiler, D., Libennan, I. S., Katz, L., & Tola, C. (1988). Awareness of phonological segments and reading ability in Italian children. *Applied Psycholinguistics, 9*, 1–16.

Critchley, M. (1970). *The dyslexic child.* Springfield, IL: Thomas.

Davis, G. W., Schuster, C. M., & Goodman, C. S. (1996). Genetic dissection of structural and functional components of synaptic plasticity. III. CREB is necessary for presynaptic functional plasticity. *Neuron, 17*, 669–679.

Decker, S. N., & Bender, B. G. (1988). Converging evidence for multiple genetic forms of reading disability. *Brain and Language, 33*, 197–215.

Decker, S. N., & DeFries, J. C. (1980). Cognitive abilities in families with reading disabled children. *Journal of Learning Disabilities, 13*, 517–522.

Decker, S. N., & Vandenberg, S. G. (1985). Colorado twin study of reading disability. In D. Gray & J. Kavanaugh (Eds.), *Biobehavioral measures of dyslexia.* Baltimore: York Press.

DeFries, J. C., & Decker, S. N. (1982). Genetic aspects of reading disability: A family study. In R. N. Malathesah & P. G. Aaron (Eds.), *Reading disorders: Varieties and treatments* (pp. 255–279). New York: Academic Press.

DeFries, J. C., Fulker D. W., & LaBuda, M. C. (1987). Evidence for a genetic aetiology in reading disability in twins. *Nature, 329*, 537–539.

DeFries, J. C., Olson, R. K., Pennington, B. F., & Smith, S. D. (1991). Colorado Reading Project: An update. In D. D. Duane & D. B. Gray (Eds.), *The reading brain: The biological basis of dyslexia* (pp. 53–88). Parkton, Maryland: York Press.

Demonet, J. F., Price, C., Wise, R., & Frackowiak, R. S. J. (1994). A PET study of cognitive strategies in normal subjects during language tasks: Influence of phonetic ambiguity and sequence processing on phoneme monitoring. *Brain, 117*, 671–682.

Durgunogu, A. Y., & Oney, B. (submitted). A cross-linguistic comparison of phonological awareness and word recognition in Turkish and English.

Dressler, G. R., & Gruss, P. (1988). Do multigene families regulate vertebrate development? *Trends in Genetics, 4*, 214–219.

Duara, R, Kushch, A., Gross-Glenn, K., Jallad, B. J., Pascal, S., Barker, W. W., Loewenstein, & Lubs, H. A. (1991). Neuroanatomic differences between dyslexic and normal subjects. *Archives of Neurology, 48*, 410416.

Duffy, F. H., Denckla, M. B., Banels, P. H., & Sandini, G. (1980). Dyslexia: Regional differences in brain electrical activity by topographical mapping. *Annals of Neurology, 7*, 412–420.

Ellis, A. W. (1985). The cognitive neuropsychology of developmental (and acquired) dyslexia: A critical survey. *Cognitive Neuropsychology, 26*, 169–205.

Eustis, R. (1947). Specific reading disability. *New England Journal of Medicine, 237*, 243–249.

Filipek, P. A., & Kennedy, D. N. (1991). Magnetic resonance imaging: Its role in the developmental disorders. In D. D. Duane & D. B. Gray (Eds.), *The reading brain: The biological basis of dyslexia* (pp. 133–160). Parkton, MD: York Press.

Finucci, J. M., Guthrie, J. T., Childs, A. L., Abbey, H., & Childs, B. (1976). The genetics of specific reading disability. *Annals of Human Genetics, 40,* 1–23.

Flowers, D. L., Wood, F. B., & Naylor, C. E. (1991). Regional cerebral blood flow correlates of language processes in reading disability. *Archives of Neurology, 48,* 637–643.

Flowers, D. L. (1993). Brain basis for dyslexia: A summary of work in progress. *Journal of Learning Disabilities, 26,* 575–582.

Flynn, J.M., Deering, W., Goldstein, M., & Rahbar, M. H. (1992). Electrophysiological correlates of dyslexic subtypes. *Journal of Learning Disabilities, 25,* 133–141.

Frith, U. (1985). Beneath the surface of developmental dyslexia. In K. E. Patterson, J. C. Marshall, & M. Coltheard (Eds.), *Surface dyslexia* (pp. 301–330). Hillsdale, NJ: Erlbaum.

Froster U., Schulte-Korne G., Hebebrand, J., & Remschmidt, H. (1993). Cosegregation of balanced translocation (1;2) with retarded speech and dyslexia. *Lancet, 342,* 178–179.

Fulker, D. W., Cardon, L. R, DeFries, J. C., Kimberling, W. J., Pennington, B. F., & Smith, S. D. (1991). Multiple regression analysis of sib-pair data on reading to detect quantitative trait loci. *Reading and Writing: An Interdisciplinary Journal, 3,* 299–313.

Galaburda, A. M. (1990). *Address to the 16th Annual Rodin Remediation Society Meeting.* Boulder, CO.

Galaburda, A. M., Sherman, G. P. Rosen, G. D. Aboitiz, F., & Geschwind, N. (1985). Developmental dyslexia: four consecutive patients with cortical anomalies. *Annals of Neurology, 18,* 222–233.

Galaburda, A. M. Schrott, L.M., Sherman, G. F., Rosen, G. D., & Denenberg, V. H. (1996). Animal models of developmental dyslexia. In C. H. Chase, G. D. Rosen, & G. F. Sherman (Eds.), *Developmental dyslexia* (pp. 3–14). Baltimore, MD: York Press.

Garret, A. S., Wood, F. B., Flowers, D. L., Absher, J. R. (1997). *Glucose metabolism in the inferior temporal cortex is related to accuracy of performance on a letter recognition task.* Unpublished manuscript.

Gilger, J. W. (1991). Differential assortative mating found for academic and demographic variables as a function of time of assessment. *Behavioral Genetics, 21,* 131–158.

Gilger, J. W., Borecki, I. B., DeFries, J. C., & Pennington, B. F. (1994). Commingling and segregation analysis of reading performance in families of normal reading probands. *Behavior Genetics, 24,* 345–356.

Glezerman, T. B. (1983). *Mozgovye disfunktsii u detei* [Minimal brain dysfunctions in children]. Moscow: Nauka.

Grigorenko, E. L. (1996). A family study of dyslexia. Unpublished dissertation.

Grigorenko, E. L., Wood, F. B., Meyer, M. S., Hart, L. A., Speed, W. C., Shuster, A., & Pauls, D. L. (1997). Susceptibility loci for distinct components of developmental dyslexia on chromosomes 6 and 15. *American Journal of Human Genetics, 60,* 27–39.

Hallgren, B. (1950). Specific dyslexia ("congenital word blindness"): A clinical and genetic study. *Acta Psychiatrica et Neurologica, 65,* 2–289.

Hanebuth, E., Gilger, J. W., Smith, S. D., & Pennington, B. F. (1994). *Parental compensation for childhood reading problems effects the risk to their offspring for developmental reading disorders.* Unpublished manuscript.

Hansen, O. Nerup, J., & Holbek, B. (1986). A common specific origin of specific dyslexia and insulin-dependent diabetes mellitus? *Heteridas, 105,* 165–167.

Harter, M. R., Anllo-Vento, L., Wood, F. B., Schroeder, M. M. (1988). Separate brain potential characteristics in children with reading disability and attention deficit disorder: Color and letter relevance effects. *Brain and Cognition, 7,* 115–140.

Harter, M. R., Diering, S., & Wood, F. B. (1988). Separate brain potential characteristics in children with reading disability and attention deficit disorder: Relevance-independent effects. *Brain and Cognition, 7,* 54–86.

Hay, D. A., O'Brien, P. J., Johnston, C. J., & Prior, M. R. (1984). The high incidence of reading disability in twin boys and its implication for genetic analyses. *Acta Geneticae Medicae et Gemellologiae, 33,* 223–236.

Hermann, K. (1959). *Reading disability: A medical study of word blindness and related handicaps.* Springfield, IL: Charles C. Thomas.

Hinshelwood, J. (1917). *Congenital word-blindness.* London: Lewis & Company.

Hohnen, B., & Stevenson, J. (1995). Genetic effects in orthographic ability: A second look. *Behavior Genetics, 25,* 271.

Hoien, T. (1989). La dyslexie: Approche developmentale et processuele [Dyslexia: A progressive developmental approach]. *Psychiatrie de l'Enfant, 32,* 617–638.

Howard, D., Patterson, K., Wise, R., Brown, D., Friston, K., Weiller, C., & Frackowiak, R. (1992). The cortical localization of the lexicons. Positron emission tomography evidence. *Brain, 115,* 1769–1782.

Hugdahl, K., Synnevag, B., & Saltz, P. (1990). Immune and autoimmune diseases in dyslexic children. *Neuropsychology, 28,* 673–679.

Hughes, J. R. (1985). Evaluation of electrophysiological studies on dyslexia. In D. B. Gray & J. F. Kavanaugh (Eds.), *Biobehavioral measures of dyslexia* (pp. 71–86). Parkton, MD: York Press.

Humphreys, P., Kautman, W. E., & Galaburda, A. M. (1990). Developmental dyslexia in women: Neuropsychological findings in three cases. *Annals of Neurology, 28,* 727–738.

Hynd, G. W. (1992). Neurological aspects of dyslexia: Comment on the balance model. *Journal of Learning Disabilities, 25,* 110–112.

Hynd, G. W., Hall, J., Novey, E. S., Etiopulos, D., Black, K., Gonzales, J.J., Edmonds, J. E., Riccio, C., Cohen, M. (1995). Dyslexia and corpus callosum morphology. *Archives of Neurology, 52,* 32–38.

Hynd, G. W., Hynd, C. R., Sullivan, H. G., & Kingsbury, T. B. (1987). Regional cerebral blood flow (rCBF) in developmental dyslexia: Activation during reading in a surface and deep dyslexic. *Journal of Learning Disabilities, 20,* 294–300.

Hynd, G. W., & Semrud-Clikeman, M. (1989). Dyslexia and brain morphology. *Psychological Bulletin, 106,* 447–482.

Hynd, G. W., Semrud-Clikeman, M., Lorys, A. R., Novey, E. S., & Etiopulos, D. (1990). Brain morphology in developmental dyslexia and attention deficit disorder/hyperactivity. *Archives of Neurology, 47,* 919–926.

Jorm, A. F. (1979). The cognitive and neurological basis of developmental dyslexia. A theoretical framework and review. *Cognition, 7,* 19–33.

Kacsmarek, L. (1993). Molecular biology of vertebrate learning: Is *c-fos* a new beginning? *Journal of Neuroscience Research, 34,* 377–381.

Kappen, C., Schughart, K., & Ruddle, F. (1989). Organization and expression of homeobox genes in mouse and man. *Annals of the New York Academy of Sciences, 567,* 243–252.

Kidd, K. K. (1991). Genes and neuropsychiatric disorders. *Social Biology, 38,* 163–178.

Kirk, S. A., & Bateman, B. (1962). Diagnosis and remediation of learning disabilities. *Exceptional Children, 29,* 72–78.

Krasowicz, G. (1993). Dysleksja a rozwoj i zaburzenia mowy [Dyslexia, development, and speech disorders]. *Psychologia Wychowawcza, 36,* 25–35.

Kussmaul, A. (1877). Disturbances of speech. In H. von Ziemssen (Ed.) & J. A. McCreery (Trans.), *Cyclopedia of the practice of medicine.* New York: William Wood.

Lahita R. G. (1988). Systemic lupus erythematosus: Learning disability in the male offspring of female patients and relations to laterality. *Psychoneuroendocrinology, 13,* 385–396.

Larsen, J. P., Hoien, T., Lundberg, I., & Odegaard, H. (1990). MRI evaluation of the size and symmetry of the planum temporale in adolescents with developmental dyslexia. *Brain and Language, 39,* 289–301.

Law, I., Kanno, I., & Fujita, H. (1992). Functional anatomical correlates during reading of morphograms and syllograms in the Japanese language. *Biomedical Research, 73,* 51–52.

LeFebvre, J. (1978). Dyslexia and simultaneous learning of French and Hebrew: Experience in the private school Lucien de Hirsch (Paris). *Revue Belge de Psychologie et de Pedagogie, 40,* 27–30.

Leonard, C. M., Voeller, K.K.S., Lombardion, L. J., Morris, M. K., Hynd, G. W., Alexander, A. W., Andersen, H. G., Garofalakis, M., Honeyman, J. C., Mao, J., Agee, O. F., & Staab, E. V. (1993). Anomalous cerebral structure in dyslexia revealed with magnetic resonance imaging. *Archives of Neurology, 50,* 461–469.

Lewitter, F. I., DeFries, J. C., & Elston, R. C. (1980). Genetic models of reading disabilities. *Behavior Genetics, 10,* 9–30.

Lubar, J. F. (1991). Discourse on the development of EEG diagnostics and biofeedback for attention deficit/hyperactivity disorders. *Biofeedback and Self-Regulation, 5,* 187–206.

Lubs, H. A., Duara, R., Levin, B., Jallad, B., Lubs, M.-L., Rabin, M., Kushch, A., & Gross-Glenn, K. (1991). Dyslexia subtypes: Genetics, behavior, and brain imaging. In D. D. Duane & D. B. Gray (Eds.), *The reading brain: The biological basis of dyslexia* (pp. 89–118). Parkton, MD: York Press.

Luh, K. E., & Levy, J. (1995). Interhemispheric cooperation: Left is left and right is right, but sometimes the twain shall meet. *Journal of Experimental Psychology: Human Perception and Performance, 21,* 1243–1258.

Lukatela, G., Carello, C., Savic, M., & Turvey, M. T. (1986). Hemispheric asymmetries in phonological processing. *Neuropsychology, 24,* 341–350.

Lukatela, G., & Turvey, M. T. (1991). Phonological access of the lexicon: Evidence from associative priming with pseudochomophones. *Journal of Experimental Psychology: Human Perception and Performance, 17,* 951–966.

Lukatela, G., & Turvey, M. T. (1993). Similar attentional, frequency, and associative effects for pseudohomophones and words. *Journal of Experimental Psychology: Human Perception and Performance, 19,* 166–178.

Lukatela, G., & Turvey, M. T. (1994). Visual lexical access is initially phonological: Evidence from associative priming words, homophones, and pseudohomophones. *Journal of Experimental Psychology, 123,* 107–128.

Lundberg, I. (1985). Longitudinal studies of reading and reading difficulties in Sweden. *Reading Research: Advances in Theory and Practice, 4,* 65–106.

Lundberg, I., Olofsson, A., Wall, S. (1980). Reading and spelling skills in the first school years predicted from phonemic awareness skills in kindergarten. *Scandinavian Journal of Psychology, 21,* 159–173.

Mann, V. A. (1985). A cross-linguistic perspective on the relation between temporary skills and early reading ability. *Remedial and Special Education, 6,* 37–42.

Martin, N. G., & Martin, P. G. (1975). The inheritance of scholastic abilities in a sample of twins. *Annals of Human Genetics, 39,* 219–228.

Mattingly, I. G. (1985). Did orthographies evolve? Special Issue: Phonology and the problems of learning to read and write. *RASE: Remedial and Special Education, 6,* 18–23.

Melton, D. A. (1991). Pattern formation during animal development. *Science, 252,* 234–241.

Morgan, W. P. (1896). A case of congenital word-blindness. *British Medical Journal, 11,* 1378.

Olson, R. K. (in press). Genes, environment, and reading disabilities. In R. J. Sternberg & L. Spear-Swerling (Eds.), *Perspective on learning disabilities.* Boulder, CO: Westview Press.

Olson, R. K., Kliegl, R., Davidson, B. J., & Foltz, G. (1985). Individual and developmental differences in reading disability. *Reading Research: Advances in Theory and Practice, 4,* 1–64.

Olson, R., Wise, B., Conners, F., Rack, J., & Fulker, D. (1989). Specific deficits in component reading and language skills: Genetic and environmental influences. *Journal of Learning Disabilities, 22,* 339–348.

Orton, S. T. (1928). Specific reading disability—strephosymbolia. *Journal of the American Medical Association, 90,* 1095–1099.

Paap, K. R., McDonald, J. E., Schvaneveldt, R. W., & Noel, R. W. (1987). Frequency and pronounceability in visually presented naming and lexical decision tasks. In M. Coltheard (Ed.), *Attention and performance XII: The psychology of reading* (pp. 221–243). Hillsdale, NJ: Erlbaum.

Paap, K. R., & Noel, R. W. (1991). Dual-route models of print to sound: Still a good horse race. *Psychological Research, 53,* 13–24.

Parkin, A. J., & West, S. (1985). Effects of spelling-to-sound regularity on word identification following brief presentation in the right or left visual field. *Neuropsychology, 23,* 315–341.

Pauls, D. L., Naylor, C., & Flowers, L. (1992). *Adult and second generation dyslexia.* Unpublished manuscript.

Pennington, B. F. (1991). Annotation: The genetics of dyslexia. *Journal of Child Psychology and Psychiatry, 31,* 193–201.

Pennington, B. F., Gilger, L. W., Pauls, D., Smith, S. A., Smith, S., & DeFries, J. C. (1991). Evidence for a major gene transmission of developmental dyslexia. *Journal of the American Medical Association, 266,* 1527–1534.

Pennington, B. F., Smith S. D., Kimberling, W. J., Green, P. A., & Haith, M. M. (1987). Left handedness and immune disorders in familial dyslexia. *Archives of Neurology, 44,* 634–639.

Perfetti, C. A. (1984). *Reading ability.* London and New York: Oxford University Press.

Perfetti, C. A., & Bell, L. C. (1991). Phonemic activation during the first 40 ms of word identification: Evidence from backward masking and priming. *Journal of Memory and Language, 30,* 473–485.

Petersen, S. E., Fox, P. T., Posner, M. I., Mintun, M., & Raichle, M. E. (1989). Positron emission tomographic studies of the processing of single words. *Journal of Cognitive Neuroscience, 1,* 153–170.

Petersen, S. E., Fox, P. T., Snyder, A. Z., & Raichle, M. E. (1990). Activation of extrastriate and frontal cortical areas by visual words and word-like stimuli. *Science, 249,* 1041–1044.

Petrill, S. A., & Thompson, L. A. (1994). The effect of gender upon heritability and common environmental estimates in measures of scholastic achievement. *Personality and Individual Differences, 16,* 631–640.

Pinker, S. (1995). *The language instinct.* New York, NY: Harper Perennial.

Preston, M. S., Guthrie, J. T., Kirsch, I., Gertman, D., & Childs, B. (1977). VERs in normal and disabled adult readers. *Psychophysiology, 14,* 8–14.

Pricep, L., John, E. R., Ahn, H., & Kaye, H. (1983). Neurometrics: Quantitative evaluation of brain dysfunction in children. In M. Rutter (Ed.), *Developmental neuropsychiatry.* London: Guilford.

Pugh, K. R., Shaywitz, B. A., Constable, R. T., Shaywitz, S. A., Skudlarski, P., Fulbright, R. K., Bronen, R. A., Shankweiler, D. P., Katz, L., Fletcher, J. M., & Gore, J. C. (1996). Cerebral organization of component processes in reading. *Brain, 119,* 1221–1238.

Pugh, K. R., Shaywitz, B. A., Shaywitz, S. E., Shankweiler, D. P., Katz, L., Fletcher, J. M., Skudlarski, P., Fulbright, R. K., Constable, R. T., Bronen, R. A., Lacadie, C., Gore, J. C. (1997). Predicting reading performance from neuroimaging profiles: The cerebral basis of phonological effects in printed word identification. *Journal of Experimental Psychology: Human Perception and Performance, 23,* 299–318.

Purves, D. (1988). *Body and brain. A trophic theory of neural connections.* Cambridge, MA: Harvard University Press.

Rabin, M., Wen, X. L., Hepburn, M., & Lubs, H. A. (1993). Suggestive linkage of developmental dyslexia to chromosome 1p34–36. *Lancet, 342,* 178–179.

Rakic, P. (1988). Defects of neuronal migration and the pathogenesis of cortical malformations. *Progress in Brain Research, 73,* 15–37.

Ramaa, S., Miles, T. R., & Lalithamma, M. S. (1993). Dyslexia: Symbol processing difficulty in the Kannada language. *Reading and Writing: An Interdisciplinary Journal, 5,* 29–41.

Read, C., Zhang, Y., Nie, H., & Ding, B. (1986). The ability to manipulate speech sounds depends on knowing alphabetic reading. *Cognition, 24,* 31–44.

Richardson, S. O. (1992). Historical perspectives on dyslexia. *Journal of Learning Disabilities, 25,* 40–47.

Roush, W. (1996). The supple synapse: An affair that remembers. *Science, 274,* 1102–1103.

Rozin, P., Poritsky, S., & Sotsky, R (1971). American children with reading problems can easily learn to read English represented in Chinese characters. *Science, 171,* 1264–1267.

Rumsey, J. M. (1992). The biology of developmental dyslexia. *Journal of the American Medical Association, 19,* 912–915.

Rumsey, J. M., Andreason, P., Zametkin, A. J., Aquino, T., King, A. C., Hamberger, S. D., Pikus, A., Rapoport, J. L., & Cohen, R. M. (1992). Failure to activate the left temporoparietal cortex in dyslexia. *Archives of Neurology, 49,* 527–534.

Rumsey, J. M., Berman, K. F., Denckla, M. B., Hamberger, S. D., Druesi, J. .T., Weinberger, D. R. (1987). Regional cerebral blood flow in severe developmental dyslexia. *Archives of Neurology, 44,* 1144–1150.

Sagar, S. M., & Sharp, F. R. (1993). Early response genes as markers of neuronal activity and growth factor action. *Advances in Neurology, 59,* 273–284.

Schuster, C. M., Davis, G. W., Fetter, R. D., & Goodman, C. S. (1996a). Genetic dissection of structural and functional components of synaptic plasticity. I. Fasciclin II controls synaptic stabilization and growth. *Neuron, 17,* 641–654.

Schuster, C. M., Davis, G. W., Fetter, R D., & Goodman, C. S. (1996b). Genetic dissection of structural and functional components of synaptic plasticity. II. Fasciclin II controls presynaptic structural plasticity. *Neuron, 17,* 655–667.

Schweiger, A., Zaidel, E., Field, T., & Dobkin, B. (1989). Right hemisphere contribution to lexical access in an aphasic with deep dyslexia. *Brain and Language, 37,* 73–89.

Shashikant, C. S., Utset, M. F., Violette, S. M., Wise, T. L., Einat, P., Einat, M., Pendleton, J. W., Schughart, K., & Ruddle, F. H. (1991). Homeobox genes in mouse development. *Eukaryotic Gene Expression, 1,* 207–245.

Shaywitz, B. A., Pugh, K. R., Constable, R. T., Shaywitz, S. E., Bronen, R. A., Fulbright, R. K., Shankweiler, D. P., Katz, L., Fletcher, J. M., Skudlarski, P., & Gore, J. C. (1995). Localization of semantic processing using functional magnetic resonance imaging. *Human Brain Mapping, 2,* 10–20.

Smith, S. D. (1992). Identification of genetic influences. *Clinics in communication disorders, 2,* 73–85.

Smith, S. D., Kimberling, W. J., Pennington, B. F., & Lubs, H. A. (1983). Specific reading disability: Identification of an inherited form through linkage analysis. *Science, 219,* 1345–1347.

Smith, S. D., Pennington, B. F., Kimberling, W. J., & Ing, P. S. (1990). Familial dyslexia: Use of genetic linkage data to define subtypes. *Journal of the American Academy of Child and Adolescent Psychiatry, 29,* 338–348.

Spear-Swerling, L. C., & Sternberg, R. J. (1996). *Off track: When poor readers become "learning disabled."* Boulder, CO: Westview Press.

Stanovich, K. E. (1988). Explaining the differences between the dyslexic and the garden-variety poor reader: The phonological-core variable-difference model. *Journal of Learning Disabilities, 21,* 590–604.

Stevenson, H. W., Lucker, G. W., Lee, S., Stigler, J. W., Kitamura, S., & Hsu, C. C. (1987). Poor readers in three cultures. In C. Super & S. Harkness (Eds.), *The role of culture in developmental disorder,* Vol. 1 (pp. 153–177). New York: Academic Press.

Stevenson, H. W., Stigler, J. W., Lucker, G. W., Lee, S., Hsu, C., & Kitamura, S. (1982). Reading disabilities: The case of Chinese, Japanese, and English. *Child Development, 53,* 1164–1181.

Stevenson, J., Graham, P., Fredman, G., & McLoughlin, V. (1987). A twin study of genetic influences on reading and spelling ability and disability. *Journal of Child Psychology and Psychiatry, 28,* 229–247.

Sutcliff, J. G. (1988). mRNA in the mammalian central nervous system. *Annual Review of Neuroscience, 11,* 157–198.

Symmes, J. S., & Rapoport, J. L. (1972). Unexpected reading failure. *American Journal of Orthopsychiatry, 42,* 8291.

Tallal, P., & Piercy, M. (1973). Defects of non-verbal auditory perception in children with developmental aphasia. *Nature, 21,* 468–469.

Tarnopol, L., & Tarnopol, M. (1981). *Comparative reading and learning difficulties.* Lexington: Lexington Books.

Taylor, I. (1981). Writing systems and reading. In G. McKinnon & T. G. Waller (Eds.), *Reading research: Advances in theory and practice.* Vol. 2 (pp. 1–51). New York: Academic Press.

Torgesen, J. K. (in press). Phonologically based reading disabilities: A coherent theory of one kind of learning disability. In R. J. Sternberg & L. Spear-Swerling (Eds.), *Perspective on learning disabilities.* Boulder, CO: Westview Press.

Tzeng, C. E. (1994). *The anomalous brain morphology in dyslexic children.* Unpublished manuscript.

van der Wissel, A., & Zegers, F. E. (1985). Reading retardation revisited. *British Journal of Developmental Psychology, 3,* 3–9.

Van Orden, G. C. (1987). A ROWS is a ROSE: Spelling, sound, and reading. *Memory and Cognition, 15,* 181–198.

Wadsworth, S. J., DeFries, J. C., Stevenson, J., Gilger, J. W., & Pennington, B. F. (1992). Gender ratios among reading-disabled children and their siblings as a function of parental impairment. *Journal of Child Psychology and Psychiatry, 33,* 1229–1239.

Wadsworth, S. J., Gillis, J. J., & DeFries, J. C. (1990). Genetic etiology of reading disability as a function of age. *Behavior Genetics, 20,* 752.

Wahlstern, D., & Gottlieb, G. (1997). The invalid separation of effects of nature and nurture: Lessons from animal experimentation. In R. J. Sternberg & E. L. Grigorenko (Eds.), *Intelligence, heredity, and environment* (pp. 163–192). New York: Cambridge University Press.

Walraven, A. M., Reitsma, P., & Kapper, E. J. (1994). Leesproblem en psychische stoornissen bij kinderen in een psychiatrisch centrum [Reading disability and behavioral problems of children in a child psychiatric clinic]. *Tijdschrift voor Psychiatrie, 36,* 195–208.

Wimmer, H. (1993). Characteristics of developmental dyslexia in a regular writing system. *Applied Psycholinguistics, 14,* 1–33.

Wimmer, H. (1996). The nonword reading deficit in developmental dyslexia: Evidence from children learning to read German. *Journal of Experimental Child Psychology, 61,* 80–90.

Wimmer, H., Landerl, K., Linortner, R., & Hummer, P. (1991). The relationship of phonemic awareness to reading acquisition: More consequence than precondition, but still important. *Cognition, 40,* 219–249.

Wood, F., Felton, R., Flowers, L., & Naylor, C. (1991). Neurobehavioral definition of dyslexia. In D. D. Duane & D. B. Gray (Eds.), *The reading brain: The biological basis of dyslexia* (pp. 1–26). Parkton, MD: York Press.

Wood, F. B., Flowers, D. L., Buchsbaum, M., & Tallal, P. (1991). Investigation of abnormal left temporal functioning in dyslexia through rCBF, auditory evoked potentials, and positron emission tomography. *Reading and Writing: An Interdisciplinary Journal, 4,* 81–95.

Wolff, P. H., & Melngailis, I. (1994). Family patterns of developmental dyslexia. *American Journal of Medical Genetics (Neuropsychiatric Genetics), 54,* 122–131.

Wright, S. F., & Groner, R. (1992). Zur Frage der Definition und Abgrensung von Lesestorungen [Dyslexia: Issues of definition and subtyping]. *Schweizerische Zeitschrift für Psychologie, 51,* 15–25.

Zaidel, E., & Peters, A. M. (1981). Phonological encoding and ideographic reading by the disconnected-right hemisphere: Two case studies. *Brain and Language, 14,* 205–234.

Zawilska, J. B., & Wawrocka, M. (1993). Chick retina and pineal gland differentially respond to constant light and darkness: In vivo studies on serotonin N-acetyltransferase (NAT) activity and melatonin content. *Neuroscience Letters, 153,* 21–24.

Zerbin-Rudin, E. (1967). Congenital word-blindness. *Bulletin of the Orton Society, 17,* 47–54

3

The Neuropsychological Basis of Learning Disabilities

George W. Hynd
Amanda B. Clinton
Jennifer R. Hiemenz

Learning disabilities are most appropriately viewed from a neuropsychological perspective. This perspective is consistent with the history of over a century of clinical and experimental reports and with accepted definitions of learning disabilities, which typically tie these disabilities to central nervous system dysfunction (Harris & Hodges, 1981; Hynd, Hooper, & Takahashi, in press). It is believed that the behavioral characteristics we associate with learning disabilities arise from abnormalities or variance in the development of important brain structures and associated connections among neurons in the cerebral cortex, which most likely arise between the fifth and seventh month of fetal gestation (Galaburda, 1993; Hynd & Semrud-Clikeman, 1989).

This chapter addresses the conceptualization of learning disabilities, particularly in the area of reading, as arising from neurological deficits. This conceptualization is based on studies of documented variability in the brains of individuals diagnosed with learning disabilities in reading. The focus herein is based on a long history of inquiry into this specific learning disability. Unfortunately, considerably less is known about other learning disabilities such as in written language or mathematics.

Various methods of investigation have been used in examining these anatomical anomalies, including postmortem procedures, neuroimaging

This research was supported in part by a grant (RO1-HD26890-03) awarded to the first author from the National Institute of Child Health and Human Development (NICHHD), National Institutes of Health (NIH).

techniques, and functional neuroimaging techniques. Investigation of these anomalies yields invaluable information regarding differences in brain morphology between individuals with reading disabilities, for example, and nondisabled individuals. But it is important to first understand when and how abnormalities might occur during neurological development. Thus we first examine the normal process of brain ontogeny and associated variability in the brains of individuals with reading disabilities, the most common of all learning disabilities. Then, we consider definitional and diagnostic issues and procedures and associated principles relevant to effective remediation. Finally, we briefly comment on the neuropsychological perspective as it relates to others noted in the literature.

Normal Brain Development and Variation Associated with Learning Disabilities

Normal Sequence of Brain Development

In the earliest stages of human prenatal development, the neural tube is formed by the process of neurulation, in which the hollow sphere of rapidly dividing cells, called the gastrula, develops an indentation that continues to extend into the interior of the ball of cells, creating a two-walled ball. The inner layer of cells forms the foundation for the neural tube, which constitutes the cellular basis of the central nervous system and develops into the brain and spinal cord. The neural tube is generally developed and closed by the sixth week of fetal gestation.

At first, the brain's surface is smooth and lacks fissures (sulci) and folds (gyri). At approximately 14 weeks, the longitudinal fissure, which divides the brain into two cerebral hemispheres, and the Sylvian fissure, dividing the parietal and frontal lobes from the temporal lobe, are visible. At 16 weeks, the parietooccipital sulcus appears, dividing the parietal from the occipital lobes. Finally, at about 20 weeks of gestation, the central sulcus becomes visible, dividing the frontal lobes from the parietal lobes (Dooling, Chi, & Gilles, 1983; Chi, Dooling, & Gilles, 1977a, b). Between the 24th and 26th weeks, the brain undergoes a rapid increase in weight, followed by a spurt in gyrification (folding) between the 26th and 28th week of gestation that follows an orderly progression (Dooling et al., 1983, Hynd & Willis, 1988). Figure 3.1 shows the major landmarks of the brain.

Originally, gyri in the cortex were thought to be formed by a passive, mechanical folding process as the brain expanded in size within the confines of the skull, thus allowing for more surface area to fit within an enclosed space (Welker, 1990). However, recent research has demonstrated

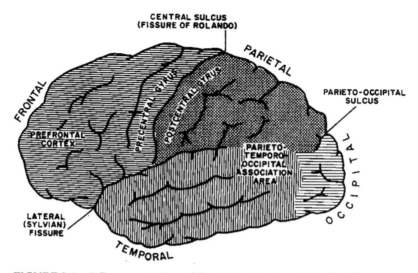

FIGURE 3.1   A Representation of the Major Landmarks in the Human Brain

that the gyrification process reflects the formation of cortical connections during the migration and development of neurons to the cortex. Neurons are originally formed in an area called the germinal matrix, near the fluid-filled cavities (lateral ventricles) of the brain. Once formed, a neuron migrates from the germinal matrix to the outer part of the brain, called the cortex. The arriving neurons migrate in waves to form layers, forming the deepest layer (VI) first and the most superficial layer (II) last, so that they are eventually arranged in columns. Layer I contains no neurons; it is referred to as the molecular or cell-free layer. Once the neurons are arranged in columns, they then begin to form connections with other neurons in various areas of the cortex. As connections form, the cortex itself becomes folded, producing the gyri and sulci that are seen in the normal human brain. Figure 3.2 shows a magnetic resonance imaging (MRI) scan of a brain in which the gyri and sulci are clearly visible.

Although gyri and sulci develop in an orderly progression that is the same across individuals, some variation does occur among individuals in the exact pattern of gyri and sulci. Because gyral patterns vary a great deal, it is necessary to determine a "normal range" of variance in order to identify patterns that can be classified as abnormal. These variations in the gyral pattern must come about between the fifth and seventh month of fetal gestation, since it is during this time that the gyral pattern is determined. Since the gyral pattern is a visible indicator of an individual's patterns of intracortical connection, it follows that variations that are out-

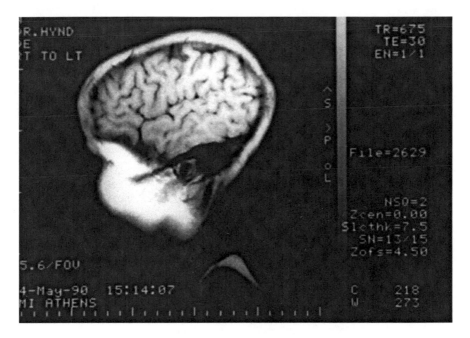

R.HYND
E
T TO LT

TR=675
TE=30
EN=1/1

S

P

File=2629

O
L

NSO=2
Zcen=0.00
Slcthk=7.5
SN=13/15
Zofs=4.50

5.6/FOV

4-May-90 15:14:07
MI ATHENS

C   218
W   273

FIGURE 3.2   A Magnetic Resonance Image (MRI) Scan of a Child's Brain in Which the Gyri and Major Fissures Can Be Seen

side the normal range of variance should be associated with deviations in cortical connections. These deviations should then, in turn, reflect some type of cognitive or behavioral deficit, depending upon the location of the abnormality. For example, abnormal gyral patterns in the left-central language zones may be associated with deficits in functions related to that area, such as language and reading. Thus these deficits in language and reading must also necessarily be associated with abnormal gyral development between the fifth and seventh month of gestation.

Normal Patterns of Sulci/Gyri in the Cerebral Cortex

Before the 1960s, very little information was available regarding normal variations in sulci and gyri in the cerebral cortex. Early studies presented evidence of normal left-right asymmetries of the Sylvian fissure; the right Sylvian fissure was shorter and was angled sharply upward compared to the left Sylvian fissure (Connolly, 1950; Rubens, Mahowald, & Hutton, 1976). In 1968, however, Geschwind and Levitsky published their seminal study documenting neuroanatomical asymmetry in a postmortem investigation of 100 adult brains. This study reported that 65 percent of the

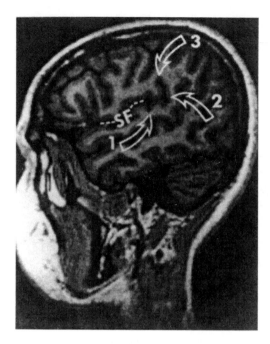

FIGURE 3.3. A Sagittal MRI Section of the Brain Showing the Topography of the Planum Temporale Buried Within the Sylvian Fissure

The tip of arrow 1 points to the anterior border of the temporal bank of the planum temporale; arrow 2 points to the termination of the temporal bank of the planum temporale. The tip of arrow 3 points to the superior termination of the planum parietal. Reprinted with permission from Jancke et al., 1994.

brains in their sample had a left-greater-than-right asymmetry of the region called the planum temporale, which is composed of the superior surface of the temporal lobe in the posterior portion of the Sylvian fissure (see Figure 3.3). Since this percentage corresponded well to ideas on the functional importance of right-handedness and language lateralization, they concluded that this asymmetry must be linked to both right-handedness and language lateralization. This finding was supported by earlier case studies by Broca, Wernicke, and others that linked language functions to this area (Witelson, 1982).

The importance of this finding by Geschwind and Levitsky (1968) has been underscored by many studies that followed their report. For example, a recent study by Foundas and her colleagues examined the relationship between this leftward asymmetry of the planum temporale region as visualized on MRI scans and language lateralization. Eleven subjects with language known to be lateralized in the left hemisphere all had a larger left than right planum temporale. One subject with language lateralized to the right hemisphere had a larger right than left planum temporale and was left-handed (Foundas, Leonard, Gilmore, Fennell, & Heilman, 1994).

The idea that planum temporale asymmetry may be linked to language lateralization inevitably led to studies investigating the possible relationship between reversed or mixed asymmetry of the planum temporale region and language and reading disorders (Hynd & Cohen, 1983; Witelson, 1982). Current studies of this relationship have primarily used measurements made from MRI scans to document the degree of asymmetry found in this region, but some recent studies have also utilized functional magnetic resonance imaging (fMRI) to investigate which areas of the brain are activated during language and reading tasks.

MRI Studies of Sulcal/Gyral Patterns in Dyslexia

More recent studies of the asymmetry of the planum temporale using MRI have presented evidence that reading disabilities may not be due to a reversed asymmetry of the planum temporale but rather linked to symmetrical plana, with the right planum being longer than in normal individuals (Larsen et al., 1990). However, Hynd and colleagues (1990) attributed the symmetry found in their reading-disabled sample to a smaller left planum rather than a larger right planum. Because of these conflicting results, other studies have examined both the temporal banks (planum temporale) and the parietal banks (planum parietale) of the planum in order to determine if differences in symmetry of these banks were related to reading disabilities (Leonard et al., 1993). This approach was theoretically important because whereas the temporal bank is thought to be critically involved in linguistic processing, the parietal bank is believed to be vital to nonverbal or visuospatial processing. This and other studies examining the temporal and parietal banks of the planum indicate that no significant differences in the asymmetry of the total plana are displayed between groups of reading-disabled and nondisabled individuals but that left planum temporale length, and thus L > R asymmetry, itself tends to be positively related to language scores for nondyslexic individuals and that right planum temporale length is negatively related to language measures for individuals with reading disabilities (Morgan, Hynd, Hall, Novey, Eliopulos, & Riccio, 1996). Specifically, for individuals with reading disabilities, having a longer right planum temporale tends to be associated with lower language ability. For individuals without reading disabilities, having a longer left planum temporale tends to be associated with higher language ability. Therefore, levels of expressive and receptive language ability as well as measures of reading ability most frequently correlated with measurements of the planum temporale as seen on MRI scans. In particular, the leftward asymmetry of the temporal bank of the planum temporale is linked to higher levels of linguistic and reading ability.

It is important that this relationship between asymmetry of the planum temporale and language and reading ability seems to be generalized to

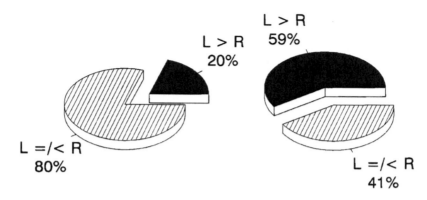

Achievement <85 SS   Achievement >85 SS

FIGURE 3.4. The Relationship Between the Direction of Asymmetry of the Planum Temporale and Receptive Language Abilities As Measured on the Clinical Evaluation of Language Functions—Revised (CELF-R) Test

It can be seen that when performance is below average (standard score < 85), significantly fewer children have L > R asymmetry of the planum temporale.

the population in general; below-average language and reading scores (< 85 standard score) are associated with less asymmetry of the planum temporale than in those with average or better language and reading abilities. For example, from our studies at the University of Georgia (Figures 3.4 and 3.5) it can be seen that when plana asymmetry is examined in children whose receptive language and passage reading comprehension scores are classified as below average (< 85 standard score), normal L > R plana asymmetry occurs in only 20 percent and 24 percent of the children, respectively. When plana asymmetry is examined in children who achieve scores in the normal or above-normal range of performance (< 85 standard score) on a measure of receptive language and passage reading comprehension, plana asymmetry shifts to 59 percent and 58 percent, respectively (Morgan et al., 1996). Thus there seems to be some compelling support for the conclusion that L > R asymmetry in this region of the central language zone is positively related to receptive language and passage reading comprehension abilities.

Although measurements of planum temporale asymmetries made using MRI technology have shown some promise in clarifying our view of the neural bases of language and learning disorders, particularly in reading, this approach is limited in that it examines only a small area of the classical language cortex, that of the planum temporale itself, while ignoring surrounding areas that may also be related to language functions.

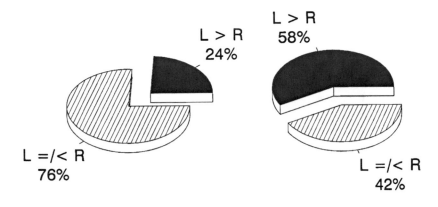

FIGURE 3.5. The Relationship Between the Direction of Asymmetry of the Planum Temporale and Passage Reading Comprehension from the Woodcock Reading Mastery Test—Revised (WRMT-R)

It can be seen that when performance is below average (standard score < 85), significantly fewer children have L > R asymmetry of the planum temporale.

Because of this limitation, recent research has begun to examine variations in overall patterns of sulci and gyri in the area surrounding the Sylvian fissure in an attempt to discern whether these variations impact language or learning ability (Hynd & Hiemenz, 1997). Since the sulcal patterns themselves are a visible indicator of cellular cortical connections, variations or disturbances of these patterns may reflect abnormal cortical connections that may in turn influence behavior, depending upon the cortical location. Although most individuals have sulcal patterns that vary from others' patterns somewhat, in the manner of fingerprints, commonalities exist in the arrangements of major sulci and gyri in the cortex. It would be possible to quantitatively classify every area of the cerebral cortex by patterns of sulci and gyri, but so far classification systems have been limited to the region surrounding the Sylvian fissure, which is of note because of its involvement in language functions associated with the classical Wernicke's region. To date, two classification systems have been developed for the sulcal/gyral patterns of this region, that of Steinmetz and his colleagues (1990) and that of Witelson and Kigar (1992).

The Steinmetz and colleagues (1990) classification system examines the physical relationship between the Sylvian fissure and other major sulci surrounding it, including the central sulcus and the postcentral sulcus. Variations in the placement and physical characteristics of these sulci have been classified into four distinct subtypes, which Steinmetz and colleagues hypothesize to be related to variations in language ability. To date, however, only one published study has applied this classification system using MRI in individuals with and without severe reading disabilities, or dyslexia. Leonard and her colleagues (1993) found evidence of greater incidences of Type I morphology in the left hemispheres of individuals without dyslexia, as well as a higher rate of Type 3 morphology in the left hemispheres of dyslexics. However, this study is limited in that the number of subjects in each group was small (10 per group) and dyslexic subjects were diagnosed solely on historical self-report, that is, whether they remembered having difficulty in reading as a child.

Witelson and Kigar's (1992) method of classification examines only the physical characteristics of the Sylvian fissure itself rather than its relation to surrounding structures. Their system yields three descriptive types of Sylvian fissures that may also show some relationship to language abilities. Whereas the Steinmetz and colleagues (1990) system examines a greater area of structures, the Witelson and Kigar system is much more analogous to the earlier studies examining asymmetries of the parietal and temporal banks of the planum temporale, which correspond to the vertical and horizontal aspects, respectively, of the Sylvian fissure itself. Although this system of classification holds much promise, no published studies have yet examined the relationship of Sylvian fissure morphology (as classified in this system) to language or reading disabilities.

Functional MRI Studies of Cerebral Activation in Reading Disabilities

Although MRI and postmortem studies have provided a great deal of insight into variations in brain morphology in reading disabilities, they have not yet provided a clear solution to the mystery of language function localization within the cerebral cortex. The best of these studies presents only correlative evidence in support of language lateralization hypotheses. However, recent studies utilizing functional imaging techniques, such as positron emission tomography (PET) and functional magnetic resonance imaging (fMRI), are beginning to provide some support for existing hypotheses concerning the language functions of the area surrounding the Sylvian fissure. Specifically, functional imaging studies of the left cortex in this area have shown activation during tasks involving listening to nonword phonemes and words (Demonet et al., 1994; Binder et al., 1994; Millen et al., 1995). Conversely, tasks involving comprehending metaphors and other nonliteral aspects of speech primarily led to right hemisphere activation in this region (Bottini et al., 1994). Although these studies do indicate that these areas of the brain are important in language comprehension, this is a rapidly growing area of research and we have only begun to scratch the surface. In particular, more functional imaging studies need to be done examining activation of these language areas in individuals with and without learning disabilities.

It should be clear that research conducted in the past several decades has significantly altered our perceptions that learning disabilities are due to some sort of "minimal brain damage" (MBD) toward a conceptualization that incorporates factors affecting the normal process of fetal brain ontogeny. Some evidence suggests that the variation we see in the brains of individuals with learning disabilities, particularly those with reading disabilities, is under genetic influences (Smith, Pennington, Kimberling, & Ing, 1990), but there still exists an appreciation for other factors, including environmental, that may affect the normal scope and sequence of brain development in persons with learning disabilities.

With these thoughts in mind, it is now appropriate to turn our attention toward definitional and diagnostic issues and their implications for treatment of learning disabilities. As will be seen, there are many different perspectives and issues related to diagnostic approaches and their implications for intervention. It is not our intention to discuss the specifics related to what tests or diagnostic procedures should or should not be administered. Rather, we discuss the broader concepts and issues germane to each approach and the neuropsychological approach as possibly the most inclusive perspective for understanding, diagnosing, and treating learning disabilities.

Defining, Diagnosing, and Treating Learning Disabilities

Despite a century-long awareness of the existence of learning disabilities, clinicians currently lack consensus regarding the most accurate and meaningful measures or methods for diagnosing and treating reading, writing, and mathematical handicaps. Although federal law mandates that a discrepancy between a child's intellectual capabilities and his or her school achievement must result in a diagnosis of learning disability, many educators and researchers prefer the information provided by alternative methods such as curriculum-based measurement (Dino, 1985) and dynamic assessment (Feuerstein, 1979). Additionally, recent research suggests a potential future role for the use of brain imaging techniques such as MRI, fMRI, or PET in the diagnosis of disabilities (Hynd et al., 1990; Rumsey, 1992) in reading, writing, and math.

The diagnostic process is further complicated by issues surrounding the effect of socioeconomic status, ethnic background, and cultural orientation on a child's test performance and subsequent placement in special instructional classes. Comorbidity, or the simultaneous existence of two or more disabling conditions, creates additional challenges to accurate diagnostics. This is especially a concern because of the relatively high rates of comorbidity between learning disabilities and Attention Deficit Hyperactivity Disorder (ADHD) (Hynd, Morgan, Edmonds, Black, Riccio, & Lombardino, 1995).

Traditional Diagnostic Methods: The Discrepancy Model

The implementation of uniform diagnostic procedures for learning disabilities evolved as a result of a U.S. Office of Education (USOE) definition of specific learning disability that focused on the presence of achievement deficits despite average learning potential (Francis, 1996). Federal legislation in the form of PL 94–142, the Education for All Handicapped Children Act, in 1975, and the Individuals with Disabilities Education Act (IDEA), most recently revised in 1996, further encouraged the development of this process, termed the discrepancy model. IDEA, a revision of PL 94–142, ensures a "free appropriate public education within the least restrictive environment for children with disabilities." In order for individual states to receive federal funding support for implementation of these federally mandated special education services, however, "nondiscriminatory evaluation procedures for identification and placement" must be utilized. IDEA also includes key provisions requiring that all tests be linked to the child's general curriculum and that assessment procedures provide information that directly contributes to the design and implementation of relevant instructional strategies for the child.

These aforementioned identification and placement procedures utilized in public schools and private-practice settings revolve around IQ testing in 46 of the 50 states. The diagnostic process for a child referred due to difficulty learning to read, write, or calculate math typically includes an analysis of the difference between a child's intellectual potential for his or her age, as measured by an individual standardized IQ measure, and performance on an achievement test, which is a standardized assessment of academic performance. The most commonly used batteries are the Weschler Individual Scales for Children—Revised (WISC III-R; Weschler, 1974) and the Woodcock-Johnson Psychoeducational Battery—Revised (WJ-R; Woodcock & Johnson, 1989), although many, many others exist. Criterion for the classification of learning disabled varies according to state law, but a difference of 15 to 20 points between the child's IQ and level of academic functioning on a basic reading skill, reading comprehension, math calculation, or writing subtest generally meets the criterion for a diagnosis of a specific learning disability (SLD).

Children whose intellectual quotient and achievement are adequately discrepant do not typically qualify for support services if their reading, writing, or math are within the average range, however. In other words, a child with an above-average IQ who is not achieving to his or her potential in school, as shown by academic achievement scores that may be 15–20 standard score points lower than the intellectual quotient, may not receive a diagnosis of learning disabled. The discrepancy criterion is considered diagnostic only if a child's performance is below average (generally defined as below a standard score of 85 on a measure of achievement) as compared to a national sample of children his or her age, not if academic progress is below his or her individual potential.

Numerous concerns surround the use of the discrepancy model to diagnose learning disabilities. It has been noted that clinicians administer IQ tests without considering the relevance to diagnostics on a case-by-case basis. Specifically, Reschly and Grimes (1990) report the existence of "recognized limitations of intellectual assessment in developing educational programs or other interventions for students" and the "lost opportunities for the delivery of other, potentially more effective services due to the time and energy devoted to intellectual assessment" (p. 427). In other words, if a student is struggling to read, write, or calculate math, the child's parents and teachers are well aware of this without the diagnostic label provided by an IQ measure and an achievement test.

A larger issue regarding the discrepancy model questions the validity of IQ scores as tools for identification of learning disabilities. Concerns center around conceptual and empirical issues, both of which are addressed in detail by Francis and his colleagues (1996). The notion that a child's cognitive capabilities, such as memory, attention, and learning, result directly from her intellectual quotient is contrasted to the greater possibility that a child's IQ score results directly from the interaction of these cognitive capacities. One would logically conclude, then, that the learning-disabled child's performance on an IQ measure would be negatively impacted by his or her difficulty. Empirically, Francis and colleagues express concerns regarding the statistical constructs underlying tests of IQ. They report that the discrepancy model fails to identify a large population of children who do indeed suffer from academic impairment yet are not recognized due to insensitive statistical procedures.

Alternative Diagnostic Methods

Statistical and conceptual inadequacies and a perceived lack of practical applicability to treatment design of the traditional model encouraged the development of a broader view of learning disabilities and, subsequently, new approaches to diagnosis. Many researchers encourage a consideration of multiple developmental cognitive and performance domains rather than conceptualizing a single index influencing expected levels of achievement (Berninger & Abbott, 1994). From an assessment perspective, these may include curriculum-based measurement, dynamic assessment, and, more recently, neuropsychological methods. Although many advocate for the exclusive use of one or another or these perspectives on assessment and diagnosis, it might be argued that these varying approaches are not necessarily mutually exclusive. Nonetheless, each needs to be considered individually.

Curriculum-based measurement (CBM) focuses on direct measurement of a child's skills in the subject area of concern. In contrast to other approaches, CBM is based on the premise that a handicap occurs when a "discrepancy between what is expected of a student and what is actually occurring" exists (Shinn, 1989, p. 92). The process emphasizes assessment that is tied to the curriculum, is brief in duration so as to allow for frequent progress monitoring, is presentable in multiple forms, and is sensitive to student progress over time (Marston, 1989). Diagnosis of a learning disability under the CBM rubric focuses on identification of students' levels of performance as compared to peers in their school district. Scores that fall two or more years below grade level or below the 16th percentile meet the criterion for special education service. Advantages of curriculum-based measurement are that it provides information pertaining to the appropriate materials for instruction of the referred student; provides samples of reading, writing, or math skills that may be readily tailored to the development of educational goals; and leads to a collection of samples of the types of errors commonly made by the student on the tasks utilized in his or her particular educational setting. These assessment outcomes successfully meet the letter of the IDEA law.

Similar to the discrepancy model, CBM has limitations. As noted by Meltzer (1994), the developmental and cognitive status of the student is disregarded in favor of evaluation of incongruence between the performance of the referred student and that student's peer group. CBM also fails to address the dynamic process of learning and does not tap into complex school tasks such as writing papers or completing projects. Finally, development of a database of children's scores at the local level, which can be used comparatively when diagnosing a child as learning disabled, is a lengthy and complex process that lacks practicality for most educators. Further issues of significant concern are the reliability of measurement on small samples of behavior, the match between the assessment measures and the frequently changing scope and sequence of curriculum materials, and the time required to complete planned academic probes to measure academic gains.

A second popular alternative method for assessing learning disabilities is referred to as dynamic assessment. The basis for this model is the assumption that a child's learning processes and response to instruction may be measured using a test-teach-test approach wherein the examiner embeds learning experiences in the assessment. Thus a dynamic assessment focuses not on a static test product such as an IQ score but on the student's ability to profit academically in a teaching context. The goal is to identify the amount of change made by a child in response to teaching by the examiner in order to design effective teaching strategies. Dynamic assessment provides information pertinent to the intensity of instruction required for documenting academic progress in the child (Lidz, 1991).

Dynamic-assessment advocates emphasize its function as a source of information complementary to traditional methods rather than as an independent means of diagnosing a learning disability. Similar to curriculum-based measurement, this method is particularly useful in that it addresses IDEA's requirement that diagnostic procedures be directly linked to intervention. It is particularly time consuming, however, and therefore difficult to implement in the school setting with the traditionally high student-to-teacher ratios.

A rapidly expanding area of interest in learning disability diagnostics for children is that derived from neuropsychology. Consistent with the increasingly impressive body of research linking variation in brain development to learning disabilities, as noted previously, assessment of impairment from a neuropsychological perspective focuses on the relationship between brain-behavior relations and deficient cognitive, behavioral, and academic processes. Neuropsychological procedures have been referred to as the "most comprehensive psychological evaluation available" (Kelly & Dean, 1990, p. 491) due to the integration of cognitive, sensorimotor, academic, and emotional aspects of behavior.

Unfortunately, neuropsychological assessment is rarely included in a standard psychoeducational evaluation. The reasons are twofold: First, most school-based psychologists do not possess the specialized training required to conduct such an evaluation. Second, the discrepancy model utilized in most diagnostic settings seeks no information pertaining to the underlying cause or origin of the disability. This focus on etiology is of primary relevance in the neuropsychological evaluation, however, as it is believed that it is important to distinguish between constitutional influences (e.g., genetic, neurological) and other, potentially relevant influences (e.g., social, environmental) that may be more easily remediated. Implementation of neuropsychological assessment results, therefore, typically takes the form of a complement to traditional methods wherein the school psychologist acts as a consultant and liaison for professionals from the educational and medical communities (Riccio & Hynd, 1995).

Further Considerations

Diagnosing learning disabilities challenges educators and psychologists not only because of the nature of assessment practices but because of the nature of children as individuals who possess myriad uniquenesses. Most salient to the diagnostic process is the presence of a coexisting but independent disorder, or comorbidity, and socioeconomic, racial, and cultural differences.

Research suggests high rates of coexistence between learning disabilities and both externalizing and internalizing disorders. For example, a notably strong association between ADHD and learning disabilities appears to exist (Shaywitz & Shaywitz, 1991; Semrud-Clikeman et al., 1992), and increased rates of mild depressive disorder have been found in those with learning disabilities (Fristad et al., 1992). Whereas most of the research addressing comorbidity utilizes samples of children currently receiving treatment for behavioral or emotional and learning difficulties, it is likely that many of the children referred for special education evaluation and subsequently diagnosed as learning disabled in the public school setting experience coexisting impairments.

The presence of more than one disorder complicates the diagnostic process considerably. The issue of primacy of one disorder over another may be particularly relevant in the school setting, where educational support is oftentimes contingent upon a specific diagnostic category (e.g., placement and treatment for learning disabilities *or* emotional disturbance, not both). Questions also arise regarding the relationship between impairments. Consider comorbidity of a reading disability and ADHD: It is possible that difficulties in reading classroom material may create a tendency for children to become fidgety, inattentive, and even impulsive in the sense that they guess at answers to questions because it is impossible to read the information upon which assignments are based. Habitual inattention may then negatively affect reading achievement, whereupon the maladaptive behaviors increase in frequency or severity. Although research currently does not support the view that learning disabilities cause ADHD (Hynd et al., 1995), this notion remains popular among parents, teachers, and some professionals.

It is interesting that a growing body of evidence suggests a possible future role for neuropsychological differentiation of the genetic basis of reading disabilities and the familial psychopathological basis of ADHD (Hynd et al., 1995; Hynd & Hiemenz, 1997). As these diagnostic techniques evolve, practitioners may be better able to differentiate one disability from another when a child suffers from comorbid disorders. For example, Lombardino, Riccio, Hynd, and Pinheiro (1997) found that linguistic deficits such as those referred to as phonological coding deficits, which are in turn linked to variation in planum temporale asymmetry (Morgan et al., 1996), characterize children with reading disability. In this regard, tests of linguistic and phonological processing known to be associated with a specific brain region may provide valuable information about brain-behavior linkages in learning-disabled children. Thus from this line of research, measures may be available to differentially diagnose children whose reading or other learning disabilities are indeed related to a neurodevelopmentally based disorder.

An additional diagnostic challenge concerns accurate identification of children from low socioeconomic or minority racial and cultural backgrounds. Surveys of proportionate numbers of African American, Hispanic, and Caucasian children enrolled in special education consistently report that smaller percentages of minorities than whites are identified as learning disabled (Tucker, 1980). In many inner-city schools, the mean IQ does not equal the national norm of 100 but instead hovers 10–15 points below the national average at 90 or 85. Utilization of the discrepancy model for diagnosis of these populations as learning disabled requires shifting the criterion for qualification to the left of the normal distribution or reducing it in order to avoid overidentifying these children as mentally impaired. Although this solution strives for fairness, it inadvertently creates a situation wherein children with academic difficulties that would otherwise meet diagnostic criterion as learning disabled may not receive needed additional or appropriate instructional support.

Unique challenges also surround evaluation of children who speak English as a second language. Of particular concern for this population is assessment of reading and language disabilities. Diagnosis of learning disabilities in bilingual children is plagued by the use of inappropriate tests based on theories that may lack relevance to these populations and inaccurate differentiation between a disorder and language differences (Jitendra & Rohena-Diaz, 1996).

Conclusions

Despite vast progress in our understanding of the neuropsychological basis of learning and the nature of learning disabilities, diagnostics and treatment remain in transition and plagued by controversy. Debate centers largely around the federally and state mandated procedures that rely upon the discrepancy between a child's IQ and academic achievement. Provision of special education services for students struggling to develop reading, writing, or math skills remains dependent on meeting the 15–20 point criterion despite its questionable validity and practicality. Curriculum-based assessment, dynamic assessment, and neuropsychological assessment represent divergent efforts aimed at improving on the traditional diagnostic and treatment models. Although issues of comorbidity, socioeconomic status, and different racial and cultural backgrounds may continue to complicate the diagnosis of learning disabilities, it is possible that these approaches will eventually complement one other in a holistic assessment process that draws on the strengths of each.

New developments are sure to come, especially from those who believe that the symptoms we see in learning-disabled children and adults reflect some basic, constitutional variability or dysfunction in the central nervous system, as is presumed in the federal definition of learning disabilities. Perhaps most promising in this regard is the work of Tallal and colleagues (1996), where evidence seems to indicate that children with language, and perhaps reading, disabilities suffer from deficits in perceiving temporal-order effects in speech. Based on her early research, Tallal has developed a computer-based intervention program that facilitates a developing sensitivity to the temporal-order perception of speech stimuli. Although she reports significant gains in the accurate perception of temporal speech stimuli and gains academically, the results are still too preliminary to draw conclusions as to the validity of these notions. It is promising, however, that two independent researchers have validated psychophysiologically the existence of temporal-order deficits in children with learning difficulties (Kraus, McGee, Carrell, Zecker, Nicol, & Koch, 1996) and in six-month-old infants at familial risk for learning disabilities (Lyytinen, 1997). Clearly, the most exciting and promising advances toward understanding why some people suffer learning disabilities will occur at the boundaries between the perspectives derived from the neurological, behavioral, and educational sciences.

References

Berninger, V., & Abbott, R. (1994). Redefining learning disabilities. In G. R. Lyon (Ed.), *Frames of Reference for the Assessment of Learning Disabilities*. Baltimore: Brookes.

Binder, J., Rao, S., Hammeke, T., Yetkin, F., Jesmanowicz, A., Bandettini, P., Wong, E., Estkowski, L., Goldstein, M., Haughton, V., & Hyde, J. (1994). Functional magnetic resonance imaging of the human auditory cortex. *Annals of Neurology, 35*, 662–672.

Bottini, G., Corcoran, R., Sterzi, R., Paulesu, E., Schenone, P., Scarpa, P., Fraclowik, R., & Frith, C. (1994). The role of the right hemisphere in the interpretation of figurative aspects of language: A positron emission tomography activation study. *Brain, 117*, 1241–1253.

Chi, J. G., Dooling, E. C., & Gilles, F. H. (1977a). Gyral development of the human brain. *Annals of Neurology, 1,* 86–93.

Chi, J. G., Dooling, E. C., & Gilles, F. H. (1977b). Left-right asymmetries of the temporal speech areas of the human fetus. *Archives of Neurology, 34,* 346–348.

Connolly, C. J. (1950). *External morphology of the primate brain.* Springfield, IL: Charles C. Thomas.

Demonet, J. F., Price, C., Wise, R., & Frackowiak, R. (1994). Differential activation of right and left posterior Sylvian regions by semantic and phonological tasks: A positron emission tomography study in normal human subjects. *Neuroscience Letters, 183,* 25–28.

Deno, S. (1985). Curriculum-based measurement: The emerging alternative. *Exceptional Children, 52,* 219–232.

Dooling, E.C., Chi, J.G., & Gilles, F.H. (1983). Telencephalic development: Changing gyral patterns (pp. 94–104). In F.H. Gilles, A. Levitan, & E.C. Dooling (Eds.), *The developing human brain.* Boston, MA: John Wright.

Egnor, D. (1996). Individuals with disabilities education act amendments of 1996: Overview of the U.S. Senate bill (S. 1578). *Focus on Autism and Other Developmental Disabilities, 11,* 194–206.

Feuerstein, R. (1979). *Dynamic assessment of retarded performers.* Baltimore: University Park Press.

Foundas, A.L., Leonard, C., Gilmore, R., Fennell, E., & Heilman, K. (1994). Planum temporale asymmetry and language dominance. *Neuropsychologia, 32,* 1225–1231.

Francis, D., Fletcher, J., Shaywitz, B., Shaywitz, S., & Rourke, B. (1996). Defining learning and language disabilities: Conceptual and psychometric issues with the use of IQ tests. *Language, Speech, and Hearing Services in Schools, 27,* 132–143.

Fristad, M., Topolosky, S., Weller, E., & Weller, R. (1992). Depression and learning disabilities in children. *Journal of Affective Disorders, 26,* 53–58.

Galaburda, A. (1993). *Dyslexia and development: Neurobiological aspects of extra-ordinary brains.* Cambridge, MA: Harvard University Press.

Geschwind, N., & Levitsky, W. (1968). Human brain: Left-right asymmetry in temporal speech region. *Science, 161,* 186–187.

Harris, T.L., & Hodges, R.E. (Eds.) (1981). *A dictionary of reading and related terms.* Newark, NJ: International Reading Association.

Hynd, G., Morgan, A., Edmonds, J., Black, K., Riccio, C., & Lombardino, L. (1995). Reading disabilities, comorbid psychopathology, and the specificity of neurolinguistic deficits. *Developmental Neuropsychology, 11,* 311–322.

Hynd, G.W., & Cohen, M.J. (1983). *Dyslexia: Neuropsychological theory, research and clinical differentiation.* Needham Heights, MA: Allyn & Bacon.

Hynd, G.W., & Hiemenz, J. (1997). Dyslexia and gyral morphology variation (pp. 38–58). In C. Hulme & M. Snowling (Eds.), *Dyslexia: Biology, cognition, and intervention.* London: Whurr.

Hynd, G.W., Hooper, S., & Takahashi, T. (in press). Dyslexia and language-based learning disabilities. In C.E. Coffey & R.A. Brumback (Eds.). *Textbook of pediatric neuropsychiatry.* Washington, DC: American Psychiatric Press.

Hynd, G.W., & Semrud-Clikeman, M. (1989). Dyslexia and brain morphology. *Psychological Bulletin, 106,* 447–482.

Hynd, G., Semrud-Clikeman, M., Lorys, A.R., Novey, E.S., & Eliopulos, D. (1990). Brain morphology in developmental dyslexia and attention deficit disorder/hyperactivity. *Archives of Neurology, 47*, 919–926.

Hynd, G.W., & Willis, W.G. (1988). *Pediatric neuropsychology.* Needham Heights, MA: Allyn & Bacon.

Jitendra, A., & Rohena-Diaz, E. (1996). Language assessment of students who are linguistically diverse: Why a discrete approach is not the answer. *School Psychology Review, 25*, 40–56.

Kelly, M., & Dean, R.S. (1990). Best practices in neuropsychology. In A. Thomas & J. Grimes (Eds.), *Best Practices in School Psychology.* Washington, DC: NASP.

Kraus, N., McGee, T.J., Carrell, T.D., Zecker, S.G., Nicol, T.G., & Koch, D.B. (1996). Auditory neurophysiologic responses and discrimination deficits in children with learning problems. *Science, 273*, 971–973.

Larsen, J.P., Hoien, T., Lundberg, I., & Odegaard, H. (1990). MRI evaluation of the size and symmetry of the planum temporale in adolescents with developmental dyslexia. *Brain and Language, 39*, 289–301.

Leonard, C., Voeller, K.K.S., Lombardino, L., Morris, M.K., Hynd, G.W., Alexander, A., Andersen, H., Garofalakis, M., Honeyman, J., Mao, J., Agee, O., & Staab, E. (1993). Anomalous cerebral structure in dyslexia revealed with magnetic resonance imaging. *Archives of Neurology, 50*, 461–469.

Lidz, C.S. (1991). *Practitioner's guide to dynamic assessment.* New York: Guilford Press.

Lombardino, L., Riccio, C.A., Hynd, G.W., & Pinheiro, S.B. (1997). Linguistic deficits in children with reading disabilities. *American Journal of Speech-Language Pathology, 6*, 71–78.

Lyytinen, H. (1997). In search of the precursors of dyslexia: A prospective study of children at risk for reading problems. In C. Hulme & M. Snowling (Eds.), *Dyslexia: Biology, cognition, and intervention.* London: Whurr.

Marston, D.B. (1989). A curriculum-based measurement approach to assessing academic performance: What it is and why do it. In M.R. Shinn (Ed.), *Curriculum based measurement: Assessing social children.* New York: The Guilford Press.

Meltzer, L.J. (1994). Assessment of learning disabilities: The challenge of evaluating the cognitive strategies and processes underlying learning. In G.R. Lyon (Ed.), *Frames of Reference for the Assessment of Learning Disabilities.* Baltimore: Brookes.

Millen, S., Haughton, V., & Yetkin, Z. (1995). Functional magnetic resonance imaging of the central auditory pathway following speech and pure-tone stimuli. *Laryngoscope, 105*, 1305–1310.

Morgan, A.E., Hynd, G.W., Hall, J., Novey, E., & Eliopulos, D. (1996). Planum temporale morphology and linguistic abilities. Manuscript submitted for publication.

Reschly, D.J., & Grimes, J.P. (1990). Best practices in intellectual assessment. In *Best Practices in School Psychology.* Washington, D.C.: NASP.

Riccio, C., & Hynd, G. (1995). Contributions of neuropsychology to our understanding of developmental reading problems. *School Psychology Review, 24*, 415–425.

Rubens, A.B., Mahowald, M.W., & Hutton, J.T. (1976). Asymmetry of the lateral (Sylvian) fissures in man. *Neurology, 26*, 620–624.

Rumsey, J.M., Anderson, P., Ametkin, A.J., Aquino, T., King, A.C., Hamberger, S.D., Pikus, A., Rapoport, J.L., & Cohen, R.M. (1992). Failure to activate the left temporoparietal cortex in dyslexia. *Archives of Neurology, 49*, 527–534.

Semrud-Clikeman, M., Biederman, J., & Sprich-Buckminster, S. (1995). Comorbidity between ADHD and learning disability: A review and report in a clinically referred sample. *Journal of the American Academy of Child & Adolescent Psychiatry, 31*, 448.

Shaywitz, B.A., & Shaywitz, S.E. (1991). Comorbidity: A critical issue in attention deficit disorder. *Journal of Child Neurology, 6* (Suppl), S13–S20.

Shinn, M. (Ed.). (1989). *Curriculum-based measurement: Assessing special children*. New York: Guilford Press.

Steinmetz, H., Ebeling, U., Huang, Y., & Kahn, T. (1990). Sulcus topography of the parietal opercular region: An anatomic and MRI study. *Brain and Language, 38*, 515–533.

Tallal, P., et al. (1996). *Science, 271, 27, 77,* 81.

Tucker, J. (1980). Ethnic proportions in classes for the learning disabled: Issues in nonbiased assessment. *Journal of Special Education, 14*, 93–105.

Wechsler, D. (1974). *Wechsler Intelligence Scales for Children—Revised*. New York: Psychological Corporation.

Welker, W. (1990). Why does cerebral cortex fissure and fold? A review of determinants of gyri and sulci. (pp. 3–136). In E.G. Jones & A. Peters (Eds.), *Cerebral cortex, 8B,* New York: Plenum Press.

Witelson, S.F. (1982). Bumps on the brain: Right-left anatomic asymmetry as a key to functional lateralization. In S.J. Segalowitz (Ed.), *Language functions and brain organization*. (pp. 117–143). New York: Academic Press.

Witelson, S.F., & Kigar, D.L. (1992). Sylvian fissure morphology and asymmetry in men and women: Bilateral differences in relation to handedness in men. *Journal of Comparative Neurology, 323*, 326–340.

Woodcock, R.W., & Johnson, M.B. (1989). *Woodcock-Johnson Psychoeducational Test Battery-Revised*. Boston: Teaching Resources.

PART TWO

Cognitive Approaches

4

Learning Disabilities in Perspective

Richard K. Wagner
Tamara Garon

Without question, this is a time of remarkable progress in understanding the nature of learning disabilities in general and of reading disabilities in particular. Researchers appear to be converging on possible genetic loci of a common form of specific reading disability. The results of longitudinal studies of reading acquisition make it possible to identify children at risk for the development of reading disabilities with considerable accuracy and then to begin interventions even prior to the onset of reading instruction. The excitement at conferences devoted to reading disabilities is nearly palpable.

The purpose of this chapter is to attempt to place this progress in perspective and to consider its implications for an account of learning disabilities. We begin by considering competing analogies and perspectives that seek to define the fundamental nature of reading disability. Next we review several behavioral markers of learning disabilities that have been widely held previously. Then we turn to a discussion of the behavioral marker that is the cause of much of the recent excitement, namely, a deficit in phonological processing. Finally, we discuss implications of research on phonological processing for understanding the nature of reading disabilities and for application of this understanding to diagnosis and treatment.

Which Is the Better Analogy: Obesity or Dwarfism?

On any given day, we come across people of varying weights and heights. Occasionally, we encounter individuals who fall outside the norm in weight, height, or both.

Dwarfism is a genetically transmitted condition in which the inability to produce a sufficient amount of growth hormone results in atypically short stature. Diagnosis is straightforward. The vast majority of individuals fall within a normal height distribution, or bell curve. Individuals with dwarfism stand out as a lump in the distribution at its extreme end. Routine interventions such as changing the quantity or quality of food consumed has no effect on the condition. However, a specialized treatment involving supplementary growth hormone can have a recognizable effect on height.

Obesity has been linked to both environmental and genetic factors. Obesity typically is defined as a certain number of pounds over average adult weight for the individual's height and bone structure. Although the range in human adult height is considerable—the tallest basketball players are roughly four times the height of individuals with dwarfism—the range of human adult weight is even greater: Recorded weights have exceeded 1,000 pounds. This is over ten times the weight of the individuals at the bottom of the distribution for healthy adults, who are expected to weigh just under 100 pounds.

With a greater range of weight than height, it is at first surprising that individuals with dwarfism are more easily identified than are individuals with obesity. Although extreme cases of obesity are clear-cut—no one would question that an individual who weighs 500 pounds is obese—the problem is where to draw the line. Currently, obesity is defined as being 20 pounds heavier than the appropriate norm for one's height and bone structure, but a decade ago, one would have had to have been far heavier to be classified as obese. The problem is that the distribution of weight is nearly continuous. There is no obvious break or lump in the distribution to provide a natural cut-point for diagnosis. At the base of all treatment is reducing calories consumed and increasing calories burned, but this approach is not a specialized one. The same prescription applies to individuals who are not obese but wish to lose a few pounds before putting on their bathing suits.

What differentiates dwarfism and obesity, then, are (1) the underlying distribution (continuous and normal for obesity), (2) evidence of a specific problem (inability to produce growth hormone for dwarfism), and (3) the existence of a specialized treatment for the condition.

The Nature of Learning Disabilities

Which condition, dwarfism or obesity, provides the better analogy for learning disabilities? This key question forms the basis of our discussion of the nature, diagnosis, and treatment of learning disabilities in the remaining sections of the chapter. We begin by showing that the dwarfism-versus-obesity analogy maps nicely onto a distinction between two perspectives on learning disabilities.

TABLE 4.1   Comparison of Social-System and Medical-Model Learning
Disabilities

	Type of Disability	
Attribute	*Social System*	*Medical Model*
Severity	Mild	Moderate, high
Impact	Primarily affects school performance	Affects school and out-of-school performance
Incidence rate	High, 10% of school-age population	Low, 1% of school-age population
Etiology	Unknown	Biological anomaly
Initial diagnosis	By school personnel in elementary grades	By medical personnal in infancy
Prognosis	Largely time-limited to school years	Life-long disability

Medical-Model and Social-System Perspectives on Learning Disabilities

When children with learning disabilities are placed in the larger context of all children with disabilities, two general categories of disability are apparent: children who are disabled from a medical-model perspective and children who are disabled from a social-system perspective (Reschly, 1996). These categories represent different fundamental views of the nature of disabilities. These two views have implications for theorizing about the etiology of learning disabilities and for professional practices associated with diagnosis and treatment.

Attributes that differentiate social-system and medical-model disabilities are presented in Table 4.1. Social-system disabilities are mild on the severity scale, and their impact primarily is limited to the school setting. Medical-model disabilities are moderate to severe, and the impact extends to the home and neighborhood settings. The incidence rate for social-system disabilities is roughly 10 percent of school-age children. The incidence rate for medical-model disabilities is only about 1 percent. The etiology of medical-model disabilities typically is a biological anomaly in the form of verifiable damage to the central or peripheral nervous systems, sensory systems, or motoric systems and may be associated with a known syndrome. The etiology of social-system disabilities is less well established and may involve the surrounding context (e.g., organizational structure of schooling) in addition to or instead of factors that are intrinsic to the individual. The initial diagnosis of a social-system disability typically is made by school personnel during the elementary school years, and the disability is less apparent or even absent when schooling is completed. For medical-model disabilities, the diagnosis usually is made by medical personnel within the first years of life, and the consequences of the disability endure throughout the lifetime.

Social-system disabilities include the vast majority of specific learning disabilities such as speech and language disabilities, mild mental retardation, and some behavioral problems. Medical-model disabilities include sensory and physical impairments, moderate and severe retardation, and more severe behavioral disabilities such as autism.

Defining Learning Disabilities

The most influential definition of learning disabilities has been the one contained in the Individuals with Disabilities Education Act (IDEA) (Code of Federal Regulations, Title 34, Subtitle B, Chapter III, Section 300.7 [b][10]):

> "Specific learning disability" means a disorder in one or more basic psychological processes involved in understanding or in using language, spoken or written, that may manifest itself in an imperfect ability to listen, speak, read, write, spell, or to do mathematical calculations. The term includes such conditions as perceptual disabilities, brain injury, minimal brain dysfunction, dyslexia, and developmental aphasia. The term does not apply to children who have learning problems that are primarily the result of visual, hearing, or motor disabilities, of mental retardation, of emotional disturbance, or of environmental, cultural, or economic disadvantage.

This definition implies that learning disabilities are intrinsic to the individual, a consequence of a disorder in an unspecified basic psychological process that itself is rooted in some kind of "minimal brain dysfunction." The disorder is relatively specific as opposed to general, as acknowledged by the label "specific learning disability" and also by the ruling out of mental retardation as the cause of poor performance. Learning disabilities also are distinguished from poor performance attributable to factors associated with poverty.

Three assumptions are common to just about all definitions of learning disabilities. The first assumption is that the locus of the learning disability is within the individual. Early work focused on a neurological origin of learning disabilities in the form of minimal brain dysfunction. Later, learning disabilities were attributed to deficiencies in academically related information processes. Most recently, application of magnetic resonance imagery (MRI) and other scanning procedures has awakened interest in the possible role of neurological structural defects in causing learning disabilities.

The second assumption is that individuals with learning disabilities do not achieve in one or more areas at a level predicted by their intellectual ability. The issue of a discrepancy between intellectual potential and achievement has provoked a great deal of debate about how best to measure intellectual potential and achievement and how much of a discrepancy ought to be required for the diagnosis of learning disabled. But the basic notion that children with learning disabilities will achieve at a lower level than their IQ would predict remains fundamental, and the discrepancy between intellectual ability and achievement is what differentiates children with learning disabilities from children who are slow learners.

The third assumption is that of specificity. Individuals with learning disabilities showed impaired performance in one or several areas, but not all. If performance is impaired generally, the problem is attributed to limited intellectual ability, motivation, or some other factor more general than specific learning disabilities.

Definitions of learning disabilities, including that contained in IDEA, reflect the medical-model perspective—the dwarfism analogy rather than the obesity one. Further, although not specifically stated in the definition, qualifying for services as a learning-disabled student requires that the student evidence a need for *special education* services—the specialized treatment uniquely required by students with learning disabilities.

Behavioral Markers of Learning Disabilities

Historically, a number of behavioral markers or indices have been proposed as the basis for diagnosing children with learning disabilities. We briefly consider the three most influential behavioral markers historically before turning to the latest and most widely used behavioral marker.

Scatter.   When the first author was trained as a school psychologist, he was taught that a hallmark of learning disabilities was scatter on the Wechsler IQ tests. The Wechsler scales typically have 10 subtests, each with a standard score mean of 10 and a standard deviation of 3. Given the assumption that learning disabilities are characterized by a specific processing disorder, one would expect the profiles of students with learning disabilities to be characterized by a mix of high scores (i.e., areas of strength) and low scores (areas of weakness). Scatter simply refers to variability in subtest performance for an individual.

It was this author's experience that scatter was indeed common in the profiles of students with learning disabilities. It was not unusual to have a number of subtest scores in the average (7 to 13) or even above-average (14+) range along with one or more below-average scores (6 or less).

Kaufman (1976) had the good sense and, being employed by the Psychological Corporation at the time, the opportunity, to answer a fundamental question: How much scatter is typical for students without disabilities? The assumption was that there ought to be minimal scatter. A child without learning disabilities who has an IQ of 100—the middle of the average range—would be expected to have subtest scores near 10. But school psychologists wouldn't know from direct experience because they routinely give IQ tests only to children who have been referred because of suspected learning or behavioral disabilities.

Kaufman calculated the range (difference between highest and lowest) in subscale scores for the 2,200 children in the standardization sample for the Wechsler Intelligence Scale for Children—Revised. Because this is a random sample of children, the vast majority of them would not have learning disabilities. The mean subscale-score range for the standardization sample was 7.0 with a standard deviation of 2.1. Scale scores for an average child without disabilities commonly ranged from a low of 6 or 7 to a high of 13 or 14. Thus average children show a surprising amount of scatter. Rather than being a behavioral marker for learning disabilities, scatter is characteristic of children in general.

Reversals.   Children with learning disabilities were observed to reverse letters such as "b" and "d" and even to read whole words backward. This suggested that they suffered from a visual-perceptual problem that resulted in their seeing mirror images of the letters and words they were trying to decode.

However, further studies revealed that young children without disabilities make similar errors when learning to read. Letters such as *b* and *d* are commonly confused by many beginning readers because they are similar both in the sounds they represent and in their visual features. Beginning readers also commonly read words backward simply because they have not yet mastered the convention that all words are read in a single direction (e.g., left to right in English, right to left in Hebrew). When students with learning disabilities were compared to a control group of younger students without learning disabilities matched in reading level, there was no difference in the frequency of reversals (Vellutino, 1978).

Sex differences.   A quick scan of a list of names of children who have been referred for evaluation for possible learning disabilities or merely visiting a classroom for children with reading disabilities reveals what is perhaps the most obvious characteristic of children with learning disabilities: Boys appear to be afflicted at a much higher rate than girls. The ratio of boys to girls in referrals for evaluation and in class rolls of children receiving special education services is almost always at least 2 to 1 and routinely approaches or exceeds 4 to 1. This empirical fact leads to hypotheses about a sex-linked genetic basis for learning disability (Crowder & Wagner, 1991).

However, the difference in the prevalence of reading disability between boys and girls appears to be an artifact of referral bias. Boys tend to be more disruptive than girls and consequently are more likely to be referred for evaluation. For example, Shaywitz and colleagues (1990) obtained an epidemiologic sample of 215 girls and 199 boys. This sample came from the Connecticut Longitudinal Study, research that began with a representative sample of children attending public school kindergarten in the 1983–1984 school year and continued until the children were graduated. From the overall epidemiologic sample, Shaywitz, Shaywitz, Fletcher, and Escobar (1990) identified two samples of reading-disabled students. One sample consisted of students who had been identified as reading disabled by their schools. A research-identified sample consisted of students whose reading achievement lagged 1.5 or more standard deviations behind IQ-based expectations.

The school-identified sample showed the familiar pattern of a greater prevalence of reading disabilities for boys. For second-grade students, 27 (13.6 percent) of 198 boys and only 7 (3.2 percent) of 216 girls were identified by schools as reading disabled. For third-grade students, 20 (10.0 percent) out of 199 boys and 9 (4.2 percent) out of 215 girls were identified as reading disabled. The ratio of boys to girls was 4.25 to 1 in second grade and 2.4 to 1 in third grade. In contrast, the prevalence of reading disabilities was more comparable for the research-identified sample. For second-grade students, 17 (8.7 percent) of 196 boys and 15 (6.9 percent) of 216 girls met the research criterion for categorization as reading disabled. For third-grade students, 18 (9.0 percent) out of 199 boys and 13 (6.0 percent) out of 215 girls met the research criterion. The resultant ratios of boys to girls were 1.3 to 1 in second grade and 1.5 to 1 in third grade.

Similar results were obtained in a comparison of prevalence rates by Finucci and Childs (1981). They reported that although many more boys than girls were served by special schools for reading-disabled children, the ratio of boys to girls in a companion study of randomly selected students from a parochial school who met criteria for reading disabilities was only 1.2 to 1.

In summary, none of the behavioral markers just reviewed support the medical-model disability implied by current definitions of learning disabilities. Scatter on IQ subtest scores is common among individuals without learning disabilities. Reversals are common among individuals who are reading at a beginning level regardless of whether they are beginning readers without disabilities or older children with learning disabilities.

Sex differences in prevalence of learning disabilities appear to be largely an artifact of referral bias.

Deficit in Phonological Processing

Reading disability is by far the most common learning disability. Much of the recent excitement in the field of reading disabilities is attributable to the discovery of a new behavioral marker. Students with reading disabilities appear to suffer from a deficit in one or more areas of phonological processing. Might a deficit in phonological processing finally be the marker that supports the medical model implied by definitions of learning disabilities? In the next section, we provide a brief description of reading-related phonological processes; then we consider implications for understanding the nature of learning disabilities and for diagnosing and treating them.

What Are Reading-Related Phonological Processing Abilities?

Understanding the nature of reading-related phonological processes requires a brief digression to review some basic levels of speech perception.

Spoken words are conveyed through space as varying waves of *acoustic energy* (Crowder & Wagner, 1991). This energy can be viewed in a spectrogram, which displays the amount of acoustic energy present at various frequencies. Analysis of spectrograms produced by spoken words reveals that the separation of words into distinct sounds, or even sentences into discrete words, is not a feature of the acoustic signal but rather a cognitive/perceptual phenomenon. Although we readily perceive individual words in sentences and individual speech sounds in words, the acoustic signal that travels from the speaker's voice to the listener's ear is largely continuous. This continuous aspect of speech is apparent to us when we hear fluent speech in a language that we do not understand—or even when we listen to a different dialect, as when the first author listened to Scottish brogue while on vacation. The words seem to run together.

One level up from the acoustic signal is the *phonetic level* of speech representation. At the phonetic level, speech is represented by phones. (The root of a number of terms in this literature such as *phone, phoneme,* and *phonological* derives from the Greek word *phone,* which means "sound" or "voice.") Phones are the universal set of speech sounds found in languages. Individual phones are produced by manipulating the placement of the tongue in the mouth and the position of the lips, by vibrating the vocal cords, and by opening and closing the mouth. The sounds corresponding to the letter "t" in the words "top," "pot," and "stop" represent different phones despite the fact that they are represented by a single letter in written English. To verify that the "t" phones in the three words really are produced by subtle differences in articulation, hold your hand several inches in front of your mouth while saying each word. You will feel a pronounced burst of air associated with the "t" in "top"; a lesser burst of air associated with the "t" in "pot," and virtually no burst of air associated with the "t" in "stop."

The next higher level is the *phonological level,* at which related phones (called allophones) are combined into families called phonemes. Phonemes represent differences in speech sounds that signal differences in meaning—they are differences we hear when attending to speech in everyday conversation. At this level, the three phones associated with the "t" in "top," "pot," and "stop" are allophones of the single phoneme /t/. The phoneme /t/ is distinguished from the phoneme /p/, which signals the fact that the words "top" and "pop" have different meanings. Midwestern American English (i.e., what is spoken by anchorpersons of national news networks—except Canadian-born Peter Jennings) can be represented with a set of from 35 to 45 phonemes depending on which classification system is used (Denes & Pinson, 1963).

Above the phonological level, phonemes are combined into larger units. Important units include onsets and rimes. The onset of a syllable refers to its initial consonant or consonant cluster. Rime refers to the remaining vowel and consonant or consonant cluster. Together, onsets and rimes compose syllables, and in turn, syllables compose words.

An almost infinite number of possible combinations of phonemes is possible, but only a relatively small number actually are found in a language, and many of these combinations occur in more than a single word. For written alphabetic orthographies such as English, letters roughly correspond to the phonemes. Thus the word "tap" consists of the three phonemes /t/, /a/, and /p/ and is spelled with letters representing those phonemes. The word "rap," is spelled the same except for a different initial letter. Given the correspondence between letters and phonemes, it would appear that knowledge of sound structure of one's oral language ought to be useful in learning to read. This possibility has motivated research on relations between the development of phonological processing abilities and the acquisition of reading skills.

Three Kinds of Phonological Processing Abilities

Three bodies of potentially related research on phonological processes developed in relative isolation (Wagner & Torgesen, 1987). The first body of research centers on the concept of *phonological awareness*. Phonological awareness refers to one's awareness of and access to the sound structure of one's spoken language (Mattingly, 1972). Phonological awareness tasks typically require individuals to identify and/or manipulate speech segments. For example, young children may be asked to distinguish words that rhyme (e.g., "Which word doesn't belong? fan, pan, house."). Older children and adults may be asked to blend sounds (e.g., /k/ + /a/ + /t/ = cat) or delete a speech segment to produce a different word (e.g., flat − /l/ = fat). Because of the correspondence between letters and phonemes in alphabetic writing systems such as English, a child with well-developed phonological awareness should find such systems reasonable and orderly. A child lacking such awareness may perceive alphabetic writing systems to be largely arbitrary.

A second body of research centers on the concept of *phonological memory*. Phonological memory refers to coding information in a sound-based (i.e., phonological) representation for efficient short-term storage (Baddeley, 1986; Conrad, 1964). You rely on phonological memory when you attempt to remember a phone number after looking it up in a phone book. It is not the visual images that you store but rather the names of the digits. Although it used to be believed that a speech-based short-term store was fundamentally involved in all language activities including reading, this view has given way in the face of mounting evidence that a surprising amount of language processing can occur outside the confines of traditional short-term memory (Crowder, 1982, 1993; Wagner, 1996a). Nevertheless, individual and developmental differences in phonological memory may be more of a factor when beginning readers attempt to decode words. As parts of words are decoded, children need to store the sounds of the letters they have decoded as they process the rest of the word. Presumably, efficient phonological memory proves helpful by providing the reader with an accurate list of sounds that have been retrieved and by freeing up cognitive resources to be applied to the difficult task of blending the sounds into words (Baddeley, 1982; Torgesen, 1995).

The third body of research centers on the construct of retrieval of phonological codes from permanent memory, and because of the tasks commonly used to measure this construct, it commonly is referred to as *phonological naming*, or rapid naming. Much of the processing of written and spoken language involves retrieving phonological codes or pronunciations associated with letters, word segments, and whole words. The efficiency with which phonological codes are retrieved may influence the success with which phonological processing is used in decoding printed words (Wolf, 1991). Tasks commonly used to assess this ability require naming objects or symbols as rapidly as possible. To perform well, individuals must be able to access and articulate symbol names quickly.

Although individual differences in performing each of the three kinds of phonological processing tasks have been found to be predictive of later reading abilities, most studies have included only a single phonological task, thereby precluding analyses that could determine whether the different kinds of tasks represented different constructs or, alternatively, whether the tasks might merely be imperfect measures of the same construct despite differences in their surface structures.

To clarify relations between the different kinds of phonological processing tasks and the constructs themselves, we carried out a series of studies in which relatively large groups of children were given multiple measures of each of the three kinds of phonological processing abilities. Confirmatory factor analysis then was used to test alternative models of the nature of these abilities.

In a study of preschoolers, multiple measures of each of the three kinds of phonological processing abilities were administered to 111 four- and five-year-old prereading children (Wagner et al., 1987). The phonological awareness measures included counting syllables, elision (dropping) of syllables from words, elision of syllables from nonwords, blending syllables, and sound categorization (picking the odd sound out of "pin," "pit," and "peg"; Bradley & Bryant, 1985). The phonological memory tasks included memory for letter strings presented orally, memory for visually presented series of pictures of common objects, and articulation rate. The phonological naming tasks included rapid naming of strings of common objects, rapid naming of strings of colors, rapid naming of strings of letters, and the Posner task using line drawings of animals. Measures of general cognitive ability included the vocabulary and block-design subtests of the Wechsler Preschool and Primary Intelligence Scale.

The results were that prereaders' phonological processing abilities were well represented by a model that consisted of two kinds of abilities. The first accounted for individual differences on both awareness and memory tasks. The second accounted for individual differences in phonological naming tasks. The interesting result was that two kinds of phonological processing tasks, awareness and memory, each emerging from a different literature and having markedly different surface structures, have the same origin of individual differences. In short, different tasks were measuring the same construct.

In a second cross-sectional study, multiple measures of each of the three kinds of phonological processing abilities were administered to samples of 95 kindergarten and 89 second-grade students (Wagner, Torgesen, Laughon, Simmons, & Rashotte, 1993). Measures of phonological awareness included segmenting phonemes, eliding phonemes, isolating sounds, categorizing sounds, blending onsets and rimes, blending phonemes into words, and blending phonemes into nonwords. The phonological memory tasks included memory for digits presented orally, memory for digits presented visually, memory for sentences, and a working-memory task. Measures of phonological code retrieval included naming digits and naming letters with isolated-trial and serial versions of each task. The results replicated and extended those obtained from the preschool study. For the kindergarten sample, a model with two kinds of phonological processing, awareness/memory and naming, again provided a good fit to the data. By second grade, the pattern of results was similar except that awareness and memory no longer could be represented by a single factor, although their respective factors remained highly correlated: $r = .78, p < .001$.

Follow-up longitudinal studies have supported these findings (Wagner, Torgesen, & Rashotte, 1994; Wagner et al., 1997). Young children's phonological processing abilities are well described by a set of three distinct yet correlated abilities. These include phonological awareness, which can be subdivided into analysis and synthesis; phonological memory; and phonological naming. For very young children, analysis and phonological memory are indistinguishable. But with development, analysis and phonological memory become distinct individual-difference factors.

Relations Between the Development of Phonological Processing Skills and the Acquisition of Reading

Children's phonological processing abilities are of particular interest because they appear to be causally related to the acquisition of beginning reading skills, although the magnitude and even the direction of proposed causal relations remain the subject of debate (Ball & Blachman, 1988; Bradley & Bryant, 1985; Bryant, Bradley, MacLean, & Crossland, 1989; Ehri, 1987; Lundberg, Frost, Petersen, 1988; Perfetti, Bell, Beck, & Hughes, 1987; Stanovich, 1986; Treiman, 1991; Tunmer & Nesdale, 1985; Wagner, 1988; Wagner & Torgesen, 1987).

Three alternative views of causal relations between the development of phonological processing abilities and the acquisition of word-level reading skills have been proposed. The first view is that the development of phonological processing abilities facilitates the acquisition of beginning reading skills (Jorm & Share, 1983; Liberman, 1983; Liberman, Shankweiler, & Liberman, 1989; Wagner & Torgesen, 1987). Evidence in support of this view includes a large number of longitudinal studies in which a phonological task given in kindergarten or first grade predicts subsequent word decoding (Bradley & Bryant, 1985; Bryant, MacLean, Bradley, & Crossland, 1990; Byrne, Freebody, & Gates, 1992; Foorman, Francis, Novy, & Liberman, 1991; Juel, Griffith, & Gough, 1986; Lundberg, Olofsson, & Wall, 1980; Stanovich, Cunningham, & Cramer, 1984; Tunmer, Herriman, & Nesdale, 1988; Tunmer & Nesdale, 1985; Vellutino & Scanlon, 1987).

TABLE 4.2   Stability of Phonological Processing Abilities and Word-Level
Reading

Variable	First Grade	Second Grade	Third Grade	Fourth Grade
Awareness	0.83	0.62	0.64	0.63
Memory	1.00	0.93	0.89	0.77
Naming	0.84	0.64	0.60	0.55
Word-level reading	0.69	0.39	0.33	0.27

The second view is that the causal arrow goes the other way: Learning
to read facilitates the development of phonological processing abilities
(Ehri, 1984, 1987; Morais, 1991; Morais, Alegria, & Content, 1987). Evidence in support of this view includes the fact that adult illiterates and
young prereaders perform poorly on phonological tasks that require
identification or manipulation of phonemes (Liberman, Shankweiler, Fischer, & Carter, 1974; Morais, Cary, Alegria, & Bertelson, 1979, Wagner et
al., 1987). The fact that children sometimes make "spelling errors" on
phonological awareness tasks—for example, when they count more
phonemes in "pitch" than in "rich" because the former has more letters—
provides indirect evidence of the knowledge of printed words affecting
performance on phonological awareness measures (Ehri & Wilce, 1980;
Tunmer and Nesdale, 1985).

The final view is that the causal relations are reciprocal (Perfetti, Beck,
Bell, & Hughes, 1987; Stanovich, 1986; Tunmer & Rohl, 1991). According
to this view, rudimentary phonological awareness—perhaps up to an
awareness of onset and rime—facilitates learning to read. Learning to
read, in turn, facilitates the development of a more full-blown awareness
that results in the ability to segment words completely into phonemes.

We carried out a five-year longitudinal study of 216 children that began
when they entered kindergarten (Wagner et al., 1994, in press). Each year
we gave them a battery of phonological tasks and reference measures, including multiple measures of each of the three kinds of phonological processing abilities and of word-level reading. We used structural equation
modeling to estimate the magnitudes and directions of causal relations between phonological processing abilities and word-level reading.

Two results were of interest. First, individual differences in phonological processing abilities were remarkably stable from year to year. Stability
coefficients (i.e., correlations between phonological processing abilities
from one year to the next) are presented in Table 4.2. The stability of individual differences in phonological processing abilities actually equaled
or exceeded that of reading or verbal ability.

The second result of interest was evidence of bidirectional causal relations. Table 4.3 contains the independent causal influences of individual

TABLE 4.3   Causal Influences of Individual Differences in Phonological
Processing Abilities, Vocabulary, and the Autoregressive Effect of Prior
Reading (at K, 1st, and 2nd grades) on Subsequent Individual Differences
in Word-Level Reading (at 2nd, 3rd, and 4th grades)

Exogenous Causes	K to 2nd	1st to 3rd	2nd to 4th
Phonological processing variables			
Awareness	.37[1]	.29[2]	.27[1]
Memory	.12	−.03	.07
Naming	.25[2]	.21[2]	.07
Control variables			
Vocabulary	.10	.22[1]	−.01
Autoregressor	.02	.27[2]	.57[1]

[1] $p<.001$
[2] $p<.01$

differences in phonological processing abilities on subsequent word-level
reading. For every time period examined, individual differences in
phonological awareness exerted a causal influence on subsequent individual differences in word-level reading. Individual differences in naming and vocabulary exerted independent causal influences on subsequent individual differences in word-level reading initially, but these
influences faded with development as individual differences in word-
level reading become increasingly stable. The increase in stability of
word-level reading is represented by the increasing autoregressive effect
of prior word-level reading on subsequent word-level reading. Individual differences in phonological memory did not exert an independent
causal influence on subsequent individual differences in word-level
reading for any time period.

Regarding reciprocal causal relations between both word-level reading
and letter-name knowledge on subsequent phonological processing abilities, there was no evidence of a causal influence of word-level reading on
subsequent phonological processing for any time period examined.
However, letter-name knowledge did exert a causal influence on subsequent phonological processing abilities, as shown by the results presented in Table 4.4.

Causal influences of individual differences in letter-name knowledge
were found for subsequent individual differences in both phonological
awareness and naming. The absence of a causal influence of letter-name
knowledge on subsequent phonological memory appears to reflect the
greater stability of individual differences in phonological memory relative to phonological awareness and naming (see Table 4.2).

TABLE 4.4   Causal Influences of Individual Differences in Letter-Name Knowledge (at K and 1st grades) on Subsequent Individual Differences in Phonological Processing Abilities (at 2nd and 3rd grades)

Exogenous Causes	K to 2nd	1st to 3rd
Awareness		
Letter-name knowledge	.23[2]	.12[3]
Control variables		
Vocabulary	.19[3]	.17[2]
Autoregressor	.43[1]	.70[1]
Memory		
Letter-name knowledge	.05	.10
Control variables		
Vocabulary	−.06	−.14
Autoregressor	.97[1]	1.00[1]
Naming		
Letter-name knowledge	.22[3]	.13[3]
Control variables		
Vocabulary	.08	−.09[2]
Autoregressor	.52[1]	.74[1]

[1] $p<.001$
[2] $p<.01$
[3] $p<.05$

Deficits in Phonological Processing as a Cause of Reading Disabilities

In recent years, a consensus has emerged that a deficit in phonological processing is a likely cause of the majority of cases of reading disability (Bruck, 1990; Bruck & Treiman, 1990; Felton & Wood, 1990; Olson, Wise, Conners, Rack, & Fulker, 1989; Siegel & Ryan, 1988; Shankweiler & Liberman, 1989; Stanovich, 1988; Torgesen, 1991, Wagner, 1986). Torgesen (this volume) provides a coherent and up-to-date statement of this position. The majority of children with reading disabilities are believed to have a deficit in some aspect of phonological processing that greatly impairs their ability to learn to read yet leaves their ability to understand and produce speech largely intact. Whether subtle indications of a deficit in phonological processing are evident in children's speech perception or production has yet to be resolved but promises to be an area of keen interest.

What are the implications for the issue we began with—namely, whether obesity or dwarfism provides the more apt analogy for reading disabilities—of the consensus that a deficit in phonological processing is the basis for the majority of cases of reading disability, and what are the implications for diagnosis and treatment? Recall that three considerations are important in determining medical-model-based conditions such as dwarfism as opposed to social-system-model-based conditions such as obesity: (1) whether the underlying distribution is continuous and normal; (2) whether there is evidence of a specific problem; and (3) whether a specialized treatment exists that is uniquely beneficial to individuals who have the condition.

Underlying Distribution.   Is there a bump in the lower tail of the distribution of reading skill that represents a subpopulation of children with reading disabilities? Although some early studies suggested that this might be the case (see, e.g., Rutter & Yule, 1975), more extensive recent studies suggest no evidence of a bump in the lower tail of the distribution of reading skill. For example, Shaywitz and colleagues (1992) examined the distribution of reading skill for 414 children from the Connecticut Longitudinal Study. They operationalized reading disability in terms of several kinds of discrepancy scores that quantified deviation of reading skill from predictions based on IQ. The discrepancy scores followed a univariate normal distribution, and correlations among the various discrepancy scores they examined followed a bivariate normal distribution. They concluded that reading disability is part of a continuum of reading skill that includes normal reading.

Specificity of the Problem.   A specific learning disability, including reading disability, is defined as a disorder in one or more basic psychological processes. Excluded are learning problems that are the result of more general causes such as mental retardation, poor instruction, and economic disadvantage. In particular, a discrepancy between predicted levels of achievement and actual achievement has been a requirement for diagnosis. The assumption is that children whose levels of achievement are discrepant from their IQs differ in cognitive characteristics and potential for remediation from children whose levels of achievement are consistent with their IQs.

Fletcher and others (1994) compared a reading-disabled sample made up of poor readers whose reading level was discrepant from their IQs with a sample of "garden variety" poor readers whose reading level was consistent with their IQs. Despite the fact that phonological awareness reliably discriminated both groups of poor readers from good readers, there were no differences between the reading-disabled sample and the garden-variety poor readers on any cognitive variable examined including measures of phonological processing. Thus a deficiency in phonological processing ought to be viewed as a characteristic of poor reading regardless of its cause, not as a specific indicator of reading disability (Stanovich & Siegel, 1994).

Existence of a Specialized Treatment.   Roughly 25 studies have been carried out to date in which a training program has been employed to boost phonological awareness. Some of the studies have involved young children at risk for reading failure or students with reading disabilities. Other studies involved random samples of beginning readers or prereaders. A meta-analysis of this literature indicates that training phonological awareness improves word-level reading skills, particularly phonetic decoding of nonwords (Wagner, 1996b). But does this finding constitute evidence of a specialized treatment for reading disabilities?

It is too early to tell, although the completion of long-term prospective treatment studies in the next few years should help to answer this question. The reason for caution is that phonological awareness training, particularly when it is coupled with training in letter-sound correspondences and in other aspects of phonics, may prove to be beneficial to many children whether or not they have reading disabilities. Further, when the effects of training are examined for individuals as opposed to just at the group level, it routinely is the case that a group of children do not respond to training. These children may represent those children in the samples who actually have a reading disability, or perhaps a severe form of reading disability.

Summary and Implications

From its early history, the field of learning disabilities has been characterized by a split between basic assumptions about the nature of learning disabilities and a research literature that suggests these assumptions are unfounded. These basic assumptions are evident from definitions of learning disabilities, including the dominant definition provided by the Individuals with Disabilities Act (IDEA), all of which assume that (1) the locus of the disability is within the individual, (2) achievement is below predictions based on intellectual ability, and (3) impaired performance can occur in one or several areas but not all. This definition represents a medical-model perspective; the preferred analogy is that of dwarfism as opposed to obesity.

We evaluated behavioral markers that traditionally have been proposed as markers of learning disabilities (e.g., scatter, reversals, sex differences) using three criteria: (1) whether the underlying distribution is continuous and normal, (2) whether there is evidence of a specific problem, and (3) whether a specialized treatment exists that is uniquely beneficial to individuals who have the condition. None of the traditional behavioral markers met the criterion for establishment of a medical-model-based disability. Had we more space, the same conclusion would have been reached for other efforts that did not pan out, for example, eye-movement training and remediation of purported psy-cholinguistic or visual-perceptual disabilities evidenced by poor perfor-mance on measures such as the Illinois Test of Psycholinguistic Abilities (ITPA).

With a growing consensus that a deficit in phonological processing is the cause of the majority of cases of reading disability, we revisited the is-sue of the better analogy for reading disabilities. For now, the conclusion remains as it was for other behavioral markers. Analysis of the distribu-tion of reading skill indicates that reading disability is part of a normally distributed continuum of reading skill that includes normal reading, as opposed to a lump in the lower tail of the distribution. A deficit in phono-logical processing is general to children who are poor readers for a vari-ety of causes as opposed to specific to children who fit the definition of reading disability. Finally, although phonological awareness training pro-grams improve word-level reading skills on average, there is as yet no evidence that this training represents a specialized treatment for children with reading disabilities. In fact, analysis of the effects of treatment at the level of the individual as opposed to the group indicates that some chil-dren—perhaps those with real or severe disabilities—do not respond to training.

Reading disability remains best characterized as a social-system phe-nomenon that emerges from a conflict between the educational needs of some children and traditional educational practices. Where does this leave us with respect to diagnosis and remediation?

We consider diagnosing and labeling children as though they suffered from a medical-model-type disability, when in fact the problem is a so-cial-system-type misfit between educational needs and traditional educa-tional practice, to be scapegoating. We recommend eliminating this prac-tice for all social-system disabilities, which apply to the majority of children with learning disabilities. Diagnosis and labeling should be re-served for verifiable medical-model disabilities. Our working with chil-dren and reading of the literature suggest to us that a severe form of reading disability exists that would meet most, if not all, of the medical-model criteria (see Table 4.1). However, the prevalence of this disability is likely to be closer to 1–3 percent of school-age children as opposed to re-cent estimates of 20–30 percent (Lyon, 1996).

We believe our view to be largely consistent with Spear-Swerling and Sternberg's (1996) analysis of the development of reading disabilities. Similarities are apparent between the intrinsic and extrinsic aspects of their interactive model and the medical-model and social-system per-spectives we have described. However, although it clearly is necessary to consider both intrinsic and extrinsic factors in describing how children become identified as having reading disabilities, at another level it is important to recognize a fundamental antagonism. If there is no convincing evidence of a medical-model type, intrinsic disorder, and we suggest that there is not for the vast majority of poor readers, it approaches dishonesty to act as though we had identified such a disorder when working with students and their families. Further, progress in our understanding of reading problems through research is likely to be impeded by a futile search for a high-incidence, nonexistent syndrome.

We don't mean to suggest that poor reading is not a pervasive problem or that we do not need to devote a great deal of effort to helping children who have trouble learning to read. As Ellis noted in the case of obesity, "For people of any given age and height there will be an uninterrupted continuum from painfully thin to inordinately fat. It is entirely arbitrary where we draw the line between the normal and obese, but that does not prevent obesity being a real and worrying condition, nor does it prevent research into the causes and cures of obesity being both valuable and necessary" (Ellis, 1985, p. 172, cited in Crowder & Wagner, 1992).

What does change is our expectations about potential causes and cures of common cases of poor reading. We ought not to expect magic bullets, distinctive syndromes, or cognitive deficits for the vast majority of poor readers. The best hope is a marked increase in individualization in reading instruction, perhaps made more practical as technology including computer-based reading tutorial programs becomes more effective and commonplace. If the label of reading disability is to be maintained, it ought to be applied to schools rather than children (with the possible exception of a rare, severe form of reading problem), and identifying and treating schools with reading disabilities ought to be our highest priority.

References

Baddeley, A. (1982). Reading and working memory. *Bulletin of the British Psychological Society, 35,* 414–417.

Baddeley, A. (1986). *Working memory.* New York: Oxford University Press.

Ball, E., & Blachman, B. (1988). Phonological segmentation training: Effects of reading readiness. *Annals of Dyslexia, 38,* 208–225.

Bradley, L., & Bryant, P. (1985). *Rhyme and reason in reading and spelling.* Ann Arbor, MI: University of Michigan Press.

Bruck, M. (1990). Word recognition skills of adults with childhood diagnoses of dyslexia. *Developmental Psychology, 26,* 439–454.

Bruck, M., & Treiman, R. (1990). Phonological awareness and spelling in normal children and dyslexics: The case of initial consonant clusters. *Journal of Experimental Child Psychology, 50,* 156–178.

Bryant, P. E., Bradley, L., MacLean, M., & Crossland, D. (1989). Nursery rhymes, phonological skills and reading. *Journal of Child Language, 16,* 407–428.

Bryant, P., MacLean, M., Bradley, L., & Crossland, J. (1990). Rhyme and alliteration, phoneme detection and learning to read. *Developmental Psychology, 26,* 429–438.

Byrne, B., Freebody, P., & Gates, A. (1992). Longitudinal data on the relations of word-reading strategies to comprehension, reading time, and phonemic awareness. *Reading Research Quarterly, 27,* 141–151.

Conrad, R. (1964). Acoustic confusions in immediate memory. *British Journal of Psychology, 55,* 75–84.

Crowder, R. G. (1982). The demise of short-term memory. *Acta Psychologica, 50,* 291–293.

Crowder, R. G. (1993). Short-term memory: Where do we stand? *Memory & Cognition, 21,* 142–145.

Crowder, R. G., & Wagner, R. K. (1991). *The psychology of reading.* New York: Oxford University Press.

Denes, P. B., & Pinson, E. N. (1963). *The speech chain.* Murray Hill, NJ: Bell Telephone Laboratories.

Ehri, L.C. (1984). The development of spelling knowledge and its role in reading acquisition and reading disability. *Journal of Learning Disabilities, 22,* 356–365.

Ehri, L. C. (1987). Learning to read and spell words. *Journal of Reading Behavior, 19,* 5–31.

Ehri, L. C., & Wilce, L. S. (1980). The influence of orthography on readers' conceptualization of the phonemic structure of words. *Applied Psycholinguistics, 1,* 371–385.

Felton, R. H., & Wood, F. B. (1990). Cognitive deficits in reading disability and attention deficit disorder. In J. K. Torgesen (Ed.), *Cognitive and behavioral characteristics of children with learning disabilities.* Austin, TX: PRO-ED.

Finucci, J. M., & Childs, B. (1981). Are there really more dyslexic boys than girls? In A. Ansara, N. Geshwind, A. Galaburda, M. Albert, & N. Gartrell (Eds.), *Gender differences in dyslexia* (pp. 1–9). Townson, MD: Orton Dyslexia Society.

Fletcher, J. M., Shaywitz, S. E., Shankweiler, D. P., Katz, L., Liberman, I. Y., Stuebing, K. K., Francis, D. J., Fowler, A. E., & Shaywitz, B. A. (1994). Cognitive profiles of reading disability: Comparisons of discrepancy and low achievement definitions. *Journal of Educational Psychology, 86,* 6–23.

Foorman, B. R., Francis, D. J., Novy, D. M., & Liberman D. (1991). How letter-sound instruction mediates progress in first-grade reading and spelling. *Journal of Educational Psychology, 83,* 456–469.

Jorm, A. F., & Share, D. L. (1983). Phonological recoding and reading acquisition. *Applied Psycholinguistics, 4,* 103–147.

Juel, C., Griffith, P., & Gough, P. (1986) Acquisition of literacy: A longitudinal study of children in first and second grade. *Journal of Educational Psychology, 78,* 243–255.

Kaufman, A. S. (1976). A new approach to the interpretation of test scatter on the WISC-R. *Journal of Learning Disabilities, 9,* 33–41.

Liberman, I. Y., (1983). A language-oriented view of reading and its disabilities. In H. Myklebust (Ed.), *Progress in learning disabilities* (Vol. 5, pp. 81–101). New York: Grune & Stratton.

Liberman, I. Y., Shankweiler, D., Fischer, F. W., & Carter, B. (1974). Explicit sylla-ble and phoneme segmentation in the young child. *Journal of Experimental Child Psychology, 18,* 201–212.

Liberman, I. Y., Shankweiler, D., & Liberman, A. M. (1989). The alphabetic princi-ple and learning to read. In D. Shankweiler & I. Y. Liberman, (Eds.), *Phonology and reading disability: Solving the reading puzzle.* Ann Arbor, MI: U. of Michigan Press.

Lundberg, I., Frost, J., & Petersen, O. (1988). Effects of an extensive program for stimulating phonological awareness in preschool children. *Reading Research Quarterly, 23,* 263–284.

Lundberg, I., Olofsson, A., & Wall, S. (1980). Reading and spelling skills in the first school years predicted from phonemic awareness skills in kindergarten. *Scandinavian Journal of Psychology, 21,* 159–173.

Mattingly, I. G. (1972). Reading, the linguistic process and linguistic awareness. In J. Kavanagh & I. Mattingly (Eds.), *Language by ear and by eye* (pp. 133–147). Cambridge, MA: MIT Press.

Morais, J. (1991). Phonological awareness: A bridge between language and liter-acy. In D. Sawyer & B. Fox (Eds.), *Phonological awareness in reading: The evolution of current perspectives* (pp. 31–71). New York: Springer-Verlag.

Morais, J., Alegria, J., & Content, A. (1987). The relationships between segmental analysis and alphabetic literacy: An interactive view. *Cahiers de Psychologie Cog-nitive, 7,* 1–24.

Morais, J., Cary, L., Alegria, J., & Bertelson, P. (1979). Does awareness of speech as a sequence of phones arise spontaneously? *Cognition, 7,* 323–331.

Olson, R., Wise, B., Conners, F., Rack, J., & Fulker, D. (1989). Specific deficits in component reading and language skills: Genetic and environmental influ-ences. *Journal of Learning Disabilities, 22,* 339–348.

Perfetti, C. A., Beck, I., Bell, L. C., & Hughes, C. (1987). Phonemic knowledge and learning to read are reciprocal: A longitudinal study of first grade children. *Merrill-Palmer Quarterly, 33,* 283–319.

Reschly, D. J. (1996). Identification and assessment of students with disabilities. *Special Education for Students with Disabilities, 6,* 40–53.

Rutter, M., & Yule, W. (1975). The concept of specific reading retardation. *Journal of Child Psychology and Psychiatry, 16,* 181–197.

Shankweiler, D., & Liberman, I. (1989). *Phonology and Reading Disability.* IARLD Monograph, No. 6. Ann Arbor, MI: University Press.

Shaywitz, S. E., Shaywitz, B. A., Fletcher, J. M., & Escobar, M. D. (1990). Preva-lence of reading disability in boys and girls. *Journal of the American Medical As-sociation, 264,* 998–1002.

Shaywitz, S. E., Escobar, M. D., Shaywitz, B. A., Fletcher, J. M., & Makuch, R. (1992). Evidence that dyslexia may represent the lower tail of a normal distrib-ution of reading ability. *New England Journal of Medicine, 326,* 145–150.

Siegel L. S., & Ryan, E. B. (1988). Reading disability as a language disorder. *Reme-dial and Special Education, 5(3),* 28–33.

Spear-Swerling, L., & Sternberg, R. J. (1996). *Off track: When poor readers become "learning disabled."* Boulder, CO: Westview Press.

Stanovich, K. E. (1986). Matthew effects in reading: Some consequences of individual differences in the acquisition of literacy. *Reading Research Quarterly, 21,* 360–407.

Stanovich, K. E. (1988). The right and wrong places to look for the cognitive locus of reading disability. *Annals of Dyslexia, 38,* 154–177.

Stanovich, K. E., Cunningham, A. E., & Cramer, B. (1984). Assessing phonological awareness in kindergarten children: Issues of task comparability. *Journal of Experimental Child Psychology, 38,* 175–190.

Stanovich, K. E., & Siegel, L. S. (1994). The phenotypic performance profile of reading-disabled children: A regression-based test of the phonological-core variable-difference model. *Journal of Educational Psychology, 86,* 24–53.

Torgesen, J. K. (1991). Cross-age consistency in phonological processing. In S. Brady & D. Shankweiler (Eds.), *Phonological processes in literacy.* Hillsdale, NJ: Lawrence Erlbaum Associates.

Torgesen, J. K. (1995). A model of memory from an information-processing perspective: The special case of phonological memory. In R. Lyon & N. Krasnegor (Eds.), *Attention, memory, and executive function* (pp. 157–184). Baltimore, MD: Brooks.

Treiman, R. (1991). Phonological awareness and its roles in learning to read and spell. In D. J. Sawyer & B. J. Fox (Eds.), *Phonological awareness in reading: The evolution of current perspectives* (pp. 159–189). New York: Springer-Verlag.

Tunmer, W. E., Herriman, M. L., & Nesdale, A. R. (1988). Metalinguistic abilities and beginning reading. *Reading Research Quarterly, 23,* 134–158.

Tunmer, W. E., & Nesdale, A. R. (1985). Phonemic segmentation skill and beginning reading. *Journal of Educational Psychology, 77,* 417–427.

Tunmer, W. E., & Rohl, M. (1991). Phonological awareness and reading acquisition. In D. Sawyer & B. Fox (Eds.), *Phonological awareness in reading: The evolution of current perspectives* (pp. 1–30). New York: Springer-Verlag.

Vellutino, F. R. (1978). Toward an understanding of dyslexia: Psychological factors in specific reading disability. In A. L. Benton & D. Pearl (Eds.), *Dyslexia: An appraisal of current knowledge.* New York: Oxford University Press.

Vellutino, F., & Scanlon, D. M. (1987). Phonological coding, phonological awareness, and reading ability: Evidence from longitudinal and experimental study. *Merrill-Palmer Quarterly, 33,* 321–364.

Wagner, R. K. (1986). Phonological processing abilities and reading: Implications for disabled readers. *Journal of Learning Disabilities, 19,* 623–630.

Wagner, R. K. (1988). Causal relations between the development of phonological processing abilities and the acquisition of reading skills: A meta-analysis. *Merrill-Palmer Quarterly, 34,* 261–279.

Wagner, R. K. (1996a). From simple structure to complex function: Major trends in the development of theories, models, and measurements of memory. In R. Lyon & N. Krasnegor (Eds.), *Attention, memory, and executive function* (pp. 137–156). Baltimore, MD: Brooks.

Wagner, R. K. (1996b, April). *Does phonological awareness training enhance children's acquisition of written language? A meta-analysis.* Paper presented at the Annual Meeting of the American Educational Research Association, New York.

Wagner, R. K., Balthazor, M., Hurley, S., Morgan, S., Rashotte, C., Shaner, R., Simmons, K., & Stage, S. (1987). The nature of prereaders' phonological processing abilities. *Cognitive Development, 2,* 355–373.

Wagner, R. K., & Torgesen, J. K. (1987). The nature of phonological processing and its causal role in the acquisition of reading skills. *Psychological Bulletin, 101,* 192–212.

Wagner, R. K., Torgesen, J. K., Laughon, P., Simmons, K., & Rashotte, C. A. (1993). Development of young readers' phonological processing abilities. *Journal of Educational Psychology, 85,* 83–103.

Wagner, R. K., Torgesen, J. K., & Rashotte, C. A. (1994). Development of reading-related phonological processing abilities: New evidence of bi-directional causality from a latent variable longitudinal study. *Developmental Psychology, 30,* 73–87.

Wagner, R. K., Torgesen, J. K., Rashotte, C. A., Hecht, S. A., Barker, T. A., Burgess, S. R., Donahue, J., & Garon, T. (1997). Changing relations between phonological processing abilities and word-level reading as children develop from beginning to fluent readers: A five-year longitudinal study. *Developmental Psychology, 33,* 468–479.

Wolf, M. (1991). Naming speed and reading: The contribution of the cognitive neurosciences. *Reading Research Quarterly, 26,* 123–141.

5

Phonologically Based Reading Disabilities:
Toward a Coherent Theory of One Kind
of Learning Disability

Joseph K. Torgesen

This book shows that it is possible to have multiple, and perhaps quite divergent, perspectives on the nature of learning disabilities. Disagreement and varying perspectives on the concept of learning disabilities have been part of the field since its beginning. However, it is my view that our discussions about the nature of learning disabilities should be constrained to a much narrower range of opinion than they usually are. The starting place for these discussions should be the definition of learning disabilities that has been at the core of the field since the beginning (Torgesen, 1991). Although achieving a consensus about a specific definition of learning disabilities has been difficult, there has never been serious disagreement among those most closely involved in the field about its central elements. These elements are reflected in the definition offered by the National Joint Committee on Learning Disabilities, which is probably the one most widely agreed upon in the field today (Hammill, 1990):

> Learning disabilities is a general term that refers to a heterogeneous group
> of disorders manifested by significant difficulties in the acquisition and use
> of listening, speaking, reading, writing, reasoning, or mathematical abilities.

The research reported in this chapter was supported by grant numbers HD23340 and HD30988 from the National Institute of Child Health and Human Development, and by grants from the National Center for Learning Disabilities, and the Donald L. Hammill Foundation.

These disorders are intrinsic to the individual, presumed to be due to central nervous system dysfunction, and may occur across the life span.

Problems in self-regulatory behaviors, social perception, and social inter-action may exist with learning disabilities but do not by themselves consti-tute a learning disability.

Although learning disabilities may occur concomitantly with other hand-icapping conditions (for example, sensory impairment, mental retardation, serious emotional disturbance) or with extrinsic influences (such as cultural differences, insufficient or inappropriate instruction), they are not the result of those conditions or influences. (NJCLD Memorandum, 1988)

This definition contains three important elements that should con-strain our thinking and speculations about the nature of learning disabil-ities: (1) the idea that the term "learning disabilities" refers to more than a single type of learning disorder, (2) the statement that these learning dis-orders are intrinsic to the individual and the result of some type of dys-function in the central nervous system, and (3) the assertion that they are different from those caused by pervasive or general mental deficiency or lack of opportunities or motivation to learn. These elements should direct our attention to learning problems that are specific, or limited, in their impact on cognitive development and that are caused by brain-based dif-ferences in cognitive functioning that are intrinsic to the individual. Al-though it is undoubtedly true that there are many types of learning prob-lems *not* covered by this definition, if our intent is to answer questions about the nature of *learning disabilities*, our efforts should focus on the kinds of problems identified in this definition. In other words, I believe that we should take this definition seriously as a specification of the kind of learning problems we should address in any discussion of learning disabilities. Others are certainly free to discuss learning problems that are different than the type specified in this definition. However, I would ar-gue that in doing so, they are changing the focus of the discussion from learning disabilities to learning problems in general.

Differences Between the Scientific and Educational Uses of the Definition

Part of the problem in deciding how to focus discussions on the nature of learning disabilities arises from the fact that learning disabilities are both a phenomenon for scientific study and the basis for a social/political/ed-ucational movement (Doris, 1993; Torgesen, 1991). The definition of learning disabilities just presented contains theoretical statements about which there may be some disagreement. However, in order to validate the theoretical elements in the definition of learning disabilities from a scientific perspective, all that is required is to show that children with neurologically based, intrinsic learning disabilities do, in fact, exist. Even one case of a child with this type of disorder can serve as an "existence proof" for the definition and concept.

However, validation of the definition from the perspective of learning disabilities as a field in special education (which can be considered a so-cial/political/educational movement) is much more difficult. This type of validation requires nothing less than evidence that a *significant portion* of children currently being served in learning-disabilities programs fits the essential elements of the definition. It is on this point that the theoretical assumptions of the definition are most frequently attacked. For example, Jim Ysseldyke and his colleagues have reported on a program of research showing that school-identified learning-disabled (LD) children cannot be differentiated from other kinds of poor learners on the basis of their patterns of intellectual abilities (Ysseldyke, Algozzine, Shinn, and McGue, 1982). In his book *The Learning Mystique*, Gerald Coles (1987) has also mounted an extensive attack on the idea that most school-identified LD children have neurological problems as the basis of their learning difficulties. In fact, he is right in showing that the evidence for this idea is exceedingly weak.

The central point here is that the concept of learning disabilities, from a scientific point of view, is not threatened by our current inability to show that a majority of school-identified LD children have intrinsic cognitive limitations resulting from neurological impairment. Historically, it is almost certainly true that the field of learning disabilities as a social/political movement has *overgeneralized* the concept of learning disabilities in order to create improved educational opportunities for the largest possible number of children (Senf, 1986; Torgesen, 1991). Given that school-identified LD children are a group defined by shifting political realities, local expediencies, and questionable psychometrics (Fletcher, Francis, Rourke, Shaywitz, & Shaywitz, 1992; Ysseldyke, 1983), they are hardly a population about which we can hope to make coherent theoretical statements. That is, we should not attempt to describe the nature of "learning disabled" children as they are identified by school systems because these children are not identified in a scientifically or definitionally principled way. It may be interesting to develop models that explain the process by which children are identified for services as learning disabled, but this would not be a theory about the nature of learning disabilities so much as a sociological theory of the placement process.

Of course, if the definition of learning disabilities I have been discussing does *not* apply to a significant proportion of children currently being served under special education law, this would seriously undermine the field of learning disabilities as a social/political/educational movement. Children currently identified as learning disabled receive special services because they qualify under a public law that assumes they have an intrinsic "handicap" preventing them from learning normally. If this turns out not to be the case for most of the 5–6 percent of schoolchildren currently being served in learning-disabilities programs, then the importance of the concept as an instrument of public educational policy should diminish.

Secondary Characteristics of Children with Learning Disabilities

Another point of confusion in thinking about the nature of learning disabilities arises from the fact that early failure in school has, itself, profound effects on the child's continuing development (Stanovich, 1986). That is, the early and consistent failure caused by a primary or intrinsic learning disorder frequently results in the development of secondary characteristics that further interfere with the child's ability to perform successfully in school, on the job, or in social situations (Kistner & Torgesen, 1987; Schumaker, Deshler, & Ellis, 1986). Although such characteristics as a limited knowledge base, low self-esteem, low motivation to learn, or confused, inactive, or nonstrategic learning style might be secondary consequences of early reading failure, for example, these characteristics could easily be primary causes of school dropout, delinquency, or even poor grades in middle school.

The study of secondary characteristics in LD children is an area ripe for the development of systematic theories. For example, there is considerable controversy at present as to whether strategic, or metacognitive, inefficiencies in children with learning disabilities should be considered primary (Denkla, 1994; Meltzer, 1993; Swanson, 1988) or secondary (Spear-Swerling & Sternberg, 1994; Torgesen, 1994; Torgesen & Licht, 1983; Wong, 1991) characteristics. Theories about secondary characteristics promise to be as important as those focusing on primary characteristics in helping us to understand the development of individuals with learning disabilities. However, theories about the nature and development of secondary characteristics need to be clearly differentiated from those that seek to identify primary, intrinsic learning disabilities. Theories about the development and effects of secondary characteristics on academic, social, or work performance will be helpful in understanding and working with learning-disabled individuals, but they do not address the essential nature of learning disabilities as specified in the definition.

Elements Required in a Complete Theory of the Nature of Learning Disabilities

In keeping with the definition of learning disabilities that is most widely accepted in the field, statements about the nature of learning disabilities should contain at least four elements. The first element should clearly indicate which type of learning disability, in terms of specific academic or behavioral outcome, is to be explained. From the definition, it is clear that it is possible to have multiple and equally valid theories about learning disabilities. Efforts to produce a single, general description of the nature of learning disabilities (that is specific enough to have educational and diagnostic implications) are inconsistent with the definition. Since the definition covers a heterogeneous group of disorders of a general type, we should expect that there will be multiple explanations of learning disabilities that are correct.

Any attempt to describe the nature of learning disabilities must start with a clear specification of the academic or behavioral outcome to be explained in order that the remaining three elements of the description may be coherent. Such descriptions as "reading difficulties," "learning problems," or "math disabilities" are not good starting points for useful theoretical explanation because they might encompass several different types of learning disabilities. A useful example of the level of specificity required can be found in the area of reading. At a basic level, reading skills can be divided into those involved in translating from visual to oral or semantic representations of words (word identification) and those involved in constructing the meaning of text (comprehension). Explanations of the nature of these two types of reading problems may require quite different theories. The point here is that the starting point for any description of the nature of learning disabilities should be as specific as possible and take full advantage of all we know about academic or other learning tasks in order to specify a coherent family of skill deficits to be explained (Brown & Campione, 1986).

The next part of any explanation of the nature of a particular learning disability should involve identification of the cognitive processing limitations that underlie the academic or developmental learning failure. This psychological level of explanation is required by the definition because of the statement that *intrinsic* processing limitations are the proximal cause of all learning problems that can be categorized as learning disabilities. This level of explanation is also important because it provides a logical link between academic failure, on the one hand, and brain pathology, on the other—it helps pinpoint the phenomena to be explained by deeper layers of theory involving brain-behavior relationships. It should be noted here that identification of the cognitive processing limitations responsible for a given academic disability does not, by itself, establish that the academic problem has its basis in *brain pathology*. It is clearly possible to have cognitive processing deficits that are the results of experiential rather than intrinsic factors. My point is simply that any complete account of the nature of a learning disability must have, as one of its elements, a specification of the psychological processing disability that underlies the academic failure.

The definition next requires that any explanation of the nature of learning disabilities involves identification of the locus or pattern of brain abnormality that is responsible for the intrinsic cognitive limitations that are the proximal cause of the disability. Much of the current excitement in the field of learning disabilities derives from the development of new technologies that will make possible the collection of better data to test the hypothesis about abnormal brain functioning in these children (Shaywitz, 1996). Although validation of the learning-disabilities concept at this level is still relatively weak, a number of large projects are currently under way to employ recently developed brain imaging technology to examine brain-behavior links in learning disabilities.

The last element in a complete description of the nature of a learning disability should address the etiology of the brain dysfunction that is part of the description. Here, it is important to show that the dysfunction itself could not be caused by the learning failure it is used to explain. For example, in explaining specific kinds of reading disability by reference to brain-based differences, we must be sure that the failure to learn to read was not itself the cause of the apparent brain abnormality (Coles, 1987).

Current Theories of Learning Disabilities That Contain Appropriate Levels of Explanation

It is my view that the theory of phonologically based reading disabilities (PRD) is currently the best developed, most coherent explanation of learning disabilities that addresses all four elements previously outlined. The theory of nonverbal learning disabilities developed by Byron Rourke (1989) is also a coherent theory of the nature of a particular learning disability, but it does not contain adequate description of the problem at the level of cognitive processing operations (Torgesen, 1993). I will now outline the nature of one specific learning disability as proposed by the theory of phonologically based reading disabilities.

The Specific Academic Outcome

The most salient academic difficulty experienced by children with PRD involves problems learning to understand and apply the alphabetic principle in translating between written and oral language (Bruck, 1988; Rack, Snowling, & Olson, 1992; Siegel, 1989; Siegel & Faux, 1989; Stanovich & Siegel, 1994). Children with this particular learning disability are slow to grasp the principle that letters bear a systematic relationship to the sounds in words, they have difficulties learning correspondences between individual letters and the sounds (phonemes) they represent, and they have special problems in applying letter-sound knowledge in "sounding out" novel words. These difficulties not only interfere with early independence (and thus limit practice) in reading but also interfere with the processes by which children gradually acquire the large vocabularies of "sight words," which are the basis for the development of reading fluency and which are critical for good reading comprehension (Adams, 1990; Ehri, 1992; Share & Stanovich, 1995).

Share and his colleagues (Share, 1995; Share & Jorm, 1987; Share & Stanovich, 1995; see also Ehri, 1992) have recently presented a convincing case for the role of phonological, or alphabetic, reading skills as a critical foundation for the development of "sight word" representations (researchers call these orthographic representations because they represent the letter patterns in words). These orthographic representations allow words to be recognized as whole units, which greatly speeds up the reading process. Although a complete presentation of Share's model is beyond the scope of this chapter, the basic idea is that children who are able to utilize partial or complete phonological cues to supplement contextual information are much more likely to arrive at a correct pronunciation of novel words in text than children who cannot use phonological cues accurately. Since orthographic representations are acquired by repeated associations of a word's correct pronunciation with its visual representation, good alphabetic reading skills provide support for acquisition of orthographic representations from the earliest stages of reading growth. Additionally, the *prior attention* to individual letters that is involved in alphabetic decoding provides a solid basis for acquisition or refinement of orthographic representation for words, since good orthographic representations contain information about all the letters in a word and not just its shape or initial or final letters.

A current point of ambiguity in the theory of phonologically based reading disabilities is whether the intrinsic processing problems underlying difficulties in acquiring alphabetic reading skills are sufficient to explain both the initial problems in acquiring accurate word-reading skills and the lingering problems in reading fluency that are characteristic of many children with reading disabilities. Share and Stanovich's (1995) analysis suggests that phonological reading skills provide necessary, but not entirely sufficient, support for the development of good orthographic reading skills. For example, a child may be able to accurately identify words by using a combination of phonological reading skills and context, but if these skills are not practiced in extensive exposure to print, the child will not develop a rich orthographic reading vocabulary. We also know that variation among children in orthographic reading skills cannot be fully explained empirically by a combination of general verbal ability, phonological abilities, and print exposure (Barker, Torgesen, & Wagner, 1992; Cunningham & Stanovich, 1991; Stanovich & West, 1989). That is, when the influence of these factors on orthographic reading skills is controlled, children and adults still show variation in the levels of their orthographic skills. Whereas it is quite possible that this unexplained variability in orthographic skill is due to unreliable or incomplete measurement of phonological reading skills or only partial assessment of reading experience, it might also be due to an as-yet-unidentified information-processing ability that directly affects the rate at which orthographic representations are formed (Bowers, Golden, Kennedy, & Young, 1994). If this latter possibility is the case, an intrinsic processing limitation that affects initial acquisition of alphabetic reading skills would be only a partial explanation of word-level reading problems in children with reading disabilities. I turn now to a discussion of these intrinsic processing limitations.

Intrinsic Cognitive Limitations of Children with PRD

There is now a broad consensus that the problems children experience in acquiring alphabetic, or phonological, reading skills are caused by variation among children "in the phonological component of their natural capacity for language" (Liberman, Shankweiler, and Liberman, 1989, p. 1). The human brain is specifically adapted for the processing of various kinds of linguistic information. One set of linguistic processing abilities allows us to make sense of the complex array of phonological information in speech. Children with PRD have a subtle dysfunction of the phonological processing module that does not necessarily affect their ability to speak or to understand speech but does interfere with their ability to take advantage of the alphabetic principle in reading. In their original thinking about reading disabilities, Isabelle Liberman and her colleagues began by asking the question, "What is required of the child in reading a language but not in speaking or listening to it?" (Liberman et al., 1989, p. 4). Their answer was that the child must master the alphabetic principle: "This entails an awareness of the internal phonological structure of words of the language, an awareness that must be more explicit than is ever demanded in the ordinary course of listening and responding to speech. If this is so, it should follow that beginning learners with a weakness in phonological awareness would be at risk" (p. 5).

Empirical research on this hypothesis has indeed amply verified that children who experience difficulties acquiring alphabetic reading skills are, as a group, substantially impaired in their performance on oral-language tasks that assess awareness of the phonological structure of words (Bowey, Cain & Ryan, 1992; Fletcher et al., 1994; Stanovich & Siegel, 1994;

Wagner, Torgesen, & Rashotte, 1994). Tasks used to assess phonological awareness do not involve letters; they assess a child's ability to notice, think about, or manipulate the sounds in words that are presented orally. They involve operations such as indicating similarities or differences among words on the basis of their first, last, or middle sounds; telling how many different sounds a word contains; or blending separately presented sounds to form a word.

The difficulties that children with PRD experience in processing phonological information have also been shown in tasks that assess subtle forms of speech perception (Manis, McBride, Seidenberg, Doi, & Custodio, 1993), the ability to rapidly access phonological representations for familiar verbal material (Wolf, 1991), and short-term retention of verbal material presented either aurally or visually (Torgesen, 1995). Measures of rapid-naming ability typically require children to name, as rapidly as possible, series of approximately 36 to 50 digits, colors, objects, or letters. Measures of short-term verbal memory typically involve immediate recall of short sequences of digits or words. A more recently developed measure of short-term verbal retention involves immediate repetition of single nonwords that vary in length from two or three phonemes to 8–10 phonemes.

In my own work, my colleagues and I have shown that it is best to conceptualize phonological awareness, rapid naming, and verbal short-term memory as correlated but distinct abilities (Wagner, Torgesen, Laughon, Simmons, & Rashotte, 1993). That is, the tasks used to assess each of these skills are not simply alternative measures of the same underlying ability but rather appear to assess a family of related abilities that may influence reading growth in slightly different ways.

In fact, the evidence that these abilities are causally related to the growth of word-reading skill is strongest for phonological awareness, next strongest for rapid automatic-naming ability, and weakest for phonological coding in working memory. Evidence that individual differences in phonological awareness are causally related to the early growth of alphabetic reading skills comes from (1) both standard and causal modeling studies of longitudinal-correlational data (Mann, 1993; Stanovich, Cunningham, & Cramer, 1984; Wagner, Torgesen, & Rashotte, 1994; Wagner, Torgesen, Rashotte, Hecht, Barker, Burgess, Donahue, & Garon, 1997); (2) studies showing that older reading-disabled children are more impaired in phonological awareness than younger, normal readers matched to them on reading level (Bowey, Cain, & Ryan, 1992); and (3) true experiments that show improved growth in word-level reading skills as a result of prior training in phonological awareness (Cunningham, 1990; Hatcher, Hulme, & Ellis, 1994; Lundberg, Frost, & Peterson, 1988; Torgesen, Morgan, & Davis, 1992).

The evidence to support rapid naming's role in early development of word-reading ability comes from two sources: (1) standard and causal modeling analyses of longitudinal-correlational data (Felton & Brown, 1990; Wagner et al., 1994, in press; Wolf & Goodglass, 1986) and (2) differences between younger normal and older reading-disabled children matched for reading level (Bowers et al., 1994). Although individual differences in verbal short-term memory can predict subsequent reading development (Brady, 1991; Mann & Liberman, 1984), differences in performance on these tasks do not appear to explain variability in reading growth beyond that explained by phonological awareness and rapid-naming ability (Wagner et al., 1994; Wagner et al., 1997). However, most of the prominent case studies of phonological reading disability in both children and adults report limitations in verbal short-term memory as one of the prominent cognitive characteristics of these subjects (Torgesen, 1995). Clearly, further research is required to determine what unique role, if any, problems in phonological coding in working memory play in causing difficulties acquiring alphabetic reading skills.

The major controversy within the theory of phonologically based reading disabilities at the level of intrinsic cognitive limitations concerns the question of whether rapid automatic-naming tasks belong within the family of phonological measures or whether they measure different skills that influence aspects of reading growth other than the initial attainment of accuracy in using alphabetic reading strategies. For example, Patricia Bowers (Bowers et al., 1994) and Maryanne Wolf (Bowers & Wolf, 1993a; Wolf, 1991) and their colleagues have argued against viewing rapid automatic-naming tasks as primarily phonological in nature; instead they emphasize the visual and speed components of these tasks. They propose that rapid-naming tasks assess the operation of a "precise timing mechanism" that is important in the formation of orthographic codes for words. They hypothesize that "slow letter (or digit) naming speed may signal disruption of the automatic processes which support induction of orthographic patterns, which, in turn, result in quick word recognition" (Bowers & Wolf, 1993a, p. 70).

The controversy about the nature and role of individual differences in rapid automatic-naming ability in causing reading difficulties is related to the controversy discussed earlier about whether difficulties in alphabetic reading skill are a sufficient explanation for problems establishing orthographic representations and moving into fluent reading. In fact, Bowers and Wolf (1993b) have proposed a "double deficit hypothesis" in which problems in phonological abilities (primarily assessed by difficulties performing phonological awareness tasks) interfere with acquisition of alphabetic reading strategies, and deficiencies in a "precise timing mechanism" (assessed by rapid automatic-naming tasks) cause difficulties acquiring orthographic representations and becoming fluent readers. It is beyond the scope of this chapter to detail the evidence on either side of this controversy (see Bowers et al., 1994; Bowers & Wolf, 1993b; Torgesen, Wagner, Rashotte, Burgess, & Hecht, 1997; and Torgesen & Burgess, in press, for a more complete discussion of this controversy).

However, if Bowers and Wolf are correct, combinations of deficiencies in phonological ability and rapid-naming skill would produce three different patterns of reading disability: (1) children with only a phonological deficiency who might show initial delays in word-reading accuracy but then, with proper instruction and practice, eventually become accurate and fluent readers; (2) children with only rapid-naming problems who might show no delays in early acquisition of accurate word-reading strategies but would be limited in growth of fluent reading skills; and (3) children with both kinds of difficulties who would remain more severely impaired in reading than children in either of the other two groups. While there can be little doubt that these different patterns of word-reading growth do exist (Spear-Swerling & Sternberg, 1994), whether they result from a single family of cognitive limitations (phonological disability) and are produced by different patterns of instruction, practice, and motivation or whether they reflect the operation of two different intrinsic cognitive limitations is still open to question.

Locus of Brain Abnormality Responsible for Phonologically Based Reading Disabilities

As indicated at the beginning of the last section, the intrinsic cognitive limitations associated with PRD are attributed to isolated difficulties in one aspect of the uniquely human capacity for language. Studies of normal brain function locate phonological processing operations in the left temporal region of the brain (Damasio & Geschwind, 1984). Thus, this is a likely locus to look for abnormalities of brain development and function in individuals with PRD. In fact, three converging strands of research provide strong initial evidence that children with PRD do frequently show anomalies of development in this region of the brain. First, Al Galaburda's microexaminations of the brains of diseased individuals with PRD consistently found disturbances of brain development in this region (Galaburda, 1988). Furthermore, the particular anomalies identified in his work arise very early in development and thus could not be the result, rather than the cause, of reading problems. A second strand of evidence comes from studies involving measurement of regional cerebral blood flow during reading (Flowers, Wood, & Naylor, 1991). This work has also verified that the temporal region of the brain functions less efficiently in adults with PRD than in individuals with normal reading ability. Finally, a study using magnetic resonance imaging technology to examine a carefully selected sample of children with PRD provides quite strong evidence of differences in brain structure along the temporal plane between reading-disabled and normal children (Hynd, Semrud-Clikeman, Lorys, Novey, & Eliopulos, 1990). Much work remains to be done in verifying the specific nature of the brain dysfunction in children with PRD and in establishing its generality as a cause of phonological disabilities in significant numbers of children. However, these three sources of information, taken together, provide important beginning validation of the concept of PRD from a scientific perspective: Apparently children and adults do exist who have alphabetic reading difficulties associated with inefficiencies in processing phonological information that are, in turn, associated with differences in brain structure and function in the left temporal region of the brain.

At this point, I would like to make a small digression to comment on two points that are often a source of contention in describing the nature of learning disabilities. Frequently, validation for the concept of learning disabilities has been sought in evidence that they exist outside the normal continuum of learning *abilities*. In the case of reading disabilities, evidence that extremely poor word-level reading skills (dyslexia) occurs with greater frequency than is predicted by a normal distribution function (i.e., a "hump" of poor readers at the bottom of the normal distribution of reading skill) is taken as evidence that reading disabilities are caused by biological abnormalities that do not occur in children within the normal distribution of reading skill (Rutter & Yule, 1975). Conversely, evidence that reading disabilities exist on a continuum within the normal distribution (Shaywitz, Escobar, Shaywitz, Fletcher, & Makugh, 1992) is sometimes taken as evidence that reading-disabled children are not biologically abnormal (see, for example, Spear-Swerling & Sternberg, 1994). However, if phonologically based reading disabilities are caused by anomalies of development in the left temporal region of the brain, there are no compelling reasons to believe that these anomalies may not exist on a continuum from completely normal (or even hypernormal) to severely impaired. Thus just because individuals with PRD may occupy the low end of a continuum of normally distributed phonological processing abilities does not mean that their problems are not linked to brain-based differences in processing ability.

Second, evidence that weak processing skills can be improved by specific instructional interventions is sometimes taken as evidence that they are not the result of brain anomalies but rather result from lack of appropriate instruction and experience. However, such evidence is quite irrelevant to the issue of what caused the processing weakness in the first place. There is voluminous evidence that cognitive dysfunctions caused by verifiable, overt brain damage can be improved by specific instructional and practice activity (Levin, Benton, & Grossman, 1982). Similarly, there is no a priori reason to believe that brain-based limitations in phonological processing ability cannot be compensated for by appropriate instruction and practice in reading.

Etiology of Phonologically Based Reading Disabilities

At present, the best candidate for "ultimate cause" of the biologically based processing inefficiencies responsible for phonologically based reading disabilities is genetic transmission. There is now considerable evidence that phonological disabilities are highly heritable (Olson, Forsberg, & Wise, 1994). Although the heritability of phonological disabilities is well established, there is still considerable controversy about the specific genetic locus (chromosome location) of the disorder (Fulker, Cardon, DeFries, Kimberling, Pennington, & Smith, 1991). Another important limitation of the evidence in this area is that genetic factors have not been linked directly to the kinds of brain anomalies studied by Galaburda and others but only to difficulties in processing phonological information.

Summary Statement About the Nature of Phonologically Based Reading Disabilities

To summarize the material in the preceding sections, phonologically based reading disabilities are primarily manifested at the level of overt reading ability by difficulties acquiring alphabetic or phonetic reading strategies. The intrinsic cognitive limitation that causes these difficulties involves inefficiencies in processing phonological information that, in turn, are caused by anomalies of brain development in the left temporal region of the brain. The most likely cause of the brain anomalies associated with phonologically based reading disabilities is genetic transmission. This simple summary makes clear that although it is possible to describe an academic or psychological perspective on learning disabilities and to contrast them with a medical or biological perspective, a complete description of the nature of learning disabilities is a multidisciplinary effort. Because of the different levels of description and explanation required by the definition of learning disabilities, statements about the nature of learning disabilities from the perspective of a single discipline (academic, psychological, or biological) must necessarily be incomplete.

Approaches to the Diagnosis of Phonologically Based Reading Disabilities

On the surface, the diagnostic implications of the theory of phonologically based reading disabilities are relatively straightforward. The most reliable indicator of this type of learning disability is difficulty in rapidly and accurately reading pseudowords (Bruck, 1990; Share & Stanovich, 1995; Siegel, 1989). In other words, the most important first-level marker of this type of learning disorder involves unusually delayed development of alphabetic reading skills. As implied by the theory, further indications of the disorder may be obtained by assessment of its cognitive markers. These markers can be assessed by tasks that involve processing the phonological features of language. At present, the two most reliable indicators of reading-related phonological processing difficulties are measures of phonological awareness and rapid automatic naming of familiar verbal material. Evidence from longitudinal-predictive studies (Meyer, Wood, Hunt, & Felton, 1995; Wagner et al., 1994; Wagner et al., 1997) indicates that assessment of both of these variables adds useful diagnostic information about the severity of the disorder beyond that obtained by assessment of word-level reading skills, particularly during early elementary school. For example, among children who are equally impaired in word-decoding skills in first grade, performance on phonological awareness and rapid automatic naming tasks can provide information about which children are more likely to remain severely impaired and which children are likely to improve their reading status. By the later grades in elementary school, individual differences in phonological processing skill are almost entirely reflected in measures of word-level reading ability, so nonreading measures of phonological processing ability may not add significant diagnostic information (Torgesen, Wagner, Rashotte, Burgess, & Hecht, 1997). However, in individual cases, additional assessment of the cognitive markers of PRD may contribute to an assessment of the severity or breadth of the disorder.

If we were doing diagnosis within the laboratory or within a large medical center, the next level of measurement in this theoretically driven process would involve assessment at the neurobiological level. We would look for either structural or functional anomalies in the brain. At a practical level in the schools, however, it is not possible to extend routine diagnostic activities to this third level. This lack of assessment capabilities at the neurobiological level introduces ambiguities in the identification of "pure" cases of children with PRD that cannot be easily resolved within school settings.

For example, it is obvious that a child can have poorly developed alphabetic reading skills for a number of reasons. Instruction can clearly make a difference. From one midsized school district that has not consistently emphasized early, explicit instruction in alphabetic reading skills, my colleagues and I have obtained data (Torgesen & Burgess, in press) indicating that 40 percent of a sample of approximately 200 fifth-grade children achieved scores that were two or more grade levels below their current grade placement on the Word Attack subtest of the Woodcock Reading Mastery Test—Revised (Woodcock, 1987). The Word Attack subtest is a direct measure of children's ability to apply "phonics" knowledge (letter-sound correspondences, phoneme-blending skills) to reading novel words. It is also probable that an individual child's acquisition of alphabetic reading skills can be affected by a broad variety of other factors that can influence growth in any academic skill, such as motivation, regularity of attendance at school, or home-based support for reading practice.

The problem with using assessment of the cognitive markers of phonological awareness and rapid automatic-naming skill to "confirm" a diagnosis of PRD is that they are, themselves, influenced by growth and instruction in alphabetic reading skills. That is, causal relationships between word-level reading skills and phonological skills are reciprocal (Ehri, Wilce, & Taylor, 1987; Morais, Alegria, & Content, 1987; Perfetti, Beck, Bell, & Hughes, 1987; Wagner, Torgesen, & Rashotte, 1994). Beginning levels of phonological skills exert a causal influence on ease of acquiring alphabetic reading skills, but in turn, growth in alphabetic reading skills influences subsequent growth of phonological skills. Thus a child who performs poorly on alphabetic reading skills in third grade because of lack of instruction or motivation is likely to also show deficient performance on measures of phonological awareness and rapid automatic naming. The "phonological processing difficulties" of this child may not be the result of neurological anomalies in the left temporal region of the brain but rather might be caused by a lack of opportunity to learn alphabetic reading skills.

The fact that academic deficits can have multiple causes reduces the utility of a multilevel description of the nature of the learning disability for school-based diagnosis if we are not able to assess all the markers for the disability. However, for educational purposes, it may not matter whether a child's difficulties in alphabetic reading development are caused by neurological or other factors. We do have some beginning evidence that degree of impairment in phonological processing is related to *rate of response* to instruction in alphabetic reading skills (Torgesen & Davis, 1996; Torgesen, Wagner, & Rashotte, 1996). However, this does not mean that children with "pure" PRD require a qualitatively different instructional intervention than those with problems in this area arising from instructional or motivational factors.

We should remember at this point that the definition of learning disabilities specifically excludes learning problems that are the result of lack of opportunities or lack of motivation to learn. Of course, these factors are very difficult to assess in practical diagnostic work. The issue of lack of appropriate instruction can be at least partially dealt with by using local norms when alphabetic and phonological skills are assessed. Although certain kinds of instructional programs can increase the incidence of poor word-level reading skills within a school or district, children with severe biologically based PRD should be *relatively* more impaired in alphabetic reading skills and phonological processing ability than their peers.

A final issue that should be discussed in this section involves the role that assessment of general intellectual ability, or IQ, should play in the diagnosis of phonologically based reading disabilities. Historically, a core theoretical assumption of the concept of specific reading disabilities is that the reading problems of children whose reading ability is discrepant from their level of general intelligence are qualitatively different than the reading difficulties of children whose poor reading skills are consistent with their level of general intelligence (Kavale & Forness, 1985; Stanovich, 1991; Torgesen, 1991). If we restrict our focus to alphabetic reading skills, recent research has shown that these assumptions about discrepant and nondiscrepant reading disabilities are incorrect. The alphabetic reading problems of poor readers who have low general intelligence appear to have the same proximal cause and the same etiological roots as those of children whose intelligence is higher than their reading skill (Fletcher et al., 1992; Fletcher et al., 1994; Pennington, Gilger, Olson, & DeFries, 1992; Stanovich & Siegel, 1994). Furthermore, the essential elements of instruction for prevention and remediation of both types of reading problems appear to be the same (Juel, 1996; Torgesen & Hecht, 1996).

These findings suggest that use of the term "phonologically based reading disabilities" should not be restricted to children whose reading level is discrepant from their general intelligence. Difficulties processing phonological information can co-occur with low general intelligence and they, not low IQ, should be considered the proximal cause of alphabetic reading difficulties. However, we should also clearly recognize that the performances of discrepant and nondiscrepant children will differ in important ways regarding cognitive skills that lie outside the word recognition, or phonological, module (Ellis & Large, 1987; Stanovich & Siegel, 1994). Because the general intelligence of discrepant children is higher than that of nondiscrepant children and because general verbal intelligence is strongly related to reading comprehension, the former group is likely to have higher reading comprehension levels once the basic deficit in alphabetic reading skill is remediated. In other words, children with higher general verbal skills are likely to have higher reading comprehension levels given the same level of word-reading ability. This argument implies that discrepant and nondiscrepant children do have a different prognosis with regard to the ultimate level of reading skill they are likely

to attain, given equivalent instruction. It also implies that apart from instruction to overcome the core problem of poor alphabetic reading skills,
nondiscrepant children may require additional intensive instruction to
acquire the general verbal knowledge that supports good reading comprehension.

One of the major advantages of a sound, multilevel theory of phonologically based reading disabilities is that it provides a way to diagnose
the disability *before* children experience failure in learning to read.
Clearly, one important application of the theory of phonologically based
reading disabilities involves the early identification of these disabilities
using nonreading measures of phonological skills (Torgesen & Burgess,
in press). If we are able to develop these measures into efficient predictive indices, and if we are also able to develop effective preventive interventions for the children they identify as phonologically disabled, the
prevention of early failure in school could be one of the most positive
outcomes of all the work that has contributed to the development of
sound theory in this area.

Instructional Interventions for Individuals with Phonologically Based Reading Disabilities

Both our current understanding of the normal pattern of reading growth
(early attainment of alphabetic reading skills is critical) and our understanding of the most common cognitive limitations of children with reading disabilities (they have special difficulties acquiring alphabetic reading skills because of phonological processing weaknesses) creates a
dilemma of sorts for those who are interested in preventing or remediating reading disabilities. Instruction to build alphabetic reading skills,
which are seen as essential in normal reading growth, is instruction directed toward the primary cognitive/linguistic *weakness* of most children
with severe reading disabilities. There is a strong component of instructional theory in the area of learning disabilities (Hammill & Bartel, 1995;
Mercer & Mercer, 1993) that emphasizes teaching to children's strengths
rather than their weaknesses. Thus we sometimes see recommendations
to teach reading-disabled children using "sight word" or "visually
based" approaches that do not overly stress limited phonological abilities.

In fact, until fairly recently, research and case-study information about
children with PRD tended to emphasize how extremely difficult it is to
teach generalized phonetic reading skills to children with these kinds of
disabilities (Lovett, Warren-Chaplin, Ransby, & Borden, 1990; Lyon, 1985;
Snowling & Hulme, 1989). Snowling and Hulme, for example, reported
the case of a young man with PRD who received four years of instruction

in a private residential school specializing in teaching dyslexic children. The boy's instructional regime was eclectic but focused on "multi-sensory training in the use of English spelling patterns and conventions, i.e. on the explicit teaching of phoneme/grapheme correspondences" (p. 383). Comparisons of the young man's reading skill before and after this four years of instruction showed that he had made reasonable gains in passage comprehension and ability to read familiar words but almost no gain in alphabetic reading skills. Although he showed about one month's gain in reading comprehension for each month of instruction, his reading-comprehension skills remained substantially below those expected from his general level of intelligence.

In contrast to these earlier results, more recent work by Lovett and her associates (Lovett, Borden, Deluca, Lacerenza, Benson, & Brackstone, 1994) and by others (Alexander, Andersen, Heilman, Voeller, & Torgesen, 1991; Brown & Felton, 1990; Wise & Olsen, 1995; Wilson, 1995) has reported significant success in building generalized alphabetic reading skills in children with phonologically based reading disabilities. In two ongoing studies I and colleagues are involved in (Torgesen, Wagner, Rashotte, Alexander, & Conway, 1997), we are also obtaining very encouraging results regarding the ability of children with PRD to acquire functional alphabetic reading skills when exposed to the right instructional conditions.

In one of our studies, we are working with children aged 8–10 who have already been identified by the public school system as learning disabled. These children were initially nominated by their teachers as having the greatest difficulties acquiring word-level reading skills; we then verified their difficulties in alphabetic reading and phonological awareness through a series of tests of our own.

One of the more unusual things about this study is the intensity of the instruction provided to the children. Students are seen individually in 50-minute sessions, five days a week for about eight weeks, for a total of about 67 hours of instruction. Following the intensive instruction, students are seen in their learning-disabilities classroom by the project teacher for one hour a week for eight weeks. The purpose of this follow-up instruction is to help the children generalize their newly developed reading skills to the kinds of assignments they receive in the classroom.

The children are being randomly assigned to two different instructional conditions. Although each of the programs contains relatively explicit instruction in "phonics," this instruction is provided in two different ways. The Auditory Discrimination in Depth (ADD) Program (Lindamood & Lindamood, 1984) stimulates phonological awareness by helping children discover the articulatory positions and movements associated with the different phonemes in the English language. For example, they learn to label the sounds represented by the letters "p" and "b" as *lip poppers* because of the way the lips pop open and air pops out when they are pronounced. The sounds represented by "t" and "d" are labeled *tip tappers* because of the way the tip of the tongue taps against the roof of the mouth when they are pronounced. After discovering the articulatory gestures associated with each phoneme, students are able to "feel" the identity, order, and number of sounds in words as well as hear them. They can also identify the phonemes in words by observing their mouths in a mirror as they pronounce the word. This curriculum also provides explicit instruction in letter-sound correspondences along with extensive instruction and practice in the application of these correspondences to decoding words, both out of context and within meaningful text. This approach is designed to provide a level of instruction and experience in phonological processing of words that is much deeper than most reading instructional methods.

The other approach, which we call embedded phonics (EP), provides less intensive but still systematic phonics training in the context of meaningful experiences in reading and writing text. This approach was adapted from a method that has been employed successfully in a large clinical practice in Tallahassee, Florida. Both approaches acknowledge that the children being instructed have special difficulties processing phonological information. However, the ADD program attempts to directly attack these difficulties through an intensive program of oral and phonological awareness training, whereas the EP program seeks to reduce the demands on these skills by using an approach to phonics instruction that does not place as much emphasis on full phonological decoding but rather emphasizes the early integration of partial phonological decodings with context clues to identify unknown words. The EP method also focuses on direct instruction in a core sight-word vocabulary to support fluent reading in the texts that children read during their instructional sessions.

We now have immediate post-test data on 59 children and one-year follow-up data on 47 students. The most striking feature of the results so far is the large gains that children in both instructional conditions are making in the accuracy of their generalized alphabetic reading skills. Children in both groups have moved from substantially below average (more than two standard deviations) in performance on measures of alphabetic reading up into the average range. This change represents from about one and a half (EP group) to two (ADD group) years of growth in this skill over the 67 hours of instruction. The children have also experienced substantial growth in their ability to recognize real words and to comprehend what they read, although these changes have not been as dramatic as those for alphabetic reading skills. Follow-up testing one year after the conclusion of the intervention indicates that almost all of the children are continuing to make gains in word-level reading skills relative to the performance of average children.

In our prevention study, we have provided individual tutoring in reading to children at risk for PRD from the second semester of kindergarten through the end of second grade. This study also contrasted the ADD method with the EP condition and with another condition in which children were directly supported by our tutors in the reading assignments they received in their regular classes. At the end of second grade, children receiving instruction in the ADD program performed in the average range on measures of word-level reading skills (including alphabetic reading ability) and substantially ahead of children in the other groups.

The most appropriate conclusion from recent instructional research with children who have phonologically based reading disabilities is that it is clearly possible to have a substantial impact on the growth of their alphabetic reading skills if the proper instructional conditions are in place. These conditions appear to involve instruction that is more *explicit*, more *intensive*, and more *supportive* than that which is usually offered in most public and private school settings.

It is more *explicit* in that it makes fewer assumptions about preexisting skills or children's abilities to make inferences about grapheme-phoneme regularities on their own. For example, most successful programs have involved some form of direct instruction designed to stimulate children's awareness of the phonological segments in words. Although some form of instruction in phonological awareness characterizes all successful programs, there has been substantial variability in the way this instruction was provided.

Several studies, for example, have employed techniques from the Auditory Discrimination in Depth Program (Lindamood & Lindamood, 1984), which involves extensive instruction to help children discover and learn the articulatory gestures associated with each phoneme. Although children quickly make the transition into working with letters, they do spend considerable time learning labels for sounds that help to make the phoneme more concrete and provide a way to think about the phonemes in words in terms of the way they feel in addition to the way they sound. Other successful programs (Lovitt et al., 1994; Brown & Felton, 1990; Wilson, 1995) have employed techniques for stimulating phonological awareness that attempt to make individual sounds in words more apparent, such as lengthening the duration of sounds in words, asking children to tap their fingers together for each sound they hear in a word, or explicitly teaching children techniques for blending sounds together to make words. It is also clear that phonological awareness can be stimulated through writing and spelling activities that are embedded within the context of reading and spelling instruction (Clay, 1985; Cunningham, 1990; Ehri, 1989). At present, there is no research available to indicate whether any of these techniques are more effective than others or if they might be differentially effective for children with differing degrees of impairment in phonological processing ability.

A second way in which successful instruction for children with PRD must be explicit involves direct instruction in letter-sound correspondences and in strategies for using these correspondences to decode words while reading text. Explicit instruction and practice in these skills is characteristic of *all* programs that have produced substantial growth in alphabetic reading skills in children with PRD. In a direct test of the utility of this type of instruction, Iverson and Tunmer (1993) added explicit training in phonological decoding to the popular Reading Recovery Program (Clay, 1979), which has traditionally placed less emphasis on instruction and practice in these skills. In their carefully controlled study, they found that a small amount of explicit instruction in phonics increased the efficiency of the Reading Recovery Program by approximately 25 percent.

In addition to being more explicit, effective reading instruction for children with PRD must be more *intensive* than regular classroom instruction. Increased intensity involves more teacher-student instructional interactions, or reinforced learning trials, per unit of time. Greater intensity of instruction is required because the increased explicitness of instruction for children with PRD requires that more things be taught directly by the teacher. Unless beginning reading instruction for children with PRD is more intensive (or lasts significantly longer) than normal instruction, these children will necessarily lag significantly behind their peers in reading growth. Substantially increased intensity of instruction seems especially critical in remedial settings, where children *begin* the instruction already significantly behind their peers.

The data in Figure 5.1 illustrate the dramatic alteration in growth rate for basic word-reading skills that was being achieved as a result of the intensive intervention model in our current remediation study (Torgesen, Wagner, Rashotte, Burgess, & Hecht, 1997). Raw scores on measures of alphabetic reading (Word Attack) and real-word reading (Word Identification) from the Woodcock Reading Mastery Test—Revised (Woodcock, 1987) are plotted as a function of the child's age in months. The steep portion of the graph corresponds to our eight-week intensive intervention period. The curves at the top of the graph represent normal growth on these two measures taken from the national standardization sample (top line) and also from a school district in the Southeast that represents a more appropriate local comparison group of average students. We assumed a similar starting point for all students on these measures at six years of age. It

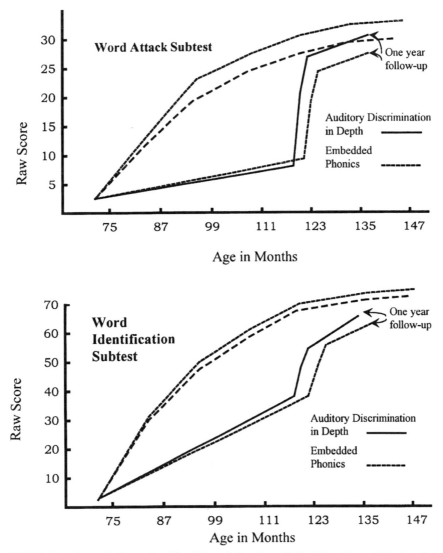

FIGURE 5.1 Growth Rates for Word-Level Reading Skills Prior To and During Intensive Reading Interventions

is obvious from this figure that both interventions (ADD and EP) have been successful in dramatically altering the course of growth in basic word-reading skills for the students as a whole. Furthermore, it is apparent from the one-year follow-up results that the children are able to maintain these dramatic gains one year after the intervention was concluded.

A third way in which instruction for children with PRD must be modified in order to be successful involves the level of *support* provided
within the instructional interactions. At least two kinds of special support are required. First, because acquiring word-level reading skills is
more difficult for children with PRD than others, they require more *emotional* support in the form of encouragement, positive feedback, and enthusiasm from the teacher in order to maintain their motivation to learn.
Second, instructional interactions must be more supportive in the sense
that they involve carefully *scaffolded* interactions with the child. In a recent investigation of the characteristics of effective reading tutors, Juel
(1996) identified the number of scaffolded interactions during each teaching session as one of the critical variables predicting differences in effectiveness across tutors. A scaffolded interaction is one in which the teacher
enables the student to complete a task (i.e., read a word) by directing the
student's attention to a key piece of information or breaking up the task
into smaller, easier-to-manage ones. The goal of these interactions is to
provide just enough support so the child can go through the processing
steps necessary to find the right answer. With enough practice, the child
becomes able to go through the steps independently. Juel's finding about
the importance of carefully scaffolded instructional interactions is consistent with the emphasis on these types of interactions in the teachers'
manuals that accompany two instructional programs shown to be effective with children with PRD (Lindamood & Lindamood, 1984; Wilson,
1988).

It is clear that we are making progress in understanding the instructional conditions that need to be in place for children with PRD to develop functional alphabetic reading skills; it is also apparent that we still
have much to learn. Richard Olson and his colleagues have pointed out
(Olson, Wise, Johnson, & Ring, in press) that the large gains in alphabetic
reading skills reported in many studies have frequently not been accompanied by similarly large gains in real-word reading ability (both accuracy and fluency) and passage comprehension. Researchers often rationalize these findings by suggesting that additional time will be necessary
for children's newly acquired alphabetic reading skills to produce corresponding gains in real-word knowledge, a hypothesis that is consistent
with Share and Stanovich's (1995) self-teaching theory of reading acquisition. However, in the only test of this hypothesis currently available
(Olsen et al., in press), it was not supported. That is, a group of children
with PRD who showed greater gains in phonological awareness and alphabetic reading skills as a result of careful instruction of the type described *did not* show greater gains in subsequent real-word reading ability than another group who had received less phonologically based
instruction.

One obvious possibility that needs to be explored in further research is that our initial attempts to train children with PRD in alphabetic reading skills have lead to substantial increases in accuracy, but the training has not been sufficient to produce phonological processing that is sufficiently fast, automatic, and flexible to be routinely used while reading text. In other words, although children may be able to consciously apply alphabetic reading skills when asked to do so on a test, if these skills are not fluent they may not be routinely applied when children read text. Thus even though alphabetic reading skills have improved through instruction, newly remediated skills may not contribute to reading growth in PRD children the same way they do in children who learn to read normally. This line of reasoning suggests that future studies should monitor the fluency and flexibility of application of alphabetic reading skills as well as accuracy on standardized tests. It also suggests that once good levels of accuracy are reached, additional training may need to focus specifically on increasing the fluency of processing as well as on flexible application of skills during the processing of text.

It is also possible, of course, that factors other than phonological deficits limit the growth of word-reading skills in many children. In addition to the possibility that some children may have a specific additional deficit in rapid automatic-naming ability that directly affects their ability to form orthographic representations (Bowers et al., 1994), such things as size of vocabulary (Plaut, McClelland, Seidenberg, & Patterson, 1996), amount of print exposure (Stanovich, 1993), and effective use of context (Tunmer & Chapman, 1995) can also influence the growth of real-word reading ability. Particularly in the case of remedial work with children who have already undergone a period of failure in reading growth, these other factors may also need to be addressed before increases in alphabetic reading ability can be fully utilized to support continued reading growth in children with PRD.

References

Adams, M.J. (1990). *Beginning to read: Thinking and learning about print*. Cambridge, MA: MIT Press.

Alexander, A., Anderson, H., Heilman, P.C., Voeller, K.S., & Torgesen, J.K. (1991). Phonological awareness training and remediation of analytic decoding deficits in a group of severe dyslexics. *Annals of Dyslexia, 41*, 193–206.

Barker, T.A., Torgesen, J.K., & Wagner, R.K. (1992). The role of orthographic processing skills on five different reading tasks. *Reading Research Quarterly, 27*, 334–345

Barron, R.W. (1986). Word recognition in early reading: A review of the direct and indirect access hypothesis. *Cognition, 24*, 93–119.

Bowers, P.G., Golden, J., Kennedy, A., & Young, A. (1994) Limits upon orthographic knowledge due to processes indexed by naming speed. In V.W. Berninger (Ed.). *The varieties of orthographic knowledge I: Theoretical and developmental issues* (pp. 173–218). Dordrecht, Netherlands: Kluwer Academic.

Bowers, P.G., & Wolf, M. (1993a). Theoretical links between naming speed, precise timing mechanisms and orthographic skill in dyslexia. *Reading and Writing: An Interdisciplinary Journal, 5*, 69–85.

Bowers, P. G., & Wolf, M. (1993b). *A double-deficit hypothesis for developmental reading disorders*. Paper presented to meetings of the Society for Research in Child Development, March 1993, New Orleans.

Bowey, J.A., Cain, M.T., & Ryan, S.M. (1992). A reading-level design study of phonological skills underlying fourth-grade children's word reading difficulties. *Child Development, 63*, 999–1011.

Bradey, S.A. (1991). The role of working memory in reading disability. In S.A. Bradey & D.P. Shankweiler (Eds.). *Phonological Processes in Literacy* (pp. 129–152). Hillsdale, NJ: Lawrence Erlbaum.

Brown, A.L., & Campione, J.C. (1986). Psychological theory and the study of learning disabilities. *American Psychologist, 14*, 1059–1068.

Brown, I.S., & Felton, R.H. (1990). Effects of instruction on beginning reading skills in children at risk for reading disability. *Reading and Writing: An Interdisciplinary Journal, 2*, 223–241.

Bruck, M. (1988). The word recognition and spelling of dyslexic children. *Reading Research Quarterly, 23*, 51–69.

Bruck, M. (1990). Word-recognition skills of adults with childhood diagnoses of dyslexia. *Developmental Psychology, 26*, 439–454.

Clay, M.M. (1979). *Reading: The patterning of complex behavior*. Auckland, New Zealand: Heinemann.

Clay, M.M. (1985). *The early detection of reading difficulties*. Portsmouth, NH: Heinemann.

Coles, G.S. (1987). *The learning mystique: A critical look at "learning disabilities."* New York: Pantheon.

Cunningham, A.E. (1990). Explicit versus implicit instruction in phonemic awareness. *Journal of Experimental Child Psychology, 50*, 429–444.

Cunningham, A.E., & Stanovich, K.E. (1991). Tracking the unique effects of print exposure in children: Associations with vocabulary, general knowledge, and spelling. *Journal of Educational Psychology, 83*, 264–274.

Damasio, A.R., & Geschwind, N. (1984). The neural basis of language. *Annual Review of Neurosciences, 7*, 127–147.

Denkla, M. (1994). Measurement of executive function. In G. Reid Lyon (Ed.), *Frames of Reference for the Assessment of Learning Disabilities: New Views on Measurement Issues* (pp. 143–162). Baltimore, MD: Brookes.

Doris, J.L. (1993). Defining learning disabilities: A history of the search for consensus. In R. Lyon, D. Gray, N. Krasnegor, and J. Kavenagh (Eds.), *Better understanding learning disabilities: Perspectives on classification, identification, and assessment and their implications for education and policy*. Baltimore, MD: Brookes.

Ehri, L.C. (1989). The development of spelling knowledge and its role in reading acquisition and reading disability. *Journal of Learning Disabilities, 22*, 356–365.

Ehri, L.C. (1992). Reconceptualizing the development of sight word reading and its relationship to recoding. In P.B. Gough, L.C. Ehri, & R. Trieman (Eds.), *Reading Acquisition* (pp. 107–143). Hillsdale, NJ: Erlbaum.

Ehri, L.C., Wilce, L., & Taylor, B.B. (1987). Children's categorization of short vowels in words and the influence of spellings. *Merrill-Palmer Quarterly, 33,* 393–421.

Ellis, N., & Large, B. (1987). The development of reading: As you seek so shall you find. *British Journal of Psychology, 78,* 1–28.

Felton, R., & Brown, I.S. (1990). Phonological processes as predictors of specific reading skills in children at risk for reading failure. *Reading and Writing: An Interdisciplinary Journal, 2,* 39–59.

Fletcher, J.M., Francis, D.J., Rourke, B.P., Shaywitz, S.E., & Shaywitz, B.A. ((1992). The validity of discrepancy-based definitions of reading disabilities. *Journal of Learning Disabilities, 25,* 555–561.

Fletcher, J.M., Shaywitz, S.E., Shankweiler, D.P., Katz, L., Liberman, I.Y., Stuebing, K.K., Francis, D.J., Fowler, A.E., & Shaywitz, B.A. (1994). Cognitive profiles of reading disability: Comparisons of discrepancy and low achievement definitions. *Journal of Educational Psychology, 86,* 6–23.

Flowers, L., Wood, F.B., & Naylor, C.E. (1991). Regional cerebral blood flow correlates of language processes in reading disabilities. *Archives of Neurology, 48,* 637–643.

Fulker, D.W., Cardon, L.R., DeFries, J.C., Kimberling, W.J., Pennington, B.F., & Smith, S.D. (1991). Multiple regression analysis of sib pair data on reading to detect quantitative trait loci. *Reading and Writing: An Interdisciplinary Journal, 3,* 299–313.

Galaburda, A.M. (1988). The pathogenesis of childhood dyslexia. In F. Plum (Ed.), *Language, Communication, and the Brain* (pp. 127–137). New York: Raven Press.

Hammill, D.D. (1990). On defining learning disabilities: An emerging consensus. *Journal of Learning Disabilities, 23,* 74–84.

Hammill, D.D., & Bartel, N.R. (1995). *Students with learning and behavior problems.* (6th Edition). Austin, TX: PRO-ED.

Hatcher, P., Hulme, C., & Ellis, A.W. (1994). Ameliorating early reading failure by integrating the teaching of reading and phonological skills: The phonological linkage hypothesis. *Child Development, 65,* 41–47.

Hynd, G.W., Semrud-Clikeman, M., Lorys, A.R., Novey, E.S., & Eliopulos, D. (1990). Brain morphology in developmental dyslexia and attention deficit disorder/hyperactivity. *Archives of Neurology, 47,* 919–928.

Iversen, S., & Tunmer, W.E. (1993). Phonological processing skills and the reading recovery program. *Journal of Educational Psychology, 85,* 112–126.

Juel, C. (1996). What makes literacy tutoring effective? *Reading Research Quarterly, 31,* 268–289.

Kavale, K., & Forness, S.R. (1985). *The science of learning disabilities.* San Diego, CA: College-Hill Press.

Kistner, J., & Torgesen, J.K. (1987). Motivational and cognitive aspects of learning disabilities. In A.E. Kasdin & B.B. Lahey (Eds.), *Advances in Clinical Child Psychology* (pp. 289–333). New York: Plenum Press.

Levin, H.S., Benton, A.L., & Grossman, R.G. (1982). *Neurobehavioral consequences of closed head injury.* New York: Oxford University Press.

Liberman, I.Y., Shankweiler, D., & Liberman, A.M. (1989). The alphabetic principle and learning to read. In D. Shankweiler & I.Y. Liberman (Eds.), *Phonology and reading disability: Solving the reading puzzle* (pp. 1–33). Ann Arbor, MI: U. of Michigan Press.

Lindamood, C.H., & Lindamood, P.C. (1984). *Auditory Discrimination in Depth.* Austin, TX: PRO-ED.

Lovett, M.W., Borden, S.L., Deluca, T., Lacerenza, L., Benson, N.J., & Brackstone, D. (1994). Treating the core deficits of developmental dyslexia: Evidence of transfer of learning after phonologically- and strategy-based reading training programs. *Developmental Psychology, 30,* 805–822.

Lovett, M.W., Warren-Chaplin, P.M., Ransby, M.J., & Borden, S.L. (1990). Training the word recognition skills of reading disabled children: Treatment and transfer effects. *Journal of Educational Psychology, 82,* 769–780.

Lundberg, I., Frost, J., & Peterson, O. (1988). Effects of an extensive program for stimulating phonological awareness in pre-school children. *Reading Research Quarterly, 23,* 263–284.

Lyon, G.R. (1985). Identification and remediation of learning disability subtypes: Preliminary findings. *Learning Disabilities Focus, 1,* 21–35.

Manis, F.R., McBride, C., Seidenberg, M.S., Doi, L., & Custodio, R. (1993, March). *Speech perception and phonological awareness in normal and disabled readers.* Paper presented at the meeting of the Society for Research in Child Development, New Orleans.

Mann, V.A. (1993). Phoneme awareness and future reading ability. *Journal of Learning Disabilities, 26,* 259–269.

Mann, V.A., & Liberman, I.Y. (1984). Phonological awareness and verbal short-term memory. *Journal of Learning Disabilities, 10,* 592–599.

Meltzer, L.J. (1993). Strategy use in students with learning disabilities: The challenge of assessment. In L.J. Meltzer (Ed.), *Strategy assessment and instruction for students with learning disabilities* (pp. 94–140). Austin, TX: PRO-ED.

Mercer, C.D., & Mercer, A.R. (1993). *Teaching students with learning problems* (4th Ed.). Columbus, OH: Charles E. Merrill.

Meyer, M.M., Wood, F.B., Hunt, L.A., & Felton, R.H. (1995). *Predictive value of rapid automatized naming for later reading.* Unpublished manuscript, Bowman Gray School of Medicine, Winston-Salem, North Carolina.

Morais, J., Alegria, J., & Content, A. (1987). The relationships between segmental analysis and alphabetic literacy: An interactive view. *Cahiers de Psychologie Cognitive, 7,* 414–438.

Olsen, R., Forsberg, H., & Wise, B. (1994). Genes, environment, and the development of orthographic skills. In V.W. Berninger (Ed.), *The varieties of orthographic knowledge I: Theoretical and developmental issues* (pp. 27–71). Dordrecht, Netherlands: Kluwer Academic.

Olson, R.K., Wise, B., Johnson, M., & Ring, J. (in press). The etiology and remediation of phonologically based word recognition and spelling disabilities: Are phonological deficits the "hole" story? In B. Blachman (Ed.), *Foundations of reading acquisition.* Mahwah, NJ: Lawrence Erlbaum.

Pennington, B.F., Gilger, J.W., Olson, R.K., & DeFries, J.C. (1992). The external validity of age- versus IQ-discrepancy definitions of reading disability: Lessons from a twin study. *Journal of Learning Disabilities, 25,* 562–573.

Perfetti, C.A., Beck, I., Bell, L., & Hughes, C. (1987). Phonemic knowledge and learning to read are reciprocal: A longitudinal study of first grade children. *Merrill-Palmer Quarterly, 33,* 283–319.

Plaut, D.C., McClelland, J.L., Seidenberg, M.S., & Patterson, K. (1996). Understanding normal and impaired word reading: Computational principles in Quasi-Regular Domains. *Psychological Review, 103,* 56–115.

Rack, J.P., Snowling, M.J., & Olson, R.K. (1992). The nonword reading deficit in developmental dyslexia: A review. *Reading Research Quarterly, 27,* 29–53.

Rourke, B.P. (1989). *Nonverbal learning disabilities: The syndrome and the model.* New York: Guilford.

Rutter, M., & Yule, W. (1975). The concept of specific reading retardation. *Journal of Child Psychology and Psychiatry, 16,* 181–197.

Schumaker, J.B., Deshler, D.D., & Ellis, E.S. (1986). Intervention issues related to the education of learning disabled adolescents. In J.K. Torgesen & B.Y.L. Wong (Eds.), *Psychological and Educational Perspectives on Learning Disabilities* (pp. 329–365). New York: Academic Press.

Senf, G.M. (1986). LD research in sociological and scientific perspective. In J.K. Torgesen & B.Y.L. Wong (Eds.), *Psychological and Educational Perspectives on Learning Disabilities.* New York: Academic Press.

Share, D.L. (1995). Phonological recoding and self-teaching: S*ine qua non* of reading acquisition. *Cognition, 55,* 151–218.

Share, D.L., & Jorm, A.F. (1987). Segmental analysis: Co-requisite to reading, vital for self-teaching, requiring phonological memory. *European Bulletin of Cognitive Psychology, 7,* 509–513.

Share, D.L., & Stanovich, K.E. (1995). Cognitive processes in early reading development: A model of acquisition and individual differences. *Issues in Education: Contributions from Educational Psychology, 1,* 1–35.

Shaywitz, S.E. (1996). Dyslexia. *Scientific American,* xx, 98–104.

Shaywitz, S.E., Escobar, M.D., Shaywitz, B.A., Fletcher, J.M., & Makuch, R. (1992). Evidence that dyslexia may represent the lower tail of a normal distribution of reading ability. *New England Journal of Medicine, 326,* 145–150.

Siegel, L.S. (1989). IQ is irrelevant to the definition of learning disabilities. *Journal of Learning Disabilities, 22,* 469–479.

Siegel, L.S., & Faux, D. (1989). Acquisition of certain grapheme-phoneme correspondences in normally achieving and disabled readers. *Reading and Writing: An Interdisciplinary Journal, 1,* 37–52.

Snowling, M. and Hulme, C. (1989). A longitudinal case study of developmental phonological dyslexia. *Cognitive Neuropsychology, 6,* 379–401.

Spear-Swerling, L., & Sternberg, R.J. (1994). The road not taken: An integrative theoretical model of reading disability. *Journal of Learning Disabilities, 27,* 91–103.

Stanovich, K.E. (1986). Matthew effects in reading: Some consequences of individual differences in the acquisition of literacy. *Reading Research Quarterly, 21,* 360–406.

Stanovich, K.E. (1991). Discrepancy definitions of reading disability: Has intelligence led us astray? *Reading Research Quarterly, 26,* 1–29.

Stanovich, K. (1993). Does reading make you smarter? Literacy and the development of verbal intelligence. In H. Reese (Ed.), *Advances in child development and behavior* (Vol. 24, pp. 133–180). San Diego, CA: Academic Press.

Stanovich, K.E., Cunningham, A.E., & Cramer, B.B. (1984). Assessing phonological awareness in kindergarten children: Issues of task comparability. *Journal of Experimental Child Psychology, 38,* 175–190.

Stanovich, K.E., & Siegel, L.S. (1994). The phenotypic performance profile of reading-disabled children: A regression-based test of the phonological-core variable-difference model. *Journal of Educational Psychology, 86,* 24–53.

Stanovich, K.E., & West, R.F. (1989). Exposure to print and orthographic processing. *Reading Research Quarterly, 24,* 402–433.

Swanson, H.L. (1988). Information processing theory and learning disabilities: A commentary and future perspective. *Journal of Learning Disabilities, 20,* 155–166.

Torgesen, J.K. (1991). Learning disabilities: Historical and conceptual issues. In B.Y.L. Wong (Ed.), *Learning about learning disabilities* (pp. 3–37). San Diego, CA: Academic Press.

Torgesen, J.K. (1993). Variations on theory in learning disabilities. In R. Lyon, D. Gray, N. Krasnegor, and J. Kavenagh (Eds.), *Better understanding learning disabilities: Perspectives on classification, identification, and assessment and their implications for education and policy.* Baltimore, MD: Brookes.

Torgesen, J.K. (1994). Issues in the assessment of executive function: An information processing perspective. In G. Reid Lyon (Ed.), *Frames of Reference for the Assessment of Learning Disabilities: New Views on Measurement Issues* (pp. 143–162). Baltimore, MD: Brookes.

Torgesen, J.K. (1995). A model of memory from an information processing perspective: The special case of phonological memory. In G. Reid Lyon (Ed.), *Attention, Memory, and Executive Function: Issues in Conceptualization and Measurement.* Baltimore, MD: Brookes.

Torgesen, J.K., & Burgess, S.R. (in press). Consistency of reading-related phonological processes throughout early childhood: Evidence from longitudinal correlational and instructional studies. In J. Metsala and L. Ehri (Eds.), *Word recognition in beginning literacy.* Mahwah, NJ: Lawrence Erlbaum.

Torgesen, J.K., & Davis, C. (1996). Individual difference variables that predict response to training in phonological awareness. *Journal of Experimental Child Psychology, 63,* 1–21.

Torgesen, J.K., & Hecht, S. (1996). Preventing and remediating reading disabilities: Instructional variables that make a difference for special students. In M.F. Graves, B.M. Taylor, and P. van den Broek (Eds.), *The First R: A Right of All Children* (pp. 133–159). Cambridge: MIT Press.

Torgesen, J.K., & Licht, B. (1983). The learning disabled child as an inactive learner: Retrospect and prospects. In J.D. McKinney & L. Feagans (Eds.), *Topics in learning disabilities* (Vol. 1, pp. 3–32). Rockville, MD: Aspen Press.

Torgesen, J.K., Wagner, R.K., & Rashotte, C.A. (1996, April). *Predicting individual differences in response to early instruction in reading.* Paper presented at meetings of the Council for Exceptional Children, Orlando, FL.

Torgesen, J.K., Wagner, R.K., Rashotte, C.A., Alexander, A., & Conway, T. (1997). Preventive and remedial interventions for children with severe reading disabilities. *Learning Disabilities: An Interdisciplinary Journal, 8,* 51–62.

Torgesen, J.K., Wagner, R.K., Rashotte, C.A., Burgess, S.R., Hecht, S. (1997). The contributions of phonological awareness and rapid automatic naming ability to the growth of word reading skills in second to fifth grade children. *Scientific Studies of Reading, 1,* 161–185.

Tunmer, W.E., & Chapman, J.W. (1995). Context use in early reading development: Premature exclusion of a source of individual differences? *Issues in Education, 1,* 97–100.

Wagner, R.K., & Barker, T.A. (1994). The development of orthographic processing ability. In V.W. Berninger (Ed.), *The varieties of orthographic knowledge I: Theoretical and developmental issues* (pp. 173–218). Dordrecht, Netherlands: Kluwer Academic.

Wagner, R.K., Torgesen, J.K., Laughon, P., Simmons, K., & Rashotte, C. (1993). The development of young readers' phonological processing abilities. *Journal of Educational Psychology, 85,* 83–103.

Wagner, R.K., Torgesen, J.K., & Rashotte, C.A. (1994). The development of reading-related phonological processing abilities: New evidence of bi-directional causality from a latent variable longitudinal study. *Developmental Psychology, 30,* 73–87.

Wagner, R.K., Torgesen, J.K., Rashotte, C.A., Hecht, S.A., Barker, T.A., Burgess, S.R., Donahue, J., & Garon, T. (1997). Changing causal relations between phonological processing abilities and word-level reading as children develop from beginning to fluent readers: A five-year longitudinal study. *Developmental Psychology, 33,* 468–479.

Wilson, B.A. (1995). *Wilson reading system: MSLE research report.* Unpublished report from Wilson Language Training, Millbury, MA.

Wilson, B.A. (1988). *Instructor manual.* Millbury, MA: Wilson Language Training.

Wise, B.W., & Olsen, R.K. (1995). Computer-based phonological awareness and reading instruction. *Annals of Dyslexia, 45,* 99–122.

Wolf, M., & Goodglass, A. (1986). Dyslexia, dysnomia, and lexical retrieval: A longitudinal investigation. *Brain and Language, 28,* 154–168.

Wolf, M. (1991). Naming speed and reading: The contribution of the cognitive neurosciences. *Reading Research Quarterly, 26,* 123–141.

Woodcock, R.W. (1987). *Woodcock Reading Mastery Tests-Revised.* Circle Pines, MN: American Guidance Service.

Ysseldyke, J.E. (1983). Current practices in making psycho-educational decisions about learning disabled students. *Journal of Learning Disabilities, 16,* 209–219.

Ysseldyke, J.E., Algozzine, B., Shinn, M., & McGue, M. (1982). Similarities and differences between underachievers and students labeled learning disabled. *Journal of Special Education, 16,* 73–85.

6

Reading Disabilities and the Interventionist

Michael G. Pressley

I spend much of my professional life thinking about children who experience difficulties with reading. There is much to think about, for many children do not learn to read as a result of the instruction they experience in the primary grades. By the end of grade 1, it is not at all unusual for 20–30 percent of a class to be behind in reading, most often manifested as difficulties in decoding text. Problems in learning to read during grade 1 predict continuing reading difficulties during the schooling years (see, e.g., Satz, Taylor, Friel, & Fletcher, 1978; Spreen, 1978). Problems in reading during childhood are predictive of poor reading during adulthood (Bruck, 1990, 1992; Finucci, Gottfredson, & Childs, 1985; Fraunheim & Heckerl, 1983; Schonhaut & Satz, 1983; Spreen, 1988).

Since the late 1970s, there has been steady accumulation of evidence that there are important biological differences between good and at least some poor readers. The information-processing differences between good and poor readers often are many. The contemporary reading interventionist knows that there is a daunting challenge with respect to the prevention and remediation of reading disabilities, at least with respect to some children: That is, some children who experience difficulties in learning to read probably suffer biological differences that translate into a variety of information-processing differences which undermine the development of skilled reading (e.g., see Bruck, 1990; Gaddes, 1994, Chapter 8; Olson, 1994).

The work covered in this chapter was supported in part by the National Reading Research Center, headquartered at the Universities of Maryland and Georgia.

136

More positively, the work in recent years also permits the conclusion that we must make great efforts to teach children to read before seriously entertaining the idea they cannot. Many children who experience difficulties learning to read are not victims of their biology; rather, their environments have been deficient in some important way. Thus there has been a variety of attempts to enrich children's environments in order to prevent or remediate reading disabilities. As a result, an impressive array of findings about interventions that work are making more certain children's progress in literacy development. There is much that parents and teachers can do to decrease the likelihood of poor reading and to remediate poor reading for many children; the various possibilities are reviewed briefly in the sections that follow.

Many readers of this volume will have no problem accepting that the explicit interventions covered in this chapter make sense. Throughout the chapter, however, I will point out the controversial nature of many of these recommendations relative to the dominant language arts education perspective in the middle 1990s—whole language. This theme appears throughout the chapter, rather than being considered in a single section, in order to emphasize the many differences between instructional interventionists and whole language theorists.

Language-Rich Emergent Literacy Experiences During the Preschool Years

A great deal of literacy development occurs during the preschool years, the period of emergent literacy (Clay, 1966, 1967). Emergent literacy experiences begin with plastic "bathtub" books filled with colorful pictures and continue as mothers and fathers read and reread nursery rhymes and stories to and with their children and as children scribble letters to Grandma. Environments that support emergent literacy include (1) rich interpersonal experiences with parents, brothers and sisters, and others; (2) physical environments that include literacy materials from plastic refrigerator letters to storybooks to writing materials; and (3) high positive regard by parents and others for literacy and its development in children (Leichter, 1984; Morrow, 1996). Put more concretely, in homes in which emergent literacy is fostered, children are exposed to paper-and-pencil activities, letters, and even printed words at an early age. Parents read to the children, and they help children as they attempt to read (e.g., by holding a book upright and pretending to read by recalling the story as they remember it). Books and other reading materials are prominent in homes supporting emergent literacy (Briggs & Elkind, 1973; Clark, 1976; Durkin, 1966; King & Friesen, 1972; Morrow, 1983; Plessas & Oakes, 1964; Teale, 1978).

Storybook reading has high potential for fostering emergent literacy. There are strong and positive correlations between the amount of storybook reading during the preschool years and subsequent vocabulary and language development, children's interest in reading, and early success in reading (Sulzby & Teale, 1991). Given the apparent power of storybook reading in stimulating children's literacy development, caregiver and child interactions during storybook reading have been studied in some detail.

Storybook reading can foster rich and animated discussions between reader and child. They can work out the meaning of the text, and they have a lot of fun doing it (Morrow, 1996). There can be questioning by both adults and children; modeling of dialogue by adults with children sometimes participating; praising children's efforts to get meaning from the pictures and print; offering information to children and responding to their reactions to the text; and both adults and children relating what is happening in the text to their lives and the world around them all enrich the experience (Applebee & Langer, 1983; Cochran-Smith, 1984; Flood, 1977; Pellegrini, Perlmutter, Galda, & Brody, 1990; Roser & Martinez, 1985; Taylor & Strickland, 1986).

Scaffolding is prominent when storybook reading is going well, when it is engaging to youngsters. Parents who are good at storybook reading encourage children to respond to the reading and participate as much as possible in the reading itself, providing support as children need it and providing input that children can understand (e.g., DeLoache & DeMendoza, 1987). With increasing age during the preschool years, children are attentive to longer sections of text (Heath, 1982; Sulzby & Teale, 1987). With increasing experience reading storybooks, adults and children have more complex discussions about the text (Snow, 1983; Sulzby & Teale, 1987). Children who experience a lot of storybook reading are accustomed to interacting with an adult about story content; they are appropriately attentive during storybook reading, much more so than same-age children who have not experienced storybook reading (Bus & Van Ijzendoorn, 1989).

There has been some research on differences in style of storybook reading and the effects of such variation on cognitive development. For example, children who interact with adults who are skillful at eliciting verbal interactions from their children during reading develop better vocabularies (e.g., Ninio, 1980). Heath (e.g., 1982) established a correlation between the degree to which parents prompted and provided elaborations of book content and the eventual literacy attainment of their children: Children who experienced rich elaborations of text meaning did better on higher-order comprehension tasks than other children.

The correlations between storybook reading and the development of emergent literacy competencies related to later literacy development prompted Whitehurst and colleagues (1988) to study whether it might be possible to improve parental skills during storybook interactions and thus positively affect the development of emergent literacy in children. The parents of 14 children between one year, nine months, and three years of age participated in a one-month intervention designed to improve interactions between parents and children during storybook reading. Parents were taught to ask more open-ended questions and more questions about the functions and attributes of objects in stories as they read with their preschoolers. The parents were also given instruction about how to respond appropriately to their children's comments during story reading and how to expand on what the children had to say. The parents in this treatment group were also taught to reduce the amount of straight reading they did as well as to eliminate questions that the child could answer simply by pointing to something in an illustration. Fifteen other children and their parents served as control participants in the study; these families were encouraged to continue reading storybooks as they normally did with their children.

First, the intervention parents were able to implement the treatment. That is, they learned to interact differently with their children during storybook reading and in ways that increased the qualities of parent-child interactions. Although there were no differences between intervention and control children at the beginning of the study with respect to language variables, there were clear differences at the end of the month of treatment that favored the intervention participants: They outscored the control subjects on a standardized measure of psycholinguistic ability and on two vocabulary tests. What was most striking in this study was that when the same measures were repeated nine months later, the intervention subjects still had an advantage over the control participants, although the differences were not as large on the 9-month follow-up as at immediate posttesting. Notably, Valdez-Menchaca and Whitehurst (1992) replicated and extended the Whitehurst and colleagues (1988) finding with Mexican children.

In summary, there can be interactions between adults and preschoolers involving materials and activities related to reading and writing. A rich history of such interactions is predictive of subsequent success in literacy acquisition. That some preschoolers do not have consistent, excellent emergent literacy experiences has stimulated researchers such as Whitehurst to study ways of increasing interactions between parents and children that promote emergent literacy. The successes to date fuel enthusiasm for the possibility that many more children could be much better prepared for formal schooling through efforts to increase the quality and quantity of literacy interactions during the preschool years.

Although emergent literacy experiences are somewhat predictive of success in early reading (Bus, van Ijzendoorn, & Pellegrini, 1995; Scarborough & Dobrich, 1994), a more powerful predictor is a kindergarten student's phonemic awareness, that is, awareness that words are composed of separable sounds (phonemes) and that phonemes are combined to say words. Reading interventionists have focused on phonemic awareness because it is the best predictor of success in early reading (e.g., Adams, 1990); reading intervention researchers are very aware that poor phonemic awareness at four to six years of age is predictive of reading difficulties throughout the elementary years (Juel, 1988; Stuart & Masterson, 1992).

The one out-of-school literacy experience that predicts phonemic awareness is parental teaching of letters and their sounds (Crain-Thoreson & Dale, 1992). Many parents, however, do not engage in such teaching, so that education that impacts phonemic awareness typically occurs in school. For phonemic awareness to develop completely in normal readers, formal instruction in reading seems essential (only a very small proportion of children develop the ability to carry out the most demanding of phonemic-awareness tasks in the absence of instruction; e.g., see Lundberg, 1991).

Many experiments have demonstrated that phonemic awareness in five- and six-year-olds can be increased with instruction that heightens children's attention to the component sounds in words (e.g., Ball & Blachman, 1988, 1991; Blachman, 1991; Bradley & Bryant, 1983, 1985; Cunningham, 1990; Lie, 1991; Lundberg, Frost, & Peterson, 1988; Tangel & Blachman, 1992; Vellutino & Scanlon, 1987; Williams, 1980). Without a doubt, however, the best known phonemic-awareness intervention study was conducted in England by Lynette Bradley and Peter Bryant (1983).

Bradley and Bryant hypothesized, based on previously established correlations between children's rhyming and alliteration skills (which require understanding that words are composed of sounds, i.e., which require phonemic awareness) and later reading achievement (e.g., see Calfee, Chapman, & Venezsky, 1972; Calfee, Lindamood, & Lindamood, 1973), that providing instruction to children about how to categorize words on the basis of their sounds would increase phonemic awareness and hence, long-term reading achievement. An important principle emphasized in the Bradley and Bryant (1983) instruction was that the same word can be categorized in different ways on the basis of sound when it is in different sets of words. Thus, if *hen* is in a group of words that include *hat*, *hill*, *hair*, and *hand*, it would make sense to categorize all of these words together as starting with *h*, especially in contrast to other words starting with another letter (e.g., *b* words such as *bag, band, bat,* etc.). If *hen* were on a list with *men* and *sun,* however, these three words could be categorized as ones ending in *n.* If *hen* were on a list of words that included *bed* and *leg,* it would be possible to categorize the words as ones with a *short e* in the middle.

The training in the study involved 40 10-minute sessions spread out over two years, although a more recent version of the instruction was implemented over a period of four months (Bradley, 1988). During the first 20 sessions, five- and six-year-olds who initially lacked phonemic awareness were taught to categorize words on the basis of common sounds using pictures of the objects (i.e., pictures of a hen, men, and a leg). For example, in one lesson a set of pictures representing the letter *b* was shown to the child who named the objects. The child repeated the names with the teacher urging the child to listen to the sounds. The child then was asked if he or she could hear a sound common in each word. This activity continued, with the adult providing help and hints if the child experienced difficulty, until the child could identify the common sound.

The sound-identification task was repeated a number of times during training, and there were variations (e.g., presentation of *bus* with the child required to pick out a picture starting with the same sound from an array of pictures; presentation of *bus* with the direction to pick out pictures of objects starting with a different sound than the one at the beginning of *bus*). Children were given sets of pictures and asked to group them together on the basis of common sounds and also to justify their classifications. In the odd-one-out activity, the child was required to eliminate a word starting with (or ending or containing) a sound different from the other pictures in a set. Many such exercises were given for each sound (e.g., *b*) with the teacher moving on to a new sound only when the child seemed to be proficient with the sound previously introduced. Of course, as new sounds accumulated, the difficulty of tasks increased (e.g., depictions of many items starting with different sounds rather than one or two sounds, as is the case at the beginning of training).

The 20 sessions with pictures were followed by 20 sessions with words, with children required to determine whether words rhymed or began with the same sound (alliteration). After the child was proficient at this task, there were lessons on end sounds (e.g., odd-word-out exercise requiring elimination of the word ending in a sound different than the others). After the child could manage categorizing on the basis of final sounds, there was instruction of categorization based on middle sounds in words.

Pictures yielded to purely aural presentations in this training. Various discrimination exercises eventually gave way to production exercises, so that children had to recall words containing particular sounds in particular positions. In the latter half of the curriculum, children were required to spell words using plastic letters, with the teacher providing help up to and including spelling the word for the child if that was needed to move the lesson along. Spelling exercises included sets of words sharing common features. Thus for a set involving *hat, cat,* and *rat,* an efficient strategy was simply to change the first plastic letter as each new word was requested. Such spelling tests illustrated the saliency of many different sound patterns.

This training produced substantial gains in standardized reading performance (about a year's advantage) relative to a control condition in which children were trained to categorize pictures and words conceptually (e.g., cat, bat, and rat are all animals). The sound-categorization-trained students were even further ahead of control participants who had received no supplementary categorization training.

Even more striking, however, were the results of a five-year follow-up. Even though many of the control subjects had received substantial remediation during the five-year interval following participation in the study, there were still striking reading advantages for students who had experienced the sound-categorization training when they were in the primary grades (Bradley, 1989; Bradley & Bryant, 1991).

Goswami and Bryant (1992) elegantly summarized the findings with respect to phonemic awareness:

> There can be little doubt that [phonemic] awareness plays an important role in reading. The results of a large number of studies amply demonstrate a strong (and consistent) relationship between children's ability to disentangle and to assemble the sounds in words and their progress in learning to read. . . . There is also evidence that successful training in [phonemic] awareness helps children learn to read. . . . Put together, these two sets of data are convincing evidence that [phonemic] awareness is a powerful causal determinant of the speed and efficiency of learning to read. . . . [This metalinguistic research] has immediate educational implications, and it will also undoubtedly play a great part in theories about learning to read. (p. 49)

In closing this discussion of phonemic awareness, I emphasize that most children's emergent literacy interactions with parents will not result in phonemic awareness; but a heavy dose of such interactions with children between four and six years of age seems to go far in promoting success in reading. For phonemic awareness to develop, adults must lead children to think about the sounds of words and how sounds are blended to produce words.

Unfortunately, explicit instruction for such skills is antagonistic to the whole language tenets that children should be oriented to the meaning of whole text. Thus many children do not receive phonemic-awareness instruction, and some experience difficulties in learning to read because of this lack (see Pressley & Rankin, 1994), especially those readers most at risk. They are often the least likely to discover on their own that words can be decomposed into sounds that correspond to letters and letter sequences. It is not hard to understand why decoding instruction, which often is operationalized as analyzing words into component sounds and blending the sounds, should be difficult for a child who is unaware that words are composed of component sounds that are blended.

Decoding Instruction

There is little doubt that learning to decode words is critical during the primary years of schooling. By the time children arrive at grade 1, where instruction in decoding has traditionally been emphasized for the first time, there are vast individual differences in children with respect to their preparedness for literacy, differences largely determined by previous interactions. The child who has had rich emergent literacy experiences is better prepared for decoding instruction than the child who has experienced limited language interactions. A history of interactions with adults about the sounds in words and the relationships of sounds to one another to produce words is also predictive of success in early reading. Most predictive of all, however, is receiving systematic instruction in decoding (see Adams, 1990, Chapter 4).

Sounding Out and Blending

The most common form of decoding instruction emphasizes using letter-sound relations and blending them to sound out words. Most children can learn to decode in this way (see Adams, 1990, Chapter 4; Harris & Sipay, 1990, Chapter 12). Many trials of successfully sounding out a word strengthen the memory of a word as a particular pattern of letters (Adams, 1990, Chapter 9; Ehri, 1980, 1984, 1987, 1991, 1992). For example, on initial exposure to a word say, *frog*, the word is sounded out. Such sounding out begins a process in which the connections between each letter and adjacent letters are strengthened (e.g., between *fr* and *og*). Eventually the word is represented in memory as a whole. With increased exposure, the word is recognized automatically.

Phonics Rules

Students can be taught phonics rules (e.g., "When there is an *e* at the end of a syllable . . . "). There are a manageable number of such rules (Clymer, 1963, produced a list of 45), and they work much of the time; that is, termed rules and phonics generalizations never hold 100 percent of the time. For example, "When two vowels go walking, the first does the talking" works about two-thirds of the time. Teaching children phonics rules does improve early reading (Adams, 1990; Anderson, Hiebert, Scott, & Wilkinson, 1985; Ehri, 1991).

Orthographic Recognition

As a child experiences alphabetic reading, letter strings encountered often (i.e., in a number of different words) eventually are perceived as wholes (e.g., repeated co-occurrence of *i, n,* and *g* in that order results eventually in *ing* being perceived as a unit; see, e.g., Stanovich & West, 1989). Prefixes and suffixes are obvious examples, but there are other recurring combinations, many of which are root words (*-take, mal-, ben-, rog-, do-*). When familiar orthographic patterns are encountered, it is not necessary to decode alphabetically. It makes good sense to increase children's awareness of prefixes, suffixes, and root words and to teach them to make use of orthographic units to decode words.

Words that sound the same often have the same spelling patterns. Thus a child who knows how to pronounce *beak* could make a good guess at *peak* the first time it is encountered simply by decoding by analogy (i.e., This is like *beak* only it starts with a *p!*). That same *beak*-word knower would have a fighting chance with *bean, bead,* and *beat* using the analogy strategy.

For the most part, analogy has been considered an advanced strategy used only by children who have been reading awhile or by adults; Marsh and his colleagues are especially strong advocates of this position (e.g., Marsh, Desberg, & Cooper, 1977; Marsh, Friedman, Welch, & Desberg, 1981). At a minimum, use of orthographic recognition as a strategy probably depends on phonological decoding skills. Ehri and Robbins (1992) found that only children who already had some phonological decoding skills were able to decode words by analogy. Peterson and Haines (1992) produced results complementary to the Ehri and Robbins outcome. In addition, Bruck and Treiman (1992) demonstrated that even when young children can use analogies, they rely greatly on decoding of individual phonemes and orthographs when encountering new words. In short, teaching students to decode by analogy is a sensible strategy but one that complements rather than replaces phonological decoding strategies.

Explicit Decoding Instruction with Students
Experiencing Severe Reading Difficulties

Explicit decoding instruction to analyze and blend component sounds is effective even for children who experience great difficulties learning to read—that is, children who leave the primary grades without having learned decoding. For example, Lovett, Ransby, Hardwick, Johns, and Donaldson (1989) succeeded in improving the decoding of dyslexic students ages 9 to 13 through intensive instruction of letter-sound analyses and blending, instruction that also improved student performance on a measure of standardized reading comprehension. Lovett and colleagues (1994) also succeeded in teaching dyslexic readers to decode using phonological analysis and blending; again, there was improved performance on a standardized comprehension measure relative to a control condition.

Summary and Commentary

There is considerable evidence that explicit teaching of decoding positively affects children's learning to read. As uncontroversial as that conclusion may seem based on the evidence reported here, in fact, explicit decoding instruction has been largely out of favor in North American classrooms since the late 1980s. Opposition to decoding instruction is almost a defining characteristic of whole language—oriented educators. Yet various analyses of the failures of contemporary beginning reading instruction have focused on the possibility that much of the failure has been due to lack of primary-level instruction in decoding (Pressley & Rankin, 1994; Smith, 1994)—that in fact, much of primary reading failure is due to poor decisionmaking by teachers: Teachers are deciding not to teach decoding explicitly, errantly believing that decoding skills can be a natural by-product of immersion in print experiences (e.g., group reading and rereading of big books, listening to stories, and writing using invented spelling). In general, it is true that when children read more, their phonological decoding skills increase as their knowledge of orthographs improves (see Allen, Cipielewski, & Stanovich, 1992; Allington, 1977; Cipielewski & Stanovich, 1992; Cunningham & Stanovich, 1990, 1991; Juel, 1988; Stanovich, 1986; Taylor, Frye, & Maruyama, 1990). Thus children should indeed be encouraged to read, read, and read, which is a predominant strategy for increasing reading skills in whole language classrooms. The research on decoding instruction, however, makes clear that many children are going to learn how to decode so that they can read, read, and read only if they experience more explicit, systematic decoding instruction than is recommended by whole language theorists and educators (e.g., Weaver, 1994).

Comprehension Strategies Instruction

For more than a decade, reading researchers have believed that readers who can decode but still experience comprehension difficulties can benefit from instruction in comprehension strategies. Palincsar and Brown's (1984) work on reciprocal teaching of comprehension strategies did much to inspire educator experimentation with comprehension strategies instruction. In the late 1980s and early 1990s my colleagues and I studied how educators effectively adapted comprehension strategies instruction to classroom realities, with us dubbing the educator approach to be transactional strategies instruction. Such strategies instruction has proven effective with readers experiencing difficulties in comprehending what they read.

Reciprocal Teaching

Reciprocal teaching, as defined by Palincsar and Brown (1984), involved teaching students to use four comprehension strategies: prediction, questioning, seeking clarification when confused, and summarization. In Palincsar and Brown's (1984) Study 1, on each of 20 days of intervention, an adult teacher began by discussing the topic of the day's text with the seventh-grade students who were the targets of the intervention. The targeted students were capable decoders but experienced comprehension problems. The teacher called for predictions about the content of the passage based on the title if the passage was completely new or for a review of the main points covered for passages that had been begun the previous day. The teacher then assigned one of the two students being taught to be the "teacher." Adult teacher and students then read silently the first paragraph of the day's lesson. When everyone had finished reading, the student teacher posed a question about the paragraph, summarized it, and then either predicted upcoming content or sought clarification if there was some confusion about the information or ideas in the paragraph. If the student teacher faltered, the adult teacher scaffolded these activities with prompts (e.g., "What question do you think a teacher might ask?"), instruction (e.g., "Remember, a summary is a shortened version."), and modification (e.g., "If you're having a hard time thinking of a question, why don't you summarize first?"). Students were praised for their teaching and given feedback about its quality (e.g., "You asked that question well" or "I might have asked the question . . . "). Students took turns as the student teacher with a session lasting about 30 minutes.

Throughout the intervention, the students were explicitly informed that questioning, summarization, prediction, and seeking clarification were strategies that would help them understand better and that they should try to use them when they read on their own. The students were also informed that being able to summarize passages and predict the questions on upcoming tests were good ways to assess whether what was read was understood.

Reciprocal teaching in this initial study positively affected all of the comprehension measures taken, providing much reason for enthusiasm about the method. Palincsar and Brown (1984, Study 2) also validated reciprocal teaching in a realistic classroom situation, again with middle-school-age poor comprehenders.

Much more research on the method followed, summarized by Rosen-shine and Meister (1994). There were consistent, striking effects on cognitive-process measures, such as those tapping summarization and self-questioning skills. With respect to standardized comprehension, however, the effects were less striking, with an average effect size of 0.3 SDs. Perhaps the most important conclusion to emerge from the Rosen-shine and Meister (1994) analysis was that reciprocal teaching was more successful when there was more direct teaching of the four comprehension strategies than when there was not, important in light of subsequent results presented in this section.

Educator-Devised Comprehension Strategies Instruction: Transactional Strategies Instruction

My colleagues and I used a variety of qualitative methods as we documented comprehension strategies instruction that was developed by educators and was apparently effective in their settings (Brown & Coy-Ogan, 1993; El-Dinary, Pressley, & Schuder, 1992; Gaskins, Anderson, Pressley, Cunicelli, & Satlow, 1993; Pressley, El-Dinary, Gaskins et al., 1992; Pressley, El-Dinary, Stein, Marks, & Brown, 1992; Pressley, Gaskins, Cunicelli et al., 1991; Pressley, Gaskins, Wile, Cunicelli, & Sheridan, 1991; Pressley, Schuder, SAIL Faculty and Administration, Bergman, & El-Dinary, 1992). Although the instructional programs studied differed in their particulars, a number of conclusions held across programs, all of which served weaker readers; two of the three programs especially targeted weaker readers.

In all of the programs studied, a small repertoire of strategies was taught, typically including prediction based on prior-knowledge activation, question generation, seeking clarification when confused, mental imagery, relating prior knowledge to text content, and summarization. In general, students were taught to use these strategies to comprehend, interpret, and remember text.

There were also commonalities in the ways the comprehension instruction occurred: (1) Instruction was long-term, optimally occurring over a number of school years. (2) Teachers initially explained and modeled the comprehension strategies, generally in-line with the direct-explanation approach as conceived by Roehler and Duffy (1984). (3) Following introduction of the strategies, teachers coached students to use them, providing hints as needed as to when students might make strategic choices. There were many minilessons about when it was appropriate to use particular strategies. (4) Students modeled use of strategies for one another, for example, thinking aloud as they read. Students explained to one another how they used strategies to process text. (5) Throughout instruction, the usefulness of strategies was emphasized. Information about when and where various strategies could be applied was discussed often. (6) Teachers consistently modeled flexible use of strategies, for example, when they read stories to students.

Much of the strategies instruction occurred in small groups with the intent that students would internalize the procedural skills practiced in those groups (Pressley, El-Dinary, Gaskins, et al., 1992). Consistent with the Vygotskian approach (Vygotsky, 1978), the assumption was that thinking skills can be developed by engaging in cognitively rich interactions with other people. In particular, the strategies were used as vehicles for coordinating dialogue about text as students read aloud in groups (see especially Gaskins et al., 1993). That is, they were encouraged to relate text to their prior knowledge, talk about their summaries of text meaning as they read, report the images they experienced during reading, and predict what might transpire next. As students read aloud, they engaged in and exchanged personal interpretations of and responses to text (Brown & Coy-Ogan, 1993).

The Pressley group described such teaching as "transactional strategies instruction" because it emphasized reader transactions with texts (Rosenblatt, 1978), interpretations constructed by readers thinking about text together (e.g., Hutchins, 1991), and teacher's and students' reactions to text affecting each other's individual thinking about text (e.g., Bell, 1968).

The descriptive studies conducted by the Pressley group were in anticipation of a comparative evaluation of the educator-developed approach to comprehension strategies instruction. Brown, Pressley, Van Meter, and Schuder (1996) conducted a year-long quasi-experimental investigation of the effects of transactional strategies instruction on second-grade children's reading. Five second-grade classrooms receiving transactional strategies instruction were matched with classrooms taught by teachers who were well regarded as language arts teachers but who were not using a strategies-instruction approach. In each classroom, a group of readers who were low achieving at the beginning of grade 2 were identified.

In fall, students in the strategies-instruction condition and control participants did not differ on standardized measures of reading comprehension and word-attack skills. By spring, there were clear differences on these measures favoring the transactional strategies-instruction classrooms. In addition, there were differences favoring the strategies-instructed students on strategies-use measures as well as interpretive measures (i.e., strategies-instructed students made more diverse and richer interpretations of what they read than controls).

One of the most compelling differences between Brown and colleagues (1996) transactional strategies-instruction students and control students was that the students who had learned strategies acquired more content from their daily lessons. All children in the study were presented a common reading as part of their regular instruction. When tested later on what they remembered from the material they had read, the strategies-instruction students remembered more than controls. When students learn comprehension strategies and use them, they get much more from the texts they encounter than students not taught to be strategic as they read.

In addition to the Brown and colleagues (1996) study with weak second-grade students, Valerie Anderson (1992; see also Anderson & Roit, 1993) conducted a three-month experimental investigation of the effects of transactional strategies instruction on reading-disabled students in grades 6 through 11. Students were taught comprehension strategies in nine small groups; there were seven control groups. Although both strategies-instructed and control students made gains on standardized comprehension measures, the gains were greater in the trained group. Anderson (1992) also collected a variety of qualitative data supporting the conclusion that reading for meaning improved in the strategies-instructed condition: For example, strategies instruction increased students' willingness to read difficult material and attempt to understand it, collaborate with classmates to discover meanings in text, and react to and elaborate text.

The work of Donald Deshler, Jean Schumaker, and their colleagues must be acknowledged here. Although they summarize their work in cognitive-behavioral terms, from my firsthand observation of their methods it is obvious that they are teaching learning-disabled students to use comprehension strategies in a transactional fashion. They have been doing so for more than a decade in schools across North America, producing various types of evidence that such instruction improves the comprehension of struggling middle-school and high-school students (e.g., Deshler & Schumaker, 1988).

Closing Comments

Comprehension in weak readers can be improved through teaching of comprehension strategies. Rather than providing students with a crutch, such teaching orients young readers to comprehend as skilled readers do. There is considerable evidence from verbal protocol (think-aloud) studies of skilled reading that good readers use the strategies that are taught as part of transactional strategies instruction (Pressley & Afflerbach, 1995).

Unfortunately, comprehension strategies instruction is not commonplace. Even 20 years after Durkin (1978–79) documented that instruction in comprehension strategies can improve children's understanding of text (Pressley, in press; Pressley, El-Dinary, Wharton-McDonald, & Brown, in press), this teaching method is anything but universal.

During 1995–1996, my colleagues and I (Pressley, Wharton-McDonald, Mistretta, & Echevarria, 1996) observed 10 fourth- and fifth-grade classrooms. One of the most striking observations was that little comprehension strategies instruction took place. One of the reasons that some children have difficulty in becoming good comprehenders is that they are not receiving instruction about how to comprehend. What I and colleagues (1996) observed instead was a great deal of sustained, silent reading consistent with the whole language philosophy that if children read a lot, they will naturally become good comprehenders (Weaver, 1994). My view is that for at least some students, highly strategic comprehension is not likely to develop in the absence of instruction.

More positively, many special educators are more likely to teach comprehension strategies to their students than are the regular educators in the same building. This is because of the generally greater awareness of special educators of the value of direct instruction as well as the conceptual leadership of the likes of Deshler and Schumaker. In general, special education is an arena in which cognitively oriented instruction has thrived (see Pressley, Woloshyn, & Associates, 1995).

Conclusions

Adults can interact in many ways with children who are at risk for or experiencing failure in reading. From infancy to high school, children's experiences with caregivers and teachers can make a difference in this respect.

It is disturbing that there actually is opposition to much of the intervention described in this chapter. Proponents of the whole language approach clamor against explicit and systematic skills instruction both to promote phonemic awareness and to teach comprehension strategies (Smith, 1994). My view is that the scientific community needs to continue to determine when and for whom such instruction is effective. I suspect that at least some of the interventions described in this chapter make an impact even on some students who are biologically different from normal readers. For example, recall Lovett's work, described earlier in this chapter: Students who had experienced exceptional difficulties learned to decode in school.

Until it is known who benefits from which forms of interaction and instruction, I believe that when a child experiences difficulties in learning to read, the informed educator should try to intervene in ways described in this chapter. The preschooler whose language is underdeveloped relative to peers might benefit from efforts to improve the emergent literacy interactions in the family. The kindergarten student who lacks phonemic awareness might benefit from teaching aimed at orienting the child to the individual sounds of words and how those sounds can be combined. The child who fails to learn to decode by the end of grade 1 might benefit from systematic decoding instruction. Instruction aimed at analyses of words and blending of their component sounds is helpful for some children; other children benefit from instruction aimed at learning the major orthographs of English and using them to decode new words by analogy (e.g., using knowledge of *cat* to decode *mat*). The child who can decode but who has difficulty with comprehension should be a candidate for comprehension strategies instruction. Especially heartening is that there is at least a little evidence that instruction aimed at particular competencies does have a range of effects beyond the particular aspect of reading targeted by the intervention. For example, Lovett and colleagues (1989, 1994) succeeded in improving comprehension when they targeted decoding. Brown and others (1996) succeeded in improving word-level skills when they targeted comprehension.

I close with the suggestion I have made many times. Sustained efforts will most likely be needed to help weaker students perform near the norm for their developmental level. There were no quick fixes outlined in this chapter but rather a series of interventions that make sense at different points in the learning-to-read progression. I suspect a child would be best served by encountering a rich language environment in preschool, instruction aimed at developing phonemic awareness in the kindergarten year, explicit decoding instruction during the primary grades, and systematic comprehension instruction in the later elementary grades. I hope that in my lifetime there will be a serious effort to determine whether sustained, high-quality instruction can make a difference that results in qualitatively better reading abilities during adulthood—which translates into greater economic success, political freedom, and personal happiness. A start in that direction is to root out the current anti-instructional biases fostered by whole language philosophy in the past decade or so, for until those biases are gone, there are going to be children who need explicit instruction to foster emerging language skills, phonemic awareness, decoding, and comprehension who are not going to receive it. Philosophies that argue against providing much-needed instruction to students who might benefit from it are dangerous philosophies (Pressley & Rankin, 1994).

References

Adams, M. J. (1990). *Beginning to read.* Cambridge, MA: Harvard University Press.

Allen, L., Cipielewski, J., & Stanovich, K. E. (1992). Multiple indicators of children's reading habits and attitudes: Construct validity and cognitive correlates. *Journal of Educational Psychology, 84,* 489–503.

Allington, R. (1977). If they don't read much, how they ever gonna get good? *Journal of Reading, 21,* 57–61.

Anderson, R. C., Hiebert, E. H., Scott, J. A., & Wilkinson, I.A.G. (1985). *Becoming a nation of readers.* Washington, DC: National Institute of Education.

Anderson, V. (1992). A teacher development project in transactional strategy instruction for teachers of severely reading-disabled adolescents. *Teaching & Teacher Education, 8,* 391–403.

Anderson, V., & Roit, M. (1993). Planning and implementing collaborative strategy instruction for delayed readers in grades 6–10. *Elementary School Journal, 94,* 121–137.

Applebee, A. N., & Langer, J. A. (1983). Instructional scaffolding: Reading and writing as natural language activities. *Language Arts, 60,* 168–175.

Ball, E. W., & Blachman, B. A. (1988). Phoneme segmentation training: Effect on reading readiness. *Annals of Dyslexia, 38,* 203–225.

Ball, E. W., & Blachman, B. A. (1991). Does phoneme segmentation training in kindergarten make a difference in early word recognition and developmental spelling? *Reading Research Quarterly, 26,* 49–66.

Bell, R. Q. (1968). A reinterpretation of the direction of effects in studies of socialization. *Psychological Review, 75,* 81–95.

Blachman, B. A. (1991). Phonological awareness: Implications for prereading and early reading instruction. In S. A. Brady & D. P. Shankweiler (Eds.), *Phonological processes in literacy: A tribute to Isabelle Y. Liberman* (pp. 29–36). Hillsdale NJ: Erlbaum & Associates.

Bradley, L. (1988). Making connections in learning to read and to spell. *Applied Cognitive Psychology, 2,* 3–18.

Bradley, L. (1989). Predicting learning disabilities. In J. Dumont & H. Nakken (Eds.), *Learning disabilities, 2; Cognitive, social, and remedial aspects* (pp. 1–18). Amsterdam Netherlands: Swets.

Bradley, L., & Bryant, P. E. (1983). Categorizing sounds and learning to read—a causal connection. *Nature, 301,* 419–421.

Bradley, L., & Bryant, P. (1985). *Rhyme and reason in reading and spelling.* International Academy for Research in Learning Disabilities Series. Ann Arbor MI: University of Michigan Press.

Bradley, L., & Bryant, P. (1991). Phonological skills before and after learning to read. In S. A. Brady & D. P. Shankweiler (Eds.), *Phonological processes in literacy: A tribute to Isabelle Y. Liberman* (pp. 37–45). Hillsdale, NJ: Lawrence Erlbaum Associates.

Briggs, C., & Elkind, D. (1973). Cognitive development in early readers. *Developmental Psychology, 9,* 279–280.

Brown, R., & Coy-Ogan, L. (1993). The evolution of transactional strategies instruction in one teacher's classroom. *Elementary School Journal, 94,* 221–233.

Brown, R., Pressley, M., Van Meter, P., & Schuder, T. (1996). A quasi-experimental validation of transactional strategies instruction with low-achieving second grade readers. *Journal of Educational Psychology, 88,* 18–37.

Bruck, M. (1990). Word-recognition skills of adults with childhood diagnoses of dyslexia. *Developmental Psychology, 26,* 439–454.

Bruck, M. (1992). Persistence of dyslexics' phonological awareness deficits. *Developmental Psychology, 28,* 874–886.

Bruck, M., & Treiman, R. (1992). Learning to pronounce words: The limits of analogies. *Reading Research Quarterly, 27,* 374–398.

Bus, A. G., van Ijzendoorn, M. H., & Pellegrini, A. D. (1995). Joint book reading makes for success in learning to read: A meta-analysis on intergenerational transmission of literacy. *Review of Educational Research, 65,* 1–21.

Calfee, R. C., Chapman, R., & Venezsky, R. (1972). How a child needs to think to learn to read. In L. W. Gregg (Ed.), *Cognition in learning and memory.* New York: Wiley.

Calfee, R. C., Lindamood, P., & Lindamood, C. (1973). Acoustic-phonetic skills and reading—kindergarten through twelfth grade. *Journal of Educational Psychology, 64,* 293–298.

Cipielewski, J., & Stanovich, K. E. (1992). Predicting growth in reading ability from children's exposure to print. *Journal of Experimental Child Psychology, 54,* 74–89.

Clark, M. M. (1976). *Young fluent readers: What can they teach us?* London: Heinemann.

Clay, M. M. (1966). *Emergent reading behavior.* Unpublished doctoral dissertation. University of Auckland, NZ.

Clay, M. M. (1967). The reading behavior of five-year-old children: A research report. *New Zealand Journal of Educational Studies, 2,* 11–31.

Clymer, T. (1963). The utility of phonic generalizations in the primary grades. *Reading Teacher, 16,* 252–58.

Cochran-Smith, M. (1984). *The making of a reader.* Norwood, NJ: Ablex.

Crain-Thoreson, C., & Dale, P. S. (1992). Do early talkers become early readers? Linguistic precocity, preschool language, and emergent literacy. *Developmental Psychology, 28,* 421–429.

Cunningham, A. E. (1990). Explicit versus implicit instruction in phonemic awareness. *Journal of Experimental Child Psychology, 50,* 429–444.

Cunningham, A. E., & Stanovich, K. E. (1990). Assessing print exposure and orthographic processing skill in children: A quick measure of reading experience. *Journal of Educational Psychology, 82,* 733–740.

Cunningham, A. E., & Stanovich, K. E. (1991). Tracking the unique effects of print exposure in children: Associations with vocabulary, general knowledge, and spelling. *Journal of Educational Psychology, 83,* 264–274.

DeLoache, J. S., & DeMendoza, O.A.P. (1987). Joint picturebook interactions of mothers and 1-year-old children. *British Journal of Developmental Psychology, 5,* 111–123.

Deshler, D. D., & Schumaker, J. B. (1988). An instructional model for teaching students how to learn. In J. L. Graden, J. E. Zins, & M. J. Curtis (Eds.), *Alternative educational delivery systems: Enhancing instructional options for all students* (pp. 391–411). Washington, DC: National Association of School Psychologists.

Durkin, D. (1966). *Children who read early.* New York: Teachers College Press.

Durkin, D. (1978–1979). What classroom observations reveal about reading comprehension instruction. *Reading Research Quarterly, 15,* 481–533.

Ehri, L. C. (1980). The development of orthographic images. In U. Frith (Ed.), *Cognitive processes in spelling* (pp. 311–338). London: Academic Press.

Ehri, L. C. (1984). How orthography alters spoken language competencies in children learning to read and spell. In J. Downing & R. Valtin (Eds.), *Language awareness and learning to read* (pp. 119–147). New York: Springer-Verlag.

Ehri, L. C. (1987). Learning to read and spell words. *Journal of Reading Behavior, 19,* 5–31.

Ehri, L. C. (1991). Development of the ability to read words. In R. Barr, M. L. Kamil, P. B. Mosenthal, & P. D. Pearson (Eds.), *Handbook of reading research,* Vol. 2 (pp. 383–417). New York: Longman.

Ehri, L. C. (1992). Reconceptualizing the development of sight word reading and its relationship to recoding. In P. B. Gough, L. C. Ehri, & R. Treiman (Eds.), *Reading acquisition* (pp. 107–143). Hillsdale, NJ: Lawrence Erlbaum Associates.

Ehri, L. C., & Robbins, C. (1992). Beginners need some decoding skill to read words by analogy. *Reading Research Quarterly, 27,* 12–27.

El-Dinary, P. B., Pressley, M., & Schuder, T. (1992). Becoming a strategies teacher: An observational and interview study of three teachers learning transactional strategies instruction. In C. Kinzer & D. Leu (Eds.), *Forty-first Yearbook of the National Reading Conference* (pp. 453–462). Chicago: National Reading Conference.

Finucci, J. M., Gottfredson, L. S., & Childs, B. (1985). A follow-up study of dyslexic boys. *Annals of Dyslexia, 35,* 117–136.

Flood, J. (1977). Parental styles in reading episodes with young children. *Reading Teacher, 30,* 864–867.

Frauenheim, J. G., & Heckerl, J. R. (1983). A longitudinal study of psychological and achievement test performance in severe dyslexic adults. *Journal of Learning Disabilities, 16,* 339–347.

Gaddes, W. H. (1994). *Learning disabilities and brain function* (3rd ed.). New York: Springer-Verlag.

Gaskins, I. W., Anderson, R. C., Pressley, M., Cunicelli, E. A., & Satlow, E. (1993). Six teachers' dialogue during cognitive process instruction. *Elementary School Journal, 93,* 277–304.

Goswami, U., & Bryant, P. (1992). Rhyme, analogy, and children's reading. In P. B. Gough, L. C. Ehri, & R. Treiman (Eds.), *Reading acquisition* (pp. 49–63). Hillsdale, NJ: Lawrence Erlbaum Associates.

Harris, A. J., & Sipay, E. R. (1990). *How to increase reading ability: A guide to developmental & remedial methods.* New York: Longman.

Heath, S. B. (1982). What no bedtime story means: Narrative skills at home and school. *Language in Society, 11,* 49–76.

Hutchins, E. (1991). The social organization of distributed cognition. In L. Resnick, J. M. Levine, & S. D. Teasley (Eds.), *Perspectives on socially shared cognition* (pp. 283–307). Washington, DC: American Psychological Association.

Juel, C. (1988). Learning to read and write: A longitudinal study of 54 children from first through fourth grades. *Journal of Educational Psychology, 80,* 417–447.

King, E. M., & Friesen, D. T. (1972). Children who read in kindergarten. *Alberta Journal of Educational Research, 18,* 147–161.

Leichter, H. P. (1984). Families as environments for literacy. In H. Goelman, A. Oberg, & F. Smith (Eds.), *Awakening to literacy.* Exeter, NH: Heinemann Educational Books.

Lie, A. (1991). Effects of a training program for stimulating skills in word analysis in first-grade children. *Reading Research Quarterly, 26,* 234–250.

Lovett, M. W., Borden, S. L., DeLuca, T., Lacerenza, L., Benson, N. J., & Blackstone, D. (1994). Treating the core deficits of developmental dyslexia: Evidence of transfer of learning after phonologically- and strategy-based reading training programs. *Developmental Psychology, 30,* 805–822.

Lovett, M. W., Ransby, M. J., Hardwick, N., Johns, M. S., & Donaldson, S. A. (1989). Can dyslexia be treated? Treatment-specific and generalized treatment effects in dyslexic children's response to remediation. *Brain and Language, 37,* 90–121.

Lundberg, I. (1991). Phonemic awareness can be developed without reading instruction. In S. A. Brady & D. P. Shankweiler (Eds.), *Phonological processes in literacy: A tribute to Isabelle Y. Liberman* (pp. 47–53). Hillsdale NJ: Lawrence Erlbaum Associates.

Lundberg, I., Frost, J., & Peterson, O. (1988). Effects of an extensive program for stimulating phonological awareness in preschool children. *Reading Research Quarterly, 23,* 263–84.

Marsh, G., Desberg, P., & Cooper, J. (1977). Developmental strategies in reading. *Journal of Reading Behavior, 9,* 391–394.

Marsh, G., Friedman, M., Welch, V., & Desberg, P. (1981). A cognitive-developmental theory of reading acquisition. In G. E. MacKinnon & T. G. Waller (Eds.), *Reading research: Advances in theory and practice,* Vol. 3 (pp. 199–221). New York: Academic Press.

Morrow, L. M. (1983). Home and school correlates of early interest in literature. *Journal of Educational Research, 76,* 221–230.

Morrow, L. M. (1996). *Literacy development in the early years: Helping children read and write* (3rd ed.). Englewood Cliffs, NJ: Prentice-Hall.

Ninio, A. (1980). Picture-book reading in mother-infant dyads belonging to two subgroups in Israel. *Child Development, 51,* 587–590.

Olson, R. K. (1994). Language deficits in "specific" reading disability. In M. A. Gernsbacher (Ed.), *Handbook of psycholinguistics* (pp. 895–916). San Diego: Academic Press.

Palincsar, A. S., & Brown, A. L. (1984). Reciprocal teaching of comprehension-fostering and monitoring activities. *Cognition and Instruction, 1,* 117–175.

Pellegrini, A. D., Perlmutter, J. C., Galda, L., & Brody, G. H. (1990). Joint reading between black Head Start children and their mothers. *Child Development, 61,* 443–453.

Peterson, M. E., & Haines, L. P. (1992). Orthographic analogy training with kindergarten children: Effects of analogy use, phonemic segmentation, and letter-sound knowledge. *Journal of Reading Behavior, 24,* 109–127.

Plessas, G. P., & Oakes, C. R. (1964). Prereading experiences of selected early readers. *Reading Teacher, 17,* 241–245.

Pressley, M. (in press). Comprehension strategies instruction. In volume based on 1996 Wingspread Conference on Balanced Reading Instruction. New York: Guilford Press.

Pressley, M., & Afflerbach, P. (1995). *Verbal protocols of reading: The nature of constructively responsive reading.* Hillsdale, NJ: Lawrence Erlbaum Associates.

Pressley, M., & Associates (1990). *Cognitive strategy instruction that really works with children.* Cambridge, MA: Brookline Books.

Pressley, M., El-Dinary, P. B., Gaskins, I., Schuder, T., Bergman, J., Almasi, L., & Brown, R. (1992). Beyond direct explanation: Transactional instruction of reading comprehension strategies. *Elementary School Journal, 92,* 511–554.

Pressley, M., El-Dinary, P. B., Stein, S., Marks, M. B., & Brown, R. (1992). Good strategy instruction is motivating and interesting. In A. Renninger, S. Hidi, & A. Krapp (Eds.), *The role of interest in learning and development* (pp. 333–358). Hillsdale, NJ: Lawrence Erlbaum Associates.

Pressley, M., El-Dinary, P. B., Wharton-McDonald, & Brown, R. (in press). Transactional instruction of comprehension strategies in the elementary grades. In D. Schunk & B. Zimmerman (Eds.), *Self-regulation book.* New York: Guilford Press.

Pressley, M., Gaskins, I. W., Cunicelli, E. A., Burdick, N. J., Schaub-Matt, M., Lee, D. S., & Powell, N. (1991). Strategy instruction at Benchmark School: A faculty interview study. *Learning Disability Quarterly, 14,* 19–48.

Pressley, M., Gaskins, I. W., Wile, D., Cunicelli, B., & Sheridan, J. (1991). Teaching literacy strategies across the curriculum: A case study at Benchmark School. In J. Zutell & S. McCormick (Eds.), *Learner factors/teacher factors: Issues in literacy research and instruction: Fortieth yearbook of the National Reading Conference* (pp. 219–228). Chicago: National Reading Conference.

Pressley, M., & Rankin, J. (1994). More about whole language methods of reading instruction for students at-risk for early reading failure. *Learning Disabilities Research & Practice, 9,* 157–168.

Pressley, M., Schuder, T., SAIL Faculty and Administration, Bergman, J. L., & El-Dinary, P. B. (1992). A researcher-educator collaborative interview study of transactional comprehension strategies instruction. *Journal of Educational Psychology, 84,* 231–246.

Pressley, M., Wharton-McDonald, R., Mistretta, J., & Echevarria, M. (1996). *The nature of literacy instruction in ten grade–4/5 classrooms in upstate New York.* Manuscript under review. Albany, NY: University at Albany, State University of New York, Department of Educational Psychology and Statistics.

Pressley, M., Woloshyn, V. E., & Associates (1995). *Cognitive strategy instruction that really works with children* (2nd ed.). Cambridge, MA: Brookline Books.

Roehler, L. R., & Duffy, G. G. (1984). Direct explanation of comprehension processes. In G. G. Duffy, L. R. Roehler, & J. Mason (Eds.), *Comprehension instruction: Perspectives and suggestions* (pp. 265–280). New York: Longman.

Rosenblatt, L. M. (1978). *The reader, the text, the poem: The transactional theory of the literary work.* Carbondale: Southern Illinois University Press.

Rosenshine, B., & Meister, C. (1994). Reciprocal teaching: A review of nineteen experimental studies. *Review of Educational Research, 64,* 479–530.

Roser, N., & Martinez, M. (1985). Roles adults play in preschool responses to literature. *Language Arts, 62,* 485–490.

Satz, P., Taylor, H. G., Friel, J., & Fletcher, J. M. (1978). Some developmental and predictive precursors of reading disabilities: A six-year followup. In A. L. Benton & D. Pearl (Eds.), *Dyslexia: An appraisal of current knowledge.* New York: Oxford University Press.

Scarborough, H. S., & Dobrich, W. (1994). On the efficiency of reading to preschoolers. *Developmental Review, 14,* 245–302.

Schonhaut, S., & Satz, P. (1983). Prognosis for children with learning disabilities: A review of follow-up studies. In M. Rutter (Ed.), *Developmental neuropsychiatry.* New York: Guilford Press.

Smith, C. B. (Moderator) (1994). *Whole Language: The Debate.* Bloomington, IN: ERIC/REC.

Spreen, O. (1978). Prediction of school achievement from kindergarten to grade five: Review and report of a follow-up study. *Research Monograph No. 33.* Victoria, BC: Department of Psychology, University of Victoria.

Spreen, O. (1988). *Learning disabled children growing up: A follow-up into adulthood.* New York: Oxford University Press.

Stanovich, K. (1986). Matthew effects in reading: Some consequences of individual differences in the acquisition of literacy. *Reading Research Quarterly, 21,* 360–407.

Stanovich, K. E., & West, R. F. (1989). Exposure to print and orthographic processing. *Reading Research Quarterly, 24,* 402–433.

Stuart, M., & Masterson, J. (1992). Patterns of reading and spelling in 10-year-old children related to prereading phonological abilities. *Journal of Experimental Child Psychology, 54,* 168–187.

Sulzby, E., & Teale, W. (1987). *Young children's storybook reading: Longitudinal study of parent-child instruction and children's independent functioning.* (Final Report to the Spencer Foundation). Ann Arbor: University of Michigan Press.

Sulzby, E., & Teale, W. (1991). Emergent literacy. In R. Barr, M. L. Kamil, P. B. Mosenthal, & P. D. Pearson (Eds.), *Handbook of reading research,* Vol. II (pp. 727–758). New York: Longman.

Tangel, D. M., & Blachman, B. A. (1992). Effect of phoneme awareness instruction on kindergarten children's invented spellings. *Journal of Reading Behavior, 24,* 233–261.

Taylor, B. M., Frye, B. J., & Maruyama, G. M. (1990). Time spent reading and reading growth. *American Educational Research Journal, 27,* 351–362.

Taylor, D., & Strickland, D. (1986). *Family storybook reading.* Exeter, NH: Heinemann Educational Books.

Teale, W. H. (1978). Positive environments for learning to read: What studies of early readers tell us. *Language Arts, 55,* 922–932.

Valdez-Menchaca, M. C., & Whitehurst, G. J. (1992). Accelerating language development through picture book reading: A systematic extension to Mexican day care. *Developmental Psychology, 28,* 1106–1114.

Vellutino, F. R., & Scanlon, D. M. (1987). Phonological-coding, phonological awareness, and reading ability: Evidence from a longitudinal and experimental study. *Merrill-Palmer Quarterly, 33,* 321–363.

Vygotsky, L. S. (1978). *Mind in society: The development of higher psychological processes.* Cambridge, MA: Harvard University Press.

Weaver, C. (1994). *Reading process and practice: From socio-psycholinguistics to whole language.* Portsmouth, NH: Heinemann.

Whitehurst, G. J., Falco, F. L., Lonigan, C. J., Fischel, J. E., DeBaryshe, B. D., Valdez-Menchaca, M. C., & Caulfield, M. (1988). Accelerating language development through picturebook reading. *Developmental Psychology, 24,* 552–559.

Williams, J. P. (1980). Teaching decoding with an emphasis on phoneme analysis and phoneme blending. *Journal of Educational Psychology, 72,* 1–15.

7

Learning Disabilities: The Roads We Have Traveled and the Path to the Future

Linda S. Siegel

Learning disabilities are defined as significant difficulties in reading, spelling, arithmetic, and/or writing in spite of average or above-average intelligence. Learning disabilities have traditionally been defined by a diagnosis of exclusion; to be considered learning disabled, individuals must have average or above-average IQ test scores, have had access to adequate instruction, and not have had neurological problems or significant emotional disturbances that might be considered to be responsible for their difficulties in acquiring skills. For over 100 years, we have known about the existence of learning disabilities in some form, but often it seems as if we have made little progress in our understanding of this complex problem.

In this chapter, I discuss where we have traveled in our attempt to understand learning disabilities, the problems, the pitfalls, and the dead ends. I will provide (1) arguments and evidence that the identification of learning disabilities has been made an unnecessarily complex and complicated process, (2) a discussion of the major types of learning disabilities, (3) an outline of the role of IQ tests in the identification of learning disabilities, (4) suggestions for how we can help individuals with learning disabilities, and (5) some directions for the future.

The research described in this chapter was supported by a grant from the Natural Sciences and Engineering Research Council of Canada. I would like to thank Kim Kozuki for secretarial assistance.

Identification of a Learning Disability

In order to determine whether there is a learning disability, the individual is tested by a psychologist, learning-disabilities specialist, psychometrician, or some presumably qualified professional. This testing often takes between three and eight hours, sometimes even longer. Then the tests must be scored and interpreted and a report written. When a meeting is called, the psychologist or psychometrist or learning-disability specialist must attend to explain the results and discuss the diagnosis and the possible educational treatments. It is obvious that this is a very complicated process. Typically, a great deal of time and money is used to identify which individuals have a learning disability. I will demonstrate that the process can be made much simpler, less costly, and more efficient and provide a simple system to identify learning disabilities.

Efficiency can be achieved by reducing this excessive testing—by eliminating intelligence testing, using simple and objective tests of achievement, and using psychoeducational testing to reveal patterns of strengths and weaknesses in areas that are directly relevant to providing remediation in specific academic areas. In this chapter, evidence and information will be provided to show how these goals can be accomplished. I know of no empirical evidence that extensive testing leads to different choices of remediation strategies or a better outcome for those with learning disabilities.

It is important to have some system for the identification of learning disabilities. This identification should be based on objective measures of achievement, including reading, spelling, arithmetic, and if possible, writing (Siegel, 1989a; Siegel & Heaven, 1986). If an individual receives a low score on any of these measures and if there are no extenuating circumstances, such as being educated in a nonnative language or having a sensory or neurological disorder or an emotional disturbance, the individual should be said to have a learning disability. Some argue that what I call a learning disability may be just a problem with inadequate education or education not directed at the child's "learning style." My assumption is that the children who we say have learning disabilities have been exposed to appropriate educational techniques. Most children in the school system learn to read, spell, write, and do arithmetic calculations with a reasonable degree of proficiency, so it is hard to imagine that severe difficulties in these areas are a result of inadequate instruction.

Of course, there can be further psychoeducational assessment, but if additional testing is used, it should be related to developing a remedial educational program for the individual and not merely assessment for its own sake.

Subtypes of Learning Disabilities

Educational testing should be designed to identify specific learning disabilities. There are three major types. One of these is a reading disability, sometimes called dyslexia, in which the individual has difficulties understanding the sounds of letters and recognizing words and shows problems in the areas of memory and language and usually with spelling (e.g., Siegel & Ryan, 1984, 1988; Stanovich, 1988a, b; Vellutino, 1978). A phonological processing problem is a fundamental problem of this disability. (For detailed discussions, see Siegel, 1993b, 1994a, b; Snowing, Rack, & Olson, 1992; Stanovich, 1988.) All dyslexics have this phonological processing deficit. There are some individuals who have reading-comprehension and not word-recognition or phonological problems. However, those with a reading-comprehension deficit do have problems with short-term and working memory (Siegel & Ryan, 1989). Another is a disability called developmental output failure, writing-arithmetic disability, or a "nonverbal learning disability." Individuals with this problem have difficulty with computational arithmetic and written work and, often, spelling and have problems with fine-motor coordination and short-term memory but, typically, have good oral language skills (Levine, Oberklaid, & Meltzer, 1981; Morrison & Siegel, 1991; Rourke, 1987, 1988; Rourke & Tsatsanis, 1996; Siegel & Feldman, 1983; Siegel & Linder, 1984). The third type of disability is called attention deficit hyperactivity disorder (ADHD). Hyperactivity is another, but not as accurate, name for this problem. It involves difficulties with concentration and impulse control. It is actually quite controversial as to whether this is a learning disability because the problems are related to behavior and cannot be assessed objectively with standardized tests. There is a lack of agreement on the manner in which ADHD should be assessed.

To measure these learning disabilities, there are several types of tests that should be used. Specifically, an assessment of an individual for the possibility of a reading disability should include a measure of word-recognition skills. These word-recognition skills are the basis of gaining meaning from print, and it is important to know if skills in this area are significantly below average (e.g., Stanovich, 1982). An assessment should include a reading test that involves the reading of what are called pseudowords. These pseudowords are pronounceable combinations of English letters that can be sounded out with the basic rules of phonics. This type of test assesses the awareness of phonics, which is the key to decoding words in an alphabetic language such as English. There should be a test of spelling involving words dictated to the individual. This parallels the type of spelling required for writing. There should be a test of computational arithmetic skills to determine what the individual understands about the fundamental arithmetic operations.

Performance on these tests should be compared to age-related, not grade-related, norms. Grade norms are commonly used, but they have a number of methodological difficulties and are not valid in a psychometric sense. (For an extended discussion of this issue see Siegel & Heaven, 1986.)

If an individual has a low score on any of these types of tests, it is appropriate to consider this problem as a learning disability. We consider a score below the 25th percentile as evidence of a learning disability. This is admittedly arbitrary, but it seems to correlate well with the observations of teachers and parents. Obviously, there can be other reasons for poor performance, and this possibility should be examined. However, a low score is usually an indication of a problem and should not be ignored.

It is considered important to measure reading comprehension, and on the surface, this seems quite reasonable. It is logical to expect that we can understand what we read, and comprehension is critical to reading. There are, however, many problems with standardized reading-comprehension tests. For example, most of the questions do not require an inference; finding the answer directly in the text is sufficient. Many can be answered without reading the text, for example, "Bananas are not grown in which of the following places: Central America, South America, India, or Alaska?" Often, these tests are very poorly constructed(see Tal, Siegel, & Maraun, 1994 for a discussion of these issues). Also, these reading-comprehension tests emphasize speed, and most of the difference between the children who do well and those who do not is in reading speed (Biemiller & Siegel, 1995). In addition, children who have only a reading-comprehension problem and no difficulty with reading individual words do not have difficulties with phonological processing or syntax, for example, as do children who have a deficit in word recognition (Siegel & Ryan, 1989). The children who have reading-comprehension problems with no associated word-recognition problems do have significant problems with short-term and working memory (Siegel & Ryan, 1989).

There are often fallacies in the interpretation of what a test actually measures. For example, an "arithmetic" test in which the individual has to compute answers to problems in his or her head may be assumed to measure arithmetic, but this is not necessarily a correct assumption because a task such as this places heavy demands on memory. An individual may be able to solve the problem with a paper and pencil, a situation that obviously reduces memory demands. However, without a careful consideration of the task demands of the test, an incorrect inference might be made about the child's arithmetic skills.

Attention deficit hyperactivity disorder can be detected by questionnaires such as the Connors Rating Scale (Goyette, Connors, & Ulrich, 1978) for children and the Wender Utah Rating Scale for adults. For this type of scale, the parent rates the child on a variety of dimensions of behavior, such as inattention, impulsivity, and antisocial behavior; in the case of the adult, the individual provides a self-rating. These ratings are subjective and difficult to verify with any type of objective evidence. However, they remain the best measures we have. More detailed testing can be done, but any testing should be related to remediation and not just used automatically without consideration of what the test really measures and whether it is really necessary.

IQ Tests

The IQ score as part of the definition of a learning disability has been absent from this discussion so far. The prevailing wisdom is that the IQ test is essential to the identification of learning disabilities. I would like to argue that IQ scores are irrelevant to the identification of learning disabilities and that intelligence testing does not contribute to the understanding of the educational needs of the individual.

In this chapter, I will summarize the issues associated with the use of IQ tests in the definition of learning disabilities. These issues are discussed in detail in Siegel (1989a, b), Toth & Siegel (1994) and Siegel (1993a). There are at least two reasons the IQ test is considered necessary. The definition of a learning disability requires that a child be of average or above-average intelligence, and it has been traditional to separate individuals who are learning-disabled from those who are retarded. This distinction is made on the basis of the IQ test. Therefore, to maintain this distinction, an IQ test must be administered. In addition, it is common in many systems to require that there be a discrepancy between an individual's "potential" (IQ) and his or her achievement levels. In other words, a child's reading or arithmetic skills need to be significantly below what would be predicted by the IQ score for the child to be considered learning disabled. I will illustrate the problems with the use of the IQ test in each of these cases, the separation of learning-disabled children from nonlearning disabled individuals and the use of the IQ score to calculate a discrepancy between "potential" and achievement.

I would like to demonstrate some of the problems with the use of IQ tests with a specific case, as outlined in Siegel (1990). This is the story of a real individual whose name has been changed to protect his privacy. Larry, age 8, received a score of 78 on an IQ test. He was placed in a class for mentally retarded children. This is a case in which the IQ score was used to make a decision that he was mentally retarded, and this fact should be kept in mind as the rest of the case is reviewed. He remained in classes for the mentally retarded until age 14. Today, at age 34, he is en-rolled in a graduate program in a major Canadian university after com-pleting a BA in psychology with an A average.

Larry had great difficulty learning to read, spell, write, and do arith-metic calculations. When tested at age 34, his IQ score was in the high-av-erage range; however, he still had significant problems with reading and spelling. His score on the reading (word recognition) subtest of the Wide Range Achievement Test (WRAT) was at the 18th percentile, and his score on the spelling subtest of the WRAT was at the 4th percentile. His score on the Woodcock Word Attack subtest, a measure of phonic skills, was at the 6th percentile. These are all extremely low scores. He had diffi-culties on short-term memory tasks and had occasional difficulty with verb tenses and word finding in spontaneous speech. He had good gen-eral knowledge and vocabulary and an average score on a reading-com-prehension test. Larry at age 34 displays a profile of a reading-disabled individual; yet at age 8 he was called mentally retarded.

Larry's case is a very dramatic example of the consequences of using an IQ test score as part of the definition of a reading disability. At age 8, Larry was *reading disabled* but, instead, was called mentally retarded. Larry was fortunate enough to have a very determined personality and very supportive parents who fought for his rights to be educated.

Fortunately, this case has a happy ending, but for many children with genuine learning problems, the ending is not university or graduate school but jail, alcohol abuse, or suicide (e.g., Barwick & Siegel, in press; McBride & Siegel, 1997). Larry's supportive environment did not prevent or cure his reading disability; his reading problem remained throughout his schooling and into adulthood. However, his environment probably prevented Larry from developing the serious social problems that are of-ten a consequence of an undetected and untreated learning disability. Is Larry a rare exception? No. Today a child with poor reading skills and an IQ of 78 would be labeled "mentally retarded" or a "slow learner" or said to have a "general learning disability" and, in any case, would usually not be labeled as reading disabled. He would not receive intensive help with reading because it would be argued, incorrectly, that we should not expect better reading from an individual with this IQ level. Unfortu-nately, children with low IQ scores who show signs of severe reading problems are still called mentally retarded.

A great deal of importance is still given to the IQ score in the definition of a reading disability, or, in fact, any other learning disability. In many schools, colleges, and universities, the intelligence test is one of the pri-mary ones used in the identification of learning disabilities. One of the criteria for the existence of a learning disability is the presence of a discrepancy between IQ test score and achievement. I will argue that the presence of this discrepancy is not a necessary part of the definition of a learning disability and, furthermore, that it is not even necessary to administer an IQ test to determine whether there is a learning disability.

Will the "Real" IQ Please Stand Up?

A key assumption of the proponents of the use of IQ test scores is that intelligence can be measured in the same way as height or weight. However, height is a physical dimension that has a physical reality. Intelligence is not a physical dimension but is a *construct*. There is no yardstick for the real IQ. Independent observers with different rulers would arrive at the same number, within a centimeter, for the height of a person. Independent IQ tests often arrive at quite different numbers for the IQ of a particular individual. There is universal agreement among scientists on what constitutes a millimeter, centimeter, inch, yard, and so on; however, there is a great deal of controversy about the nature of intelligence and how to measure it.

IQ and LD: A Case of Bias

There is an additional problem in the use of IQ tests with individuals who have learning disabilities. IQ tests are quite diverse in the abilities they measure. Some require a great deal of verbal skills and others, reading skills; some require memory, visual spatial skills, and/or fine-motor coordination. It is a logical paradox to use IQ scores with learning-disabled individuals because most of these people are deficient in one or more of the component skills that are part of these IQ tests; therefore, their scores on IQ tests will be an underestimate of their competence. It seems illogical to recognize that a child has deficient memory and/or language and/or fine-motor skills and then say that an individual is less intelligent because he or she has these problems. Of course, IQ tests differ in the skills they measure, but the problem that the individuals with learning disabilities will receive a spuriously low score is characteristic of all of them.

There is another possible bias in the use of IQ tests. I and colleagues have shown that children from lower socioeconomic backgrounds with reading problems have, on the average, lower scores on IQ tests than do children from higher socioeconomic backgrounds who have the same degree of reading problems (Siegel & Himel, in press). Therefore, children from lower socioeconomic backgrounds are more likely to be denied access to services because they have lower IQ scores.

Matthew Effects

Another issue in assessing the validity of the discrepancy definition is the problem of "Matthew effects," as described by Stanovich (1986). The Matthew effect means that individuals who are good readers read more and thus gain vocabulary, knowledge, and language skills and, consequently, obtain higher IQ scores because the IQ test measures all these skills. Poor readers, in contrast, show a decline in vocabulary, language, and knowledge because of fewer opportunities for exposure to print. Stanovich reviews studies to show that IQ scores decrease over time for reading-disabled children. My colleagues and I have shown that the IQ scores of older children with a reading disability are significantly lower than the IQ scores of younger children with the same severity of reading disability (Siegel & Himel, in press). The existence of these Matthew effects is particularly relevant to the discussion of the role of IQ in the measurement of reading disability because the Matthew effects cast doubts on the validity of the IQ measure, particularly for children with reading and other learning problems.

The intelligence test and scores based on it are not useful in the identification of learning disorders. There are both logical reasons for and empirical data to support this statement. It is often argued that we need IQ tests to measure the "potential" of an individual. This type of argument implies that there is some entity that is real that will tell us how far an individual can go, how much he or she can learn, and what we can expect of that child. Presumably, this IQ score is a measure of logical reasoning, problem solving, critical thinking, and whatever we mean by intelligence. This sounds quite reasonable until one examines the content of the IQ test. IQ tests measure factual knowledge, word-meaning recognition, memory, fine-motor coordination, and the fluency of expressive language and do not measure reasoning or problem-solving skills. They measure, for the most part, what a child has learned, not what he or she is capable of doing in the future. Typical items on the IQ test consist of definitions of certain words, questions about geography and history, tasks involving fine-motor coordination such as doing puzzles, memory tasks in which individuals are asked to remember a series of numbers, and mental arithmetic problems for which children must calculate answers without the benefit of paper and pencil. It is obvious that these types of questions measure what a child has learned, not problem-solving or critical thinking skills.

One assumption behind the use of an IQ test is that IQ scores predict and set limits on academic performance. Thus if an individual has a low IQ score, we presumably should not expect much in the way of academic skills. In other words, by using the IQ test in the psychoeducational assessment of possible learning disabilities, we are assuming that the score on the IQ test indicates how much progress in reading, arithmetic, and other areas we can expect from an individual. However, there is some evidence that contradicts this assumption. There are children who have low scores on IQ tests, that is, scores less than 90 or even 80, and yet have average or even above-average scores on reading tests (Siegel, 1988). Logically, this should not occur if the level of reading competency can be determined by IQ scores.

Empirical Evidence

There is also empirical evidence that suggests it is not necessary to use the concept of intelligence in defining reading disabilities. I have conducted studies in which I divided children with reading disabilities into groups based on their IQ level. I then compared these groups on a variety of language, memory, spelling, and phonological tasks (Siegel, 1988b). In spite of wide differences in their IQ levels, there were no differences between the IQ groups on these reading tasks. Thus administering an IQ test would not provide useful information about performance differences on *reading*-related tasks.

One typical use of the IQ test is to measure the discrepancy between IQ and academic achievement. In some systems, if there is a discrepancy, the child is said to have a learning disability. If the child is a poor reader but has no discrepancy between his or her IQ and reading scores, the child is not considered reading disabled. However, I have conducted a study and collected data to show that there is no reason to require that there be a discrepancy between IQ scores and reading scores for the child to be considered learning disabled (Siegel, 1992, 1996).

An assumption of the discrepancy definition is that children who are *dyslexic* and who have a discrepancy between their reading and IQ scores are different from those children who are *poor readers* and who have lower IQ scores and no discrepancy between reading and IQ. I have studied the differences between dyslexics and poor readers on a variety of phonological processing, language, and memory tasks (Siegel, 1996). Although the dyslexics had significantly higher IQ scores than the poor readers, these two groups did not differ in their performance on reading, spelling, phonological processing, and most of the language and memory tasks. There were also no differences in reading comprehension between the dyslexics and poor readers. In all cases, the performance of *both* reading-disabled groups was significantly below that of normal readers. Reading-disabled children, whether or not their reading is significantly below the level predicted by their IQ scores, have significant problems in phonological processing, short-term and working memory, and syntactic awareness. On the basis of these data, there does not seem to be a need to differentiate between dyslexics and poor readers. Both of these groups are *reading disabled* and have deficits in phonological processing, verbal memory, and syntactic awareness. There does not appear to be any empirical evidence to justify the distinction between dyslexics and poor readers.

The Verbal-Performance Discrepancy

One rationale offered for the use of intelligence tests in the assessment of who is learning disabled has been that the patterns of performance on the parts of the IQ test can provide useful information about the learning disability. For example, it is still believed that if an individual has a discrepancy between the verbal scale and the performance scale on the WISC-R, this is a sign of a learning disability. I have never understood the logic of this type of definition. The questions on an IQ test do not directly measure achievement in the areas related to school learning, so it is not clear why scores on an IQ test have anything to tell us about reading, spelling, writing, or arithmetic. My own data of a sample of over 200 children with learning disabilities indicate that approximately 40 percent had no significant discrepancy between their verbal and performance IQ scores and yet were having major problems in school. In addition, 10 percent of children who were having *no* difficulties in school had a significant discrepancy between verbal and performance scores. These relationships clearly show that a verbal-performance discrepancy is *not* a reliable indicator of a learning disability. It is true that many learning-disabled children show patterns of having low scores on the subtests that measure memory or fine-motor performance; however, many children with normal achievement scores and no learning disabilities do also.

Remediation and IQ

One of the arguments given for the use of intelligence tests is that scores on these tests can be used to place the child in the appropriate educational program. The underlying assumption of this approach is that IQ scores predict the child's ability to benefit from a remedial program. In fact, there is not much evidence on this point, but from the little there is, it appears that *IQ scores do not predict the ability to benefit from remediation.*

Studies that have actually *measured* the relation between IQ and the effects of remediation have found that *learning-disabled children with lower scores showed gains from remediation similar to those of children with higher IQ scores* (Arnold, Smeltzer, & Barneby, 1981; Kershner, 1990; Lytton, 1967; van der Wissel & Zegers, 1985). Torgesen, Dahlem, and Greenstein (1987) found that in some cases, gains in reading performance among reading-disabled children were not related to IQ scores but in some cases there was a small but statistically significant relationship. One study (Yule, 1973) even found that "reading backward" children (poor readers) with lower IQ scores made *more* gains than "specifically reading disabled" children (dyslexics) with higher IQ scores.

One of the difficulties with the excessive reliance on psychoeducational testing and the IQ score is that remediation is often neglected. That is, there is no attempt to relate the test scores to what educational methods and strategies might be used to help the individual. People in the field need to encourage the development of specific and detailed assessment of academic skills to give us useful clues about how to provide remediation for individuals with learning problems.

Where We Have Been

I have argued that in the field of learning disabilities, we have traveled along some roads that are dead ends. Excessive assessment and the use of IQ scores are two of these roads. Another is the issue of subtypes. There have been a number of attempts to define subtypes within the field of learning disabilities. These studies often have serious logical and methodological flaws (see Metsala & Siegel, 1992; Morrison & Siegel, 1991; Siegel, Levey, & Ferris, 1985 for an extended discussion of these issues). The three subtypes (or two if we eliminate ADHD) described earlier seem to be as close as possible to the reality of learning disabilities, although there are many individual variations.

What We Can Do to Help Individuals
with Learning Disabilities

There are two general types of methods that can be used in the treatment of learning disabilities. The first involves direct attempts to treat the problems and eliminate the source of the difficulty; the second attempts to find some alternate educational strategies that do not eliminate the problem but provide the child with ways to cope with the problem. In general, the most effective treatment for learning disabilities is teaching strategies to compensate for the problem; direct remediation is sometimes not effective. I will describe the various alternatives for each of the subtypes.

Individuals with a reading disability read slowly and with a great deal of effort; they have difficulty understanding what they have read; they cannot interpret new or long words in the text easily; they cannot remember what they have read; and, most important, they often hate reading. A very useful technique is to provide books on tape so that they can look at the print and hear the words at the same time. This strategy helps build up reading fluency, speed, and basic vocabulary. Of course, these textbooks must be at an appropriate reading level. Another technique appropriate for children is to use high-interest, low-vocabulary books that stimulate their interest in reading but are not so challenging as to make reading impossible. Another technique suitable for young children is the Bridge Reading Program, in which the children learn to associate words and pictures. Gradually, they read simple sentences in books with a combination of words and pictures. Then, they read sentences with only some of the pictures and, finally, with none of them. This technique has proven successful in helping young children who have reading difficulties (Biemiller & Siegel, 1997).

Computers are important for individuals who have learning problems. The computer can help with fine-motor coordination because the skills involved in typing are much simpler than those involved in handwriting. And if handwriting is a serious problem, the computer makes the writing legible. Computers also have software that enables writers to check their spelling. The computer notes words that it cannot find in its dictionary and suggests alternate spellings. This is invaluable for individuals with learning disabilities. For individuals with writing and arithmetic problems, computers are very helpful and can provide important aids to improve writing skills, as demonstrated by Yau, Siegel, and Ziegler (1991). We showed that children who had access to computers improved in the quality and quantity of what they wrote.

Tape recorders are also useful for developing oral skills and allowing the teacher to hear the quality of the child's ideas. Calculators are useful for children who have difficulty with number facts and multiplication tables. It is still necessary that the children learn estimating and problem-solving skills, but the calculator provides an important aid for memory problems.

The Road to the Future

We need to follow three directions simultaneously in order to understand learning disabilities and help those who have faced these problems throughout their life. First, we need to agree on a definition of who is learning disabled. Second, we need to try to understand the strengths and talents of individuals with a learning disability. Third, we need to concentrate our efforts on the early detection of learning problems. I will discuss all of these issues below.

Who Has a Learning Disability?

I have discussed an identification process that is simple and makes conceptual sense. The two cornerstones of this process are objective mea-

surements of achievement (as described previously) and the abandon-
ment of the use of an IQ-achievement discrepancy. The process can be
made simple and cost effective without reliance on excessive testing.

Strengths of Individuals with Learning Disabilities

In my experience, individuals with learning disabilities are extremely talented in one or more of the following areas: music, art, dance, sports,
drama, and mechanical skills. I believe it is very important for the educational system to try to develop these talents and to recognize these abilities when they exist. For example, two very talented individuals, Agatha
Christie (Siegel, 1988) and Yeats (Miner & Siegel, 1992), both showed evidence of significant learning disabilities. Agatha Christie had great difficulties with spelling, arithmetic, handwriting, and learning a foreign language. She in fact changed the titles of two of her books because she did
not know how to spell the words she wanted to include. Yet she had a
vivid imagination and was able to write books that have been translated
into many languages and are known all over the world. Yeats experienced great difficulties in reading, spelling, learning Latin, and memoriz-
ing historical facts. His poor handwriting, spelling, and punctuation
earned him very low grades in composition in school: yet he won the No-
bel Prize for his writing.

People with learning disabilities often experience difficulties with self-
esteem and self-concept and, as they proceed in school, experience more
and more failure. Psychological problems and even antisocial behavior
are often consequences of this low self-esteem. For these reasons it is important to identify learning disabilities early and provide remediation as
soon as possible.

Why We Must Provide Solutions to the Problems of Learning Disabilities

The correct identification of learning disabilities is critical for the health
of our society and individuals. If we fail to identify these individuals and
do not provide the help that is necessary, the results can be disastrous.
We have shown that 82 percent of the homeless youth in Toronto ("street
kids") have learning disabilities (Barwick & Siegel, in press). This star-
tling statistic means that most of these youth did not receive the help
they needed (all had at least a grade 10 education) and had to deal with
the emotional, academic, and social consequences of their learning disabilities. Perhaps this lack of help is one of the reasons they have ended
up homeless and jobless. It is interesting in this regard that the 18 percent
who did not have obvious learning problems were as likely as those who
did to come from backgrounds with social problems, substance abuse,

and sexual and/or physical abuse; so it is difficult to argue that these factors are causally related to learning disabilities. We have also shown, through an analysis of suicide notes, that a significant number of adolescent suicides can be attributed to learning disabilities (McBride & Siegel, 1997). We can prevent many social problems if we identify learning disabilities early, before secondary emotional problems develop. After this, identification, remediation, and the provision of accommodations such as those described earlier are the next steps. We have taken many false steps and followed many paths that have led nowhere. I think we can arrive at our goal to help all individuals with learning disabilities only if we analyze and think logically about the problem and abandon the dogmas and false beliefs that have been part of the field.

References

Arnold, L. E., Smeltzer, D. J., & Barneby, N. S. (1981). Specific perceptual remediation: Effects related to sex, IQ, and parents' occupational status; behavioral change pattern by scale factors; and mechanism of benefit hypothesis tested. *Psychological Reports, 49*, 198.

Bell, L., & Perfetti, C. A. (1989). Reading ability, "reading disability" and garden variety low reading skill: Some adult comparisons. Unpublished manuscript.

Biemiller, A., & Siegel, L. S. (1997). A longitudinal study of the effects of the *Bridge* Reading Program for children at risk for reading failure. *Learning Disabilities Quarterly, 20*, 83–92.

Bloom, A., Wagner, M., Reskin, L., & Bergman, A. (1980). A comparison of intellectually delayed and primary reading disabled children on measures of intelligence and achievement. *Journal of Clinical Psychology, 36*, 788–790.

Cobrinik, L. (1974). Unusual reading disability in severely disturbed children. *Journal of Autism and Childhood Schizophrenia, 4*, 163–175.

Das, J. P., Mensink, D., & Mishra, R. K. (1990). Cognitive processes separating good and poor readers when IQ is covaried. *Learning and Individual Differences, 2*, 423–436.

Ellis, N., & Large, B. (1987). The development of reading: As you seek so shall you find. *British Journal of Psychology, 78*, 1–28.

Fischer, F. W., Liberman, I. Y., & Shankweiler, D. (1977). Reading reversals and developmental dyslexia: A further study. *Cortex, 14*, 496–510.

Fletcher, J. M. (1992). The validity of distinguishing children with language and learning disabilities according to discrepancies with IQ: Introduction to the special series. *Journal of Learning Disabilities, 25*, 546–548.

Francis, D. J., Espy, K. A., Rourke, B. A., & Fletcher, J. M. (1990). Validity of intelligence scores in the definition of learning disability: A critical analysis. In B. P. Rourke (Ed.), *Neuropsychological validation of learning disability subtypes* (pp. 15–44). New York: Guilford.

Friedman, G., & Stevenson, J. (1988). Reading processes in specific reading retarded and reading backward 13 year olds. *British Journal of Developmental Psychology, 6*, 97–108.

Goyette, G. H., Conners, C. K., & Ulrich, R. F. (1978). Normative data on the revised Conners Parent and Teacher Rating Scales. *Journal of Abnormal Child Psychology, 6,* 221–236.

Hall, J. W., Wilson, K. P., Humphreys, M. S., Tinzmann, M. B., & Bowyer, P. M. (1983). Phonetic similarity effects in good vs. poor readers. *Memory and Cognition, 11,* 520–527.

Johnston, R. S., Rugg, M. D., & Scott, T. (1987a). The influence of phonology on good and poor readers when reading for meaning. *Journal of Memory and Language, 26,* 57–68.

Johnston, R. S., Rugg, M. D., & Scott, T. (1987b). Phonological similarity effects, memory span and developmental reading disorders: The nature of the relationship. *British Journal of Psychology, 78,* 205–211.

Johnston, R. S., Rugg, M. D., & Scott, T. (1988). Pseudohomophone effects in 8 and 11 year old good and poor readers. *Journal of Research in Reading, 11,* 110–132.

Jorm, A., Share, D. L., Matthews, R. J., & Maclean, R. (1986). Behaviour problems in specific reading retarded and general reading backward children: A longitudinal study. *Journal of Child Psychology and Psychiatry, 27,* 33–43.

Kershner, J. R. (1990). Self-concept and IQ as predictors of remedial success in children with learning disabilities. *Journal of Learning Disabilities, 23,* 368–374.

Liberman, I. Y., Shankweiler, D., Orlando, C., Harris, K. S., & Berti, F. B. (1971). Letter confusions and reversals of sequence in the beginning reader: Implications for Orton's theory of developmental dyslexia. *Cortex, 7,* 127–142.

Lytton, H. (1967). Follow up of an experiment in selection of remedial education. *British Journal of Educational Psychology, 37,* 1–9.

McBride, H., & Siegel, L. S. (1997). Learning disabilities and adolescent suicide. *Journal of Learning Disabilities, 30,* 652–659.

Merrell, K. W. (1990). Differentiating low achieving students and students with learning disabilities: An examination of performances on the Woodcock-Johnson Psycho-Educational Battery. *Journal of Special Education, 24,* 296–305.

Rack, J. P. (1989, April). Reading-IQ discrepancies and the phonological deficit in reading disability. Paper presented at the biennial meeting of Society for Research in Child Development, Kansas City, MO.

Saloner, M. R., & Gettinger, M. (1985). Social interference skills in learning disabled and nondisabled children. *Psychology in the Schools, 2,* 201–207.

Scarborough, H. S. (1989a). A comparison of methods for identifying reading disabilities in adults. Unpublished manuscript.

Scarborough, H. S. (1989b). Prediction of reading disability from familial and individual differences. *Journal of Educational Psychology, 81,* 101–108.

Seidenberg, M. S., Bruck, M., Fornarolo, G., & Backman, J. (1985). Word recognition processes of poor and disabled readers: Do they necessarily differ? *Applied Psycholinguistics, 6,* 161–180.

Share, D. L., Jorm, A. F., McGee, R., Silva, P. A., Maclean, R., Matthews, R., & Williams, S. (1987). Dyslexia and other myths. Unpublished manuscript.

Siegel, L. S. (1984). A longitudinal study of a hyperlexic child: Hyperlexia as a language disorder. *Neuropsychologia, 22,* 577–585.

Siegel, L. S. (1988a). Evidence that IQ scores are irrelevant to the definition and analysis of reading disability. *Canadian Journal of Psychology, 42,* 202–215.

Siegel, L. S. (1988b). Definitional and theoretical issues and research on learning disabilities. *Journal of Learning Disabilities, 21*, 264–266.

Siegel, L. S. (1989a). IQ is irrelevant to the definition of learning disabilities. *Journal of Learning Disabilities, 22*, 469–478, 486.

Siegel, L. S. (1989b). Why we do not need IQ test scores in the definition and analyses of learning disability. *Journal of Learning Disabilities, 22*, 514–518.

Siegel, L. S. (1990a). IQ and learning disabilities: R.I.P. In H. L. Swanson & B. Keogh (Eds.), *Learning disabilities: Theoretical and research issues*. Hillsdale, NJ: Erlbaum.

Siegel, L. S. (1990b). Siegel's reply. [Letter to the editor]. *Journal of Learning Disabilities, 23*, 268–269, 319.

Siegel, L. S. (1991). The identification of learning disabilities: Issues in psychoeducational assessment. *Education and Law Journal, 3*, 301–313.

Siegel, L. S. (1992). An evaluation of the discrepancy definition of dyslexia. *Journal of Learning Disabilities, 25*, 618–629.

Siegel, L. S. (1993a). Alice in IQ land or why IQ is still irrelevant to learning disabilities. In R. M. Joshi and C. K. Leong (Eds.), *Reading disabilities: Diagnosis and component processes* (pp. 71–84). Dordrecht, Netherlands: Kluwer.

Siegel, L. S. (1993b). Phonological processing deficits as the basis of a reading disability. *Developmental Review, 13*, 246–257.

Siegel, L. S. (1994a). The modularity of reading and spelling: Evidence from Hyperlexia. In G. D. A. Brown & N. C. Ellis (Eds.), *Handbook of Spelling: Theory, process and intervention* (pp. 227–248). Sussex, UK: John Wiley.

Siegel, L. S. (1994b). Phonological processing deficits as the basis of developmental dyslexia: Implications for remediation. In M. J. Riddoch & G. W. Humphreys (Eds.), *Cognitive neuropsychology and cognitive rehabilitation* (pp. 379–400). Hove, UK: Erlbaum.

Siegel, L. S., & Heaven, R. K. (1986). Categorization of learning disabilities. In S. J. Ceci (Ed.), *Handbook of cognitive, social and neuropsychological aspects of learning disabilities* (Vol. 2, pp. 95–121). Hillsdale, NJ: Erlbaum.

Siegel, L. S., & Himel, N. (in press). Socioeconomic status, age and the classification of dyslexic and poor readers: Further evidence of the irrelevancy of IQ to reading disability. *Dyslexia*.

Siegel, L. S., & Ryan, E. B. (1988). Development of grammatical sensitivity, phonological, and short-term memory skills in normally achieving and learning disabled children. *Developmental Psychology, 24*, 28–37.

Siegel, L. S., & Ryan, E. B. (1989a). The development of working memory in normally achieving and subtypes of learning disabled children. *Child Development, 60*, 973–980.

Siegel, L. S., & Ryan, E. B. (1989b). Subtypes of developmental dyslexia: The influence of definitional variables. *Reading and Writing: An Interdisciplinary Journal, 1*, 257–287.

Silva, P. A., McGee, R., & Williams, S. (1985). Some characteristics of 9-year old boys with general reading backwardness or specific reading retardation. *Journal of Child Psychology and Psychiatry, 26*, 407–421.

Stanovich, K. E. (1986). Matthew effects in reading: Some consequences of individual differences in the acquisition of literacy. *Reading Research Quarterly, 21,* 360–407.

Stanovich, K. E. (1988a). Explaining the differences between the dyslexic and garden variety poor reader: The phonological-core variance-difference model. *Journal of Learning Disabilities, 21,* 590–604, 612.

Stanovich, K. E. (1988b). The right and wrong places to look for the cognitive locus of reading disability. *Annals of Dyslexia, 38,* 154–177.

Stanovich, K. E. (1991). Discrepancy definitions of reading disability: Has intelligence led us astray? *Reading Research Quarterly, 26,* 1–29.

Tal, N. F., Siegel, L. S., & Maraun, M. (1994). Reading comprehension: The role of question type and reading ability. *Reading and Writing: An Interdisciplinary Journal, 6,* 387–402.

Taylor, H. G., Satz, P., & Friel, J. (1979). Developmental dyslexia in relation to other childhood reading disorders: Significance and clinical utility. *Reading Research Quarterly, 15,* 84–101.

Torgesen, J. K., Dahlem, W. E., & Greenstein, J. (1987). Using verbatim text recordings to enhance reading comprehension in learning disabled adolescents. *Learning Disabilities Focus, 3,* 30–38.

Toth, G., & Siegel, L. S. (1994) A critical evaluation of the IQ-achievement discrepancy based definition of dyslexia. In K. P. van den Bos, L. S. Siegel, D. J. Bakker, & D. L. Share (Eds.), *Current directions in dyslexia research* (pp. 45–70). Lisse, Netherlands: Swets & Zeitlinger.

van der Wissel, A., & Zegers, F. E. (1985). Reading retardation revisited. *British Journal of Developmental Psychology, 3,* 3–9.

Yau, M., Siegel, L. S., & Ziegler, S. (1991). Laptop computers and the learning disabled student. *ERS Spectrum, 9,* 22–30.

Yule, W. (1973). Differential prognosis of reading backwardness and specific reading retardation. *British Journal of Educational Psychology, 43,* 244–248.

8

Developing Reading Fluency in Learning-Disabled Students

S. Jay Samuels

In this chapter I focus on the identification and remediation of a difficulty commonly encountered by learning-disabled students as they learn to read. The difficulty to which I refer is the lack of reading fluency—or automaticity. Without automaticity students find that although it is possible to comprehend a text, doing so requires so much effort that reading becomes a most unpleasant experience. Although lack of automaticity is experienced by most students with a learning disability, it is a problem that can be overcome. In this chapter I present specific techniques that teachers can easily use to determine if students are decoding text automatically and also suggest a variety of techniques for developing this skill.

For present purposes, we can think of a learning disability as a disorder that hampers learning in a specific domain such as reading. According to Eggen and Kauchak (1997, p. 164), learning-disabled students are characterized by their lack of reading fluency.

The following scenario, which accurately describes the lack of fluency experienced by learning-disabled students, was reported by an inner-city St. Paul teacher who had taken a cognitive psychology course with me that included material on automaticity theory. This teacher was trying to understand why one of her third-grade students had such a low score on the reading portion of the Metropolitan Achievement Test, a test that her school district uses to assess districtwide academic achievement. The test was given early in fall about a month after the students had returned from vacation. During classroom discussions, the student who had scored poorly on the reading test showed himself to be an eager participant, and what he had to say during discussions indicated that he had considerable general knowledge. He seemed highly motivated to do well and attended school regularly.

In order to understand the nature of the student's problem, the teacher administered several informal tests that she had learned about in my course. When she asked the student to read orally from an easy passage, she discovered that his reading rate was slow; there were many errors in word recognition; and, most telling, there was a lack of expression in his voice. After the student had read the passage orally, the teacher asked him to explain what it was about, but he had difficulty recalling what he had read. Next, she asked him to listen while she read the passage to him. Again, she asked him to recall the passage; this time he did much better in his comprehension and recall. This simple diagnostic reading test provided the teacher with several good clues as to why the student had done so poorly on the standardized reading test. At least part of the problem seemed attributable to a lack of automatic decoding skills when reading. The student was then referred to a school psychologist, who diagnosed the student as having a learning disability.

The Extent to Which a Reading Disability Can Be Remediated

Is a learning disability a "kiss of death," a handicapping condition of such grave magnitude that the barriers to learning to read are insurmountable? The answer to this question is no! Even though the learning-to-read process may be hard at first for learning-disabled students, with good instruction, opportunities for practice, and sufficient motivation, they can learn to read well. For example, Fink (1996) interviewed prominent adults who had been diagnosed as dyslexic youngsters; as seen in Table 8.1, all of them became eminent in their chosen fields.

Fink's interview data revealed some factors that were important in helping them to overcome their handicaps. These same factors should be considered by parents and educators who want to help learning-disabled students become good readers. The successful dyslexics had not as children tried to circumvent reading as a way to learn. Although it took them longer to develop fluency skills, they persisted, and this persistence led to the practice they needed to develop automatic decoding skills.

Fink (1996) notes that although many of the successful dyslexics she interviewed continued to have difficulty with lower-level decoding skills such as letter identification and phonics, "they eventually developed basic fluency." What the successful dyslexics seemed to share as children was a passionate interest in a topic they pursued through reading. This intense reading about a favorite subject enhanced their depth of background knowledge and, at the same time, enabled them to gain practice, which fostered fluency. "By reading in depth about a single domain of knowledge, each became a virtual 'little expert' about a subject" (p. 275).

TABLE 8.1   Dyslexic Students Who Overcame Their Reading Difficulties

Profession	Names
Attorney	Amy Symons, assistant state attorney, Dade County, FL
Biochemist	Ronald Davis, National Academy of Sciences, Stanford University Medical School
Businessman	Joe Jones, CEO, Jones Company, Salem, MA
Gynecologist	Robert Knapp, Harvard Medical School, Boston, MA
Immunologist (Nobel Prize)	Baruj Benacerraf, Harvard Medical School
Neurologist	Charles Bean, Jefferson Hospital, Philadelphia, PA
Physicist	James Bensinger, Brandeis University, Waltham, MA
Special Educator	Charles Drake, director, Landmark School, Prides Crossing, MA

Fink's observations (1996) fit nicely with what is known about automaticity theory and decoding fluency. Even the most advanced "normal" reader does not automatically decode all printed words, only those that have been identified previously. The high-frequency words, those that have been seen in print over and over again, involve the highest rate of automaticity.

Stanovich (1986) has written about Matthew effects in reading: Students who read a lot get better and better and those who seldom read get worse and worse. Fink (1996) acknowledges that the redundant text in discipline-specific texts may provide the necessary drill and practice required to develop basic automaticity skills for a large corpus of words.

My own research at the University of Minnesota on the development of automaticity has shown that virtually all students reach the automatic stage if they persist long enough. Development of automaticity is an individual-difference variable, but the variability shows up in the amount of time and practice required to attain automaticity and not in whether one attains this level of skill. Assume, for example, that learning how to recognize words automatically is a complex skill that can be separated into two stages: the accuracy stage and the automatic stage. During the first, the student can recognize printed words but must apply considerable attention and effort. At the automatic stage, not only is the student accurate but very little cognitive effort or attention is required in order to recognize words.

Students differ greatly in the amount of time and practice required to reach the accuracy stage. With repeated practice at reading, they go beyond accuracy to automaticity. Again, the amount of time and practice needed to attain automaticity varies, but eventually, all students become competent at automatically recognizing printed words. At least with regard to this important reading skill, students seem to be more alike than different. Once the automaticity stage in word recognition is reached, learning-disabled and nonhandicapped students are alike in that they can recognize the printed words with accuracy, speed, and little effort. If learning-disabled students have the drive and motivation to persist and have good instruction and opportunities to practice, almost all of them can become fluent, automatic readers.

One of the best predictors of which learning-disabled students will become fluent readers is the socioeconomic status of the family (Rawson, 1968). In general, learning-disabled students from high-socioeconomic-status families seem to be more successful in overcoming their handicaps than students from lower-socioeconomic-status families, primarily because upper-class families highly value education and have the resources to pay for the extra tutoring and instructional help needed by learning-disabled students.

A Definition and Example of Automaticity

The general notion that practice is one of the essential prerequisites for skilled performance is certainly not a new idea. This principle was expressed in William James's (1890) *Principles of Psychology*: "If an act became no easier after being done several times, if the careful direction of consciousness were necessary to its accomplishment on each occasion, it is evident that the whole activity of a lifetime might be confined to one or two deeds—that no progress could take place in development" (p. 37).

In Huey's (1908) classic book *The Psychology and Pedagogy of Reading*, now considered to be one of the early precursors to modern cognitive psychology, we can find similar ideas:

> Perceiving being an act, it is, like all other things that we do, performed more easily with each repetition of the act. To perceive an entirely new word or other combination of strokes requires considerable time, close attention, and is likely to be imperfectly done, just as when we attempt some new combination of movements, some new trick in the gymnasium or new serve at tennis. In either case, repetition progressively frees the mind from attention to details, makes facile the total act, shortens the time, and reduces the extent to which consciousness must concern itself with the process. (p. 104)

Two more recent publications have directed attention to the importance of automaticity. A LaBerge and Samuels (1974) article explained from a theoretical position why automatic decoding was an essential prerequisite for fluent reading, and Bloom's (1986) analysis of highly skilled performance in reading, writing, and mathematics detailed how the automization of the lower-order subskills made possible the higher-order thinking required in these subjects. What James (1890), Huey (1908), LaBerge and Samuels (1974), and Bloom (1986) suggest in their writings is that *automaticity may be defined as the ability to perform complex skills with minimal attention to the task and with minimal effort.*

Now that automaticity has been defined as the ability to execute complex processes with little attention, an example of automaticity in everyday life would be helpful. Driving an automobile is a complex act that is an important part of life in this country. There are so many tasks in driving that must be performed quickly and accurately and all at the same time. First, there are the simple mechanics of driving the car, getting it to move, turn, and stop. In addition, there is the job of monitoring the traffic, stoplights, sideroads, pedestrians, road signs, and advertising, and on top of all this, the driver often listens to news on the car radio or is involved in conversation with a passenger or is thinking about topics unrelated to the driving task. Performing all these tasks at the same time is possible only after a certain level of automaticity is reached.

As a person who has done research on automaticity for many years, I am continually impressed by how many complex skills can get done simultaneously once some of the tasks become automatized to the point where little attention and effort are needed.

Two decades ago, when LaBerge and Samuels (1974) published their theoretical article on automatic information processing in reading, automaticity was seen as playing a role only in decoding, but in the intervening years the role of automaticity in reading has been extended. Automaticity has been shown to be vital in a variety of comprehension subprocesses such as generating essential inferences while reading (Thurlow and Van den Broek, 1997) and gaining automatic access to the meanings of words after they have been identified (Samuels and Naslund, 1994; Naslund and Samuels, 1992). The Samuels and Naslund article explains in detail how the combination of slowness and lack of automaticity in gaining access to word meanings acts as a contributing factor in the comprehension problems of learning-disabled children.

Let me take a moment to explain how the speed and automaticity of accessing word meanings is a factor in reading comprehension. Imagine a situation in which gaining access to word meaning requires three steps. In step one, the person decodes the word. In step two, using a mental dictionary, the person locates the word and its meaning. Since many words contain multiple meanings (i.e., are polysemous), step three requires selecting the correct word meaning for the context in which the word is found. Each of the three steps requires time and cognitive resources for its execution. If selecting word meaning is slow and consumes a disproportionate share of cognitive resources, it will have a dampening effect on all of the reading process (Samuels and Naslund, 1994).

Why Automaticity Is an Important Requirement for Skilled Reading

Regardless of how one prefers to teach reading, whether by using a whole-language, skills-based, or an eclectic approach, virtually everyone agrees that the purpose of reading is to comprehend the information printed on the page. However, there is a vast difference in the strategies used to construct meaning when one compares beginning and fluent readers.

Every act of reading requires decoding the words printed in the text, comprehending what has been decoded, and paying attention. By decoding I mean that when the words are seen on the page, the student can pronounce the words either out loud or silently. Another reading-related process is comprehension. In order to comprehend the decoded material, the student must access word meanings and construct a message using information from the page as well as from the student's own personal knowledge and experience.

The third element necessary for reading is attention. Attention may be thought of as the cognitive energy or effort required to perform tasks such as decoding or comprehending. Both decoding and comprehension are difficult, especially for beginning readers, and require considerable attention for their proper execution. Unfortunately, the amount of attention is limited. If the demands of decoding and comprehension exceed the attention capacity of the individual, a strategy must be employed. Beginning readers' skills at decoding the material printed on the page are so limited that decoding demands may exceed their attention capacity. Hence they cannot decode and comprehend at the same time. Consequently, they use a clever divide-and-conquer strategy in order to understand what is on the page. First they direct attention to the words in order to decode the material because that is all that can be done with the limited supply of attention available. Then, holding the decoded material in short-term memory, they direct attention to the comprehension process. By switching attention back and forth from decoding to comprehension, they are able to understand what is printed on the page; but this switching takes great effort and places a heavy load on memory.

Samuels, LaBerge, and Bremer (1978) have demonstrated that the unit of word recognition for beginning compared to experienced readers is quite different. For beginning readers the size of the unit of recognition is the letter, a unit that most of the time has no meaning. For skilled readers the unit is the entire word, a unit that has meaning. These units have to be held in short-term memory long enough to construct a meaning for the text. No wonder beginning readers and learning-disabled children find the learning-to-read stage a difficult period. With practice at reading, the picture changes dramatically.

Largely due to extended practice in reading, skilled readers can decode automatically. In line with the definition of automaticity given earlier, they can decode with little attention and effort. They have sufficient attention and cognitive resources available to handle both the decoding and the comprehension processes at the same time. Students who decode automatically may find the reading task easier simply because there is less load on memory and what is put into short-term memory is meaningful.

In order to understand the reading problems students encounter, it is important to recognize the student's reading stage (Spear-Swerling & Sternberg, 1994). Some students may be able to decode words accurately but not automatically. Lack of automaticity in decoding creates a problem with comprehension. Other students may decode both accurately and automatically. These students may also have comprehension difficulties, but the cause will be other than a decoding difficulty, for example, a lack of proper background knowledge of a text topic. Thus for diagnostic purposes, it is important to distinguish between the beginning and fluency stages in reading development.

Characteristics of Automatic and
Nonautomatic Performances

In order to understand the development of complex skills such as those involved in reading, as a convenience we can separate the learning into stages. The beginning stage can be thought of as "controlled" and the final stage as "automatic" (Shiffrin & Schneider, 1977; Schneider & Shiffrin, 1977). Controlled processing of a text is slow, requires considerable effort and attention, and is performed at the conscious level. The controlled stage in reading is much like the stage in beginning driving when one must direct behavior with thoughts such as "now the key, now the clutch, release clutch, and more gas." At the automatic level performance is fast, accurate, seemingly effortless, and not under conscious control. Posner and Snyder (1975) have noted that automatic performance usually occurs without intention or awareness, and since it occurs unconsciously, it is difficult to suppress or modify.

At this point we can extend the definition of automaticity by stating that in contrast to the beginning stage, the automatic stage involves all of the tasks being done simultaneously. The principle remains the same in many fields of endeavor. In complex activities such as driving a car, reading a text, writing a letter at a computer, and reading music and playing it with feeling, the many subprocesses involved occur simultaneously after they have each become automatic.

Advantages and Disadvantages of Automaticity

In summary, there are some impressive reasons that skills should be developed to the automatic level:

- Tasks learned to the automatic level are usually executed with speed, accuracy, and minimal effort.
- When a skill is automatic, sufficient attention is available to simultaneously perform other tasks.
- Skills learned to the automatic level are often retained for a lifetime and are highly resistant to memory loss.

Unfortunately, automaticity has some negative effects:

- Automatic skills are often difficult to control, suppress, or modify. For example, because skilled readers read automatically, when driving they often find themselves reading billboards rather than paying attention to traffic conditions. Or a teacher may habitually scold students who use disruptive behavior to get attention even though she knows that scolding reinforces the very behavior she wants to discourage. The classic example of how hard it is to modify an automatic response comes from the Stroop color-word test. In this test GREEN, for example, is printed in blue and the word BLUE is printed in green. Instructions to a person might be "Ignore the printed word, just name the color." There is so much response competition between the automatic reading of the printed words and the naming of the colors that good readers find this to be a very difficult task. What is most interesting is that poor readers who do not recognize words automatically find this to be an easy task. In fact, the Stroop color-word test can be used as an indicator to determine if a student recognizes words automatically.
- Usually, automaticity is developed during a long period of practice. But even though we may have attained automaticity with words or spelling patterns we have seen frequently, those we have not had much experience with can still slow us down. When we encounter such patterns we often resort to decoding

strategies used by nonautomatic readers because it takes less time to be accurate than to attain automaticity. Although Logan (1997) has some cogent arguments to support his contention that automaticity may develop rather quickly under special conditions, in general we may say that a considerable amount of time, effort, and practice must be expended to perform a complex task automatically.

- Often one forgets the separate skills that had to be mastered in order to reach the automatic stage. For example, after long training an expert pediatric cardiologist may be able to listen to an infant's heartbeat and determine if there is a malfunctioning valve. She may, however, have difficulty explaining the separate telltale indicators to medical students. Similarly, reading-instruction experts, who have reached automaticity in word recognition and comprehension, find that delineating the essential reading skills and the sequence in which they should be introduced is a most difficult task, one that has contributed to what we call "the reading pedagogy wars." As stated earlier, the task of determining what skills have to be learned to attain automaticity is so difficult that it has taken two decades for the "experts" to realize that automatic processes are involved in comprehension as well as in word recognition. Some of the skills we use in comprehension are so automatic that we are unaware that they even exist, that we are using them, and that the skills may be teachable.

Diagnostic Indicators of Automaticity in Word Recognition

Fortunately for the medical profession, numerous techniques exist for assessing people's health, ranging from thermometers and blood pressure cuffs at the low-technology end to MRIs and computer-assisted echocardiograms at the other end. Compared to the medical profession, education has few reliable and valid diagnostic procedures. Some years ago, I was a consultant on a project to establish techniques for diagnosing and remediating reading problems. One of the investigators had just successfully finished a project in which he had developed a computer program that could identify heart sounds indicating a malfunctioning heart. He planned to apply the same approaches and strategies that were successful in the medical field to reading diagnosis. The first step required that so-called reading experts be given simulated case studies of kids with reading problems. The experts were supposed to diagnose each case and recommend remediation. Two severe problems arose immediately and stopped the project. First, there was such low inter-rater reliability that the investigator was hard pressed to know which diagnosis and suggested remediation of the probable cause of the reading difficulty was correct. Second, when the same case reappeared in a somewhat different form, there was also low intra-rater reliability. It would be interesting to repeat that procedure again to see how much progress, if any, has been made in the intervening years.

Although there are no formal standardized tests of automaticity, fortunately there are a number of informal and easy-to-use procedures that can help teachers decide if a student recognizes words automatically. One I recommend to teachers is to select three reading passages at the student's estimated reading level. These passages should be unfamiliar to the student, of the same approximate length, and the same level of reading difficulty. The length of the passages can be as short as a half-page or as long as several pages depending on the student's ability to read. One of the passages is for silent reading; one is for oral reading; and the third, not read by the student but by the teacher, is for listening comprehension. For the silent- and the oral-reading passages the student should not be allowed to preread or practice the passage. Remember, this is a testing situation and not a teaching situation. The goal is to ascertain if the student processes words automatically, and practice will alter the results. We have found that even college students may be unable to decode automatically.

On the text used for silent reading, the instructions would be, "Read this silently to yourself just one time. As soon as you are finished reading, tell me everything that you can remember." On the text used for oral reading, the instructions are, "Read this out loud to me. As soon as you are done I want you to tell me everything that you can remember." For both passages the teacher should use the comprehension-recall protocol to observe the degree to which the student can understand and recall the text information. If the student omits passage details in the recall, the teacher can ask questions. For the oral reading test the teacher should record the following additional information: oral word-recognition errors, word-per-minute reading rate, estimate of oral expression, and student's comprehension. If possible, a tape recorder inconspicuously placed can be used for recording the student's oral reading and recall of the three texts.

For the test of listening comprehension, the instructions are, "I am going to read to you. I want you to listen carefully because when I am done I want you to tell me as much as you can remember of what I read to you." These three informal tests will provide the teacher with a wealth of information that can be used for diagnostic purposes.

The rationale for the oral-reading test is that it demands simultaneous decoding and comprehension. Thus only students who decode automatically will have good recall and read with expression. The latter is one of the best indicators of automaticity in decoding. It is most interesting that students who read a text for the first time with no expression often read the same text expressively after they have reread it several times, a technique known in the field simply as "repeated reading" (Samuels, 1979). The word-recognition and reading-speed scores provide additional evidence of automaticity. The silent-reading passage is included because automatic behaviors such as reading can be disrupted if the conditions of testing are different from the conditions under which the skill is usually practiced. For example, after the third grade, there is little oral reading; most of the training a student gets is in reading silently. When we ask a student who normally silent reads automatically to read orally for a test, the task requirements may be sufficiently unfamiliar that the performance is compromised. We see similar loss of automaticity when a student who has practiced a speech to perfection in his room discovers that his speech is poorly presented when given in a strange auditorium to an unfamiliar audience. Athletic coaches are familiar with the loss of automatic skills when they have to be performed under stressful conditions in locations unfamiliar to the athletes. In order to help athletes perform their best, coaches give them a few days to practice in their new surroundings (Logan, 1997).

Generally, an oral-reading word-recognition error rate of more than 10 percent indicates the student is probably at the accuracy stage. If the comprehension-recall score is much greater for the listening-comprehension text than for the other two, decoding the text likely has interfered with comprehension. When the requirement to read and decode at the same time leads to a decrement in comprehension, we have another indicator that the student is not automatic at decoding.

Remediating Word-Recognition Problems
Associated with Lack of Automaticity

Following several basic rules will help students develop reading skills to the automaticity level of decoding:

- Students must have knowledge of phonics, that is, know how to sound out words, in order to be at least accurate at word recognition.
- Accuracy in word recognition is a necessary condition for fluent reading, but it is not enough. In order to become fluent readers, students must go beyond accuracy to automaticity—and this requires lots of reading.
- Building self-esteem and motivation is important in keeping students on task. Books that are of interest to students and at

their reading level encourage the practice needed for both
accuracy and automaticity.

Now for some additional suggestions. Ask your students how one ex-
cels at any sport, such as basketball, skiing, wrestling, or at playing a mu-
sical instrument such as the piano. They will all acknowledge that the
route to competence is practice. Students should know that the same
principles work in becoming good readers. A few students will acquire
the rudiments of automaticity by the end of first grade; those who have
difficulty learning to read may not acquire this level of skill until the
fourth or fifth grade. With good instruction and lots of practice, automaticity in decoding is a reasonable goal.

Encourage students to read more by choosing books that interest them
for recreational reading on their own. Don't ask for book reports on their
independent reading; this acts only as a disincentive. Incentive systems
as simple as a gold star or a check after their names for each book read
can also be used as encouragement.

A simple, effective technique for developing automaticity in word
recognition has been recognized in nearly 100 published reports by researchers in the reading field. This method, as mentioned earlier, is
known as "repeated reading." It was developed by Samuels (1979) as a
practical application of automaticity theory. Although it has become the
most universally used method of remedial reading instruction, it has one
drawback: Reading rates and word-recognition errors are put on charts,
and thus the technique is labor intensive and usually requires adult help.
We need a simple method that captures the advantages of repeated reading as it is usually practiced in remedial reading pull-out programs. The
goal is to have students, either alone or in pairs, do their own repeated
reading, leaving the teacher or teaching aid free to do other things. Of
course, students will need some instruction on how to use the method,
but in time they should be able to work independently. This approach is
what Singer and Donlan (1989) called "phase out the teacher and phase
in the learner."

In another approach to repeated reading, the student reads a passage
three to four times and then moves on to the next portion of the text. No
charting of reading speed or errors is done. The independent repeated
reading can be done with audio assist: The student listens to someone
read the passage out loud and then practices rereading the passage on his
own several times. The rereading can be done alone or in pairs, one student listening while the other reads out loud, followed by reversal of
roles.

One final recommendation is in order. Recall Fink's (1996) study, mentioned in the beginning section of this chapter, of successful adults who

were diagnosed as having dyslexia as children. These children continued to read despite the difficulty they were having, and through perseverance, they overcame their handicaps. At present, educational practice runs counter to Fink's findings. Modifications are often made in the instruction for remedial and special education students so that they get their information verbally rather than through reading. Consequently, they read less and less and slip behind in reading with each passing year. These students should be encouraged to read more as a way to overcome their handicaps.

Summary

The ability to recognize words automatically is an important prerequisite for the reading tasks one faces as an adult because it allows the student to decode and comprehend the text simultaneously, thus reducing memory load and the effort required for reading. Two routes to automaticity in decoding are to practice reading easy texts and to use a modified form of repeated reading. Students who have a learning disability often experience difficulty learning to read with some degree of automaticity. This handicap can be overcome with proper motivation, instruction in word-recognition skills, and extended opportunities to practice reading.

References

Bloom, B. S. (1986). Automaticity: The hands and feet of genius. *Educational Leadership, 70–77.*

Eggen, P., and Kauchak, D. (1997). *Educational Psychology: Windows on Classrooms* (3rd. Ed.). Upper Saddle River, NJ: Prentice Hall.

Fink, R. P. (1996). Successful dyslexics: A constructivist study of passionate interest in reading. *Journal of Adolescent and Adult Literacy, 39*(4), 268–280.

Huey, E.B. (1908). *The Psychology and Pedagogy of Reading.* Cambridge, MA: Macmillan; Reprinted by M.I.T. Press, 1968.

James, W. (1890). *The Principles of Psychology.* New York: Holt.

Logan, D. (1997). Automaticity and Reading: Perspectives from the instance theory of automatization. *Reading and Writing Quarterly: Overcoming Learning Difficulties 13,* 2, 123–146.

Naslund, J., and Samuels (1992). Automatic access to word sounds and meaning in decoding written text. *Reading and Writing Quarterly: Overcoming Learning Difficulties, 2,* 135–156.

Posner, M. I., & Snyder, C. R. R. (1975). Attention and cognitive control. In R. L. Solso, (Ed.), *Information processing and cognition: The Loyola Symposium.* Hillsdale, NJ: Erlbaum.

Rawson, M. B. (1968). *Developmental Language Disabilities: Adult Accomplishments of Dyslexic Boys.* Baltimore: Johns Hopkins Press.

Samuels, S. J. (1979). The method of repeated reading. *The Reading Teacher, 39,* 403–408.

Samuels, S. J., LaBerge, D., and Bremer, C. (1978). Units of word recognition: Evidence for developmental changes. *Journal of Verbal Learning and Verbal Behavior,* 17, 715–720.

Samuels, S. J. and Naslund, J. (1994). Individual differences in reading: The case for lexical access. *Reading and Writing Quarterly: Overcoming Learning Difficulties, 4,* 285–296.

Schneider, W., & Shiffrin, R. M. (1977). Controlled and automatic human information processing: I. Detection, search, and attention. *Psychological Review, 84,* 1–66.

Shiffrin, R. M., & Schneider, W. (1977). Controlled and automatic human information processing: II. Perceptual learning, automatic attending, and a general theory. *Psychological Review, 84*(2), 127–190.

Singer, H., and Donlan, D. (1989). *Reading and Learning from Text.* Hillsdale, NJ: Lawrence Erlbaum Associates.

Spear-Swerling, L., & Sternberg, R. J. (1994). The road not taken: An integrative theoretical model of reading disability. *Journal of Learning Disabilities, 27*(2) 91–103.

Stanovich, K. E. (1986). Matthew effects in reading: Some consequences of individual differences in the acquisition of literacy. *Reading Research Quarterly, 21,* 360–406.

Thurlow, R., and Van den Broek, P. (1997). Automaticity and inference generation during reading comprehension. *Reading and Writing Quarterly: Overcoming Learning Difficulties, 13*(2), 165–184.

PART THREE

Contextual Approaches

9

Learning Disabilities as Organizational Pathologies

Thomas M. Skrtic

The common view of organizations is that they are merely social tools, mechanisms that societies use to achieve goals that are beyond the reach of individual citizens (Parsons, 1960). But organizations do more than achieve social goals: The nature and needs of organizations shape the very goals that society uses them to achieve (Allison, 1971; Scott, 1981). For example, although we seek "health" when we visit the hospital, what we get is "medical care." We are encouraged to see these outcomes as synonymous, of course, but there may be no relation between them, or the relation may be negative; more medical care can result in less health (Illich, 1976). Like health, education is a social goal that is shaped by the medium of an organization; society wants "education," but what it gets is a particular kind of "schooling," one that, for good or ill, is shaped by the type of organization that is used to provide it.

In this chapter I consider the kind of schooling that conventional school organizations provide and, based on this analysis, reconceptualize the nature, diagnosis, and treatment of learning disabilities from an organizational perspective. As the title indicates, my main contention is that learning disabilities are best thought of as organizational pathologies rather than as intrinsic human pathologies. By making this assertion, I am not denying that there are students who have what are known as learning disabilities or that in many cases learning disabilities are caused by a pathological condition known generally as central nervous system dysfunction. Rather, I am arguing that the very notion of pathology has outlived its usefulness in the field of special education and that learning disabilities professionals and advocates should drop it as a guide to practice and advocacy.

In the first section I trace the pathological view of learning disabilities to the theories and assumptions that have shaped and legitimized the field of special education in the twentieth century. Then I present a structural analysis of the kind of schooling that conventional school organizations provide. In the third section I use this analysis to reconsider the validity and utility of special education's grounding assumptions from an organizational perspective. As part of my structural analysis of conventional school organizations I also introduce an alternative structure for schools, one that in the fourth section I claim not only makes education more effective and equitable for all students but turns learning disabilities into an asset rather than a liability for school organizations and public education as a whole. In the concluding section I justify this alternative structure by showing how it makes possible the kind of schooling that is needed for the emerging economic and political conditions of the twenty-first century. My aim is to persuade special education professionals and learning disabilities advocates to shift their focus from reforming conventional school organizations (including the special education system) to replacing them with this alternative form. Such an undertaking, I contend, should emphasize political and economic arguments for educational excellence over moral arguments for educational equity.

Special Education's Grounding Assumptions

Professional practices (what professionals do) and discourses (what they think, say, read, and write about what they do) are grounded in a network of anonymous, historically situated assumptions that organize and give meaning to professional thought and action (Cherryholmes, 1988; Kuhn, 1970). The assumptions are anonymous because they are premised on largely unquestioned theories; they are historically situated, rather than universal or context free, because they are human constructions, temporarily valid and useful products of a particular time and place (see further on). Ultimately, I want to question the validity and utility of the assumptions that ground special education practices and discourses by considering them and the very notion of student disability from an organizational perspective. In this section I introduce these assumptions and the theories upon which they are premised, paying particular attention to the way they have shaped the conventional understanding of learning disabilities.

According to a number of authors (Bogdan & Kugelmass, 1984; Mercer, 1973; Rist & Harrell, 1982; Skrtic, 1986, 1991a; Tomlinson, 1982), special education practices and discourses are grounded in the following assumptions.

1. Student disability is a pathological condition.
2. Diagnosis of student disability is objective and useful to students so identified.
3. Special education is a rationally conceived and coordinated system of services that benefits diagnosed students.
4. Progress in special education is a rational-technical undertaking, an evolutionary process of incrementally improving conventional models and practices.

The first two assumptions have two theoretical sources. The first is the historical dominance of biological theories of human pathology (from medicine) in the field of special education (Bogdan & Knoll, 1988; Mercer, 1973), a situation that certainly holds for the area of learning disabilities (see Kavale & Forness, 1985a; Rist & Harrell, 1982). Virtually all definitions of learning disabilities identify the cause of the problem as an intrinsic human pathology (Torgesen, 1986), and this is so largely because of the dominant role played by the medical profession in the development of the field of learning disabilities both historically (Hallahan & Cruickshank, 1973; Wiederholt, 1974) and today (Lerner, 1988). The second source is the confounding of biological theories of pathology from medicine and behavioral theories of deviance from psychology (Mercer, 1973; Skrtic, 1986), which occurred first in the field of mental retardation and then later in that of learning disabilities.

As Mercer (1973) explained with regard to the confounding of these theories in the field of mental retardation, the pathological model is bipolar and evaluative. It defines normal and abnormal according to observable biological processes; those that interfere with life are "bad" (pathology) and those that enhance it are "good" (health). The behavioral or statistical model from psychology defines deviance in terms of variance from a population mean. It is evaluatively neutral; whether being above or below average on a particular attribute is good or bad depends on a social definition. According to Mercer, both models are used to define mental retardation—the pathological model for assessing biological symptoms and the statistical model for assessing behavioral manifestations, which are not comprehensible under the pathological model. Although some forms of mental retardation are associated with observable patterns of biological symptoms (i.e., syndromes) and thus are comprehensible under the pathological model, the vast majority of individuals labeled mentally retarded show no biological signs. In these instances, a low score on an intelligence (IQ) test is accepted as a symptom of pathology, a conceptual transposition that turns behavioral patterns into pathological signs.

The implicit logic that underlies this transformation is as follows: Low IQ = "bad" in American society: a social evaluation. "Bad" = pathology in the pathological model. Therefore, low IQ = pathology. Thus, IQ, which is not a biological manifestation but is a behavioral score based on responses to a series of questions, becomes conceptually transposed into a pathological sign carrying all of the implications of the pathological model. (1973, pp. 5–6)

Although Mercer limited her criticism to the disability classification of mental retardation, the learning disabilities classification is open to the same type of criticism (see Rist & Harrell, 1982). This is so because, as Lerner (1988) noted, "in many cases the neurological condition [that causes learning disabilities] is difficult, if not impossible, to ascertain by medical examination or external medical tests. Often, therefore, the central nervous system dysfunction is presumed and determined through observation of behavior" (p. 10). The primary difference, of course, is that the behavioral observation used to determine learning disabilities is a low score on an achievement test rather than an IQ test. Paraphrasing Mercer, the implicit logic that underlies the transformation for learning disabilities is as follows: Low achievement = "bad" in American society, a social evaluation. "Bad" = pathology in the pathological model. Therefore, low achievement = pathology. In the case of learning disabilities, then, academic achievement, which is a behavioral manifestation and not a biological symptom, is conceptually transposed into a pathological sign that carries all of the negative implications of the pathological model.

The problem with biological and behavioral theories of deviance (alone or confounded) is that by their very nature, they locate the cause of the problem within the person and thus tend to ignore causal factors that lie in the larger social context in which human differences occur. Moreover, this problem is reinforced by the last two assumptions, which in effect take the organizational context of schooling for granted, thus excluding it as a causal factor relative to student disability. This is so because these assumptions are derived from the theory of organizational rationality. The term "rationality" here does not refer to the common or broad sense of rationality, that is, to thoughtful, reasoned, or intelligent action (as opposed to irrational or foolish action). Rather, it refers to the narrow sense of "technical" rationality or functional efficiency, that is, to "the extent to which a series of actions is organized in such a way as to lead to predetermined goals with maximum efficiency" (Scott, 1981, pp. 57–58). Given this narrow sense of rationality, then, the theory of organizational rationality assumes that organizations are technically efficient means to achieve prespecified goals (Pfeffer, 1982; Scott, 1981) and that improving or changing them is merely a rational-technical process of increasing the efficiency of an existing system incrementally rather than changing the system in more fundamental ways or replacing it with a different one (Skrtic, 1988b).

Although the pathological view of student disability stems from a conceptual confusion within the field of special education, the rational view of school organizations comes from a similar confusion in the field of educational administration. Since its inception, educational administration has been dominated by the notion of "scientific management" (Callahan, 1962), an extremely narrow view of organization and management premised on the theory of organizational rationality. Scientific management is a method for using standardization to increase the efficiency of industrial organizations (factories), what I refer to below as "machine bureaucracies." With their great success in industry, however, scientific management and the factory model became social norms in early twentieth century America (Haber, 1964), unquestioned standards for the most efficient way to organize and manage all organizations, including schools (Callahan, 1962). As a result, when industrialization, immigration, and compulsory school attendance produced large numbers of students who failed to thrive in traditional classrooms, the problem of school failure was framed as two related problems—inefficient (nonrational) organizations and defective (pathological) students. Given this interpretation, educational administrators used the principles of scientific management to make schools more efficient by standardizing the work of teachers and removing the "defective" students from their classrooms (see Skrtic, 1991a). From the perspective of scientific management, then, special education was a rational means (narrow sense) to "serve" pathological students by simply containing them within a separate "special" education system (Lazerson, 1983; Sarason & Doris, 1979; and further on).

By considering special education's grounding assumptions from an organizational perspective, I want to question the sense of objectivity and rationality that they imply and propose the following set of alternative assumptions as a guide to practice and advocacy in the field of learning disabilities.

1. Learning disabilities are organizational pathologies.
2. Diagnosis of learning disabilities is subjective and harmful to students and to public education as a whole.
3. Special education is a nonrational and uncoordinated system of services that benefits school organizations.
4. Progress in special education is a nonrational undertaking, a revolutionary process of fundamentally replacing conventional school organizations.

As a philosophical pragmatist, I am not concerned with whether the conventional assumptions are right or wrong but with whether they are useful today as a guide to practice and advocacy in the field of learning disabilities (see Skrtic, 1991a, 1995c). That is, although the conventional assumptions may have served an important (largely political) purpose in the past (see Robinson, 1995), I am arguing that they have outlived their usefulness and that learning disabilities professionals and advocates should adopt the alternative assumptions because they are more useful for serving the best interests of all students, whether or not they have learning disabilities (pathological or not), and of society as a whole.

School Organization and Change

Although educational administration largely remains tied to scientific management and the machine bureaucracy model (Bates, 1980; Foster, 1986; Weick, 1982b), recent developments in the social sciences have produced a number of new theories of organization and change (see Burrell & Morgan, 1979; Pfeffer, 1982; Scott, 1981), many of which are applicable to schools (see Skrtic, 1987, 1988b, 1991b). In this section I use two of these newer theoretical perspectives—configuration theory (Miller & Mintzberg, 1983; Mintzberg, 1979, 1983) and institutional theory (Meyer & Rowan, 1977, 1978; Meyer & Scott, 1983; Meyer, 1979)—to characterize the structure of conventional school organizations and the way they respond to student diversity and demands for change.[1]

The central idea in configuration theory is that organizations structure themselves into a small number of somewhat naturally occurring configurations according to the means they employ to divide and coordinate their work. From this perspective, the structure of an organization can be understood as "the sum total of the ways in which it divides its labor into distinct tasks and then achieves coordination among them" (Mintzberg, 1979, p. 2). Applying this insight to the study of organizations yields several basic configurations, two of which—*machine bureaucracy* and *professional bureaucracy*—are particularly helpful for understanding the nature and functioning of conventional school organizations; a third configuration, the *adhocracy*, is helpful for conceptualizing an alternative to the conventional organizational form.

As we will see, given the means they use to divide and coordinate their work, schools configure themselves as professional bureaucracies even though, under the influence of scientific management, they are managed and governed as if they were machine bureaucracies (Meyer & Rowan, 1978; Weick, 1982b). According to institutional theory, schools deal with this contradiction by maintaining two relatively independent or "decoupled" structures—an inner professional bureaucracy structure that corresponds to the ways they divide and coordinate their work and an outer machine bureaucracy structure that conforms to the social norms of scientific management and the factory model (Meyer & Rowan, 1977, 1978; Skrtic, 1987).

Differences Between Machine and Professional Bureaucracies

Organizations configure themselves as machine bureaucracies when their work is simple enough to be divided through *rationalization*, a process in which the total work activity is task analyzed into a sequence of relatively routine subtasks, each of which can be prespecified and done by a separate worker (think of an assembly line). The process of rationalization represents the operationalization of the narrow sense of "rational" in organizations. Work that can be rationalized in this sense is coordinated through *formalization*, that is, by standardizing the procedures for doing each subtask and specifying precise rules for each worker to follow in completing his or her assigned work activity.

When their work is too complex to be rationalized and formalized, organizations configure themselves as professional bureaucracies. The best examples of this configuration are organizations that do complex client-centered work, such as hospitals, law firms, universities, and public schools. In these organizations, division of labor is achieved through *specialization*, a process in which clients are distributed among the workers on the basis of a match between the specialized skills of the worker and the presumed needs of the client. Thus in hospitals, for example, no single physician can serve the needs of every patient. So we find cardiologists, neurologists, and gynecologists, each of whom specializes in the knowledge and skills necessary to serve patients who are presumed to have a particular type of medical need. Given the same logic of specialization, in schools we find primary, elementary, and secondary teachers as well as further subject-area specialists at the middle school and secondary levels. And, of course, at all levels of public education we find teachers of students who are bilingual, gifted, or economically disadvantaged as well as teachers of students with behavior disorders, mental retardation, or learning disabilities. Complex work that can be divided among the workers through specialization is coordinated through *professionalization*, that is, intensive education and socialization carried out in professional schools such as medical schools, law schools, and schools or colleges of education. Whereas formalization standardizes the work process through rules, professionalization standardizes the knowledge and skills of the worker through education and socialization.

Together, an organization's division of labor and means of coordination shape the nature of the interdependence, or "coupling," among its

workers (Thompson, 1967; Weick, 1976; 1982b). Because machine bureaucracies divide and coordinate their work through rationalization and formalization, their workers are *tightly coupled*, a situation in which, like
links in a chain, they are highly dependent on one another. In a professional bureaucracy, however, specialization and professionalization create a *loosely coupled* form of interdependence, a situation in which each
professional works closely with her or his clients but only loosely with
other professionals. Specialization and professionalization virtually eliminate the need for coordination among professionals because each one
does virtually all aspects of the work with his or her assigned clients.
What little coordination is needed is achieved by each professional specialist knowing roughly what every other one is doing, given their common professional education and socialization within a given field.

Problems with Professionalization

As a means of coordination, formalization is premised on minimizing
worker discretion by separating theory from practice. The theory behind
the work in machine bureaucracies rests with the managers and engi-
neers who rationalize and formalize it; they do the thinking and the
workers simply follow the rules. Conversely, professionalization is
premised on maximizing discretion by uniting theory and practice in the
professional. This is necessary because the ambiguity of client-centered
work requires professionals to adapt the theory to fit the actual needs of
their clients. In principle, professionals know the theory behind their
work and have the discretion to adapt it to the unique and changing
needs of their clients. In practice, however, professionalization circumscribes the work of professionals in two ways.

First, professionalization provides professionals with only a finite
repertoire of standard practices that are matched to a particular set of
presumed client needs. For example, no elementary teacher has an infinite number of practices in her or his repertoire for teaching subtraction
with regrouping so that she or he can teach any student (with any learning needs) the place-value concepts, number facts, and regrouping skills
to perform the subtraction algorithm for problems such as 346 minus 179.
Elementary teachers may have one or two such practices in their repertoires, and these are most likely standard teaching practices designed for
typical learners. Of course, like all professionals, teachers are assumed to
have the ability and the discretion to adapt their practices to the actual
needs of their students. But the degree to which teachers can adapt their
standard practices has limits; teaching practices are not infinitely adaptable even if teachers have unlimited discretion, and they rarely do (see
further on). In schools, this means that a student whose needs fall outside

his or her teacher's repertoire of practices or beyond the bounds of the teacher's ability or opportunity to adapt must be sent to a different teacher. That is, given the logic of specialization, the student must be sent to a different specialist whose repertoire presumably contains the required practices.

The second way that professionalization circumscribes professional work is that by design, it results in convergent thinking and deductive reasoning, a situation in which "the professional confuses the needs of his clients with the skills he has to offer [them]" (Mintzberg, 1979, p. 374). A fully open-ended process—one that seeks a truly creative solution to each unique need—requires a problem-solving orientation premised on innovation rather than standardization. But professionalization is based on the standardization of skills, a process that prepares all professionals, including teachers, to function largely as performers, not problem solvers. Professionals ordinarily do not invent new practices; they perfect the standard practices in their repertoires by performing them over and over again (Simon, 1977; Weick, 1976). Instead of accommodating diversity, then, teachers tend to screen it out either by forcing their students' needs into one of their standard practices or by forcing them out of their classrooms into a professional-client relationship with a different educational specialist (see Perrow, 1970; Segal, 1974; Skrtic, 1988b).

Managing Professional Bureaucracies
Like Machine Bureaucracies

Given the dominance of scientific management in the field of educational administration, schools are managed (Clark, 1985; Weick, 1982a) and governed (Meyer & Rowan, 1978; Mintzberg, 1979) as if they were machine bureaucracies even though rationalization and particularly formalization (i.e., standardization through rules) are ill-suited to the technical demands of doing complex client-centered work. In principle, this forces the professional bureaucracy to perform like a machine bureaucracy because, by design, rationalization and formalization separate theory from practice, thus violating the discretionary logic of professionalization. This is a problem in schools because complex work cannot be coordinated through rules "except in misguided ways which program the wrong behaviors and measure the wrong outputs, forcing the professionals to play the machine bureaucratic game—satisfying the standards instead of serving the clients. . . . The individual needs of the students— slow learners and fast, rural and urban—as well as the individual styles of the teachers have to be subordinated to the neatness of the system" (Mintzberg, 1979, p. 377).

Rules take many forms in schools, including mandated textbook series, required curriculum guides, standardized tests, and even bell schedules. They are a problem because they reduce teachers' discretion and thus the degree to which they can adapt their practices to the needs of their students; thus fewer students can be retained in their classrooms.

For example, imagine that an elementary teacher has two practices for teaching subtraction with regrouping. The first practice is a largely symbolic approach in which the teacher uses standard print materials and a variety of paper-pencil exercises. This approach works well with 24 of 27 students, those who understand place value and have mastered most of the basic subtraction facts. The second practice is a constructivist approach in which the teacher uses manipulative devices and trading games to demonstrate place-value concepts and teach subtraction facts. It works well with the remaining 3 students who do not understand place value as well and have not mastered very many of the basic subtraction facts. The teacher is comfortable using either practice and is quite successful with students under both instructional formats. In fact, using the constructivist approach the teacher has been able to accelerate the learning of the 3 students, keep them relatively close to the other 24 students in terms of rate of concept and skill development, and thus avoid the need to refer the 3 students for remedial or special education services.

Now, imagine that the teacher's school district adopts a new mathematics textbook series and requires all elementary teachers to use it and its largely symbolic approach, accompanying standardized tests, and rather quick-paced scope and sequence specifications. Under this requirement—in effect, a new set of rules that forces the teacher to play the machine bureaucratic game of satisfying the *district's* standards instead of serving the *students'* instructional needs—the teacher does not have the discretion to use the constructivist approach with the 3 students who need it *even though he or she has this practice—the very practice these students need—in his or her repertoire of skills*. As a result, the teacher has no choice but to force the students' "constructivist needs" into his or her "symbolic practices." Eventually, of course, the 3 students fall far enough behind their classmates that the teacher has no other choice but to force them out of her classroom and into a different professional-client relationship with a another specialist, most likely a learning disabilities specialist, who is presumed to have the practice the students need in her or his repertoire of skills.

Fortunately, however, rationalization and formalization do not work completely in schools. According to institutional theory, misguided attempts to rationalize and formalize teaching are largely contained in schools' machine bureaucracy structure, which is decoupled from the classrooms of their professional bureaucracy structure, where the work is actually done. That is, the outer machine bureaucracy structure of schools acts largely as a myth, a collection of symbols (formal rules) and ceremonies (administrative procedures) that tend to be ignored in classrooms because they threaten the discretionary logic of professionalization. As Meyer and Rowan (1977) explained, "Decoupling enables organizations to maintain standardized, legitimating, formal structures while their activities vary in response to practical considerations" (p. 357). That is, the outer structure protects the school's legitimacy by giving it the appearance of the machine bureaucracy that central office administrators and the public expect while allowing the school to do its work according to the localized judgments of its teachers. Nevertheless, although this decoupled, two-structure arrangement protects teachers' discretion somewhat, it does not work completely either because regardless of how contradictory they may be, rationalization and formalization require at least overt conformity (Mintzberg, 1979; Dalton, 1959). Decoupled structures notwithstanding, the rationalization and formalization associated with the scientific management approach to educational administration further circumscribe professional discretion; thus ultimately, more students are forced out of general education classrooms and into the special education system.

Professional Bureaucracies and Change

Both the machine bureaucracy and the professional bureaucracy are premised on the principle of standardization, which means that in principle, both are inherently nonadaptable structures. Although change is resisted in both configurations, it can be forced on a machine bureaucracy by *re*rationalizing and *re*formalizing its work processes, that is, by using a "rational-technical" approach to change in which "rational" refers to the narrow sense of improving the "technical" rationality or functional efficiency of the system through further standardization. However, when a professional bureaucracy is required to change, it cannot respond by making such rational-technical adjustments in its rules because coordination of its work rests within each professional, by way of education and socialization, not in its official but decoupled rules. Nevertheless, because schools are managed and governed as if they were machine bureaucracies, attempts to change them typically have followed the rational-technical approach that is used in factories (see House, 1979; Wise, 1979).

Applied to school organizations, the rational-technical approach assumes that changes in or additions to the existing formalization (rules) in schools will result in changes in the way teachers do their work. However, because the formalization in schools is largely decoupled from the actual work of teachers, rational-technical reforms are largely absorbed by the mythical machine bureaucracy structure, where the new rules serve the purpose of signaling central office administrators and the public that a change has occurred (Meyer, 1979). Of course, because they are decoupled from the actual work, such reforms typically fail to bring about the desired changes (see Cuban, 1979; Elmore & McLaughlin, 1988; Skrtic, 1987). Worse yet, although they rarely produce the desired change, rational-technical reforms extend the existing (but misplaced) formalization in schools; because formalization requires at least overt conformity, rational-technical reforms drive the organization further toward the machine bureaucracy configuration (Skrtic, 1987, 1991b; Wise, 1979). This process circumscribes professional discretion further still and ultimately forces even more students out of general education classrooms and into the special education system.

Even though schools are nonadaptable structures, their status as public organizations means that they must respond to public demands for change. As we know, one way that schools deal with this problem is by using their outer machine bureaucracy structure to signal the public that a change has occurred. Another way that schools relieve pressure for change is by creating "ritual" or decoupled subunits within the organization by adding separate programs or specialists to deal with the change demand without disrupting the rest of the organization (Meyer & Rowan, 1977, 1978). Given the loosely coupled interdependence among teachers, schools signal change by simply adding separate subunits and then decoupling them from the other professionals and programs. By symbolizing change, these decoupled subunits buffer the organization from change demands, that is, they give the appearance of change without requiring any meaningful reorganization of activity (Meyer & Rowan, 1977; Zucker, 1981).

The Adhocracy Configuration

Professional bureaucracies are nonadaptable because they are premised on standardization, which configures them as performance organizations, that is, organizations geared to perfecting their existing standard practices. However, the third configuration—the adhocracy, noted previously—is premised on the principle of innovation rather than standardization; it is a problem-solving organization configured to invent new practices.

Adhocracies emerge in dynamic, uncertain environments where innovation and adaptation are necessary for organizational survival (Pugh et al., 1963). As such, they are the inverse of the bureaucratic form (Burns & Stalker, 1966; Woodward, 1965), organizations that configure themselves around work that is so ambiguous that initially the knowledge and practices required to do it are completely unknown (Pugh et al., 1963; Toffler, 1970). As Mintzberg (1979) noted, "At the outset, no one can be sure exactly what needs to be done. That knowledge develops as the work unfolds. . . . The success of the undertaking depends primarily on the ability of the [workers] to adapt to each other along their uncharted route" (p. 3). The difference between adhocracies and professional bureaucracies is that faced with a problem, the adhocracy "engages in creative effort to find a novel solution; the professional bureaucracy pigeonholes it into a known contingency to which it can apply a standard [practice]. One engages in divergent thinking aimed at innovation; the other in convergent thinking aimed at perfection" (Mintzberg, 1979, p. 436).

Perhaps the best early example of an adhocracy is the National Aeronautics and Space Administration (NASA) in the 1960s when, during its Apollo phase, its mission was a manned lunar landing. NASA configured itself as an adhocracy because at the time there were no standard practices for accomplishing such an undertaking. Thus at that point in its history, NASA had to rely on its workers to invent the necessary knowledge and practices on an ad hoc basis, on the way to the moon, as it were. Although NASA employed professional workers, it could not use specialization and professionalization to divide and coordinate its work because there were no professional specializations that had perfected the knowledge and practices for doing the type of work that was required. Thus in the 1960s, NASA's division of labor and means of coordination were premised on *collaboration* and *mutual adjustment*, respectively.

A collaborative division of labor is achieved by deploying professionals from various specializations on multidisciplinary project teams, a situation in which team members work collaboratively on the teams' project of innovation and assume joint responsibility for its completion. Collaboration is essential because innovation in organizations requires professionals to "break through the boundaries of conventional specialization," creating a situation in which they "must amalgamate their efforts [by joining] forces in multidisciplinary teams, each formed around a specific project of innovation" (Mintzberg, 1979, pp. 434–435). Under mutual adjustment, coordination is achieved through informal communication among team members as they invent and reinvent novel problem solutions on an ad hoc basis, a process that requires them to adapt their existing specialized knowledge to that of their colleagues relative to the team's progress on the tasks at hand (Chandler & Sayles, 1971; Mintzberg, 1979, 1983). Together, collaboration and mutual adjustment give rise to a *discursive coupling* arrangement premised on critical reflection and dialogical discourse (Burns & Stalker, 1966; and see further on). By contrast, during its current Space Shuttle phase, NASA has reconfigured itself as a professional bureaucracy (see Romzek & Dubnik, 1987), that is, as a performance organization that perfects a repertoire of standard Shuttle launch and recovery practices, most of which were invented during its Apollo phase.

Although NASA has shifted from adhocracy to bureaucracy over the past thirty years, the emergence of a dynamic, postindustrial economy during this period has elevated the adhocracy configuration to a position of increasing prominence in the (formerly) industrialized nations (Reich, 1983). Whereas the industrial economy of the twentieth century was premised on perfection (mass production through standardization) and thus required the machine bureaucracy configuration, the emerging postindustrial economy is premised on invention, which, as we have seen, requires the adhocracy configuration. Thus adhocracies—originally called "organic structures" (Pugh et al., 1963) and, more recently, "learning organizations" (Senge, 1990)—will become the dominant economic organizations of the twenty-first century (see Bennis & Slater, 1964; Mintzberg, 1979; Toffler, 1970).

Adhocracies invent new products and services by deploying their workers on collaborative teams and empowering them to deconstruct and reconstruct their conventional knowledge and practices (Mintzberg, 1979). Collaboration is essential because invention requires reflective problem solving through discourse, a process in which teams of workers construct new meanings in organizations, new ways to understand their work and themselves (Gray, 1989; Reich, 1990). On their own, individual workers or specialists are of little use in such organizations; innovation requires a *team* of specialists who construct new bodies of knowledge and skill from existing ones, a goal that "none of them working independently could achieve" (Gray, 1989, p. 11). As such, invention through collaboration requires a reconstruction of all meanings *and* relationships within the organization (Drucker, 1989; Jantsch, 1979). Moreover, because inventing new products and services is pointless if they are not personalized to the particular needs of those who will use them, it also requires a different kind of relationship between the organization and its consumers (Drucker, 1989; Naisbitt & Aburdene, 1985; Reich, 1983, 1990). That is, given the inexorable relationship among personalization, innovation, and collaboration, the viability of postindustrial organizations depends on a democratic relationship among the organization's members (to invent new products and services) as well as between them and their consumers (to personalize what they invent) (Dertouzos et al., 1989; Drucker, 1989; Mintzberg, 1979; Reich, 1983). The essence of this relationship is a new form of accountability.

Under the organizational contingencies of collaboration, mutual adjustment, and discursive coupling, accountability is achieved through a presumed community of interests, a sense among workers of a shared interest in a common goal. Under this form of accountability, responsibility flows from the workers' common concern for progress toward their mission rather than from an ideological identification with a professional culture (professional bureaucracy) or a formalized relationship with a hierarchy of authority (machine bureaucracy) (see Burns & Stalker, 1966; Chandler & Sayles, 1971; Romzek & Dubnik, 1987). Thus rather than the *professional-bureaucratic* mode of accountability that emerges in professional bureaucracies like schools (Martin, Overholt & Urban, 1976; Wise, 1979), the organizational contingencies of the adhocracy configuration give rise to a more democratic, *professional-political* mode of accountability. Work is controlled by professionals who, although they act with more discretion than in a professional bureaucracy, are subject to self-imposed sanctions that emerge within a political discourse among themselves and their consumers (Burns & Stalker, 1966; Chandler & Sayles, 1971; Romzek & Dubnik, 1987; Skrtic, 1991a).

Special Education's Assumptions from an Organizational Perspective

In this section I consider the legitimacy and utility of special education's conventional assumptions from the organizational perspective developed previously.[2] These assumptions (with the first two combined) are reproduced below in the form of questions about the nature, diagnosis, and treatment of learning disabilities.

Are Learning Disabilities Objective Pathologies?

Conventional school organizations are nonadaptable at the level of the professional because they use professionalization to coordinate their work. As we have seen, professionalization standardizes teachers' skills, giving each a finite repertoire of standard practices matched to a particular set of presumed student needs. Moreover, it encourages convergent thinking and deductive reasoning, which leads teachers to interpret their students' needs narrowly in terms of the practices in their repertoires. Although teachers have some discretion to adapt their practices to fit the actual needs of their students, there is a limit on how much adaptation is possible. There are creative teachers, of course, individual professionals who think divergently and reason inductively. In principle, however, professionalization does not produce problem solvers who seek creative solutions for each unique need. By design, professional education and socialization produce professionals who think convergently and reason deductively. In schools, this means that students cannot have just any needs; they must have needs that more or less match the practices in their assigned teacher's repertoire of skills. Thus given the nature of professionalization, teachers tend to screen out diversity rather than accommodate it, either by forcing their students' needs into one of their standard practices or, given the logic of specialization, by forcing them out of their classrooms and into a new professional-client relationship with a different educational specialist who is presumed to have the required practices in her or his repertoire of skills.

Given a finite repertoire of standard teaching practices and an inherently diverse and changing set of student needs, schools organized as professional bureaucracies can do nothing but create situations in which students' needs do not match the practices of their assigned teachers. As a result, students are identified as handicapped and, to one degree or another, removed from regular classrooms simply because their needs cannot be accommodated by the standard practices contained in a particular teacher's repertoire of skills (see Ysseldyke, 1987). Moreover, the situation is compounded by the scientific management approach to educational administration, which by introducing unwarranted rationalization and formalization, reduces teachers' discretion and thus the degree to which they can retain students with atypical needs in their classrooms. From an organizational perspective, having a learning disability in school is neither a pathological condition nor an objective distinction. It is an unintended consequence of organizing schools as professional bureaucracies and managing them as if they were machine bureaucracies, a matter of having needs that do not match the practices of teachers working in organizations that are not configured to accommodate diversity and so must screen it out. In these organizations, the assessment and identification process required by the Individuals with Disabilities Education Act (IDEA) functions largely to pathologize the inevitable problems encountered by classroom teachers (see Christenson & Ysseldyke, 1989; White & Calhoun, 1987; Ysseldyke, 1987; Ysseldyke & Algozzine, 1982; Ysseldyke et al., 1983), that is, to redefine as human pathologies the organizational problems created by an inherently nonadaptable bureaucratic structure.

Of course, there are some students in school for whom the handicapped designation is a pathological distinction, including some of the students labeled learning disabled. However, because of a variety of "powerful organizational influences" (Keogh, 1988, p. 240), most students identified as handicapped are not disabled in the pathological sense (see Bryan, Bay, & Donahue, 1988; Kauffman, Gerber, & Semmel, 1988; Gartner & Lipsky, 1987; Wang, Reynolds, & Walberg, 1986, 1987b). The IDEA assessment and identification process does not result in objective distinctions between "disabled" and "nondisabled" students or among the three high-incidence disability classifications of learning disabilities, emotional disturbance, and mild mental retardation (see Gartner & Lipsky, 1987; Gerber & Semmel, 1984; Kauffman, 1988; Keogh, 1988; Wang, Reynolds, & Walberg, 1986, 1987a).[3] Moreover, there are virtually no instructionally relevant reasons for making the disabled-nondisabled distinction or for distinguishing among the three high-incidence disability classifications. This is so because all students have unique learning needs and thus, for example, "one cannot assume that any two learning disabled children would be any more similar than a learning disabled child and a normally achieving child, or a normally achieving child and an underachieving child" (Bryan et al., 1988, p. 25; also see Gartner & Lipsky, 1987; Reynolds, Wang, & Walberg, 1987; Stainback & Stainback, 1984, 1989; Wang et al., 1986, 1987a). Finally, even if the assessment and identification process could make such distinctions, "effective instructional and management procedures will be substantially the same for nonhandicapped and most mildly handicapped students" (Kauffman et al., 1988, p. 8; also see Gerber, 1987; Hallahan & Kauffman, 1977; Lipsky & Gartner, 1989c; Wang, 1989a, 1989b).

It is important to note that these discouraging findings on the special education assessment and identification process do not mean that there is no place for diagnostic and evaluative testing in schools. What they do mean is that testing for the purpose of classifying students as disabled and nondisabled and differentiating among the three high-incidence classifications is ineffective, inefficient, and counterproductive. The forms of diagnostic and evaluative testing that remain useful are those that produce results that are meaningful to teachers, that is, those that are directly related to the instructional decisionmaking process, such as criterion-referenced tests, curriculum-based measures, and authentic assessments.

Is Special Education a Rational System?

Although as professional bureaucracies schools are nonadaptable structures, as public organizations they must be responsive to public demands for change. As we have seen, one way that schools deal with this contradiction between organizational capacity and public expectations is to signal that a change has occurred by building symbols and ceremonies of change into their decoupled machine bureaucracy structure. We know, too, that their loosely coupled internal structure permits schools to signal change by simply adding decoupled specialists and programs, a move that gives the organization the appearance of change without requiring any meaningful reorganization of activity. The emergence of the segregated special education classroom is the archetype of this latter process at work in schools.

At the start of this century, when public schools were required to
serve a broader range of students in the interest of the democratic ideal
of universal public education, the "ungraded" or special classroom
emerged to deal with largely poor, culturally diverse students who
could not be accommodated by the conventional practices of classroom
teachers (Bogdan & Knoll, 1988; Lazerson, 1983; Sarason & Doris, 1979).
From an organizational perspective, the segregated special classroom
served as a legitimating device, a politically expedient mechanism for
signaling the public that schools had complied with the demand for universal public education while permitting them to maintain their traditional organizational form and conventional practices. Once special
classrooms were created, they and their students and teachers were simply decoupled from the general education system.[4] Indeed, this decoupled relationship between general and special education was one of the
major criticisms leading to the passage of Public Law 94-142, the Education for All Handicapped Children Act of 1975 (now IDEA) and the introduction of the "continuum of services," or mainstreaming, model (see
Christophos & Renz, 1969; Deno, 1970; Dunn, 1968, 1973; Johnson, 1962).
Moreover, after nearly two decades of mainstreaming, the same decoupled relationship between general and special education continues to be
a major criticism of the current system of special education (see Lipsky
& Gartner, 1989a; Reynolds & Wang, 1983; Stainback & Stainback, 1984;
and further on).

Considering the function of special education from an organizational
perspective, we can consider it a "rational" system only in the narrow,
technical sense of being functionally efficient or politically expedient *for*
school organizations. It is not a rational system in the broader sense of
being the product of reasoned, intelligent action that serves the best interests of students with special educational needs. In this broader, intellectually and ethically defensible sense, special education is a nonrational
system because it is neither rationally conceived nor rationally coordinated. It is not a rationally conceived system because, historically, it has
served a political function as a legitimating device that schools use to
cope with shifting value demands in society. It is not a rationally coordinated system because, by design, it is decoupled from the general education system and the other special-needs programs (e.g., compensatory
education, bilingual education, migrant education, gifted education),
each of which is itself a decoupled subunit added to schools in response
to an unattainable public demand for change (see Kauffman et al., 1988;
Reynolds & Birch, 1977; Reynolds & Wang, 1983; Reynolds et al., 1987;
Wang, Reynolds, & Walberg, 1985, 1986). Recall that the unintended consequence of using organizations to achieve social goals is that the goals

are shaped by the nature and needs of the organizations. From an organizational perspective, special education is an unintended consequence of the particular kind of schooling that conventional school organizations provide. It and the other special-needs programs are organizational artifacts, political mechanisms that emerged to protect the legitimacy of a nonadaptable bureaucratic structure faced with the changing value demands of a dynamic and increasingly diverse democratic society.

Another way to address the question of whether special education is a rational system in the broad, intellectually and ethically defensible sense is to consider the effects of its placement and instructional practices on the students it serves. That is, even though special education is a nonrational system in the broad sense, does it nonetheless confer some instructional benefit on students whose needs cannot be met in the general education system?

Using this criterion, critics of the current system of special education reject the idea that it is a rational system in the broad sense (e.g., Lilly, 1986; Gartner & Lipsky, 1987; Reynolds, 1988; Reynolds et al., 1987; Stainback & Stainback, 1984; Wang et al., 1987a). Pointing to the weak effects of special education instructional practices and the social costs of labeling and segregation, they argue that the current system is no more rational than simply permitting most students with special educational needs to remain unidentified in general education classrooms (see Gartner & Lipsky, 1987; Lipsky & Gartner, 1989a, 1989b; Pugach & Lilly, 1984; Stainback & Stainback, 1984; Wang et al., 1987a; and further on). Although they recognize that students with special educational needs can pose problems for regular classroom teachers, their point is that, functioning separately, neither the general education system nor the special education system is sufficiently adaptable to serve them adequately (Gartner & Lipsky, 1987; Pugach & Lilly, 1984; Wang et al., 1986), a position with which most defenders of the current system agree, implicitly (Bryan et al., 1988; Kauffman, 1988) or explicitly (Kauffman et al., 1988; Keogh, 1988). Indeed, even the most avid defenders of the current system agree that special education placement and instructional practices have not been shown to benefit students (see Hallahan, Keller, McKinney, Lloyd, & Bryan, 1988; Keogh, 1988). Their defense of the current system is based on the argument that these practices are beneficial to students in a political rather than an instructional sense. In this regard, they argue that given the way resources have been allocated in schools historically, the current system of special education targets otherwise unavailable special education instructional services to designated students, the questionable effectiveness of these services notwithstanding (Council for Children with Behavioral Disorders, 1989; Kauffman, 1988, 1989; Kauffman et al., 1988).

Is Progress in Special Education a Rational-Technical Process?

In this section the question is whether the special education system can be improved incrementally using the rational-technical approach to change previously described, that is, the approach intended for machine bureaucracies but misapplied to schools historically. We can address this question by considering the implementation of the IDEA from an organizational perspective.[5]

Structurally, the problem with the IDEA is that it attempts to change professional bureaucracies into adhocracies by treating them as if they were machine bureaucracies (Skrtic, 1987, 1991a). That is, the implicit goal of the IDEA is an adhocratic school, a problem-solving organization in which educational problems are solved by multidisciplinary teams of professionals and parents who collaborate to invent personalized programs for each student designated handicapped. The problem here, of course, is that this goal contradicts the logic of the inner professional bureaucracy structure of schools in every way given that the schools are performance organizations in which individual professionals work alone to perfect their conventional standard practices. As a result, although the IDEA was intended to reduce the effects of student disability by increasing personalized instruction and regular classroom integration, for several organizational reasons it has produced virtually the opposite results.

First, although the IDEA implicitly seeks an adhocratic school organization, it approaches change from the rational-technical perspective. That is, it assumes that schools are machine bureaucracies, organizations in which worker behavior is controlled by procedural rules and thus is subject to modification through revision and extension of those rules (see Elmore and McLaughlin, 1982). Thus because the IDEA's means are completely consistent with the outer machine bureaucracy structure of schools, it extends their existing but misplaced rationalization and formalization. Structurally, this extension deflects the adhocratic ends of the IDEA from the actual work in schools by further reducing professional thought and discretion, thus intensifying professionalization and reducing personalization in regular and special education classrooms (see Gartner & Lipsky, 1987; Kauffman et al., 1988; Keogh, 1988; Pugach & Lilly, 1984; Skrtic, Guba, & Knowlton, 1985; Weatherley, 1979). This process results in even more students whose needs fall outside the standard practices of their classroom teachers, most of whom must be identified as handicapped, primarily learning disabled (Gerber & Levine-Donnerstein, 1989; U.S. Department of Education, 1988), and placed in special education (Skrtic, 1987, 1988b, 1991a; Skrtic et al., 1985).

Second, because the IDEA requires at least overt conformity, an array of symbols and ceremonies of compliance have emerged. One of the primary symbols of compliance with the law's "least restrictive environment" principle is the resource room, a new type of decoupled subunit that serves students in the high-incidence disability classifications, primarily students classified as learning disabled.[6] From an organizational perspective, the resource room (and special needs pull-out programs generally) is even more problematic than the traditional special classroom because it violates both the division of labor and the means of coordination in the professional bureaucracy configuration. Under the logic of mainstreaming, the responsibility for the student's instructional program is divided among one or more regular classroom teachers and a special education resource teacher. This arrangement contradicts the division of labor in schools because it requires that the student's instructional program be divided among two or more professionals, a requirement justified implicitly on the assumption that the professionals will collaborate to integrate the program. However, the collaboration required to integrate the instructional program contradicts the logic of specialization and professionalization and thus the loosely coupled form of interdependence among teachers. In principle, teachers collaborating in the interest of a single student for whom they share responsibility does not make sense in schools. Indeed, because professionalization locates virtually all of the necessary coordination within the individual professional, there is little need for teachers to collaborate or even communicate. If collaboration does occur in schools, it is rare, fleeting, and idiosyncratic, whether it is among regular classroom teachers (Tye & Tye, 1984) or between regular classroom teachers and special education resource teachers (Lortie, 1975, 1978; Skrtic et al., 1985; Walker, 1987).

Finally, although regular classroom placement (to the maximum extent possible) is required for students with disabilities under the IDEA, they are identified as handicapped precisely because their needs cannot be accommodated by the conventional practices of particular regular classroom teachers (see Skrtic et al., 1985; Walker, 1987). Thus mainstreaming for these students is largely symbolic; they spend time in regular classrooms, but as research on the implementation of mainstreaming has shown, they are not integrated in a meaningful way, instructionally or socially (Biklen, 1985; Skrtic et. al., 1985; Wright et. al., 1982). Given its adhocratic goals, the IDEA was meant to be a mechanism for reducing the effects of student disability by increasing personalized instruction and regular classroom integration. However, given the bureaucratic structure of schools and of the law itself, the IDEA has resulted in an increase in the number of students classified as disabled, particularly learning disabled

(Gerber & Levine-Donnerstein, 1989; U.S. Department of Education, 1988); disintegration of their instructional programs (Keogh, 1988, Skrtic, et al., 1985; Walker, 1987); and a decrease in personalization in regular and special education classrooms (Bryan et al., 1988; Carlberg & Kavale, 1980; Gartner & Lipsky, 1987; Wang et al., 1986; Reynolds, Wang, & Walberg, 1987).

Equity, Excellence, and Adhocracy

The postindustrial principles of personalization, innovation, and collaboration are implicit in the latest developments in educational reform (see Skrtic, 1991a, 1995a). For example, advocates of school restructuring in general education reject the conventional bureaucratic school outright, as well as rational-technical reform efforts that merely try to make it more efficient through further standardization (e.g., Cuban, 1983, 1989; Elmore, 1987; Goodlad, 1984; Sizer, 1984; Wise, 1979). They argue that educational excellence requires a completely new structure for schools, one that eliminates homogeneous grouping practices such as in-class ability grouping, curricular tracking, and even some forms of special needs programming (Oakes, 1985, 1996). At bottom, this new structure is premised on inventing personalized instructional practices through collaborative problem solving between and among parents and professionals at local school sites (see Goodlad, 1984; McNeil, 1986; Sizer, 1984).

The same idea is at the heart of the inclusive-education reform movement in special education.[7] Inclusion advocates reject the assessment and identification requirements of the IDEA and the placement and instructional practices associated with mainstreaming (Lipsky & Gartner, 1989a; Pugach & Lilly, 1984; Reynolds & Wang, 1983; Stainback & Stainback, 1984). Like advocates of school restructuring, they argue that educational equity requires a restructured system of public education, one that integrates the separate general and special education systems into a unified system that is "flexible, supple and responsive" (Lipsky & Gartner, 1987, p. 72), a "totally adaptive system" (Reynolds & Wang, 1983, p. 199) designed to personalize instruction through "group problem solving . . . shared responsibility, and . . . negotiation" (Pugach & Lilly, 1984, p. 52).

Although historically the relationship between general and special education has been strained by the inability to reconcile the goals of educational excellence and educational equity, today there is a convergence of interests between the proponents of school restructuring and the proponents of inclusive education. Both groups of reformers are calling for a system of education that provides "all" students with personalized instruction in heterogeneous classrooms. In both cases, such a system is to be achieved through structural reforms that increase professional discretion and promote collaborative problem solving among professionals and consumers at local schools. Although there are differences within and between the inclusive-education and school-restructuring reform movements relative to the definition of "all" students, they are differences in degree, not in kind (see Skrtic, 1991a). From an organizational perspective, both groups implicitly are calling for the elimination of specialization, professionalization, and loose coupling in schools and thus their nonadaptable inner professional bureaucracy configuration. Moreover, both groups implicitly are calling for the introduction of collaboration, mutual adjustment, and discursive coupling, the structural contingencies of the adaptable, personalizing adhocratic configuration (see Skrtic, 1991a, 1995c).[8] In organizational terms, then, achieving excellence and equity in public education requires the same thing—reconfiguring schools as adhocracies.

As we know, adhocracies configure themselves as problem-solving organizations because they do ambiguous work, that is, work for which the required practices are unknown at the outset and thus must be invented through divergent thinking and inductive reasoning by teams of professionals and consumers engaged in a reflective discourse. Uncertainty is essential if an organization is to become and remain adhocratic because without it, adhocracies reconfigure themselves as bureaucracies, as the case of NASA illustrates. Thus reconfiguring schools as adhocracies requires an enduring source of instructional uncertainty. In organizational terms, public education cannot be excellent or equitable unless schools are adhocratic. In structural terms, schools can neither become nor remain adhocratic without the instructional uncertainty of student diversity.

As we have seen, the conventional bureaucratic configuration of schools means that they are performance organizations, nonadaptable structures that must screen out diversity by forcing some students out of the system. But student diversity is not an inherent problem for school organizations; it is a problem only if they are configured as bureaucracies or performance organizations. Regardless of its causes and its extent, *student diversity is not a liability in a problem-solving organization*; in an adhocratic school it is an asset, an enduring source of uncertainty and thus the driving force behind innovation, growth of knowledge, and progress (see Skrtic, 1991a, 1991b).

Although the moral argument for educational equity has always been right, today special education professionals and learning disabilities advocates can strengthen their position by arguing that from an organizational perspective, educational equity is a precondition for educational excellence. The first step in making this argument is for them to stop thinking of learning disabilities as human pathologies and to start thinking of them and special education itself as organizational pathologies, artifacts of conventional schooling, unintended consequences of organizing schools as professional bureaucracies and managing them as if they were machine bureaucracies. The second step is to convince educators and the public that shifting from bureaucratic to adhocratic schooling will serve the best political and economic interests of America, particularly as it faces the challenges of the emerging postindustrial era.

Adhocracy and Democracy in Postindustrial America

At the start of this century, John Dewey (1976, 1988b) argued that the arrival of an industrial age had created both a problem and an opportunity for America. The problem was that industrialization put more of life, particularly work and education, under the bureaucratic administrative form. As we have seen, the problem with bureaucracy is that it virtually eliminates the need for people to solve problems and to engage in discourse. And because bureaucracy thus diminishes the human capacity for reflection and collaboration—the essential skills for democratic citizenship—Dewey believed that industrialization threatened the public's ability to govern itself democratically. The opportunity posed by industrialization was that as a mode of economic production, it created an expanding network of regional, national, and international social interdependencies. In turn, Dewey (1988a, 1988b) argued, these interdependencies created the need for a new cultural sensibility in America, a shift from the rugged or *possessive* individualism that had served it well in the eighteenth and nineteenth centuries to a *social* form of individualism that was more suited to democratic life under the new interdependent conditions.

Pointing to the mounting social and political costs of this cultural contradiction, Dewey (1988a, 1988b) argued that the new conditions of interdependence made possible and begged for a new approach to public education, one premised on returning problems to the lives of students, problems that required them to engage in reflective discourse and collaborative problem solving, thus developing in them the essential skills for democratic citizenship. Dewey (1976) believed that the goal of public education should be to restore the public's capacity for democratic citizenship by turning schools into communities of inquiry, problem-rich contexts in which thinking teachers put their students' minds to work on concrete problems—intellectual and moral—rather than simply filling their heads with abstract "facts." For Dewey, education was a social constructivist process leading to "reconstruction . . . of experience which adds to the meaning of experience, and . . . increases the ability to direct the course of subsequent experience" (Dewey, 1976, p. 93). He favored a pedagogy premised on collaborative problem solving because he saw it as the best means for developing students' capacities for critical reflection and dialogical discourse, the essential skills for reconstructing experience democratically.

The arrival of a postindustrial age makes Dewey's earlier arguments about the social and political costs of possessive individualism even more relevant today than they were at the start of the century. A postindustrial economy makes the world even more interdependent (Rosenthau, 1980), and thus social individualism even more of a necessity for meaningful democratic life. As such, postindustrialization creates a new set of opportunities and problems for America. One advantage is that a postindustrial economy requires schools to produce a different kind of worker. Dewey argued for educating reflective democratic citizens during a period when industrialists were demanding that schools produce compliant bureaucratic workers (see Callahan, 1962; Haber, 1964). Today, however, postindustrialists, in effect, are calling for democratic workers, reflective people who can identify and solve problems collaboratively through dialogical discourse (see Dertouzos, Lester, & Solow, 1989; Drucker, 1989; Kearns & Doyle, 1988; Naisbitt & Aburdene, 1985; Reich, 1983, 1990). This development is significant because it holds out the possibility of a convergence of interest on the long-standing and highly contested question of the role of public education in a capitalist democracy.

A related advantage is that postindustrialism changes the meaning of educational excellence. Far more than basic numeracy and literacy, educational excellence is the capacity for working collaboratively with others and for taking responsibility for learning (Dertouzos et al., 1989; Drucker, 1989; Kearns & Doyle, 1988; Naisbitt & Aburdene, 1985; Reich, 1983, 1990; Secretary's Commission on Achieving Necessary Skills, 1991). The redefinition of educational excellence is particularly significant for the special education advocacy community because it changes the meaning of educational equity, in effect making it a precondition for economic excellence (see Skrtic, 1991b). This is so because collaboration means learning with and from persons with varying interests, abilities, and cultural perspectives; and taking responsibility for learning means being responsible for one's own learning *and* that of others (Dertouzos et al., 1989; Drucker, 1989; Kearns & Doyle, 1988). Ability grouping, tracking, and categorical pull-out programs have no place in a postindustrial system of education because, as former secretary of labor Robert Reich noted, they "reduce young people's capacities to learn from and collaborate with one another" (1990, p. 208). Such practices work against promoting social responsibility in students and developing in them the capacity for negotiation within a community of interests, outcomes that Reich believes are unlikely unless "unity and cooperation are the norm" in schools (Reich,

1990, p. 208; also see Dertouzos et al., 1989; Secretary's Commission on Achieving Necessary Skills, 1991). Not only is inclusion possible in such a system of education, it is the central organizing principle.

Like industrialization, however, postindustrialization also creates a new set of problems for America. The most unsettling problem is the specter of a two-class society composed of elite, adhocratic "thought workers" on the one hand and low-level service workers and the permanently underemployed and unemployed on the other. Special education is implicated here because, as we have seen, in its conventional form it is a sophisticated and largely unrecognized form of tracking that is uniquely placed within public education to serve the necessary sorting function (see Skrtic, 1991a, 1995a; Tomlinson, 1995).

Like all social policy, educational policy is concerned with more than technical issues; it is concerned primarily with moral transactions and social relations (Blanco, 1994; Titmuss, 1968). And so in reconstructing educational institutions and practices for a postindustrial age, special educators and disability advocates must be explicit about what they believe is morally and politically right. Since at least the 1970s, they have been right about trying to build a more inclusive, consumer-oriented system of special education. Given the shortcomings of the resulting system, a better understanding of school organization and change, and current political and economic conditions, today they can and must set their sights on building a more inclusive, consumer-oriented system of public education. Like all those who approach social policy from a democratic perspective, they must "probe and push" the value assumptions that shape social policy toward those that unite us (Rein, 1970, 1976). From this perspective, social policy above all should be concerned with building an inclusive system, one that "includes those aspects of social life that are . . . justified by [an] appeal to . . . identity or community. . . . to build the identity of a person around some community with which he is associated" (Boulding, 1967, p. 7). Inclusion and identity are central to social policy because their opposites, exclusion and alienation, threaten community itself (Moroney, 1981). Moreover, as Dewey (1980, 1988a) and others (e.g., Guttman, 1987) have noted, because humans must learn to be democratic, educational policy in particular must promote inclusive systems because these are the types of institutional arrangements in which democratic identities, values, and communities are cultivated.

Notes

1. The structural analysis presented in this section is an admittedly narrow interpretation because it does not consider the culture of schools. For an analysis that combines structural and cultural perspectives on school organization and

change, see Skrtic (1987, 1988b, 1991a, 1991b, 1995b, 1995e). Except where noted otherwise, all of my comments on configuration theory (division of labor, coordination of work, interdependence among workers, and the implications of configuration for management, adaptability, and accountability) and institutional theory (decoupled structures and subunits and the implications of organizational symbols and ceremonies for school governance and educational reform) are based on the authors cited in this sentence, respectively.

2. My use of citations in this section is somewhat unconventional. Throughout the section I make a number of theoretical claims based on the structural analysis of school organization and change presented previously. The authors cited in association with these claims have not made such claims; I am making the theoretical claims and simply using the citations as references to empirical and interpretive research that supports them.

3. There is no argument over the fact that most disabilities in the severe to profound range of severity are associated with observable patterns of biological symptoms (or syndromes) and are thus comprehensible under the pathological model. The question of whether student disabilities are pathological refers primarily to the high-incidence disability classifications, which in most cases do not show biological signs of pathology, as noted previously.

4. Another example of decoupling is the overrepresentation of minority students in special classrooms, a process in which school organizations use an existing decoupling device—the special education system—to maintain their legitimacy in the face of failing to meet the needs of disproportionate numbers of minority students in regular classrooms. For more on this point, see Skrtic (1988a, 1991a, 1995a, 1995d) and Sleeter (1995).

5. Although in this section I use the IDEA (P.L. 101-476) to refer to the law that governs special education practice, much of the implementation research cited in this section (see note 2) was done prior to the time the law's name was changed from the Education for All Handicapped Children Act (P.L. 94-142). Nevertheless, the basic principles and requirements of the IDEA are virtually identical to those of P.L. 94-142.

6. The symbol of compliance for programs that serve students labeled severely and profoundly handicapped is the traditional decoupled subunit, the segregated special classroom. Although I will not consider these programs here, I have argued elsewhere (Skrtic, 1991a) that they are important in an organizational sense because given the unique needs of the students they serve and the interdisciplinary approach employed, they are prototypical of the adhocratic organizational form.

7. What I am calling the "inclusive education reform movement" began as the "regular education initiative" in the early 1980s and evolved into a highly contentious debate over the wisdom and feasibility of inclusive education as a replacement for mainstreaming. For reviews, see Davis (1989), Goetz and Sailor (1990), Fuchs and Fuchs (1991, 1994), and Skrtic (1987, 1988b, 1991b).

8. A comprehensive analysis of the school-restructuring and inclusive-education reform proposals would show that even though the reforms both groups want require the adhocracy structure, their reform proposals actually retain the professional bureaucracy structure. For more on this shortcoming in both reform

movements and its negative implications for special education, see Skrtic (1988, 1991a, 1991b, 1995a, 1995c).

References

Allison, G. T. (1971). *Essence of decision: Explaining the Cuban missile crisis.* Boston: Little, Brown.

Bates, R. J. (1980). Educational administration, the sociology of science, and the management of knowledge. *Educational Administration Quarterly, 16*(2), 1–20.

Bennis, W. G., & Slater, P. L. (1964). *The temporary society.* New York: Harper & Row.

Biklen, D. (1985). *Achieving the complete school: Strategies for effective mainstreaming.* New York: Columbia University.

Bledstein, B. J. (1976). *The culture of professionalism: The middle class and the development of higher education in America.* New York: W. W. Norton.

Bogdan, R., & Knoll, J. (1988). The sociology of disability. In E. L. Meyen & T. M. Skrtic (Eds.), *Exceptional children and youth: An introduction* (pp. 449–477). Denver: Love.

Bogdan, R., & Kugelmass, J. (1984). Case studies of mainstreaming: A symbolic interactionist approach to special schooling. In L. Barton & S. Tomlinson (Eds.), *Special education and social interests* (pp. 173–191). New York: Nichols.

Boulding, K. (1967). The boundaries of social policy. *Social Work, 12,* 3–11.

Bryan, T., Bay, M., & Donahue, M. (1988). Implications of the learning disabilities definition for the regular education initiative. *Journal of Learning Disabilities, 21*(1), 23–28.

Burns, T., & Stalker, G. M. (1966). *The management of innovation* (2nd Ed.). London: Tavistock.

Burrell, G., & Morgan, G. (1979). *Sociological paradigms and organizational analysis.* London, England: Heinemann.

Callahan, R. (1962). *Education and the cult of efficiency.* Chicago: University of Chicago Press.

Carlberg, C., & Kavale, K. (1980). The efficacy of special versus regular class placement for exceptional children: A meta-analysis. *Journal of Special Education, 14,* 295–309.

Chandler, M. D., & Sayles, L. R. (1971). *Managing large systems.* New York: Harper and Row.

Cherryholmes, C. H. (1988). *Power and criticism: Poststructuralist investigations in education.* New York: Teachers College Press.

Christenson, S., & Ysseldyke, J. (1989). Assessing student performance: An important change is needed. *Journal of School Psychology, 27,* 409–425.

Clark, D. L. (1985). Emerging paradigms in organizational theory and research. In Y. S. Lincoln (Ed.), *Organizational theory and inquiry: The paradigm revolution* (pp. 43–78). Beverly Hills, CA: Sage.

Collins, R. (1979). *The credential society.* New York: Academic Press.

Cuban, L. (1979). Determinants of curriculum change and stability, 1870–1970. In J. Schaffarzick & G. Sykes (Eds.), *Value conflicts and curriculum issues*. Berkeley, CA: McCutchan.

Cuban, L. (1983). Effective schools: A friendly but cautionary note. *Phi Delta Kappan, 64*(10), 695–696.

Cuban, L. (1989). The "at-risk" label and the problem of urban school reform. *Phi Delta Kappan, 70*(10), 780–784, 799–801.

Dalton, M. (1959). *Men who manage*. New York: Wiley.

Davis, W. E. (1989). The regular initiative debate: Its promises and problems. *Exceptional Children, 55*(5), 440–446.

Dertouzos, M. L., Lester, R. K., & Solow, R. M. (1989). *Made in America: Regaining the productive edge*. Cambridge, MA: MIT Press.

Dewey, J. (1938). Education, democracy and socialized economy. *The Social Frontier, 5*(40), 71–73.

Dewey, J. (1976). The school and society. In J. A. Boydston (Ed.), *John Dewey: The middle works, 1899–1924* (Vol. 1, pp. 1–109). Carbondale, IL: Southern Illinois University Press. (Original work published 1899)

Dewey, J. (1980). Democracy and education. In J. A. Boydston (Ed.), *John Dewey: The middle works, 1899–1924* (Vol. 9, pp. 1–370). Carbondale, IL: Southern Illinois University Press. (Original work published 1916)

Dewey, J. (1988a). Individualism, old and new. In J. A. Boydston (Ed.), *John Dewey: The later works, 1925–1953* (Vol. 5, pp. 41–123). Carbondale, IL: Southern Illinois University Press. (Original work published 1929–1930)

Dewey, J. (1988b). The public and its problems. In Jo Ann Boydston (Ed.), *John Dewey: The later works, 1925–1953* (Volume 2: 1925–1927), (pp. 235–372). Carbondale, IL: Southern Illinois University Press. (Original work published 1927)

Drucker, P. F. (1989). *The new realities*. New York: Harper and Row.

Dunn, L. M. (1968). Special education for the mildly retarded—Is much of it justifiable? *Exceptional Children, 35*(1), 5–22.

Elmore, R. F. (1987). *Early experiences in restructuring schools: Voices from the field*. Washington, DC: National Governors Association.

Elmore, R. F., & McLaughlin, M. W. (1982). Strategic choice in federal education policy: The compliance-assistance trade-off. In A. Lieberman and M. W. McLaughlin (Eds.), *Policy making in education: Eighty-first yearbook of the National Society for the Study of Education* (pp. 159–194). Chicago: University of Chicago Press.

Elmore, R. F., & McLaughlin, M. W. (1988). *Steady work: Policy, practice, and the reform of American education*. Santa Monica, CA: Rand Corporation.

Foster, W. (1986). *Paradigms and promises: New approaches to educational administration*. Buffalo, NY: Prometheus Books.

Foucault, M. (1973). *Madness and civilization: A history of insanity in the age of reason*. R. Howard (trans.). New York: Vintage/Random House. (Original work published 1961)

Foucault, M. (1983). The subject and power. In H. L. Dreyfus and P. Rabinow (Eds.), *Michel Foucault: Beyond structuralism and hermeneutics*, (pp. 208–226). Chicago: University of Chicago Press.

Freidson, E. (1988). *Professional powers: A study of the institutionalization of formal knowledge.* Chicago: University of Chicago Press.

Fuchs, D., & Fuchs, L. (1991). Framing the REI debate: Abolitionists versus conservationists. In J. W. Lloyd, N. N. Singh, & A. C. Repp (Eds.), *The Regular Education Initiative: Alternative perspectives on concepts, issues, and models,* (pp. 241–255). Sycamore, IL: Sycamore.

Fuchs, D., & Fuchs, L. S. (1994). Inclusive schools movement and the radicalization of special education reform. *Exceptional Children, 60*(4), 294–309.

Gartner, A., & Lipsky, D. K. (1987). Beyond special education: Toward a quality system for all students. *Harvard Educational Review, 57*(4), 367–390.

Gerber, M. M., & Levine-Donnerstein, D. (1989). Educating all children: Ten years later. *Exceptional children, 56*(1), 17–27.

Gilb, C. L. (1966). *Hidden hierarchies: The professions and government.* New York: Harper & Row.

Goetz, L., & Sailor, W. (1990). Much ado about babies, murky bathwater, and trickle-down politics: A reply to Kauffman. *Journal of Special Education, 24*(3), 334–339.

Goodlad, J. I. (1984). *A place called school: Prospects for the future.* New York: McGraw-Hill.

Gray, B. (1989). *Collaborating: Finding common ground for multiparty problems.* San Francisco: Jossey-Bass.

Guttman, A. (1987). *Democratic education.* Princeton, NJ: Princeton University Press.

Haber, S. (1964). *Efficiency and uplift: Scientific management in the Progressive Era, 1890–1920.* Chicago: University of Chicago Press.

Haskell, T. L. (1984). *The authority of experts: Studies in history and theory.* Bloomington: Indiana University Press.

Heller, K., Holtzman, W., & Messick, S. (1982). *Placing children in special education: A strategy for equity.* Washington, DC: National Academy of Sciences Press.

House, E. R. (1979). Technology versus craft: A ten year perspective on innovation. *Journal of Curriculum Studies, 11*(1), 1–15.

Illich, I. (1976). *Medical nemesis.* New York: Random House.

Jantsch, E. (1979). *The self-organizing universe.* New York: Pergamon Press

Johnson, G. O. (1962, October). Special education for the mentally handicapped— A paradox. *Exceptional Children, 62* 69.

Kauffman, J. M., Gerber, M. M., Semmel, M. I. (1988). Arguable assumptions underlying the regular education initiative. *Journal of Learning Disabilities, 21*(1), 6–11.

Kearns, D. T., & Doyle, D. P. (1988). *Winning the brain race: A bold plan to make our schools competitive.* San Francisco: Institute for Contemporary Studies.

Keogh, B. K. (1988). Improving services for problem learners: Rethinking and restructuring. *Journal of Learning Disabilities, 21*(1), 19–22.

Kuhn, T. S. (1970). *The structure of scientific revolutions.* (2nd ed.). Chicago: University of Chicago Press.

Lazerson, M. (1983). The origins of special education. In J. G. Chambers & W. T. Hartman (Eds.), *Special education policies: Their history, implementation, and finance.* Philadelphia: Temple University Press.

Lipsky, D. K., & Gartner, A. (Eds.) (1989a). *Beyond separate education: Quality education for all.* Baltimore: Paul H. Brookes.

Lipsky, D. K., & Gartner, A. (1989b). Building the future. In D. K. Lipsky & A. Gartner (Eds.), *Beyond separate education: Quality education for all* (pp. 255–290). Baltimore: Paul H. Brookes.

Lortie, D. C. (1975). *Schoolteacher: A sociological study.* Chicago: University of Chicago Press.

McNeil, L. M. (1986). *Contradictions of control: School structure and school knowledge.* New York: Methuen/Routledge & Kegan Paul.

Mercer, J. (1973). *Labeling the mentally retarded: Clinical and social system perspectives on mental retardation.* Berkeley: University of California Press.

Meyer, J. W., & Rowan, B. (1977). Institutionalized organizations: Formal structure as myth and ceremony. *American Journal of Sociology, 83,* 340–363.

Meyer, J. W., & Rowan, B. (1978). The structure of educational organizations. In M. W. Meyer (Ed.), *Environments and organizations* (pp. 78–109). San Francisco: Jossey-Bass.

Meyer, J. W., & Scott, W. R. (1983). *Organizational environments: Ritual and rationality.* Beverly Hills, CA: Sage.

Meyer, J. W. (1979). Organizational structure as signaling. *Pacific Sociological Review, 22*(4), 481–500.

Miller, D., & Mintzberg, H. (1983). The case for configuration. In G. Morgan (Ed.), *Beyond method: Strategies for social research* (pp. 57–73). Beverly Hills, CA: Sage

Mintzberg, H. (1979). *The structuring of organizations.* Englewood Cliffs, NJ: Prentice-Hall.

Mintzberg, H. (1983). *Structure in fives: Designing effective organizations.* Englewood Cliffs, NJ: Prentice-Hall.

Mintzberg, H. (1989). *Mintzberg on management: Inside our strange world of organizations.* New York: Free Press.

Moroney, R. M. (1981). Policy analysis within a value theoretical framework. In R. Haskins & J. J. Gallagher (Eds.), *Models for analysis of social policy: An introduction* (pp. 78–101). Norwood, NJ: Ablex.

Naisbitt, J., & Aburdene, P. (1985). *Re-inventing the corporation.* New York: Warner Books.

Oakes, J. (1985). *Keeping track: How schools structure inequality.* New Haven, CT: Yale University Press.

Parsons, T. (1960). *Structure and process in modern societies.* Glencoe, IL: Free Press.

Perrow, C. (1970) . *Organizational analysis: A sociological review.* Belmont, CA: Wadsworth.

Perrow, C. (1978). Demystifying organizations. In R. C. Sarri and Y. Hasenfeld (Eds.), *The management of human services* (pp. 105–120). New York: Columbia University Press.

Pfeffer, J. (1982). *Organizations and organization theory.* Marshfield, MA: Pitman.

Pugach, M., & Lilly, M. S. (1984). Reconceptualizing support services for classroom teachers: Implications for teacher education. *Journal of Teacher Education, 35*(5), 48–55.

Pugh, D. S., Hickson, D. J., Hinnings, C. R., MacDonald, K. M., Turner, C., & Lupton, T. (1963). A conceptual scheme for organizational analysis. *Administrative Science Quarterly, 8*(4), 289–315.

Reich, R. B. (1983). *The next American frontier*. New York: Penguin Books.

Reich, R. B. (1990). Education and the next economy. In S. B. Bacharach (Ed.), *Education reform: Making sense of it all* (pp. 194–212). Boston: Allyn and Bacon.

Reynolds, M. C., & Wang, M. C. (1983). Restructuring "special" school programs: A position paper. *Policy Studies Review, 2*(1), 189–212.

Reynolds, M. C., Wang, M. C., & Walberg, H. J. (1987). The necessary restructuring of special and general education. *Exceptional Children, 53*, 391–398.

Rist, R., & Harrell, J. (1982). Labeling and the learning disabled child: The social ecology of educational practice. *American Journal of Orthopsychiatry, 52*(1), 146–160.

Romzek, B. S., & Dubnick, M. J. (1987). Accountability in the public sector: Lessons from the Challenger tragedy. *Public Administration Review, 47*(3), 227–238.

Rosenthau, J. N. (1980). *The study of global interdependence*. London: Pinter.

Sarason, S. B., & Doris, J. (1979). *Educational handicap, public policy, and social history*. New York: Free Press.

Schein, E. H. (1972). *Professional education*. New York: McGraw-Hill.

Schön, D. A. (1983). *The reflective practitioner: How professionals think in action*. New York: Basic Books.

Scott, R. W. (1981). *Organizations: Rational, natural, and open systems*. Englewood Cliffs, NJ: Prentice-Hall.

Secretary's Commission on Achieving Necessary Skills (1991). *What work requires of schools: A SCANS report for America 2000*. Washington, DC: U.S. Department of Labor.

Segal, M. (1974). Organization and environment: A typology of adaptability and structure. *Public Administration Review*, 212–220.

Senge, P. M. (1990). *The fifth discipline: The art and practice of the learning organization*. New York: Doubleday.

Simon, H. A. (1977). *The new science of management decision* . Englewood Cliffs, NJ: Prentice-Hall.

Sizer, T. R. (1984). *Horace's compromise: The dilemma of the American high school*. Boston: Houghton Mifflin.

Skrtic, T. M. (1986). The crisis in special education knowledge: A perspective on perspective. *Focus on Exceptional Children, 18*(7), 1–16.

Skrtic, T. M. (1987). An organizational analysis of special education reform. *Counterpoint 8*(2), 15–19.

Skrtic, T. M. (1988a). The crisis in special education knowledge. In E. L. Meyen and T. M. Skrtic (Eds.), *Exceptional children and youth: An introduction* (pp. 415–447). Denver: Love.

Skrtic, T. M. (1988b). The organizational context of special education. In E. L. Meyen and T. M. Skrtic (Eds.), *Exceptional children and youth: An introduction*. Denver: Love.

Skrtic, T. M. (1991a). *Behind special education: A critical analysis of professional culture and school organization*. Denver: Love.

Skrtic, T. M. (1991b). The special education paradox: Equity as the way to excellence. *Harvard Educational Review*, 61(2), 148–206.

Skrtic, T. M. (Ed.) (1995a). *Disability and democracy: Reconstructing (special) education for postmodernity*. New York: Teachers College Press.

Skrtic, T. M. (1995b). The organizational context of special education and school reform. In E. L. Meyen & T. M. Skrtic (Eds.), *Special education and student disability: Traditional, emerging, and alternative perspectives*, (pp. 729–791). Denver: Love.

Skrtic, T. M. (1995c). Power/knowledge and pragmatism: A postmodern view of the professions. In T. M. Skrtic (Ed.), *Disability and democracy: Reconstructing (special) education for postmodernity* (pp. 25–62). New York: Teachers College Press.

Skrtic, T. M. (1995d). The special education knowledge tradition: Crisis and opportunity. In E. L. Meyen & T. M. Skrtic (Eds.), *Special education and student disability: Traditional, emerging, and alternative perspectives* (pp. 579–642). Denver: Love.

Skrtic, T. M. (1995e). Special education and student disability as organizational pathologies: Toward a metatheory of school organization and change. In T. Skrtic (Ed.), *Disability and democracy: Reconstructing (special) education for postmodernity* (pp. 190–232). New York: Teachers College Press.

Skrtic, T. M., Guba, E. G., & Knowlton, H. E. (1985). *Interorganizational special education programming in rural areas: Technical report on the multisite naturalistic field study*. Washington, DC: National Institute of Education.

Sleeter, C. E. (1995). Radical structuralist perspectives on the creation and use of learning disabilities. In T. Skrtic (Ed.), *Disability and democracy: Reconstructing (special) education for postmodernity* (pp. 153–165). New York: Teachers College Press.

Stainback, S., & Stainback, W. (1984). A rationale for the merger of special and regular education. *Exceptional Children*, 51, 102–111.

Thompson, J. D. (1967). *Organizations in action*. New York: McGraw-Hill.

Toffler, A. (1970). *Future shock*. New York: Bantam Books.

Tomlinson, S. (1982). *A sociology of special education*. Boston: Routledge and Kegan Paul.

Tomlinson, S. (1995). The radical structuralist view of special education and disability: Unpopular perspectives on their origins and development. In T. Skrtic (Ed.), *Disability and democracy: Reconstructing (special) education for postmodernity* (pp. 122–134). New York: Teachers College Press.

Tye, K. A., & Tye, B. B. (1984). Teacher isolation and school reform. *Phi Delta Kappan*, 65(5), 319–322.

U.S. Department of Education (1988). *Annual report to Congress on the implementation of the Education for All Handicapped Children Act*. Washington, DC: U.S. Department of Education.

Walker, L. J. (1987). Procedural rights in the wrong system: Special education is not enough. In A. Gartner & T. Joe (Eds.), *Images of the disabled/disabling images*. New York: Praeger.

Wang, M. C., Reynolds, M. C., & Walberg, H. J. (1986). Rethinking special education. *Educational Leadership*, 44(1), 26–31.

Weatherley, R. (1979). *Reforming special education: Policy implementation from state level to street level.* Cambridge, MA: MIT Press.

Weick, K. E. (1976). Educational organizations as loosely coupled systems. *Administrative Science Quarterly 21*, 1–19.

Weick, K. E. (1982a). Administering education in loosely coupled schools. *Phi Delta Kappan, 63*(10), 673–676.

Weick, K. E. (1982b). Management of organizational change among loosely coupled elements. In P. Goodman (Ed.), *Change in organizations* (pp. 375–408). San Francisco: Jossey-Bass.

White, R., & Calhoun, M. (1987). From referral to placement: Teachers' perceptions of their responsibilities. *Exceptional Children, 53*(5), 460–469.

Wise, A. E. (1979). *Legislated learning: The bureaucratization of the American classroom.* Berkeley: University of California Press.

Woodward, J. (1965). *Industrial organizations: Theory and practice.* Oxford: Oxford University Press.

Wright, A. R., Cooperstein, R. A., Reneker, E. G., & Padilla, C. (1982). *Local implementation of P.L. 94-142: Final report of a longitudinal study.* Menlo Park, CA: SRI International.

Ysseldyke, J. (1987). Classification of handicapped students. In M. Wang, M. Reynolds, & H. Walberg (Eds.), *Handbook of special education: Research and practice* Vol. 1. Oxford, England: Pergamon.

Ysseldyke, J., & Algozzine, B. (1982). *Critical issues in special and remedial education.* Boston: Houghton Mifflin.

Ysseldyke, J., Thurlow, M., Graden, J., Wesson, C., Algozzine, B., & Deno, S. (1983). Generalizations from five years of research on assessment and decision making. *Exceptional Education Quarterly, 4*(1), 75–94.

Zucker, L. G. (1981). Institutional structure and organizational processes: The role of evaluation units in schools. In A. Bank & R. C. Williams (Eds.), *Evaluation and Decision Making.* Los Angeles: UCLA Center for the Study of Evaluation.

10

Learning Disability: Issues of Representation, Power, and the Medicalization of School Failure

Carol A. Christensen

Traditional learning-disability theory grew out of pioneering work by Strauss and Lehtinen (1947). Their work was based on the observation that many children exhibiting academic and behavioral difficulties performed similarly to children who were known to have sustained brain damage. Therefore, they argued, if brain injury produced certain types of behavior, it could be inferred that children who exhibited similar behavior may also have suffered brain injury. Subsequent researchers and practitioners were less tentative in applying this logic. Consequently, in the early 1960s, prevailing professional opinion about children with normal intelligence test scores and from reasonably advantaged families who failed to achieve as expected rested strongly on the assumption that their learning problems resulted from some neurological abnormality or pathology.

The term "learning disability" was introduced by Kirk in 1962 to describe students who "displayed retardation, disorder, or delayed development in one or more of the processes of speech, language, reading, writing, arithmetic, or other school subjects resulting from a psychological handicap caused by possible cerebral dysfunction and/or emotional or behavioral disturbances. It is not the result of mental retardation, sensory deprivation, or cultural or instructional factors" (Kirk, 1962). A variety of psychophysiological variables have been used to indicate brain pathology for learning-disabled (LD) students. These have included inadequacies in motor development (Kepart, 1960), visual and auditory perception (Frostig, 1972; Wepman, 1958), psycholinguistic ability (Kirk & Kirk, 1971), and memory and information processing skills (Connor, 1983).

Over the ensuing years, a variety of labels have been invented to describe these children, including brain injured, hyperkinetic, neurologically impaired, dyslexic, and aphasic. A number of formal definitions have also been offered for learning disability. These diverse terms and definitions have a common thread in that they all accept the basic tenet that learning disability results from some imperfection in the child's brain. In other words, the source of the child's failure is a medical condition. For example, the World Federation of Neurology defined specific developmental dyslexia as "a disorder manifested by difficulty in learning to read despite conventional instruction, adequate intelligence and socio-cultural opportunity. It is dependent upon fundamental cognitive disabilities which are fundamentally constitutional in origin" (Critchely, 1970, p. 11).

The concept that school failure results from an underlying neurological deficit was formalized in public policy with the development of the Education for All Handicapped Children Act (PL 94-142). In 1977, federal regulations (U.S. Office of Education) subsumed the variety of medico-educational terms applied to low-achieving children under one category, specific learning disability, using as a definition one not substantially different from Kirk's original suggestion. According to these regulations, learning disability

> means a disorder in one or more of the basic psychological processes involved in understanding or in using language, spoken or written, which may manifest itself in an imperfect ability to listen, think, read, spell or do mathematical calculations. The term includes such conditions as perceptual handicaps, brain injury, minimal brain dysfunction, dyslexia and developmental aphasia. The term does not include children who have learning problems which are primarily the result of visual, hearing, or motor handicaps, of mental retardation, or emotional disturbance, or of environmental, cultural, or economic disadvantage.

In addition, the regulations indicated that learning disability is manifested by a significant discrepancy between the student's ability or "potential" and his or her current level of achievement. In practice this has meant that formal identification of students with learning disabilities generally involves documentation of a discrepancy between their score on an IQ test and their score on a standardized achievement test (Fletcher, 1992; Stanovich, 1991; Szuszkiewicz & Symons, 1993).

Therefore, four consistent themes emerge from definitions of learning disability:

1. There is inadequacy or failure in a particular area of academic or cognitive performance.

2. The inadequacy is caused by a medical condition related to an individual deficit or impairment that is generally neurological or psychological in nature.
3. The inadequacy is not caused by any other factor widely recognized as the basis of school failure such as sensory impairment, social or economic disadvantage, or lack of intelligence.
4. Learning disability can be identified by a discrepancy between achievement and potential.

Thus the dominant view of learning disability is that it results from an individual deficit inherent in the child and that it is manifested by a discrepancy between achievement and potential as indicated by intelligence. In other words, learning disability exists within and is a characteristic of individuals. Its origin lies within an individual's brain and as such it has an existence separate from the social and cultural experiences of the individual. It is seen to exist as a real physical entity independent of teachers, parents, or other environmental factors.

This view of learning disability is intuitively appealing to the naive observer who sees that despite teachers' and parents' best efforts, some children fail to learn to read, write, or do mathematics. When young, these children may write letters backward; when reading, they stumble over words others have long since mastered. They may be easily distracted and have difficulty settling and staying on task. Their motor coordination and handwriting may be poor or they may be left-handed. They may have trouble following directions or tracking with their eyes from left to right across the page. Clearly it seems that these children's brains function differently from those of other children. It seems that this impaired neurological functioning is related to the intransigent difficulties they have in school learning.

Early Psychological Critiques

Despite the commonsense nature of the deficit-discrepancy view of school failure, it has not been without criticism. Shortly after Kirk first articulated the term "learning disability," data began to emerge that threatened the conceptual links sustaining the belief that brain pathology is the cause of learning-disabled children's failure.

Traditional models of learning disability were based on the *medical model*. According to this model, *symptoms* of a *disease* are a sign of an underlying *pathology*. Accurate *diagnosis* will identify the pathology and indicate appropriate *treatment*. Treatment will destroy the pathology and effect a *cure*. Thus the relationships among symptoms, pathology, diagnosis, treatment, and cure are sustained through a series of conceptually logical links. When applied to learning disability, the medical model suggests that school failure (the symptom) is due to an underlying neurological deficit (the pathology). Accurate diagnosis (psychological assessment) will indicate appropriate treatment (provision of an individualized education program [IEP] and placement in a remedial program). Remediation should result in a cure (normal achievement).

The pervasive nature of the medical model is reflected in the discourse of the field. Inadequate achievement is referred to as a *disability*—teaching responses to students are often referred to as *clinical* or *remedial* interventions—and teachers employed specifically to work with students with learning disabilities are referred to as resource *specialists*. This medico-educational terminology not only reflects the conceptual basis for the field but is additionally attractive because it confers greater status and respectability through association with medicine (Bart, 1984).

Unfortunately, when they have examined the practices associated with learning disability, researchers have generally been unable to sustain the logical coherence of the medical model. They have found a chronic disparity between the formal definition, the characteristics of students identified as learning disabled, and recommended diagnostic instruments or clinical procedures (Christensen, Gerber, & Everhart, 1986).

Impairment and Discrepancy: Finding the Disability

The first problem confronting the field has been a persistent difficulty in locating the brain pathology responsible for learning disability. The identification of the neurological impairment has proved so elusive that operationally the identification of a "severe discrepancy" between achievement and ability has been substituted for documented pathology (Stanovich, 1991). The presence of an organic disorder is then inferred from the discrepancy.

This inference, however, has not been supported by data collected on identification procedures and characteristics of children labeled learning disabled. Diagnostic procedures indicate that children identified as learning disabled rarely show demonstrable signs of neurological problems or distinct forms of psychological-process disturbance. In fact, in many cases children identified by schools as learning disabled are virtually indistinguishable from other poorly achieving students. For example, Shepard, Smith, and Vojir (1983) found that of the population of students identified by schools as learning disabled, less than 1 percent demonstrated any "hard" neurological signs of brain abnormality. A small minority of students showed more ambiguous "soft" signs (sometimes regarded as indicative of neurodevelopmental differences rather than defects), 4.7 percent demonstrated clinical signs that were considered "high-quality evidence" of processing deficits, and 11.1 percent presented what was termed "medium-quality" clinical evidence of processing deficits. The vast majority (97 percent) of students identified by schools as learning disabled in this study showed no signs of physiological impairment. Similarly, Ysseldyke, Algozzine, and Epps (1983) reported that school-identified learning-disabled and low-achieving children were indistinguishable on tests of neurological functioning. Standard psychological assessment differentiated school-identified learning-disabled children from their "nondisabled" peers at about a chance level.

A series of more recent studies has indicated that the reading-related cognitive problem is the same for both LD and low-achieving poor readers—a difficulty in phonological processing (Fletcher, Shaywitz, Shankweiler, Katz, Liberman, Stuebing, Francis, Fowler, & Shaywitz, 1994; Stanovich, 1988). Similarly, in the area of learning problems in mathematics, Russell and Ginsburg (1984) state that "many LD students rather than suffering from fundamental deficits are essentially cognitively normal" (p. 243).

The issue of establishing a severe discrepancy between potential and achievement has also been of concern. In many cases, assessment personnel are confused about what psychometric or clinical results constitute evidence of a "severe" discrepancy between academic achievement and potential, and thus there is substantial unexplained variability in school practices. Even if valid statistical and clinical procedures were reliably applied to discriminating between learning-disabled students and other low achievers, the critical decision on when a "discrepancy" is so "severe" that students require differential treatment is largely based on a social judgment, one that cannot be made on a psychometric basis alone (Gerber & Semmel, 1982).

Further, the use of IQ tests to establish a student's ability or potential appears indefensible given critical analysis of the psychometric properties of these tests (Coles, 1978; Stanovich, 1991). Put simply, IQ tests measure students' existing knowledge based on their past social and cultural experiences. Neither IQ tests nor any other psychometric test can measure students' ability or potential to learn in the future.

The very notion that learning-disabled children fail to learn at a level that is commensurate with their potential is an intriguing one. Since the learning-disabled population is assumed to be a subgroup of low-achieving children, the discrepancy position relies on a further assumption that some children (i.e., nonlearning-disabled low achievers) should fail to learn in school while others (learning-disabled students) have greater "potential" and should not fail. According to advocates for the brain-pathology view of learning disability, some children, due to a disorder in "basic psychological processes," have potential beyond that indicated by their low levels of achievement. However, logic would seem to suggest that potential for achievement by neurologically impaired students would be limited by virtue of their neurological deficits. Learning-disability "specialists" have given scant attention to the reasonable position that if neurological impairment produces poor learning, then neurologically impaired students who demonstrate poor learning are achieving according to their "potential." This contradiction is further illustrated by the widespread belief that learning disability not only is a childhood condition but persists throughout life (American Association of Children and Adults with LD, 1985). In other words, children do not recover from learning disabilities as they grow into adults. The condition is permanent.

Finally, concern has been expressed about the difficulty in linking learning disability with specific instructional interventions. The medical model rests on the assumption that correct diagnosis indicates correct treatment. Thus identification of a learning disability should indicate effective instructional interventions. Unfortunately, this is not the case. There has been a failure to identify instructional methods that are specifically effective for students with learning disabilities. Rather, there is substantial overlap in effective instruction for students with learning disabilities and other groups of students identified as mildly disabled (e.g., mildly intellectually disabled, emotionally disturbed) (Algozzine, Algozzine, Morsink, & Dykes, 1984; Morsink, 1984). At the same time, the heterogeneity of the group of students identified as learning disabled means that some instructional interventions are successful with some learning-disabled students but not others (Morsink, Thomas, & Smith-Davis, 1987). Finally, effective instruction for learning-disabled students is fundamentally the same as effective instruction for normally achieving students. For example, Scruggs and Mastropieri (1992) identified a range of effective instructional strategies for mildly handicapped students placed in mainstream classrooms. Generally, these strategies are the same as those recommended for nondisabled students. Thus instruction that is effective for students with learning disabilities is also effective for other low-achieving students and for normally achieving students.

In summary, an increasing number of investigators have shown that a variety of traditional assumptions about learning disability are untenable when applied to school practice. As a result, there have been some unusually strident expressions of dissatisfaction with the continued search for psychological methods for discovering neurological and other within-student causes of learning failure. For example, Ysseldyke, Algozzine, and Thurlow (1983) have called practices in the identification and treatment of learning disability "indefensible," and Algozzine has called the category "ludicrous" (cited in Tucker, Stevens, & Ysseldyke, 1983). However, although these and other criticisms of practice have succeeded in arousing concern, they have generally failed to explain either the forces that created this current policy dilemma or the phenomenal growth and variability in classifying children as learning disabled. Psychologically oriented empiricists who have cataloged contradictions and inconsistencies between learning-disability theory and practice have not questioned the fundamental premises upon which learning disability theory rests. Following the logic of the field, they have established that the system does not work the way it should, but they have been unable to explain why this is so or to suggest how it can be changed.

Despite documented inconsistencies, the field has clung steadfastly to the assumptions underlying the medical model, holding out its promise of curative or remedial treatment. It has erected the edifice of learning disability as an innate condition. Correct "diagnosis" is assumed to lead to "prescriptive" educational, psychological, and sometimes pharmacological "treatment." The data do not support these assumptions.

Learning Disability as Social Practice

The inherent contradictions in learning-disability theory and practice can be explained only by examining the social and cultural processes through which learning disability is created. These processes medicalize school failure by transforming diversity in achievement into individual pathology or "disability." However, the idea that learning disability is created through social agency rather than neuropathology runs counter to the commonsense view of learning disability. Consequently, social analyses have had a limited impact in shaping academic debate and understanding of the field. For example, Dudley-Marling and Dippo (1995) suggest that published responses to social critiques range from "indifference to defensiveness to ridicule to near hysteria. The field of learning disabilities, although enriching itself by drawing on various traditions in medicine and cognitive psychology, remains isolated from developments in sociolinguistics, critical theory, anthropology, feminist studies, literacy education, philosophy and literary studies that challenge basic understandings in learning disabilities" (p. 408).

According to alternative perspectives, learning disability is a form of social practice. Identification and labeling of students as learning disabled is not so much the inevitable consequence of students' inherent neuropathology but is more the result of social processes that occur within classrooms, schools, and wider communities. For example, at a broad societal level, identification of students as learning disabled is often driven by funding and policy pressures rather than the characteristics of students. Hocutt, Cox, and Pelosi (1984) found that identification of students as "learning disabled," "educable mentally retarded," or "emotionally disturbed" was strongly influenced by the policies of the local education authority. The major influences on these policies were "federal and state laws and regulations, funding amounts and formulas, professional philosophy / training, and the characteristics of the students served by a school" (p. 2). Algozzine and Korinek (1985) found that during the period from 1978 to 1982 there was a significant increase in the number of students classified as learning disabled and a commensurate decrease in the number identified as educable mentally retarded. Tucker (1980) examined the ethnic composition of special education categories. He found that the shift in identification of students from educable mentally retarded to learning disabled could be accounted for by the reclassification of large numbers of African American students. Thus it appears that as the overrepresentation of ethnic minority students in the category of educable mentally retarded was critiqued, these students became overrepresented as learning disabled.

Although there has been considerable debate about the adequacy of definitions of learning disability, research has demonstrated that to the extent that children who are identified as learning disabled do share a common defining characteristic, it is that they exhibit an unacceptably low level of academic achievement (Algozzine & Ysseldyke, 1983; Kavale, Fuchs, & Scruggs, 1994). Yet the achievement profiles of children identified as learning disabled may vary dramatically. For example, Mehan, Hertweck, and Meihls (1986) found that in one school district many children who were identified as learning disabled did not meet the achievement criteria required for identification. In the same classrooms from which these learning-disabled children had come, there were numerous children who fitted the criteria perfectly but had not been identified.

Similarly, in a study we are currently undertaking in Australia, we have found that within classrooms there is substantial overlap in the achievement patterns of students identified as having learning difficulties (the Australian term that corresponds to learning disability) and those of normally achieving students. Although the mean levels of achievement for identified students was lower than for nonidentified students, in many cases students who were regarded as normally achieving performed below students who were identified as experiencing learning difficulties. The pattern became more extreme when examined across schools. In many cases the mean level of achievement for the identified group in one school was higher than the mean for normally achieving students in other schools.

Thus it appears that a learning disability is not defined by the essential characteristics of the students who are identified. Rather, it reflects how the achievement and cognitive characteristics are explained and conceptualized or represented in the classroom or school.

Learning Disability and the Politics of Representation

Social categories do not have a single essential meaning. Rather, meaning is ascribed to people, events, and objects as a result of social activity. Mehan (1993) gives the example of the many ways in which nonresident laborers can be represented: as "guest workers," as "potential citizens," as "undocumented workers," and as "illegal aliens." Each form of representation defines a different social identity. For example, "guest workers" can make a useful economic contribution to the workforce, whereas "illegal aliens" are foreign, threatening, and socially undesirable. Similarly, people with a physical disability (for example, who use a wheelchair) may be represented in many ways. They may be represented as brave and heroic in the face of adversity, as pathetic and useless cripples, as needy and helpless victims of tragedy, or as members of a socially disempowered and oppressed group.

The ways in which people are represented has a powerful influence in shaping their identities and opportunities. Carrier (1990) argues that forms of representation for disability emerge from cultural understandings that "are reflected in the ways that people evaluate and treat those who are labelled as handicapped, consistently denigrating their performance and restricting their freedom of action" (p. 213).

Issues of representation are profoundly political in that they are embedded within a set of power relationships. Fundamental to the ways in which groups of people are represented are questions about who is represented, how they are represented, who decides the form of representation, and what the consequences are of that form of representation for the individual. The way in which school success and failure, as well as ability and inability, are represented is embedded in issues of power. In other words, "Mental ability is a cultural construction that reflects the political power of different sets of people to impose their own evaluation of people's attitudes and behaviours" (Carrier, 1990, p. 214). For example, decisions about how children who fail in schools are represented are overwhelmingly made by teachers, school administrators, and school psychologists. The children who are labeled and their parents are relatively powerless in the process.

As with other social phenomena, differences in school learning, particularly school failure, may be represented in many ways. Throughout history, students who displayed unsatisfactory levels of achievement have variously been represented as illiterates, dullards, or morons or idiots; as lazy or as socially disadvantaged; as academically gifted underachievers who are bored or unmotivated. Although these terms vary, they all focus on a within-child deficit responsible for school problems.

Failure, Schools, and Social Justice

The need to represent school failure as something that resides within the neurology of the child or in his or her social or cultural background is deeply embedded within the nature of the school as a social institution. Schools are charged with providing equitable educational opportunity to all students. Thus it is essential that schools be perceived as socially just institutions and that differences in student achievement arise from factors related to students and their backgrounds rather than from factors related to the structure of schools.

Schools function on a view of social justice embedded within a notion of individual merit. One notable, recent advocate of this view was Nozick (1976). Nozick argued that critical to socially just practices is the protection of the individual right to fair and open competition and an entitlement to the products of that competition. In other words, equity requires free and open competition so that the most meritorious individual succeeds. It is the justice of competition—the way competition is conducted—not its outcomes, that is critical.

This entitlement view of social justice is central to the ways schools function. Equality (or sameness) of treatment is provided to all students in the form of standard school sites, curricula, and instructional provision. Schools are seen as essentially neutral in the distribution of educational opportunities. Schools must be seen to provide everyone with a fair and equal opportunity for educational resources and attainment. They must be seen to favor no particular individual or group of students, ensuring that students can openly compete for the benefits of educational success. Thus the distribution of outcomes (the success and failure of individual students) is supposedly merit based. It is believed that those who are most deserving—based on personal effort, talent, or "intelligence"—achieve school success through fair and open competition.

According to this merit-based view of schooling, if school success is the appropriate reward for the most deserving students, school failure is logically the student's own failure. Although failing students are represented in many ways, in each case failure is explained in terms of agencies external to the school.

For schools to be seen as fair and just, in terms of this view of social justice, they must maintain the legitimacy of the competitive processes by accounting for persistent failure of students in terms of deficiencies of the student, home environment, or society. To sustain the meritocratic assumptions of traditional schooling, schools must explain failure through factors outside the control of schools. In this context the concept of learning disability constitutes one legitimating mechanism; student failure is caused by an individual defect or pathology rather than by inequitable competitive practices whereby specific groups of students persistently experience disproportionately high failure rates (Carrier, 1983; Christensen, Gerber, & Everhart, 1986).

Learning disability helps legitimate or sustain existing school practices by providing a mechanism to attribute school failure to a deficit within the child rather than the structure and organization of schools. A learning disability label implies a pathological condition intrinsic to the individual; it fails to recognize that the concept of disability is a social construct.

Rather than being a nonproblematic feature of the individual, learning disability occurs as a consequence of diverse student characteristics interacting with the highly constraining demands of the classroom. Thus it can be argued that many students have been identified as learning disabled, stigmatized, or placed in segregated programs not because their personal characteristics necessitate this but because schooling is structured in such a way that it cannot accommodate student diversity beyond very narrowly prescribed limits. The lockstep, grade-based system of schooling requires a homogeneous school population to function efficiently (Skrtic, 1991). From this perspective, it can be argued that schooling itself is disabling, that its lack of flexibility in accommodating a diverse range of student attributes helps create learning disability. In this sense, student disability results from organizational pathology rather than student pathology. However, because the assumptions underpinning competitive meritocratic concepts of social justice allow the manner in which schools function to remain unexamined, many educators continue to identify the source of students' difficulties as defects within individuals, masking the role of educational systems in creating problems and failure (Carrier, 1983).

Historically and before universal compulsory schooling, it was accepted that illiteracy was the mark of poverty and lower socioeconomic class. Universal schooling meant that even the poor were given opportunities to learn to read. However, opportunity did not translate into educational attainment. Universal schooling resulted in large differences in academic achievement among students that corresponded to their social backgrounds. Social class interpreted as "social deprivation" or "cultural disadvantage" continued to provide an explanation and justification for failure. In other words, for children from low socioeconomic backgrounds, failure in reading was explicable. However, the belief that the frequent failure of children from low socioeconomic backgrounds was due to their own social deprivation or cultural disadvantage again masked the relationship between school practices, which systematically favored children with particular social and cultural background experiences, and inequitable achievement outcomes (Carrier, 1983). Thus the school continued to be seen as impartial in the allocation of academic success and failure.

While the concept of social disadvantage served to justify the failure of some children, there remained in schools a group of children whose failure appeared inexplicable. They simply did not achieve according to their "potential." Learning disability was introduced as a within-child pathology to explain this residual failure—the cases that could not be accounted for by inadequate intelligence or cultural background (Christensen, Gerber, & Everhart, 1986).

Definitional contradictions and inconsistencies emerge from the political agenda embedded in this form of representation. The exclusionary criteria (that the child's problems do not emerge from visual, hearing, or motor handicaps; from mental retardation or emotional disturbance; or from environmental, cultural, or economic disadvantage) are explicitly designed to eliminate competing forms of representation. Discrepancy definitions support the representation of the student as having the potential to achieve well when he or she is viewed according to conventional representations of failure (that the child is unintelligent, socially or economically disadvantaged).

Representation of school failure as a learning disability has the added advantage that it has a "no-fault, no-blame clause." If failure results from a neurological impairment, the child cannot be blamed for laziness or lack of intelligence, parents cannot be blamed for providing an inadequate home environment, and teachers cannot be blamed for providing inadequate or inappropriate instruction. Learning disability lets everyone off the hook. However, there is a price to pay for the comfort afforded by the learning-disability label. It distracts attention from classroom and school factors that could account for failure and that, if identified, could lead to productive and enduring solutions to students' problems.

Learning Disability and Classroom Life

The processes by which learning disability functions to legitimate inequitable school outcomes are situated in the day-to-day lives of teachers and students. Carrier (1990) suggests that the social processes by which a child's learning becomes represented as learning disability are "submerged in the routine of teachers' work and thoughts [so that] frequently there is no call for teachers to articulate them" (p. 211). These covert social processes stand in stark contrast to the formal, institutional processes where pupil performance is transformed from "normal" to "learning disabled" through the procedures of identification, psychological assessment, and educational planning.

The explicit procedures for identification, classification, and treatment of a learning disability are legislatively prescribed. They involve mechanisms for teacher *referral*, *nonbiased assessment*, and development of an *individualized education program* (IEP). The IEP is developed in an IEP meeting, which involves a number of participants including the classroom teacher, parents, and school psychologist and often the principal, special-education teacher, and possibly other professionals. These mandated procedures are intended to safeguard the rights of the child and to ensure that identification of a learning disability is based on impartial evidence. They are also designed to ensure that educational provision for the learning-disabled child is appropriate. Of course they are grounded on the assumption that learning disability is a real, physical entity that merely requires accurate identification.

At a superficial level, these procedures are transparently fair, politically and socially neutral, and in the best interests of the child. They are designed to seek out and classify the learning disability and to respond to it by protecting the child's rights to a fair and equal educational opportunity.

In practice, the transparent fairness of the process is an illusion. McDermott (1993) argues that "there is no such thing as LD, only a social practice of displaying, noticing, documenting, remediating and explaining it" (p. 272). In other words, the procedural safeguards in fact provide a formal mechanism for the creation of learning disability. They establish the procedures by which school failure is seen to reflect the qualities of the child rather than political processes where children are sorted, classified, and placed according to culturally determined, institutionalized procedures.

Unfortunately, relatively few researchers have systematically investigated the social processes underpinning learning disability. Mehan and McDermott are notable exceptions to the rule. Using discourse analysis they have examined the classroom processes by which learning disability becomes recognized, labeled, and treated. Discourse analysis refers to the examination of patterns of communication that characterize social contexts. It explores verbal and nonverbal interaction and both written and spoken language and the ways people use communication to pursue particular social purposes. This work provides telling insights into how learning disability is socially rather than neurologically created.

Identification and Referral of Learning Disability

Identification and referral of the child for assessment by the teacher is embedded within the social interaction patterns of the classroom. Identification as educationally normal or deviant, bright or dull, learning disabled or normally achieving, is not an objective reflection of the inherent attributes of the child. Numerous researchers have found that teachers refer many students who do not fit legislative criteria and that students who meet psychometrically prescribed criteria remain undetected in the classroom (Mehan et al., 1986; Shepard et al., 1983). Hargreaves, Hester, and Mellor (1975) argue that identification and referral of pupils can be understood only within the context of ongoing classroom interaction. For example, being identified as a disruptive student is not an issue of the level of noise a student creates. Rather, it depends on how skilled the student is in negotiating the classroom social organization—for example, some students are simply better at not being caught at making noise at times prohibited by the teacher. Similarly, Tattum (1982) found that in the process of identifying a disruptive pupil there are many pupils in schools whose behavior is "equally disruptive but is overlooked, minimised, tolerated, or handled differently, and so they are not considered for special placement" (1982, pp. 183–184).

In his case study of "Adam," McDermott (1993) found that learning disability was less an inadequacy inside Adam's head and more a consequence of "the arbitrariness of the tasks Adam is asked to work on ... and the interactional dilemmas thrown in Adam's way as he moves through school" (p. 279). According to traditional psychometric criteria, Adam qualified as learning disabled; however, McDermott found that in everyday situations, Adam's "disability" disappeared. "He proved in every way competent, and, more than most of the children he could be wonderfully charming, particularly if there was a good story to tell" (p. 278). In classroom tasks with low cognitive demand Adam performed capably provided he had a supportive social environment. For example, when working with a supportive peer, he could complete tasks successfully, sometimes reading instructions independently. However, if the interpersonal environment became more hostile, Adam's performance deteriorated dramatically. Rather than completing the task, Adam concentrated on avoiding the appearance of incompetence.

Unfortunately, use of an incompetence-avoidance strategy merely compounded the problem. For example, Adam made every effort to avoid reading instructions in situations where others might observe any errors. Thus mistakes became inevitable. As McDermott notes, "Reading 'teaspoon' for 'tablespoon' becomes more likely, not because Adam's head does not work, but because he barely looks at the page and ordinary resources for solution of the problem are disallowed" (p. 285).

Central to this cycle of avoidance and failure was public humiliation based on exposure of the learning disability. McDermott referred to this humiliation as a "degradation ceremony." Adam consistently acted to avoid such exposure; but, McDermott argues, once Adam's learning disability had been identified and named, it became a visible element of the classroom discourse. "Adam's LD generally played to a packed house. Everyone knew how to look for, recognise, stimulate, make visible and depending upon the circumstances keep quiet about or expose Adam's problem" (p. 287). Thus "looking for Adam's LD has become something of a sport in Adam's class" (p. 291). His difficulties lay not so much in the inherent difficulty of material he was required to learn or his own inherent inability to deal with that material but in the social organization and patterns of interaction within the classroom. Adam's difficulty arose because he "cannot address the material without worrying whether he can get it straight or whether anyone will notice if he does not" (p. 291).

The notion that persistent failure results in reluctance to engage in learning, which in turn inhibits further learning, is well established in the literature. For example, White (1959) developed a theory of effectance motivation. White suggested that the development of effectance motivation was cyclic. Feelings of pleasure were derived from experiences of success or competence in learning. These feelings of competence encouraged greater participation in future learning tasks. Increased participation increased the likelihood of success, and the cycle continued. Similarly, Bandura (1993) has argued that success in learning results in feelings of self-efficacy that facilitate learning in a number of ways: Children set more challenging goals and employ better strategies to achieve those goals, including persistence. Failure, in contrast, destroys a student' sense of self-efficacy and results in the avoidance of learning tasks.

Dweck (1986) argued that frequent failure can lead to a sense of helplessness or a perceived "external locus-of-control." Students who often fail feel that they have little influence over the consequences of their actions and come to "harbour doubts about their ability, yet, because ability is linked to their sense of worth, they have little choice but to maneuver to avoid failure (Covington, 1985, p. 391).

Stanovich (1986) refers to the "Matthew effect": Many children who become labeled learning disabled initially fail to learn to read because they lack critical prerequisite phonological awareness. As a result of their early failure, these children avoid reading tasks and so miss opportunities to practice their emerging reading skills, exacerbating the initial problem. The cycle of failure and avoidance continues until failure becomes chronic and the problem intractable.

Numerous studies have found that many students with learning disabilities demonstrate learned helplessness, an external locus-of-control, and a lack of self-efficacy (Hallahan & Kauffman, 1982; Seligman, 1975). However, traditional analyses adopt an individual-deficit perspective, attributing the cycle of failure, lack of self-efficacy, avoidance of tasks, and further failure to the characteristics of the individual. Findings of an external locus-of-control, low self-esteem, or lack of self-efficacy are seen as another manifestation of the learning-disabled student's pathology.

McDermott's analysis differs from traditional perspectives in that he suggests that this cycle is context dependent. Failure on a task is not the result of individual factors operating in isolation. Rather the outcome depends on the way the task is structured, the availability of social support, the presence of arbitrary restrictions on how the task can be accomplished, and the scrutiny of others as the task is performed. Moreover, McDermott argues that these social processes play a critical role in creating and sustaining the disability.

Testing and Assessment

Assessment plays a crucial role in the classification and treatment of learning disability. Both public policy and traditional learning-disability theory are based on the assumptions that assessment is scientifically objective and socially and culturally neutral and that assessment instruments measure a child's abilities and capacities independent of the social contexts of the school and the child's community.

These assumptions are erroneous from two perspectives. First, the test instruments themselves, far from representing culturally neutral measures, are culturally and socially discriminatory (Coles, 1978). Performance on standardized tests depends on an individual's access to the knowledge and skills the tests measure. Knowledge is not socially and culturally neutral. Rather, different social, ethnic, and racial groups have different access to particular types of knowledge. Standardized tests measure cultural knowledge associated with the white middle class. As Gipps and Murphy (1994) state, "The content of IQ tests is riddled with general cultural knowledge and are just as unfair to children from minority groups within a culture as they are if used across different cultures" (p. 71).

Second, the assessment situation itself is a form of social activity. It requires extended face-to-face interaction between the tester and the student. This can have a marked effect on the performance of the student. For example, Gipps and Murphy (1994) suggest that the character of the tester can exert a significant influence on students' performance. Students score lower if the tester is aloof and rigid in his or her interpersonal manner. If the tester is warm and personable, students tend to gain higher marks. Testers can communicate in subtle ways their expectations as to whether the students will do well or poorly, and students' performances tend to reflect these expectations. Similarity of backgrounds between students and the tester can also affect student performance. Students from minority ethnic or racial backgrounds do better when tested by a person from the same background (Watson, 1972).

Thus tests can measure a diversity of factors unrelated to the knowledge they are intended to assess. It is very difficult to determine the impact these factors have on any particular student's score. However, they effectively contaminate the scores, resulting in the possibility of unfair conclusions if the test is used as the sole basis for decisionmaking.

Because of its social nature, the assessment process involves a "panoply of unspoken assumptions, covert cues and responses" (Carrier, 1990, p. 21). Carrier argues that psychologists bring to assessment situations a set of expectations and assumptions that reflect their own social and cultural backgrounds. These cultural assumptions filter their perceptions of the student's behavior and subsequently help shape their analysis and interpretation of student performance.

In his analysis of Adam's learning disability, McDermott (1993) found that the testing situation was the most arbitrary and demanding of the social environments Adam encountered. Although his performance in many situations was competent, during testing "Adam stood out from his peers not just by his dismal performance but by the wild guesswork he tried to do" (p. 279). In many situations the learning disability was invisible. "Adam can blend into the crowd and do what he has to do without anyone worrying about the quality of his mind" (p. 280). During testing, the disability became highly visible; he became "learning disabled." McDermott argues that once the search for the learning disability is launched, "once our inquiry is narrowed down to the question of what is wrong with this or that child," evidence for an inherent deficit within the child is available "wherever one looks" (p. 281).

In essence, McDermott demonstrates that testing situations represent an arbitrary and highly constrained social environment. In other environments Adam can draw on a range of cognitive, social, and linguistic resources to achieve his goals: He can seek advice, employ his own reading skills, and dialogue with peers to joint problem solve. Testing represents an arbitrary situation in that the range of options normally available to him are artificially constrained. It was this arbitrariness that created his learning disability.

McDermott found that all the children in his study constantly appeared to avoid tasks they believed would be too difficult for them. They worried about appearing incompetent and offered excuses if caught not knowing something important. However, in Adam's case this fairly ubiquitous behavior became a sign of his disability. During testing it became part of the formalized evidence used to demonstrate his inherent deficit. McDermott noted that Adam barely attempted to engage in the assessment tasks. Given that they had been defined as "difficult," he simply used any extraneous information he could identify to guess an answer. For example, "If he has to choose between cup and spoon for the answer, he says, 'Cu-um-spoon' slowly enough to pick the answer that the tester seems to respond to" (p. 281).

Despite the impact of social and cultural factors on the assessment process, assessment information is generally presented as objective, scientific information that represents unbiased evidence of the students' disability. The social nature of assessment becomes masked by a cloak of scientific infallibility. As a result, assessment information is given a privileged status in decisionmaking processes that affect the labeling and treatment of students. This is particularly the case in IEP meetings.

Individualized Educational Planning

The legislative intent of the IEP mandate was to provide a safeguard mechanism to ensure that decisions regarding the identification of disability were based on sound, objective criteria and that decisions about the placement and provision of instructional support were made in the best interests of the child. It was assumed that through a process of negotiation around nondiscriminatory assessment, the participants in the meeting would establish fair and equitable educational provision for the child.

However, IEP meetings have never functioned in the way intended. They are intensely political. Ysseldyke, Thurlow, Graden, Wesson, Algozzine, and Deno (1983) report that IEP team decisions often functioned to do little more than verify the problems identified by the teacher. Ysseldyke, Algozzine, Richey, and Graden (1982) suggest that the most potent influence in IEP decisionmaking was "teacher squeak." This was an index of the degree to which the teacher wanted the removal of the student from the classroom. Reynolds (1984) referred to the IEP team decision meeting as a "capitulation conference."

Mehan et al. (1986) report that the discourse in IEP conferences focused on ensuring that all participants (particularly parents) acceded to the decision that had already been made during several informal meetings between the professional stakeholders. For example, the school psychologist and classroom teacher often met to talk over the implications of assessment results and the nature of teacher concerns about the child's classroom behavior. However, although these informal meetings appear to be the most powerful influence in shaping decisions about the child, they are rarely, if ever, referred to in the formal IEP meeting. Rather, the IEP meeting becomes an avenue to selectively provide information that substantiates the decisions already made.

Mehan (1993) argues that within an IEP meeting, the political combatants attempt to capture the dominant mode of representation. Because of the assumptions of inherent deficit that underpin the medical representation of learning disability, the psychological view, embedded in the medical model, has privileged status. Mehan provides an example of an IEP meeting for "Shane," where the participants provided competing representations of Shane and his achievement. The psychologist represented Shane as having "troubles" and "problems." For example, she reported that "he cannot switch channels" and "has some fears and anxieties." Thus Shane's difficulties were seen to reside clearly "beneath his skin, between his ears" (p. 255). The teacher's representation also focused on a within-child deficit: "The fine motor types of things are difficult for him" (p. 255). However, the teacher contextualized Shane's behavior, acknowledging that his achievements varied depending on circumstances and tasks. "He's got a very creative mind and expresses himself well orally and verbally and he's pretty alert to what's going on. . . . I've been noticing that it's just his writing and things that he has a block with. And he can reread and comprehend some things when I talk to him" (p. 252).

The mother's representation was more contextualized as well as historically embedded. She saw Shane to be developing over time: "As a small child, he didn't [write] at all. . . . He was never interested in sitting in my lap and having a book read to him . . . which I think is part of it. [Now] Shane, at night, lots of times he comes home and he'll write or draw. He's really doing a lot. . . . He sits down and is writing love notes to his girlfriend" (p. 253).

Within the decisionmaking process about Shane's performance, these competing forms of representation were not equal. The psychologist's view had privileged status and was politically the most powerful. The psychologist's recommendations were accepted unchallenged. Mehan argues that psychological language gained its authority from its technical and quasi-scientific terminology. The psychologist's representation of the child as disabled was bolstered by discourse punctuated with evidence of "scientific" observation: "I found that he had a verbal IQ of 115, performance of 111, a full scale of 115, so he's a bright child. He had very high scores in information which is his long-term memory. Vocabulary was also considerably over average, good detail awareness . . . scored in reading at 4.1, spelling 3.5 and arithmetic 3.0. . . . I gave him the Bender Gestalt and he had six errors. And his test age was 7.0 to 7.5 [and] his actual age is 9 so . . . " (p. 251).

The psychologist presented her technical account of Shane's disability as an uninterrupted monologue. Although she consistently used technical jargon that was impenetrable to the other participants, she was never asked to clarify terms or challenged on her interpretation of her numbers as indicative of learning disability. In contrast, both the teacher and parent, with their more contextualized representation of Shane's skills, were constantly interrupted with requests for clarifications and explication.

The psychological view dominated to the exclusion of all other views in the processes of identification, labeling, and treatment of Shane's learning disability. Prior to the meeting, the teacher argued that as Shane had demonstrated significant improvement from the time he was initially referred, she no longer felt that placement in special education was warranted. Shane's mother expressed concern that placement in a special program would be stigmatizing and that she did not want her child removed from the regular classroom. Despite these competing opinions, the decision to place Shane in a "pull-out" program for students with learning disabilities was accepted in the meeting without dissent or discussion. In other words, by the end of the meeting, one view of Shane prevailed—that he was learning disabled.

IEP meetings can be characterized as highly political environments where competing representations of the student are negotiated so that one emerges as dominant. This view then defines the nature of the child (learning disabled or not learning disabled) and the future educational opportunities open to him or her. These analyses contest the view that learning disability is a purely physical disorder that resides within the head of the child. Rather, learning disability is constructed through social activity within schools. It is created as participants seek to interpret and explain student behavior.

This is not to suggest that students do not vary in their learning and achievement. Clearly some students learn more quickly and more effectively than others. However, the interpretations of these differences are essentially social in nature. The classification of one student's level of achievement as "acceptable," another's as "below grade level," and another's as "learning disabled" is dependent on social activity. In this way, failure is medicalized and disability is created. As we have seen, these processes emerge from the fabric of the day-to-day lives of students, teachers, school psychologists, and administrators.

In summary, rather than constituting an individual neurological deficit, learning disability is a social category. It functions to legitimate school failure for students whose failure would otherwise be inexplicable. It is created through the social practices of schooling, but medicalizing school failure and attributing it to individual pathology mask the role of these social processes and hinder the development of more effective solutions to the problem.

References

Algozzine, B., & Korinek, L. (1985). Where is special education for students with high prevalence handicaps going? *Exceptional Children, 51,* 388–397.

Algozzine, B., & Ysseldyke, J.E. (1983). Learning disabilities as a subset of school failure: The over-sophistication of a concept. *Exceptional Children, 50*, 242–246.

Algozzine, B., Algozzine, K., Morsink, C., & Dykes, M.K. (1984). *Summary of the 1983–84 ESE classroom observation, using COKER*. Gainesville: University of Florida, Department of Special Education.

American Association for Children and Adults with Learning Disabilities (1985). Definitions of the condition of specific learning disabilities. *ACLD News Briefs, 58*, 1–3.

Bandura, A. (1993). Perceived self-efficacy in cognitive development and functioning. *Educational Psychologist, 28*, 117–148.

Bart, D. (1984). The differential diagnosis of special education: Managing social pathology as individual disability. In L. Barton & S. Tomlinson (Eds.), *Special Education and Social Interests*. London: Crook Helm.

Carrier, J. (1983). Masking the social in educational knowledge: The case of learning disability theory. *American Journal of Sociology, 88*, 948–974.

Carrier, J. (1990). Special education and the explanation of pupil performance. *Disability, Handicap and Society, 5*, 211–227.

Christensen, C.A., Gerber, M.M., & Everhart, R.B. (1986). Toward a sociological perspective on learning disabilities. *Educational Theory, 36*, 317–331.

Coles, G.S. (1978). The learning-disabilities test battery: Empirical and social issues. *Harvard Educational Review, 48*, 313–340.

Connor, F.P. (1983). Improving school instruction for learning disabled children: The Teachers' College Institute. *Exceptional Education Quarterly, 4*, (1), 23–44.

Covington, M.V. (1985). Strategic thinking and the fear of failure. In J. Segal, S. Chipman, & R. Glaser (Eds.), *Thinking and learning skills: Relating instruction to basic research* (pp. 389–416). Hillsdale, NJ: Erlbaum.

Critchley, M. (1970). *The dyslexic child*. London: Heinemann.

Dudley-Marling, C., & Dippo, D. (1995). What learning disability does: Sustaining the ideology of schooling. *Journal of Learning Disabilities, 28*, 408–414.

Dweck, C.S. (1986). Motivational processes affecting learning. *American Psychologist, 41*, 1040–1048.

Fletcher, J.M. (1992). The validity of distinguishing children with and without learning disabilities according to discrepancies with IQ: Introduction to special series. *Journal of Learning Disabilities, 25*, 546–548.

Fletcher, J.M., Shaywitz, S.E., Shankweiler, D.P., Katz, L., Liberman, I.Y., Stuebing, K.K., Francis, D.J., Fowler, A.E., & Shaywitz, B.A. (1984). Cognitive profiles of reading disability: Comparisons of discrepancy and low achieving definitions. *Journal of Educational Psychology, 86*, 6–23.

Frostig, M. (1972). Visual perception, integrative functions and academic learning. *Journal of Learning Disabilities, 1*, 1–15.

Gerber, M.M., and Semmel, M.I. (1982). Teachers as imperfect test. In M.L. Smith, *How educators decide who is learning disabled*. Springfield, IL: Charles C. Thomas.

Gipps, C., & Murphy, P. (1994). *A fair test? Assessment, achievement and equity*. Buckingham, UK: Open University Press.

Hallahan, D.P., & Kauffman, J.M. (1982). *Exceptional children*. Englewood Cliffs, NJ: Prentice-Hall.

Hammill, D.D., Leigh, J.E., McNutt, G., & Larsen, S.C. (1981). A new definition of learning disabilities. *Learning Disability Quarterly, 4,* 336–342.

Hargreaves, D., Hester, S., & Mellor, F. (1975). *Deviance in classrooms.* London: Routledge & Kegan Paul.

Hocutt, A.M., Cox, J.L., & Pelosi, J. (1984). An exploration of issues regarding the identification and placement of LD, MR, and ED students. In *A policy-oriented study of special education's service delivery system, Phase I: Preliminary study.* (RTI Report No. PT1/2706–06/OISE). Durham, NC: Research Triangle Institute, Center for Educational Studies.

Kavale, K.A., Fuchs, D., & Scruggs, T.E. (1994). Setting the record straight on learning disability and low achievement: Implications for policy making. *Learning Disabilities Research and Practice, 9,* 70–77.

Kepart, N.C. (1960). *The slow learner in the classroom.* Columbus, OH: Merrill.

Kirk, S.A. (1962). *Educating exceptional children.* Boston: Houghton Mifflin.

Kirk, S.A., & Kirk, W.D. (1971). *Psycholinguistic learning disabilities: Diagnosis and remediation.* Urbana, IL: University of Illinois Press.

McDermott, R.P. (1993). The acquisition of a child by a learning disability. In S. Chaiklin & J. Lave (Eds.), *Understanding practice: Perspectives on activity and context* (pp. 269–305). Cambridge: Cambridge University Press.

Mehan, H. (1993). Beneath the skin and between the ears: A case study in the politics of representation. In S. Chaiklin & J. Lave (Eds.), *Understanding practice: Perspectives on activity and context.* Cambridge: Cambridge University Press.

Mehan, H., Hertweck, A., & Meihls, J.L. (1986). *Handicapping the handicapped: Decision making in students' educational careers.* Stanford, CA: Stanford University Press.

Morsink, C.V., Thomas, C.C., & Smith-Davis, J. (1987). Noncategorical special education programs: Processes and outcomes. In M. Wang, M. Reynolds, & H. Walberg (Eds.), *Handbook of special education research and practice. Learner characteristics and adaptive education* (Vol. 1, pp. 287–309). New York: Pergamon.

Nozick, R. (1974). *Anarchy, state and utopia.* New York: Basic Books.

Reynolds, M.C. (1984). Classification of students with handicaps. In E.W. Gordon (Ed.), *Review of research in education* (Vol. 2, pp. 63–92). Washington, DC: American Educational Research Association.

Rourke, B.P. (1989). Coles's *Learning Mystique:* The good, the bad and the irrelevant. *Journal of Learning Disabilities, 22,* 272–277.

Russell, R.R., & Ginsburg, H.P. (1984). Cognitive analysis of children's mathematical difficulties. *Cognition and Instruction, 1,* 217–244.

Scruggs, T.E., & Mastropieri, M.A. (1992). Effective mainstreaming strategies for mildly handicapped students. *Elementary School Journal, 92,* 389–409.

Seligman, M.E. (1975). *Helplessness: On depression and death.* San Francisco: Freeman.

Shepard, L.A., Smith, M.L., & Vojir, C.P. (1983). Characteristics of pupils identified as learning disabled. *American Educational Research Journal, 20,* 309–311.

Skrtic, T.M. (1991). *Behind special education.* Denver, CO: Love.

Stanovich, K.E. (1988). Explaining the differences between dyslexic and the garden-variety poor reader: The phonological-core variable-difference model. *Journal of Learning Disabilities, 21,* 590–604.

Stanovich, K.E. (1991). Discrepancy definitions of reading disability: Has intelligence led us astray? *Reading Research Quarterly, 26,* 7–29.

Stanovich, K.E. (1996). Matthew effects in reading: Some consequences of individual differences in the acquisition of literacy. *Reading Research Quarterly, 21,* 360–370.

Strauss, A., and Lehtinen, L. (1947). *Psychopathology and education of the brain injured child.* New York: Grune & Stratton.

Szuszkiewicz, T., & Symons, D. (1993). Comment on Rosenberg et al. (1993). *Journal of Learning Disabilities, 26,* 570–571.

Tattum, D. (1982). *Disruptive pupils in schools and units.* Chichester, UK: John Wiley.

Tucker, J., Stevens, L.J., & Ysseldyke, J.E. (1983). Learning disabilities: The experts speak out. *Journal of Learning Disabilities, 16,* 6–14.

Ulman, J.D., & Rosenberg, M.S. (1986). Science and superstition in special education. *Exceptional children, 52,* 459–460.

U.S. Office of Education (1977). Education of handicapped children: Implementation of Part B of Education of the Handicapped Act. *Federal Register, 42.*

Watson, P. (1972). Can racial discrimination affect IQ? In K. Richardson & D. Spears (Eds.), *Race, culture and intelligence.* Harmondsworth: Penguin.

Wepman, J. (1958). *Auditory Discrimination Test.* Chicago: Language Research Associates.

White, R.W. (1959). Motivation reconsidered: The concept of competence. *Psychological Review, 66,* 297–333.

Ysseldyke, J., Algozzine, B., & Epps, S. (1983). A logical and empirical analysis of current practice in classifying students as handicapped. *Exceptional Children, 50,* 160–166.

Ysseldyke, J.E., Algozzine, B., Richey, L., & Graden, J. (1982). Declaring students' eligibility for learning disability services: Why bother with the data? *Learning Disability Quarterly, 5,* 37–44.

Ysseldyke J., Algozzine, B., Shinn, M.R., & McGue, M. (1979). Similarities and differences between low achievers and students classified as learning disabled. *Journal of Special Education, 16,* 1973–1983.

Ysseldyke, J., Algozzine, B., and Thurlow, M. (1983). On interpreting Institute research: A response to McKinney. *Exceptional Education Quarterly, 4,* 1945–1947.

Ysseldyke, J.E., Thurlow, M.L., Graden, J.L., Wesson, C., Algozzine, B., & Deno, S.L. (1983). Generalizations from five years of research on assessment and decision-making. *Exceptional Education Quarterly, 4* (1), 75–93.

11

Can We Get There from Here? Learning Disabilities and Future Education Policy

Louise Spear-Swerling

Contemporary educational policies for identifying learning disabilities (LD) have been widely criticized. I would like to begin this chapter with a story that illustrates some of the conundrums in these policies.

As part of a program for training preservice teachers, I have been supervising students in a fieldwork setting for the past few semesters. The students tutor children in an after-school program at an urban public elementary school, which I will call Center School, in a large city in Connecticut. The school serves a population that is close to 100 percent African American and of uniformly low socioeconomic status.

I had been told that none of the children in the after-school program were receiving remedial or special-education services, so I was dismayed to discover that several of them were functioning at extremely low reading levels. Four youngsters, all third-graders, had scores below the twelfth percentile for both Word Attack and Word Identification from the Woodcock-Johnson Tests of Achievement—Revised (Woodcock & Johnson, 1989). Two of the four children could read no higher than primer-level text; the other two could not read accurately in context even at a preprimer level. The after-school program—one 45-minute session per week for eight weeks—was completely inadequate for providing the intensity of instruction required by these youngsters.

Test results in hand, I went to talk to the principal of the school. Was there any possibility of getting the children some extra help during the schoolday, perhaps via compensatory education programs such as those funded by Title I?

"Oh, the whole school qualifies for that," the principal said bluntly. "We have to spread that money around to all the children."

What about special education? Indeed, the principal informed me, all four children had been evaluated for learning-disabilities services, but they had failed to qualify because they did not meet the IQ-achievement discrepancy criterion, which is central to most educational definitions of learning disabilities not only in Connecticut but in many other states. Although clearly the children were not mentally retarded and all were in desperate need of help in reading, their IQ scores were not high enough relative to their achievement scores for them to meet LD identification guidelines.

Ironically, a few days later, I received a phone call from a parent whose child had just begun receiving learning-disabilities services in an affluent suburban public school district. During our conversation, I discovered that this sixth-grader, whom I'll call Danny, was reading in context at about the fifth-grade level and had scored at approximately the twenty-fifth percentile in word recognition. However, although these reading problems were mild compared to those of the four Center School youngsters, Danny had not had difficulty meeting the discrepancy requirement of LD guidelines because he had scored well above average on an IQ test.

From an educational standpoint, it is difficult to see the logic in a system in which children with very serious reading difficulties cannot qualify for help, whereas those with milder difficulties can qualify. Of course, the LD category is not the only one under which children can receive extra educational services in reading. However, LD identification guidelines play a particularly important role in educators' attempts to help poor readers. For one thing, many poor readers do receive services under the LD designation, which is the single largest category of special education nationwide (Torgesen, 1991). In some schools, if poor readers do not qualify as learning disabled and if they do not fall into some other special-education category (such as "emotionally handicapped"), their remedial needs will go largely unmet, as in the case of the four Center School children. And finally, LD identification guidelines are influential in shaping how educators and others think about—and go about solving—the problem of reading difficulties.

This chapter focuses on the problems with current LD identification policies and, more optimistically, on possible improvements in educational policies for identifying and serving children with reading difficulties. I begin the chapter by discussing current definitions of learning disabilities and guidelines for identifying LD in public schools. In the second section of the chapter, I review research done by many educational and scientific investigators that reveals some of the central problems with these policies. Finally, in the third section, I present several different kinds of proposals for redefining and identifying learning disabilities that have been made by researchers. I then explore how one proposal, that involving the concept of failure to respond to treatment, might form a basis for future educational policy.

Before I begin, I must clarify three basic points about the orientation of this chapter. First, I focus on educational policies in the United States. Learning disabilities as a category is widely recognized by educators and researchers from many countries, and some of the problems with U.S. policies on learning disabilities also may exist elsewhere. However, the educational research that I cite has been conducted primarily in the United States. Furthermore, there are features of the American educational system in general, such as the lack of equity in funding across school districts, that make it different from the systems of many other developed countries (Berliner & Biddle, 1995).

Second, I highlight one particular domain, that of reading. Although children can be identified as learning disabled in a number of different domains, a full discussion of all of these domains is well beyond the scope of the chapter. I emphasize reading disability (RD) because it is the most intensively researched area of learning disabilities and because it is the domain in which children are most commonly identified as being in need of educational services. However, the policy issues for other domains of learning disabilities, such as mathematics or written expression, are likely analogous to those in reading.

A final and especially important point regards the distinction between learning disabilities as a field of education and learning disabilities as a field of scientific investigation. This chapter focuses on the former field, which dates from the early 1960s, well before the advent of most scientific research on learning disabilities. A number of investigators (e.g., Keogh, 1993; Moats & Lyon, 1993; Torgesen, 1991) have suggested that many of the current problems of learning disabilities as an educational field stem from the fact that the field "took off" for social and political reasons (e.g., pressure from parent and professional advocacy groups) before it had a solid scientific foundation.

Interestingly, recent scientific research does support some basic ideas long associated with reading disability. It is clear that some children do need much more intensive instruction in order to learn to read than do others (e.g., Felton, 1993; Torgesen & Hecht, 1996; Torgesen, Wagner, & Rashotte, 1994). Furthermore, reading difficulties can occur even when children come from an affluent family background, receive a good instructional program in reading, and are highly intelligent; and at least in some cases, these difficulties appear to be associated with biological (e.g., genetic) differences. Nonetheless, current educational policy is not congruent with scientific research on reading disability in many crucial ways that will be elaborated later in the chapter.

Scientifically, the study of even a single unusual case is justified and may ultimately yield practical benefits (Torgesen, 1991; see also Torgesen, Chapter 5, this volume). From a scientific standpoint, it may be entirely reasonable to include Danny as a subject of study and to exclude the Center School children. However, in order to be good educational policy, the current system of classifying children with LD must meet other requirements. Specifically, the classification should be valid for most school-labeled children with LD, and these children's educational needs should be distinctive enough to warrant singling them out for separate educational classification and treatment. For instance, in the case of the Center School children and Danny, it may be legitimate to classify Danny as learning disabled and not the Center School children if Danny has greater "potential" in reading or a qualitatively different type of poor reading, one that requires a special kind of remediation not beneficial to the Center School children. Indeed, these are traditional assumptions associated with reading disability, but they are among the ones not supported by scientific evidence.

Current Educational Policies on Learning Disabilities

Federal and State Regulations

Federal and state regulations are extremely influential in educational identification of RD, and in determining funding to schools for provision of special-education services. In these guidelines, RD is included under the umbrella category of learning disabilities. The federal regulations (P.L. 101-476, or the Individuals with Disabilities Education Act, and its earlier counterpart, P.L. 94-142, the Education for All Handicapped Children Act of 1975) contain the following definition of learning disabilities:

> "Specific learning disability" means a disorder in one or more of the basic psychological processes involved in understanding or in using language, spoken or written, which may manifest itself in imperfect ability to listen, think, speak, read, write, or do mathematical calculations. The term includes such conditions as perceptual handicaps, brain injury, minimal brain dysfunction, dyslexia, and developmental aphasia. The term does not include children who have learning problems which are primarily the result of visual, hearing, or motor handicaps, of mental retardation, of emotional disturbance, or of environmental, cultural, or economic disadvantage. (*Federal Register*, December 29, 1977, p. 65083)

Federal guidelines also require that children identified with learning disabilities have "a severe discrepancy between achievement and intellectual ability" (p. 65083) in at least one of seven areas: basic reading, reading comprehension, written expression, oral expression, listening comprehension, mathematics reasoning, or mathematics calculation. Thus children with RD may be identified based on deficits in basic reading (i.e., word recognition), in reading comprehension, or in both areas.

Federal guidelines do not specify a particular method for measuring "intellectual ability"; nor do they specify exactly what constitutes a "severe discrepancy." In fact, they give educators considerable latitude in deciding whether to qualify a particular child for services. However, in educational practice, an individually administered IQ test typically is used to measure intellectual ability. Furthermore, state guidelines have often sought to quantify the amount of discrepancy needed for an LD diagnosis. This amount, as well as the actual procedure for determining the discrepancy (e.g., standard-score comparison vs. the use of expectancy formulas), can vary considerably from state to state (Frankenberger & Harper, 1987; Moats & Lyon, 1993).

The discrepancy criterion is only one of three main requirements contained in the federal regulations and found in many state guidelines on LD as well. A second requirement involves the statement in the federal definition that children with learning disabilities have "a disorder in one or more of the basic psychological processes." In educational practice, processing disorders commonly are identified through the use of tests of visual processing, auditory processing, memory, or language. Deficits in these areas usually are assumed to be evidence of an intrinsic disorder in learning (and not, for example, evidence of faulty instruction or lack of experience). The third requirement involves the last sentence of the federal definition, often called the exclusion clause, which states that learning disabilities are not primarily due to other handicapping conditions, such as sensory impairment or mental retardation, or to cultural or environmental factors. Of these three requirements, the discrepancy criterion is the most emphasized in educational practice (Frankenberger & Harper, 1987; Stanovich, 1991), perhaps because it is the easiest to quantify.

Fundamental to these definitions of LD and RD are several assumptions. Children with RD are assumed to have an intrinsic problem in learning, one that is based on a biological deficit. The notion of "unexpected" reading failure also has been historically fundamental to the concept of reading disability (Stanovich, 1991). That is, reading difficulties are seen as explainable in children with limited intellectual abilities, sensory handicaps, obvious environmental deprivation, and the like, whereas reading disability involves unexpected or unexplained reading failure. And finally, educational definitions of RD assume that it involves a unique kind of poor reading that is different from generic reading failure.

The National Joint Committee on Learning Disabilities Definition

The National Joint Committee on Learning Disabilities (NJCLD) consists of representatives from a variety of influential learning-disabilities organizations and professional groups. Their definition of learning disabilities has been widely cited:

> *Learning disabilities* is a general term that refers to a heterogeneous group of disorders manifested by significant difficulties in the acquisition and use of listening, speaking, reading, writing, reasoning, or mathematical abilities. These disorders are intrinsic to the individual, presumed to be due to central nervous system dysfunction, and may occur across the life span. Problems in self-regulatory behaviors, social perception, and social interaction may exist with learning disabilities but do not by themselves constitute a learning disability. Although learning disabilities may occur concomitantly with other handicapping conditions (for example, sensory impairment, mental retardation, serious emotional disturbance) or with extrinsic influences (such as cultural differences, insufficient or inappropriate instruction), they are not the result of those conditions or influences. (National Joint Committee on Learning Disabilities, 1988, p. 1)

The NJCLD definition makes explicit what is implicit in federal and most state regulations—that RD (and other types of learning disabilities) involve intrinsic disorders in learning that are assumed to be due to central nervous system dysfunction.

Some Problems with Current Identification Policies

The Discrepancy Criterion

Many investigators have compared poor readers who have IQ-achievement discrepancies to "garden variety" poor readers (Gough & Tunmer, 1986) who lack discrepancies. Garden-variety poor readers are children whose IQs, although approximately commensurate with their reading achievement, are not low enough for them to be classified as mentally retarded—the case with the four children from Center School. A central question in these investigations has been whether the comparisons would reveal significant cognitive differences between the two groups of poor readers in support of the idea that the discrepancy criterion identifies a qualitatively different kind of poor reading. However, many more similarities than differences have been revealed. These similarities are most pronounced for the basic cognitive processes involved in reading, particularly word recognition. Both groups of poor readers appear to share a core set of deficits in phonological processing (Fletcher et al., 1994; Siegel, 1988, 1989; Stanovich & Siegel, 1994). There is now considerable scientific consensus that most cases of reading disability do not involve a unique syndrome of poor reading, but rather are best conceptualized as being on a continuum with garden-variety poor reading.

Currently, there is little evidence to support the idea that children with discrepancies necessarily have a better prognosis in reading than do children who lack discrepancies (Stanovich, 1991). Furthermore, both groups appear to benefit from similar types of remedial programs (Felton, 1993; Siegel, 1988, 1989, Chapter 7, this volume; Torgesen, 1991). Although youngsters like the Center School children are excluded, based on the discrepancy criterion, from remedial services (at least under the LD category), they might well benefit from these services as much as their peers who have discrepancies.

Yet another problem with the discrepancy criterion involves the assumption that the causal relationship between IQ (or "ability") and reading achievement runs in only one direction—from ability to achievement. In fact, it is clear that the causal relationship runs in both directions (Siegel, 1988, 1989; Stanovich, 1991). That is, reading itself helps to develop many of the abilities that are measured on IQ tests, such as vocabulary. Thus over time, "Matthew effects" (Stanovich, 1986; Walberg & Tsai, 1983) associated with poor reading, such as a lack of independent reading, may gradually erode some poor readers' performance on IQ tests.

The Use of Processing Tests

Certain measures of cognitive processing are very useful in identifying reading difficulties—whether or not those difficulties involve IQ-achievement discrepancies—and in predicting whether young children are at risk of future reading failure. Three especially important measures involve knowledge of letter names and sounds; phonological awareness, or sensitivity to sounds in spoken words; and rapid-naming tasks, in which children are required to name a variety of stimuli such as letters and digits as quickly as possible (Adams, 1990; Nation & Hulme, 1997; Torgesen, Wagner, Rashotte, Burgess, & Hecht, 1997; Wolf, 1991). A principal reading deficit in children with RD involves phonological reading, that is, the ability to decode unfamiliar words (Rack, Snowling, & Olson, 1992).

Unfortunately, however, there are a number of problems with the way processing measures tend to be used in education. A very basic problem is the lack of technical adequacy of some processing tests (Moats & Lyon, 1993). Second, sometimes the right processes are not measured. For instance, although the scientific consensus is that linguistic, particularly phonological, deficits are fundamental to most cases of reading disability and of poor reading generally, these phonological processes sometimes are not emphasized in educational assessment.

Perhaps the most serious problem with the use of processing tests in education involves how the tests are interpreted. Cognitive psychologists interested in reading-related cognitive abilities such as phonological awareness have emphasized that these abilities are shaped by experiential as well as innate influences (e.g., Mann, 1994; Olson, Rack, Conners, DeFries, & Fulker, 1991). The fact that an individual child has a low score on a processing test, by itself, permits no firm conclusions regarding the ultimate cause of the low score. In most cases, processing weaknesses likely reflect a complex interplay of both innate and experiential factors. However, in school identification of learning disabilities, these weaknesses often are assumed to be entirely the result of an intrinsic disorder in learning.

Exclusionary Criteria

Like reading disability, most of the conditions specified in the exclusion clause—emotional disturbance, cultural or economic disadvantage, and so on—are themselves difficult to define. In theory, when educators are confronted with poor readers who have one of these other conditions— such as the Center School children—they must determine the child's "primary" disability. Exactly how they are supposed to accomplish this goal, however, is not clear.

For instance, all of the Center School children are African American and poor. But Keogh, Gallimore, and Weisner (1997) point out that race and ethnicity should not be confounded with culture. Within a single racial or ethnic group, cultural attitudes that are important in educational achievement, such as the extent to which literacy is encouraged at home, vary widely. (See also Snow, Barnes, Chandler, Goodman, & Hemphill, 1991.) This variability is evident in the Center School children, some of whom appear to come from families that promote literacy and some of whom do not. Of course, there is also variability among white, middle-class families. It cannot be assumed, for example, that Danny's home literacy experiences have been ideal or that he has no serious family problems (Weissbourd, 1996). Race, ethnicity, and socioeconomic status cannot be used as simple proxies for cultural attitudes toward literacy and education or to make assumptions about whether a child's home environment is optimal for learning.

Furthermore, even if educators had the assessment tools to determine cultural attitudes toward learning or the extent of literacy in a child's home, these would probably not be particularly helpful in deciding the cause of an individual child's reading difficulties. Failure in school involves a complex interaction between characteristics that the child brings to the classroom, such as innate abilities and motivation, and extrinsic influences, such as the nature of classroom instruction (e.g., Spear-Swerling & Sternberg, 1996; Zigmond, 1993). In scientific research, it is entirely legitimate to try to tease apart these different causal influences. But in the messy reality of schools, determining ultimate causation for individual cases of poor reading usually is impossible.

The Assumption of an Intrinsic Biological Disorder

Scientific investigators interested in the biological correlates of reading disability have identified certain biological differences in some individuals with RD. For example, autopsy and magnetic resonance imaging (MRI) studies have shown an unusual symmetry in the planum temporale, a brain structure believed to be involved in language processing, in some subjects with RD (Galaburda, Sherman, Rosen, Aboitiz, & Geschwind, 1985; Hynd & Semrud-Clikeman, 1989). Other investigators (e.g., Flowers, 1993; Flowers, Wood, & Naylor, 1991) have demonstrated functional brain differences, such as different patterns of regional cerebral blood flow during the performance of certain linguistic and reading tasks, in some individuals with RD. Genetic research has shown that at least one cognitive ability that is particularly important in reading disability and in reading acquisition generally, phonological reading, appears to be highly heritable (Olson et al., 1991).

However, the extent to which these biological differences constitute actual abnormalities—as opposed to a continuum of individual differences in biology, some of which might make children more vulnerable to reading failure—is uncertain. Studies of school-identified children with RD rarely find evidence of clear-cut neurological abnormalities in these youngsters (Denckla, LeMay, & Chapman, 1985). Although poor readers whose difficulties are caused by a discrete biological disorder certainly may exist, such a disorder does not appear to characterize the vast majority of children who are labeled as learning- or reading-disabled under current educational policies. In addition, none of the biological differences that have been identified to date appear to preclude learning how to read, although they may sometimes make learning to read more difficult.

Many scientific investigators have suggested that the LD category has been overgeneralized in educational practice. As Zigmond (1993) points out, educators usually are less concerned with who is "really" learning disabled than with finding a way to get educational help for youngsters who need it. Because the LD category is a relatively palatable one compared to other special-education categories, it lends itself to overgeneralization.

Educationally, if categorizing children as learning disabled is frequently done for pragmatic reasons, simply as a way to obtain extra help, does the category influence how children are perceived by teachers? In some cases, it does. For example, Allington, McGill-Franzen, and their colleagues (Allington & Li, 1990; McGill-Franzen & James, 1990) found that special-education teachers had much lower expectations for the poor readers in their classes than did remedial-reading teachers, even though the youngsters in special-education were intellectually normal and many were not dramatically deficient in reading. Similarly, Clark (1997) found that regular-classroom teachers were more likely to expect future failure from (hypothetical) boys described as having learning disabilities than from similar boys not labeled as learning disabled.

Another concern involves how children labeled as learning disabled perceive themselves. Obviously, children who experience serious reading problems already are at risk of a negative self-concept. However, in emphasizing that children with RD have an intrinsic learning problem that is "presumed to be due to central nervous system dysfunction," the learning-disabled label may sometimes cause poor readers to view themselves even more negatively than they would otherwise. A line of work in psychology (e.g., Chiu, Hong, & Dweck, 1994; Dweck & Leggett, 1988) indicates that people's beliefs about their own abilities within a domain can exert a causal influence on their actual performance in that domain, especially when they are faced with difficult tasks. For example, Chiu and colleagues (1994) review evidence showing that incremental theorists of intelligence (individuals who believe that intelligence is malleable) were more likely to choose challenging tasks that entailed a risk of failure than were entity theorists (those who believe that intelligence is fixed). Even when the two types of theorists were initially matched in terms of ability, entity theorists were more likely to give up in the face of failure, whereas incremental theorists were more likely to persist. Moreover, analogous results were obtained for the domain of social skills and for the domain of intellectual achievement. (See also Cole, Maxwell, & Martin, 1997.)

Of course, some individuals classified as having RD, as well as their teachers, are incremental theorists about reading abilities; they believe that these abilities are malleable rather than fixed. But the concept of reading disability as an intrinsic disorder in learning does little to foster this kind of theorizing.

"Unexpected" Reading Failure

Historically, the idea of "unexpected" reading failure conveyed the fact that poor reading could exist in children who appeared to have intact intellectual and sensory abilities as well as adequate opportunities to learn. However, the idea of "unexpected" reading failure developed at a time when less was known about the cognitive processes involved in reading,

about human cognitive abilities generally, and about the complex interaction of both innate and experiential variables that contribute to reading
achievement. For instance, it is now known that reading acquisition
draws on a wide variety of cognitive abilities, not all of which correlate
highly with IQ; thus one can have weak phonological abilities and poor
decoding skills but still obtain a high score on an IQ test. Even for individual children, reading failure is often not "unexpected" if one monitors
the specific cognitive processes that are crucial to early reading achievement. Well before first grade, for instance, future poor readers frequently
evidence problems in learning letters and in phonological awareness.
Thus the idea of "unexpectedness" appears to have outlived its usefulness as a way of thinking about reading problems.

To sum up, current scientific research on reading disability has provided
important insights about the nature of poor reading, but it does not support current educational policies for identifying a reading disability. Indeed, as yet it provides no legitimate basis for singling out any subgroup
of poor readers—whether they are defined using current policies or some
other criteria—for separate educational classification and treatment. And
finally, in failing to convey the complex interactions involved in the genesis
of poor reading, the construct of reading disability does not provide educators with a useful way of conceptualizing most reading difficulties.

Future Policy Directions

An old joke about finding one's way to an unfamiliar place laments that
"you can't get there from here," an opinion one also might hold about the
possibility of improvements in future educational policy. However, I
think it is possible to reach the destination of an educational policy that
serves all poor readers well or at least makes considerable progress toward that goal—but not if future policy is based on the traditional construct of reading disability.

Weissbourd (1996) points out:

> Those who run programs and work with children need a more complex
> model for thinking about how and why individual children are vulnerable.
> Such a model would not rely on general conditions, such as poverty, or on
> multiple, static risk factors. Instead, it would enable a professional to tell a
> story about a child that captures the interactions between the child and the
> environment and that is faithful to the dynamic qualities and complexities
> of the child's life. (pp. 32–33)

Although Weissbourd's emphasis is on race and poverty, his viewpoint
is equally applicable to the problem of poor reading. We need a complex

model for thinking about reading failure that takes account of individual differences in both cognitive abilities and children's experiences, that examines the interactions among these variables, and that considers how these variables may change developmentally. The traditional concept of reading disability does not provide such a complex model for thinking about reading difficulties. Moreover, although it certainly is legitimate for scientists to try to identify and study unusual disorders of reading or specific cognitive patterns of poor reading, at present there is no scientific basis for framing *educational policy* around such a disorder or pattern. Indeed, one irony of research on reading disability is that it has been far more successful in elucidating the types of difficulties experienced by poor readers in general than it has been in identifying a distinctive reading disorder.

In this section, I begin by reviewing three types of proposals for changes in identification policies for RD: reforming the discrepancy criterion, using a low-achievement criterion in place of the discrepancy criterion, and identifying children based on either low achievement or the presence of a discrepancy. I also elaborate some reasons I believe that each of these proposals is not the right choice for framing future educational policy on reading difficulties. Finally, I review a fourth kind of proposal—incorporating the concept of persistence of difficulties or resistance to treatment—one I argue may hold more promise for designing future educational policy.

Table 11.1 contrasts all four types of proposals regarding the extent to which they retain the core components and assumptions associated with the traditional construct of RD. As the table shows, these proposals have focused largely on problems with the discrepancy criterion, and at least two have abandoned the assumption that RD constitutes a unique kind of poor reading. However, none of the proposals has abandoned the assumption that RD involves an intrinsic learning disorder or the idea of "unexpected" reading failure.

Proposal 1: Reforming the Discrepancy Criterion

Many policy recommendations have revolved around attempts to modify the discrepancy criterion. These possible modifications were examined at length by Stanovich (1991). Perhaps the most logical modification (in terms of the cognitive processes involved in reading), and one that has a long history in the reading field, is to substitute a listening comprehension–reading comprehension discrepancy for the IQ-achievement discrepancy. The basic idea behind this change is that listening comprehension is a better indicator of "potential" in reading than is IQ. Further-

TABLE 11.1 Core Components and Assumptions of RD Construct Retained by Proposals for Redefining RD

	Component				
Proposal	Discrepancy Criteria	Unique Kind of Poor Reading	Use of Some Exclusion Criteria	Intrinsic Disability in Learning	"Unexpected" Failure
REFORM	yes (but in altered form)	yes	yes	yes	yes
LA	no	no	yes	yes	yes
LA/ DISCREP	yes (but also allows low-achievement criterion)	no	yes	yes	yes
RESPONSE/ PERSIST	no	?	?	yes	yes

Note: REFORM = reformations of the discrepancy criterion (e.g., Stanovich, 1991); LA = low achievement (e.g., Siegel, 1988); LA/DISCREP = either low achievement or discrepancy criterion; RESPONSE/PERSIST = response to treatment/persistence of deficits (e.g., Berninger & Abbot, 1994).

more, because the central deficit in reading disability appears to revolve around word decoding, listening comprehension provides a measure of how well one might expect children with RD to comprehend in reading were their decoding problems remediated.

However, as Stanovich points out, the use of a listening comprehension–reading comprehension discrepancy entails certain practical problems and, like an IQ-achievement discrepancy, is subject to Matthew effects. More important from the standpoint of educational policy, there is little justification for excluding children from educational services because they lack a discrepancy, however it is formulated. Furthermore, poor readers with a listening comprehension–reading comprehension discrepancy do not appear to differ substantially in their cognitive profiles from poor readers of the same age who lack this kind of discrepancy (Fletcher et al., 1994). In the words of Yogi Bera, "It's like déjà vu all over again": The use of a listening comprehension–reading comprehension discrepancy (or any other kind of discrepancy) fails to solve the problems of the discrepancy criterion as educational policy.

Proposal 2: Using a Low-Achievement Criterion

The multitude of problems surrounding the discrepancy criterion led to Siegel's (1988, 1989) proposal that reading disability be defined and identified solely on the basis of low achievement, particularly in word recognition. Siegel also suggests (see chapter 7, this volume) that measures of pseudoword reading (e.g., the Word Attack subtest of the Woodcock-Johnson Tests of Educational Achievement, Woodcock & Johnson, 1989) be included in assessment of individuals with reading difficulties. Pseudowords provide a more sensitive indicator of decoding abilities than do real words, and decoding problems are central not only to reading disability but to poor reading in general. However, Siegel's proposal appears to retain the other aspects of the RD construct, such as the use of some exclusionary criteria, the assumption of an intrinsic deficit in learning, and the concept of "unexpected" reading failure.

Proposal 3: Using the Low-Achievement or the Discrepancy Criterion

Other proposals have suggested that poor readers be identified based either on low achievement or on an IQ-achievement discrepancy. For example, Fletcher and Foorman (see also Fletcher et al., 1994) suggest that not only low achievers, but also children with IQ-achievement discrepancies who are not low achievers, may need educational assistance and should be eligible for identification as reading disabled. Presumably, the latter would be youngsters with higher-than-average IQs and average or borderline achievement in reading, but with relative weaknesses in specific phonological skills—for instance, youngsters like Danny. These investigators also advocate only two exclusionary criteria: generalized developmental delay (i.e., mental retardation) and sensory impairment. Like Siegel's proposal, however, this one does not abandon the notion of an intrinsic deficit in learning or "unexpected" reading failure.

A different proposal incorporating both a low-achievement criterion and an IQ-achievement discrepancy criterion was presented to the U.S. Office of Special Education Programs (Division for Learning Disabilities, 1995). This proposal, developed by representatives of several major learning-disabilities organizations, relies explicitly on the notion of "unexpected" failure. Specifically, students in grades three or below would be identified as learning-disabled based on "unexpected poor performance" in one of eight areas, including basic reading skills and reading comprehension. An ability-achievement discrepancy criterion would continue to be used for students in grades four and up. Exclusionary criteria also would be used and would remain similar to those in current federal regulations.

Problems with the First Three Types of Proposals as Educational Policy

These proposals do make it easier for many children to qualify for educational help. Proposals 2 and 3, in particular, would ease the dilemma described in my opening anecdote of children with very serious reading difficulties not being eligible for extra services because they lack an ability-achievement discrepancy. The use of either a low-achievement or a discrepancy criterion is an especially liberal proposal that would allow many youngsters like Danny, as well as those like the Center School children, to be eligible for educational services.

However, the price to be paid for these services is that children are considered to have a "reading disability" that is "intrinsic to the individual" and "presumed to be due to central nervous system dysfunction." In other words, these proposals address certain problems in the construct of reading disability—most notably the discrepancy criterion and the assumption that RD constitutes a unique kind of poor reading—but not the other problems outlined in the second section of this chapter.

For instance, at a place like Center School, very large numbers of children could qualify for services as "reading disabled" under these proposals. Do we really want to assume that they all have an intrinsic disorder in learning based on a biological defect? As the research reviewed in the second section of this chapter showed, for the vast majority of poor readers in educational settings, this assumption is at best unproven and at worst actually damages children's future educational prospects.

I am not suggesting that the existence of individual differences in reading ability, or in the underlying cognitive abilities that serve reading, should be ignored. Nor should we deny that these individual differences are likely shaped in part by biological differences (as opposed to defects). However, it is one thing to convey to children that they have a significant weakness in reading that needs to be worked on; it is quite another to convey that they have an intrinsic disability in learning based on a presumed biological dysfunction. In the absence of evidence bearing on the question of an intrinsic disability, our default assumption should be that children's learning abilities are intact (Pikulski, 1996). In my opinion, a better way to think about reading difficulties is in terms of multidimensional views of abilities (e.g., Gardner, 1983; Sternberg, 1988, 1994). Many different kinds of abilities are important in life, and most people have strengths and weaknesses across different types of abilities. The goal of education is to help children, whether they are poor readers or not, to capitalize on their strengths while improving in areas of weakness.

I also do not believe that average-achieving youngsters should be classified as "reading disabled" because they have IQs that are high relative to their achievement. However, I would certainly agree that it is essential to look at component abilities in reading, such as decoding, and not just at overall reading achievement. For example, in addition to the four extremely poor readers I described in my opening story, there were several youngsters in the program at Center School who read near-grade-level text despite having Word Attack scores below the twentieth percentile. In reading connected text, they were clearly using contextual cues to compensate for poor decoding. There certainly is reason to be worried about how these *below-average* decoders will fare in reading as they encounter increasingly difficult texts in the later grades, and these children's decoding problems should be addressed, through additional educational services if necessary. However, I would not conceptualize *average* decoders with above-average IQs as having reading problems or as needing extra educational services in reading.

Proposal 4: Persistence of Difficulties or Resistance to Treatment

Another set of suggestions for conceptualizing reading disability has involved the notions of resistance to treatment or persistence of problems over time (Berninger & Abbott, 1994; Shaywitz, Escobar, Shaywitz, Fletcher, & Makuch, 1992; Vellutino, Scanlon, & Tanzman, 1991). These suggestions emphasize individual differences in how quickly poor readers respond to educational help; some respond to fairly short-term interventions, whereas others continue to experience long-term problems despite treatment.

Investigators who advocate this approach to redefining RD typically have maintained that children who fail to learn when given research-validated treatments ("treatment nonresponders") are more likely to have intrinsic disabilities in learning than are children who respond to treatment. Thus as Table 11.1 shows, this type of proposal, like the previous three, does not abandon the assumption of an intrinsic disorder based on a biological deficit. Also, "unexpected" failure would mean something slightly different here than in the other three proposals—not failure to learn despite adequate intelligence and sensory abilities but failure to learn despite exposure to treatments that typically are effective with other, similar children. (The question marks in the table indicate that it is not clear whether treatment nonresponders would be viewed as having a unique type of poor reading or whether exclusionary criteria would be used.)

Critics of this approach (e.g., Fletcher & Foorman, 1994) have high-lighted some important problems with it. These include practical difficul-ties in the adequate measurement of response to treatment, a lack of re-search evidence regarding the best way to design specific treatments, and problems with early intervention (if children have to demonstrate failure over a period of time in order to be identified as needing educational ser-vices).

Nevertheless, I believe that with some modifications, this way of view-ing reading difficulties may hold some promise for designing educa-tional policy, for at least two reasons. First, it is consistent with research showing that children who seem to have similar deficits do vary substan-tially in their responses to treatment. For example, although cognitive re-search has shown that word-recognition and phonological skills are pri-mary deficits for poor readers, it has also revealed marked individual differences in poor readers' responses to intervention in these areas (Torgesen & Hecht, 1996; Torgesen et al., 1994). And second, it appears to have a relevance to educational policy that, at least to this point, has eluded approaches that attempt to classify children according to different "types" of poor reading. For example, if some children need greater in-tensity of instruction than do others, educational policy needs to take ac-count of this fact by providing a range of instructional options.

However, we should not assume that children who are treatment non-responders are the "real" cases of RD any more than we should make this assumption based on the presence of an IQ-achievement discrepancy or phonological-processing problems. There are many reasons that individ-ual youngsters might not respond to a particular treatment—less prior experience with literacy in the home, less motivation for reading, some individual-difference variable that does not constitute an actual disabil-ity, or any number of other reasons. The fact that some children fail to re-spond to a given treatment, by itself, is not evidence of a particular etiol-ogy of poor reading. In other words, if this approach to conceptualizing reading difficulties is to form a good basis for educational policy, we must liberate it from the assumptions that have been and continue to be yoked to the traditional concept of reading disability.

Here I would like to reiterate the distinction made at the outset between science and educational policy. In scientific research, it is of course legiti-mate to explore questions such as whether some treatment nonresponders have biological anomalies—just as it is legitimate to use the first three types of proposals in research, for example, to investigate various cogni-tive patterns of poor reading. However, it is premature at best to assume that all treatment nonresponders have an intrinsic disorder of learning and to found educational policy on such an assumption. To do so would only repeat the past mistakes of learning disabilities as a field of education.

Recently, the response-to-treatment approach to redefining RD has been highlighted by a debate between several learning-disabilities organizations and the leadership of the International Reading Association (IRA). The latter has been openly critical of definitions of LD, specifically the NJCLD definition, and of the assumptions embedded in the traditional construct of reading disability (see, e.g., Pikulski, 1996). Pikulski suggests that persistence of problems over time be explored as one way of defining learning disabilities and that "intense, appropriate instruction in the area of difficulty . . . should take place prior to concluding that special education placement is needed" (1996, p. 15).

In a response to IRA criticisms of LD policy, Minskoff (1996) correctly points out that "prereferral intervention strategies are mandated or encouraged in many states and have been effective in having reading teachers provide early intervention services to students experiencing difficulty in reading" (p. 11). However, prereferral strategies not only lack universality across school districts but typically involve modifications made by the regular-classroom teacher after consultation with other educators (Lerner, 1997). They rarely involve the kind of intensive instruction advocated by Pikulski (1996).

Obviously, all regular-classroom teachers should use prereferral intervention because this kind of intervention can be very effective in addressing some children's problems. Nevertheless, the failure of prereferral strategies to solve a given child's problems does not mean that the child should immediately be consigned to special education. Rather, a range of alternatives needs to be available. A second set of options might involve the more intensive instruction that Pikulski (1996) suggests. Examples of this second group of interventions could include programs such as Reading Recovery (Clay, 1985) or Hiebert's restructured Chapter 1 program (Hiebert, 1994). If a youngster's difficulties continued to persist in the face of these more intensive interventions, the child might be considered for special education. In other words, one way to translate the response-to-treatment approach into educational policy involves the use of several tiers of intervention. These different tiers might be distinguished—at least initially—primarily by increasing intensity, individualization, and duration, with special education representing the most intensive and long-term option. In this scenario, the educational needs of both Danny and the Center School children might be met without unfounded assumptions about the nature of their poor reading.

A point to emphasize involves Pikulski's (1996) recommendation that before special-education placement is considered, children receive intensive instruction *in the area of difficulty*. For many poor readers, the most significant area of difficulty involves phonological skills, particularly the ability to decode unfamiliar words. It is essential that the initial tiers of intervention target this area when needed. This is not to mandate any one particular reading program or approach, for the evidence does not clearly favor one particular method of developing decoding skills over all others. Children might be taught initially via more analytic or more synthetic approaches to decoding; their phonological abilities might be developed through writing activities as well as through oral-language activities; and they might learn to decode in the context of a basal reading program, a whole-language program, or a literature-based program. However, research does indicate that poor readers (and children generally) benefit from explicit teaching of decoding skills that is well integrated with the kinds of texts that children are reading (e.g., Anderson, Hiebert, Scott, & Wilkinson, 1985; Chall, 1983). It surely makes no sense to refer children for special education because of poor decoding if no one has actually tried to teach them to decode. Similarly, children with reading-comprehension problems should have explicit instruction in that area well before they are considered for special education.

Of course, I am not the first person to suggest a system of multiple tiers of intervention, and indeed, such a system already does exist in some schools. However, even where this system exists, it still is tied to an invalid policy for classifying poor readers as "learning disabled" or "not learning disabled." We need a formal educational policy for identifying and serving poor readers that does not require pigeonholing them into invalid categories but that at the same time recognizes individual differences in children's instructional needs. I have already tried to suggest one possible basis for such a policy. To conclude this chapter, I would like to consider some potential problems in the implementation of that policy.

Possible Problems with Multiple Tiers of Intervention as Educational Policy

Clearly, a multiple-tier policy is only as good as the system of ongoing assessment and intervention behind it. If children's progress in reading is not carefully monitored and if the initial tiers of intervention are weak, there still will be many children whose educational needs are not being met or who are in special education unnecessarily. For example, children like the four lowest-achieving readers in the Center School program should be targeted for intervention long before reaching the third grade. It also is essential that this (or any other) educational policy attach funding in such a way as to promote rather than inadvertently discourage early intervention.

Early intervention requires monitoring not only overall reading achievement but also the underlying cognitive abilities that are important in reading acquisition. At the kindergarten and first-grade levels, for instance, three especially important predictors of reading are knowledge of letter names and sounds, phonological awareness, and rapid-naming abilities. If educators monitor these abilities closely, they can target many children for help early, before they fall far behind their peers in reading. Accomplishing these aims, however, requires that educators be knowledgeable about the cognitive processes involved in literacy and skilled in helping children to develop those processes. Many teacher-education programs, especially at the preservice level, have not caught up to the explosion of scientific knowledge about reading acquisition (Nolen, McCutcheon, & Berninger, 1990).

Furthermore, regular-classroom teachers already have a tremendous amount of knowledge to acquire in a four- or even five-year baccalaureate program. Specialists in education can have a valuable role to play in helping regular-classroom teachers to meet the needs of all youngsters— if the specialty is framed in the right way. Instead of focusing on diagnosing "learning disabilities," special educators might specialize in knowledge about the cognitive abilities that are important in various domains of achievement, including reading, and in knowledge about how best to develop those abilities. Because there are other specialists involved in working with poor readers (e.g., reading consultants and remedial-reading teachers), reframing the LD field also might require special educators to resolve some "turf" issues with other professional groups. These issues might be settled in any number of ways (e.g., based on the tier of intervention) but should be done in a manner that is flexible enough to allow the best use of the human resources available at a given school.

Another consideration involves the variability across school districts that is especially characteristic of public education in the United States (Berliner & Biddle, 1995). That is, not only is there tremendous variability in how well funded schools are, there is substantial variability in the actual content of the curriculum. For example, one school district may place a relatively strong emphasis on direct teaching of word-recognition skills at the first-grade level, whereas that emphasis may be much less in a neighboring school district. It is likely that more children will need "intensive intervention" to learn word-recognition skills in the second district than in the first. This example illustrates why we should not make assumptions about the causality behind children's need for intensive intervention. However, it also illustrates that improvements in regular-classroom reading instruction are fundamental to the design and implementation of a sound educational policy for helping children with reading difficulties. All children should experience a reading program that balances instruction in basic skills with instruction in many other crucial aspects of reading such as higher-level comprehension abilities.

Of course, exactly what constitutes a "good balance" is open to interpretation. Should first-grade teachers spend 10 percent of their reading program developing word recognition? Thirty percent? Fifty percent? Furthermore, for children who need more intensive intervention, what is "intensive"? For example, is it possible for small-group instruction to be as intensive and as effective as one-to-one tutoring? Which variables, other than level of intensity, might need to be manipulated in designing interventions? And for children who do not seem to be responding to a given tier of intervention, how long should we wait before concluding that the intervention has had a fair trial and that the children need a different or more intensive type of intervention?

Obviously, although research is beginning to provide some answers to these kinds of questions (see, e.g., Torgesen, Chapter 5, this volume), more research is needed. Nevertheless, questions about the efficacy and optimal design of various interventions are already with us. Current educational policy does not save us from answering such questions; it merely fails to focus our attention on them. A good educational policy for all poor readers, including those currently labeled as learning disabled, would provide the instructional options children need without making unwarranted assumptions about those children. We can "get there from here," but only if we fully disengage educational policy from the traditional construct of reading disability.

References

Adams, M. J. (1990). *Beginning to read: Thinking and learning about print.* Cambridge, MA: MIT Press.

Allington, R., & Li, S. (1990). *Teacher beliefs about children who find learning to read difficult.* Paper presented at the National Reading Conference, Miami, FL.

Anderson, R., Hiebert, E., Scott, J., & Wilkinson, I. (1985). *Becoming a nation of readers: The report of the Commission on Reading.* Champaign, IL: Center for the Study of Reading.

Berliner, D. C., & Biddle, B. J. (1995). *The manufactured crisis: Myths, fraud, and the attack on America's public schools.* Reading, MA: Addison-Wesley.

Berninger, V. W., & Abbot, R. D. (1994). Redefining learning disabilities: Moving beyond aptitude-achievement discrepancies to failure to respond to validated treatment protocols. In G. R. Lyon (Ed.), *Frames of reference for the assessment of learning disabilities: New views on measurement issues* (pp. 163–183). Baltimore, MD: Brookes.

Chall, J. (1983). *Learning to read: The great debate (revised).* New York: McGraw-Hill.

Chiu, C., Hong, Y., & Dweck, C. (1994). Toward an integrative model of personality and intelligence: A general framework and some preliminary steps. In R. J. Sternberg & P. Ruzgis, *Personality and intelligence* (pp. 104–130). New York: Cambridge University Press.

Clark, M. D. (1997). Teacher response to learning disabilities: A test of attributional principles. *Journal of Learning Disabilities, 30,* 69–79.

Clay, M. M. (1985). *The early detection of reading difficulties* (3rd ed.). Portsmouth, NH: Heinemann.

Cole, D. A., Maxwell, S. E., & Martin, J. M. (1997). Reflected self-appraisals: Strength and structure of the relation of teacher, peer, and parent ratings to children's self-perceived competencies. *Journal of Educational Psychology, 89,* 55–70.

Denckla, M. B., LeMay, M., & Chapman, C. A. (1985). Few CT scan abnormalities found even in neurologically impaired learning disabled children. *Journal of Learning Disabilities, 18,* 132–135.

Division for Learning Disabilities. (1995, Summer). Proposed new LD criteria. *DLD Times, 5,* 8.

Dweck, C. S., & Leggett, E. L. (1988). A social-cognitive approach to motivation and personality. *Psychological Review, 95,* 256–273.

Federal Register (1977, December 29) (65082–65085), Washington, DC.

Felton, R. H. (1993). Effects of instruction on the decoding skills of children with phonological-processing problems. *Journal of Learning Disabilities, 26,* 583–589.

Fletcher, J. M., & Foorman, B. R. (1994). Issues in definition and measurement of learning disabilities: The need for early intervention. In G. R. Lyon (Ed.), *Frames of reference for the assessment of learning disabilities: New views on measurement issues* (pp. 185–200). Baltimore, MD: Brookes.

Fletcher, J. M., Shaywitz, S. E., Shankweiler, D. P., Katz, L., Liberman, I. Y., Stuebing, K. K., Francis, D. J., Fowler, A. E., & Shaywitz, B. A. (1994). Cognitive profiles of reading disability: Comparisons of discrepancy and low achievement definitions. *Journal of Educational Psychology, 86,* 6–23.

Flowers, D. L. (1993). Brain basis for dyslexia: A summary of work in progress. *Journal of Learning Disabilities, 26,* 575–582.

Flowers, D. L., Wood, F. B., & Naylor, C. E. (1991). Regional cerebral blood flow correlates of language processes in reading disability. *Archives of Neurology, 48,* 637–643.

Frankenberger, W., & Harper, J. (1987). States' criteria and procedures for identifying learning disabled children: A comparison of 1981/82 and 1985/86 guidelines. *Journal of Learning Disabilities, 20,* 118–121.

Galaburda, A. M., Sherman, G. F., Rosen, G. D., Aboitiz, F., & Geschwind, N. (1985). Developmental dyslexia: Four consecutive patients with cortical anomalies. *Annals of Neurology, 18,* 222–233.

Gardner, H. (1983). *Frames of mind: The theory of multiple intelligences.* New York: Basic Books.

Gough, P. B., & Tunmer, W. E. (1986). Decoding, reading, and reading disability. *Remedial and Special Education, 7,* 6–10.

Hiebert, E. H. (1994). A small-group literacy intervention with Chapter 1 students. In E. H. Hiebert & B. M. Taylor (Eds.), *Getting reading right from the start: Effective early literacy interventions* (pp. 85–106). Boston, MA: Allyn and Bacon.

Hynd, G. W., & Semrud-Clikeman, M. (1989). Dyslexia and brain morphology. *Psychological Bulletin, 106,* 447–482.

Keogh, B. K. (1993). Linking purpose and practice: Social-political and developmental perspectives on classification. In G. R. Lyon, D. B. Gray, J. F. Kavanagh, & N. A. Krasnegor, *Better understanding learning disabilities: New views from re-*

search and their implications for education and public policies (pp. 311–323). Baltimore, MD: Brookes.

Keogh, B. K., Gallimore, R., & Weisner, T. (1997). A sociocultural perspective on learning and learning disabilities. *Learning Disabilities Research & Practice, 12,* 107–113.

Lerner, J. (1997). *Learning disabilities: Theories, diagnosis, and teaching strategies* (7th ed.). Boston, MA: Houghton Mifflin.

Mann, V. (1994). Phonological skills and the prediction of early reading problems. In N. C. Jordan & J. Goldsmith-Phillips (Eds.), *Learning disabilities: New directions for assessment and intervention* (pp. 67–84). Boston, MA: Allyn and Bacon.

McGill-Franzen, A., & James, I. (1990). *Teacher beliefs about remedial and learning disabled readers.* Paper presented at the National Reading Conference, Miami, FL.

Minskoff, E. (1996). IRA attacks on learning disabilities. *DLD Times,* Spring/Summer, 10–11.

Moats, L. C., & Lyon, G. R. (1993). Learning disabilities in the United States: Advocacy, science, and the future of the field. *Journal of Learning Disabilities, 26,* 282–294.

Nation, K., & Hulme, C. (1997). Phonemic segmentation, not onset-rime segmentation predicts early reading and spelling skills. *Reading Research Quarterly, 32,* 154–167.

National Joint Committee on Learning Disabilities. (1988). Letter to NJCLD member organizations.

Nolen, P. A., McCutchen, D., & Berninger, V. (1990). Ensuring tomorrow's literacy: A shared responsibility. *Journal of Teacher Education, 41,* 63–72.

Olson, R. K., Rack, J. P., Conners, F. A., DeFries, J. C., & Fulker, D. W. (1991). Genetic etiology of individual differences in reading disability. In L. V. Feagans, E. J. Short, & L. J. Meltzer (Eds.), *Subtypes of learning disabilities: Theoretical perspectives and research* (pp. 113–135). Hillsdale, NJ: Lawrence Erlbaum Associates.

Pikulski, J. J. (1996). IRA board questions definition of "learning disabilities." *Reading Today,* August/September, 15.

Rack, J. P., Snowling, M. J., & Olson, R. K. (1992). The nonword reading deficit in developmental dyslexia: A review. *Reading Research Quarterly, 27,* 28–53.

Shaywitz, S. E., Escobar, M. D., Shaywitz, B. A., Fletcher, J. M., & Makuch, R. (1992). Evidence that dyslexia may represent the lower tail of a normal distribution of reading ability. *New England Journal of Medicine, 326,* 145–150.

Siegel, L. S. (1988). Evidence that IQ scores are irrelevant to the definition and analysis of reading disability. *Canadian Journal of Psychology, 42,* 201–215.

Siegel, L. S. (1989). IQ is irrelevant to the definition of learning disabilities. *Journal of Learning Disabilities, 22,* 469–478.

Snow, C. E., Barnes, W. S., Chandler, J., Goodman, J. F., & Hemphill, L. (1991). *Unfulfilled expectations: Home and school influences on literacy.* Cambridge, MA: Harvard University Press.

Spear-Swerling, L., & Sternberg, R. J. (1996). *Off track: When poor readers become "learning disabled."* Boulder, CO: Westview Press.

Stanovich, K. E. (1986). Matthew effects in reading: Some consequences of individual differences in the acquisition of literacy. *Reading Research Quarterly, 21,* 360–406.

Stanovich, K. E. (1991). Discrepancy definitions of reading disability: Has intelligence led us astray? *Reading Research Quarterly, 26,* 7–29.

Stanovich, K. E., & Siegel, L. S. (1994). Phenotypic performance profile of children with reading disabilities: A regression-based test of the phonological-core variable-difference model. *Journal of Educational Psychology, 86,* 24–53.

Sternberg, R. J. (1988). *The triarchic mind: A new theory of human intelligence.* New York: Viking.

Sternberg, R. J. (1994). Thinking styles: Theory and assessment at the interface between intelligence and personality. In R. J. Sternberg & P. Ruzgis, *Personality and intelligence* (pp. 169–187). New York: Cambridge University Press.

Torgesen, J. K. (1991). Learning disabilities: Historical and conceptual issues. In B. Y. L. Wong (Ed.), *Learning about learning disabilities* (pp. 3–37). San Diego, CA: Academic Press.

Torgesen, J. K., & Hecht, S. A. (1996). Preventing and remediating reading disabilities: Instructional variables that make a difference for special students. In M. F. Graves, P. van den Broek, & B. M. Taylor (Eds.), *The first R: Every child's right to read* (pp. 133–159). New York: Teachers College Press.

Torgesen, J. K., Wagner, R. K., & Rashotte, C. A. (1994). Longitudinal studies of phonological processing and reading. *Journal of Learning Disabilities, 27,* 276–286.

Torgesen, J. K., Wagner, R. K., Rashotte, C. A., Burgess, S., & Hecht, S. (1997). Contributions of phonological awareness and rapid automatic naming ability to the growth of word-reading skills in second- to fifth-grade children. *Scientific Studies of Reading, 1,* 161–185.

Vellutino, F. R., Scanlon, D. M., & Tanzman, M. S. (1991). Bridging the gap between cognitive and neuropsychological conceptualizations of reading disability. *Learning and Individual Differences, 3,* 181–203.

Walberg, H. J., & Tsai, S. (1983). Matthew effects in education. *American Educational Research Journal, 20,* 359–373.

Weissbourd, R. (1996). *The vulnerable child: What really hurts America's children and what we can do about it.* Reading, MA: Addison-Wesley.

Wolf, M. (1991). Naming speed and reading: The contribution of the cognitive neurosciences. *Reading Research Quarterly, 26,* 123–141.

Woodcock, R. W., & Johnson, M. B. (1989). *Woodcock-Johnson Tests of Achievement-Revised.* Boston, MA: Houghton Mifflin.

Zigmond, N. (1993). Learning disabilities from an educational perspective. In G. R. Lyon, D. B. Gray, J. F. Kavanagh, & N. A. Krasnegor, *Better understanding learning disabilities: New views from research and their implications for education and public policies* (pp. 251–272). Baltimore, MD: Brookes.

PART FOUR

Conclusions

12

Epilogue:
Toward an Emerging Consensus About
Learning Disabilities

Robert J. Sternberg

Just what does it mean to say that John—or Jean or Jaime or anyone else—is "learning disabled"? The answer to this question proves to be maddeningly complex. Not only are there disagreements as to what *learning disabled* means, there are disagreements as to whether the concept is even meaningful.

Despite the disagreements, there is a surprising degree of emerging consensus among experts in the field regarding a number of key issues. My goal in this epilogue is to argue that the field is progressing toward some major points of consensus even if it has not fully converged toward a unified view of learning disabilities as biological, psychological, and societal phenomena. At the same time, I will mention some of the main points of disagreement.

Points of General Agreement

Here are what I view as 15 key points of broad consensus.

1. *Learning disabilities represent a diversity of distinct phenomena, not a single one.* Although *learning disability* might sound like a unitary phenomenon, the consensus of expert theoreticians, researchers, and practitioners is that it is not. We do children and adults alike a disservice simply by lumping them into a category of learning disabled (LD). Experts disagree as to the exact number of learning disabilities and even as to their exact identities. It seems clear, for example, that mathematical disability is separate from reading disability and that reading disability can manifest itself in different forms regardless of whether it is unitary in a biological

Preparation of this chapter was supported in part by grant R206A70001 from the Javits Program of the U. S. Office of Educational Research and Improvement.

sense. A task for the future is to develop a better taxonomy of the types of learning disabilities, and to determine how they are similar and different.

2. *Different types of learning disabilities need to be diagnosed and treated differently.* The existence of different types of learning disabilities implies that there is no magic bullet—no single instructional program or even means of identification—that is going to answer every question we might wish to pose either with regard to instruction or assessment. "LD classes" that provide a uniform regimen of instruction for children diagnosed as LD are bound to be inadequate because they assume that one size fits all students. Any good method of assessment and program of instruction will have to be tailored to meet the needs of the individuals being instructed or assessed.

3. *Learning disabilities, at least reading disability, have a genetic component.* Even contextualists agree in some cases learning disability is biological in nature and its origins are partially genetic. Current research suggests that chromosomes 6 and 15 may be keys to understanding the genetic origins of reading disability (see Olson, Chapter 1 in this volume, and Grigorenko, Chapter 2). There is also agreement that not all poor readers, and probably not even most poor readers, are going to be identified through chromosomal analysis.

4. *Learning disabilities run in families.* Because some kinds of learning disabilities are partially genetic in origin, they run in families. The closer the family relationship of two individuals, the more likely the two individuals are to share this particular form of disability. Similarly, identical twins are more likely than fraternal twins to share such disabilities.

5. *Environmental context affects how genetic predispositions manifest themselves.* Not even the most ardent biological theorists fail to assign a major role to the environment, often a role as large as that assigned by contextualists. Genes always have their effects through environments, and different environments can result in a given set of genes expressing itself in very different ways.

6. *Some learning disabilities show themselves in brain structures different from those of normal individuals.* The work of Hynd and his colleagues suggests that parts of the brains of certain learning-disabled individuals (such as the planum temporale) are physically different in some respects from the brains of those individuals who are normal readers. If genetic factors do partially underlie certain forms of learning disability, it would indeed make sense for them to express themselves through differences in the brain.

7. *Many children who are labeled as learning disabled aren't.* People can assign labels and then reify the constructs they have created, and they can assign labels that are doubtful and then create self-fulfilling prophecies through their assignments. The work of Skrtic, Christensen, and Spear-Swerling emphasizes the role of societal labeling in creating a nightmare where children are unfairly labeled and treated; presumably all of the

theorists in this volume would agree that we can easily create a class of unjustly labeled individuals through dubitable practices of identification. In particular, as Christensen points out, the medical model does not provide a good way of understanding, diagnosing, or treating learning disabilities.

8. *The label of learning disabled can end up reinforcing already existing forms of group discrimination.* Different groups perform differentially well on different kinds of tests. When such tests are valid in the way they are used, such group differences are a cause of valid educational concern and need to be addressed and, if possible, remedied. But if the tests are being used in an invalid way, the use of the tests can actually help reinforce already existing forms of discrimination, as pointed out by Skrtic and Christensen. IQ tests show group differences, and because they are often used in a way that is not valid for identifying the reading disabled, they can end up contributing further to discrimination against groups that do not score well on them.

9. *IQ tests are typically not useful in the diagnosis of learning disabilities.* Intelligence tests have been widely used in the diagnosis of learning disabilities, typically through the computation of a difference score between IQ and reading or other specific ability scores. The use of intelligence tests in diagnosing learning disabilities is extremely problematical, a point made by Siegel and others. One of the greatest problems is that intelligence tests measure only a portion of intelligence. Thus one is not truly computing a difference between a level of intelligence and a level of reading but rather a difference between only an aspect of intelligence and reading. If one uses verbal tests in the IQ battery, reading may be measured by the IQ test as well as by the reading test; if one does not use verbal tests, one is looking at an even narrower portion of intelligence. The bottom line is that IQ tests typically serve no useful function in identifying the learning disabled.

10. *Difference scores are an undesirable means of identifying the learning disabled.* Again, as pointed out by Siegel, Spear-Swerling, and others, difference scores are extremely problematical in identifying learning disabilities or, really, anything else. For one thing, difference scores tend to be unreliable, and the more highly correlated the two things are that are being compared, the more unreliable the difference scores are. For another thing, the difference is usually with respect to IQ, which, as was discussed earlier, is a questionable measure. Finally, difference scores mean different things at different points along a continuum. For example, a difference of 10 points between an IQ score and a reading score means something different for above-average students than for below-average students.

11. *The current U.S. system of funding actually encourages irresponsibility in the identification of the learning disabled.* The current system of funding education in the United States has created the perverse situation where

schools and school districts are rewarded financially for identifying children as learning disabled. They are likely to receive extra funding for each child so identified. This method of funding actually encourages irresponsible identification of children as learning disabled and further encourages parents to want their children to be labeled so that the children will receive extra services. What helps in the short run may not help in the long run, however. Once identified, the children have a label assigned to them that tends to stick with them and that may result in their being treated as intellectually inferior to their not-so-identified peers.

12. *The best means of identification we have for reading-disabled individuals are tests of phonological processing.* There are no perfect tests of anything. But tests of phonological processing, described in some detail by Wagner and Garon (Chapter 4, this volume), Torgesen (Chapter 5), and Pressley (Chapter 6), provide the best means currently available to identify the reading disabled. Indeed, even biologically oriented theorists such as Shaywitz and her colleagues have identified phonological processing as key to understanding reading disabilities. We are less far along in identifying individuals with other kinds of learning disabilities. The phonological tests do not specifically distinguish garden-variety poor readers from disabled readers; but (1) it is debatable as to how much of a difference there is between the two groups, and (2) even if the two groups are different, it is not clear at this point that there is any way at all in which the appropriate treatment interventions are different.

13. *Automatization failure is also a common sign of learning disability.* As pointed out by Samuels in Chapter 8, reading-disabled individuals show deficits in phonological processing in particular and in their automatization of phonological processing and other kinds of information processing in general. Cognitive processing that for other people is effortless, automatic, and relatively painless can be effortful, controlled, and even painful for the reading disabled.

14. *Comprehension as well as phonological processing is affected in the case of reading disability.* Experts on reading disability tend to focus on deficits in phonological processing, but over the long haul and sometimes over the short haul, reading-disabled individuals show deficits in higher-order comprehension skills as well, a point emphasized by Pressley. Such deficits may well be a long-term product of the phonological deficits. Because reading-disabled persons invest more resources in their efforts at phonological decoding, they have fewer resources left over to cope with higher-order verbal comprehension. Particularly as children get older, deficits in verbal comprehension are likely to become more and more salient.

15. *Training programs to help reading-disabled individuals need to take into account and remediate identified cognitive deficits.* Reading programs for

poor readers of any stripe need to develop phonological, automatization, and comprehension skills. Programs need to be tailored to specific forms of reading or other disability, and thus a program that works for one individual may not necessarily work for another.

Most important, instructional programs need to focus on scientifically identified deficits rather than hype. There is an enormous amount of hype and faddism in the reading field, resulting in points of view and even programs that are affectively satisfying to their users but that have no scientific basis. Such programs are almost never adequately evaluated, for obvious reasons, but nevertheless continue to be used. They do a disservice to children and teachers alike. Training programs should help students build on strengths as well as helping them remediate and compensate for weaknesses. They need to be based on a science of learning disabilities, a science to which all the authors of this book have attempted to contribute.

Points of Disagreement

In this epilogue, I have concentrated upon points of consensus. Of course, consensus does not underlie every issue. Three major points of disagreement stand out.

1. *Are poor reading in general and reading disability in particular continuous?* The experts in this volume disagree as to whether garden-variety poor reading and learning disability are simply different points along a continuum (e.g., Wagner & Garon) or are qualitatively different phenomena (e.g., Grigorenko). Presumably, time will tell which of these points of view is correct.

2. *At what level of analysis is learning disability best studied?* The experts disagree as to whether learning disability is best approached as a biological phenomenon (e.g., Olson; Hynd, Clinton, & Hiemenz), a cognitive one (e.g., Torgesen; Samuels), or a contextual one (e.g., Skrtic, Christensen). But differences in level of analysis generally reflect preferences in theoretical and research strategies. As the authors point out, the biological and cognitive levels can be mapped onto each other (see, e.g., the chapter by Grigorenko), the cognitive and contextual levels can be mapped onto each other (see, e.g., the chapters by Pressley and Spear-Swerling), and the biological and contextual levels can be mapped onto each other (see, e.g., the chapters by Olson and Hynd et al.). Thus the three levels of analysis are complementary rather than conflicting.

3. *To what extent are learning disabilities within the organism and to what extent are they in the society?* The experts disagree as to the extent to which learning disabilities should be understood as a phenomenon occurring within an individual. Here, the contextualists diverge most from the bio-

logical and cognitive theorists. The latter do their research primarily on individuals. The former view learning disabilities primarily as labels assigned by a system that can be as much a cause as an effect of educational problems. Ultimately, again, both points of view are probably needed fully to understand learning disabilities at all levels of analysis.

Conclusion

In this epilogue, I have tried to outline some of the main points of consensus in the field of learning disabilities, as well as more briefly to mention some of the disagreements. Although all our questions about learning disabilities have not been answered, we have come a long way since the days when we believed that learning-disabled children might be identified primarily by, say, visual impairment or a tendency to reverse letters. We still have a long way to go.

About the Editors and Contributors

Carol A. Christensen is a senior lecturer in educational psychology at the University of Queensland, Brisbane, Australia. Her research has focused on the cognitive characteristics of students with learning disabilities as well as the social factors that result in the identification and classification of learning disabilities. She has published work on the role of phonological awareness in reading, the development of cognitive and metacognitive skills, and the social construction of learning disabilities. She recently edited a book with Fazal Rizvi titled *Disability and the Dilemmas of Education and Justice.*

Amanda B. Clinton is a doctoral student in school psychology at the University of Georgia. She has worked as a school psychologist and is currently completing clinical and research experiences in Medellin, Colombia. She is interested in language and the brain, particularly neuropsychological issues related to second-language learning.

Tamara Garon is a doctoral candidate in cognitive and behavioral psychology at Florida State University. Her research focuses primarily on the effects of linguistic complexity on children's oral- and written-language skills.

Elena L. Grigorenko is a research scientist at Yale and associate professor at Moscow State University. Her current interests include learning disabilities, developmental dyslexia, and broader issues concerning the effects of ill health on children's cognitive development.

Jennifer R. Hiemenz is a doctoral student in school psychology at the University of Georgia. Her research interests are related to the application of neuroimaging procedures in developing a better understanding of brain-behavior relations in reading disorders. She recently completed research at the University of Jyvaskyla in Finland using functional magnetic resonance imaging procedures (fMRI) in familial dyslexics.

George W. Hynd is research professor of special education and psychology and director of the School of Professional Studies at the University of Georgia. He also directs the Center for Clinical and Developmental Neuropsychology. Dr. Hynd's research has focused on the relationship between planum temporale morphology and reading disability and on the frequent co-occurrence of learning disabilities and ADHD.

Richard K. Olson is professor of psychology at the University of Colorado and associate director of the Center for the Study of Learning Disabilities at the Institute for Behavioral Genetics. His research has focused on the genetic and environmental etiology of reading disabilities and on the remediation of reading disabilities through the use of computer speech programs.

Michael G. Pressley is professor of psychology and director of the Masters Program in Teaching at the University of Notre Dame. He currently serves as the editor of the *Journal of Educational Psychology*. In recent years, he has conducted research on the nature of teaching that produces high literacy achievement.

S. Jay Samuels was the coeditor of *Reading Research Quarterly*. He holds the William S. Gray Distinguished Research Award from the International Reading Association and the Oscar Causey Research Award from the National Reading Conference. He is a member of the Reading Hall of Fame.

Linda S. Siegel is professor in the Department of Educational Psychology and Special Education at the University of British Columbia in Vancouver, BC, and holds the Dorothy C. Lam Chair in Special Education. She has conducted research in language and cognitive development, the role of psychoeducational assessment in the identification of learning disabilities, bilingualism, premature and high-risk infants, and the early identification of learning disabilities. She was the editor of the *International Journal of Behavioral Development* and an associate editor of *Child Development*.

Thomas M. Skrtic is professor of special education policy and administration at the University of Kansas. His published works include *Behind Special Education: A Critical Analysis of Professional Culture and School Organization* (1991), *Special Education and Student Disability: Traditional, Emerging, and Alternative Perspectives* (1995), and *Disability and Democracy: Reconstructing (Special) Education for Postmodernity* (1995). His academic interests are philosophical pragmatism, organization theory, policy implementation, and democratic education.

Louise Spear-Swerling is professor of special education at Southern Connecticut State University in New Haven, Connecticut. She has taught in public schools in both special-education and regular-classroom settings. Her specialties are reading acquisition, reading difficulties, and literacy instruction with at-risk youngsters and individuals with learning disabilities.

Keith E. Stanovich is currently professor of human development and applied psychology at the Ontario Institute for Studies in Education,

University of Toronto. He has twice received the Albert J. Harris Award from the International Reading Association for influential articles on reading disabilities and in 1995 was elected to the Reading Hall of Fame. He is a recipient of the Oscar Causey Award from the National Reading Conference for contributions to research, and he is a fellow of both the American Psychological Association (Divisions 3 and 15) and the American Psychological Society. In 1997, he received the Sylvia Scribner Award from the American Education Research Association. Author of over 125 scientific papers, since 1986 he has been the associate editor of the *Merrill-Palmer Quarterly*, a leading journal of human development.

Robert J. Sternberg is IBM Professor of Psychology and Education in the Department of Psychology at Yale University. A fellow of eight divisions of the American Psychological Association, Sternberg is also a fellow of the American Academy of Arts and Sciences, the American Association for the Advancement of Science, and the American Psychological Society. He is past editor of the *Psychological Bulletin* and incoming editor of *Contemporary Psychology*. Sternberg is the author of roughly 650 articles, books, and book chapters and coauthor of two books on reading disabilities, *Off Track*, with Louise Spear-Swerling, and *The LD Lottery* with Elena Grigorenko. Sternberg has won numerous awards from organizations such as the American Psychological Association, the American Educational Research Association, and the Society for Multivariate Experimental Psychology.

Joseph K. Torgesen received his PhD in developmental and clinical psychology from the University of Michigan in 1976, and he is currently Distinguished Research Professor of Psychology at Florida State University. Over the past 20 years, he has published over 100 research articles, book chapters, or books on the subject of learning disabilities and reading development, and he is on the editorial board of five professional research journals. He and his colleague Richard Wagner have been studying the development of reading and phonological processes for the past ten years, and he is currently directing one of two five-year grants from the National Institute of Child Health and Human Development to study the prevention and remediation of reading disabilities in young children. With Richard Wagner, he is also working on the development of a comprehension diagnostic test of phonological processes in reading.

Richard K. Wagner is professor of psychology at Florida State University. He earned a PhD in cognitive psychology from Yale University in 1985. He previously earned a master's degree in school psychology from the University of Akron, and before embarking on his research career, he completed a year of internship and two years as a school psychologist. His major area of research interest is the acquisition of complex cognitive knowledge and skills, which he has pursued in two domains. In the domain of reading, his research has focused on the role of reading-related phonological processing abilities in the normal and abnormal development of reading skills and on the prediction, prevention, and remediation of dyslexia. In the domain of human intelligence, his research has focused on the role of practical knowledge and intelligence in intellectual performance manifested outside the classroom setting.

Index

3 5282 00627 8439

Printed in the United States
69271LVS00003B/185

9 780813 331768